WAR: ITS CONDUCT AND LEGAL RESULTS

By T. BATY, D.C.L., LL.D.
FORMERLY FELLOW OF UNIVERSITY COLLEGE, OXFORD, JOINT HONORARY GENERAL SECRETARY OF THE INTERNATIONAL LAW ASSOCIATION

AND

J. H. MORGAN, M.A.
PROFESSOR OF CONSTITUTIONAL LAW AT UNIVERSITY COLLEGE, LONDON, LATE SCHOLAR OF BALLIOL COLLEGE, OXFORD

The great resource of Europe was in England; not in a sort of England detached from the rest of the world, but in that sort of England who considered herself as embodied with Europe; in that sort of England who, sympathetic with the adversity or the happiness of mankind, felt that nothing in human affairs was foreign to her.—BURKE.

THE LAWBOOK EXCHANGE, LTD.
Clark, New Jersey

ISBN 978-1-58477-573-7 (hardcover)
ISBN 978-1-61619-402-4 (paperback)

Lawbook Exchange edition 2005, 2014

The quality of this reprint is equivalent to the quality of the original work.

THE LAWBOOK EXCHANGE, LTD.
33 Terminal Avenue
Clark, New Jersey 07066-1321

Please see our website for a selection of our other publications and fine facsimile reprints of classic works of legal history:
www.lawbookexchange.com

Library of Congress Cataloging-in-Publication Data

Baty, T. (Thomas), 1869-1954.
    War: its conduct and legal results / by T. Baty and J. H. Morgan.
      p. cm.
    Originally published: London: J. Murray, 1915.
    Includes bibliographical references and index.
    ISBN 1-58477-573-4 (cloth: alk. paper)
    1. War and emergency powers—Great Britain. 2. War (International law) I. Morgan, J. H. (John Hartman), 1876-1955. II. Title.

KD5110.B38 2005
343.41 '0 1—dc22   2004058789

Printed in the United States of America on acid-free paper

WAR: ITS CONDUCT AND LEGAL RESULTS

By T. BATY, D.C.L., LL.D.

FORMERLY FELLOW OF UNIVERSITY COLLEGE, OXFORD, JOINT HONORARY
GENERAL SECRETARY OF THE INTERNATIONAL LAW ASSOCIATION

AND

J. H. MORGAN, M.A.

PROFESSOR OF CONSTITUTIONAL LAW AT UNIVERSITY COLLEGE,
LONDON, LATE SCHOLAR OF BALLIOL COLLEGE, OXFORD

> The great resource of Europe was in England; not in a sort of England detached from the rest of the world, but in that sort of England who considered herself as embodied with Europe; in that sort of England who, sympathetic with the adversity or the happiness of mankind, felt that nothing in human affairs was foreign to her.—BURKE.

LONDON
JOHN MURRAY, ALBEMARLE STREET, W.
1915

All rights reserved.

TO THE RIGHT HON.
SIR JOHN SIMON, K.C.V.O., K.C., M.P.
HIS MAJESTY'S ATTORNEY-GENERAL

PREFACE

PART I. (The Crown and the Subject), Part II. (The Crown and the Enemy), with the exception of Chap. III., and Part III. (The Neutrality of Belgium) of this book are the work of Professor Morgan. The remaining three parts are from the pen of Dr Baty. The authors have, however, written throughout in constant consultation with one another, and we accept a joint and several liability for the whole of the book.

There are many books on war in international law; there is, we believe, not one on the effect of war upon the laws of this realm. This must be the chief justification for the appearance of this book. Works on war in international law, of which there are many and admirable examples, are not, and perhaps could not be expected to be, concerned with this municipal aspect. They say little of the effect of war upon contracts, and nothing of martial law. The prerogative concerns them but little, and statute not at all. The English law reports make but a fitful appearance in their pages. Our books on common law and constitutional law are almost equally silent. *Inter arma silent leges.* Yet the common law has much to say, even though its words be largely negative, of the safety of the realm and the prerogative in relation thereto. This debatable land which marches between War and Peace, the power of the Crown when England is "at war" without the English realm being in a state of war, has never yet been explored by any writer, still less has it been secured by the title of effective occupation.

Moreover, there are many international problems arising out of war which in this country at any rate have never been thoroughly examined, and upon which great doubt and confusion exists. The right of alien enemies to sue is one; the nature of enemy domicile is another. New problems—or shall we say old problems in a new guise?—have arisen about occasional contraband. Our happy immunity from a European war for just a century—with one brief interval—has created a close season for problems of this kind, and they are now very strong on the wing. It is not surprising, therefore, that legal marksmanship is not conspicuously good.

The war has brought these things very close home to us, and there can be few patriotic Englishmen at the present moment who are not deeply concerned with their legal aspect in one form or another. We have borne this consideration in mind, and while striving to write a book which shall not be lacking in learning, we have written with an eye to all sorts and conditions of men—the man who is concerned about his duties, in the event of invasion, at home and the soldier with his rights abroad, the special constable, the sheriff, the magistrate, the recruit, the trader, the shipowner, and the newspaper proprietor. And we have studied with some care those drastic Regulations under the Defence of the Realm Act, which place every citizen under military law. They are the most remarkable example of delegated legislation that this country has yet witnessed. We have criticised them with some freedom, not so much because we doubt their wisdom as because we question their authority. It may well be that the Act might have been more stringent; the Regulations could not have been more arbitrary. We do not forget that within a four hours' journey of Charing Cross this country is fighting for its existence, but we venture to think that of the many glorious aspects of England's part in this great struggle not the least glorious in the eyes of future historians should be the fact (and may it continue a fact!) that the courts continued open, the king's writ ran, Parliament was in session, and the Press was free.

It seems almost superfluous to say that though we sometimes hint a legal doubt, we never insinuate a political dislike. Whatever be one's political opinions to-day (if indeed opinions are still political), we are all united in the conviction that never was a cause more just or a war more righteous. That conviction, as will be seen from the chapter on the Neutrality of Belgium, the authors share to the full. As regards that chapter, and the one on the Laws of War on Land, we have striven to present these matters in a new light by going to German sources for a statement of the law, and nothing more damning, both of the wantonness with which Germany provoked the war and the brutality with which she has conducted it, could possibly be found. We would particularly invite the attention of the reader to two things. First, the strong words—stronger than anything to be found in English jurists—used by German lawyers as to the inviolability of Belgian neutrality, and the impossibility of its ever being outraged. Second, the amazingly cynical declarations of the German General Staff as to "the flabby emotionalism" of the Hague Conventions and as to the beatitude of cruelty in the field. That such opinions should be authoritatively expressed in the official manual of the German General Staff (*Kriegsbrauch im Landkriege*), issued for the guidance of officers in the field, will probably come as a shock to many English readers. This remarkable publication appears to be unknown in this country, and it has never been translated.[1] As the reader will see, it throws quite a new light, a lurid light and tragic, upon the German conception of the laws of war. Nothing more cynical has been written since Machiavelli wrote *The Prince*, and of it may be said what was said of the sombre Florentine, its authors are seldom indignant and never surprised. It is the true child of the Prussian military tradition.

The recent discussion of the status of foreign companies appears to have proceeded in ignorance of Story's important dicta in *S. P. G.* v. *Wheeler*, and the general discussion of the status of enemy aliens, in disregard of the special terms of the Declarations of War under which *Wells* v. *Williams* was decided. "Trading with the Enemy" is spoken of and legislated about, as though it meant all com-

[1] A translation of this book, with a critical introduction, is issued by Mr John Murray under the title of *The German War Book*.

PREFACE

mercial transactions, instead of being a technical term for transport. Sweeping assumptions have been made that all such transactions are penal, in apparent ignorance of the absence of conclusive authority to that effect, and the fact that Georgian legislation imposed only very light penalties even on the insurance of enemy ships. We have tried to examine these and kindred obscure points in the light of history and scientific principle.

The fundamental alterations which have been made in the Declaration of London; the atrocious German attempts to introduce as a weapon of warfare mines which may strike any peaceful voyager; the neglected *minutiæ* of the law of prize; the provisions of the Hague Conventions on sea warfare—are instances of topics in the sphere of maritime law which are well worth examination, and we have endeavoured to deal with them as succinctly as possible.

It is our privilege to inscribe this work to His Majesty's Attorney-General, Sir John Simon, but it will be understood that we alone are responsible for any statements made therein.

We desire to express our cordial thanks to Mr Pickering, the Librarian of the Inner Temple, for his courtesy in facilitating our use of the library in the prosecution of this work.

T. BATY.
J. H. MORGAN.

1 MITRE COURT BUILDINGS,
TEMPLE, *January* 1915.

CONTENTS

PREFACE ix

PART I

THE CROWN AND THE SUBJECT

CHAPTER I

A STATE OF WAR

The Prerogative to Declare War—War within the Realm—War and the Common Law—What is a "State of War"?—Emergency and "Public Danger"—What the Crown may or may not do—Trespass upon Land—Closing of the Ports—Stuart Doctrines of the Prerogative—Martial Law—Theories of Martial Law—Offences against the State—Treason—Treason in Time of War—Aliens and Treason—Sedition—Conspiracy—Espionage 3

CHAPTER II

THE DEFENCE OF THE REALM

Proclamations—Invasion—Duty of the Subject and Right of the Crown at Common Law—The Militia Ballot and Impressment—Police and Special Constables—Aliens—Precautionary Statutes—The Customs and Inland Revenue Acts—Defence Acts and Military Manœuvres Acts—Regulation of the Forces Act and Control of Railways—Aerial Navigation Acts and the Freedom of the Air—The Army Act (Billeting and Requisitions). Exercise of these Statutory Powers on the outbreak of War 43

CHAPTER III

THE DEFENCE OF THE REALM (*continued*)

I. The New Emergency Legislation.

The Emergency Legislation: The Defence of the Realm Acts I. and II., Scope of the Regulations, Effect on Personal Liberty and on Rights of Property, A *Lex Regia*, Specified Statutory Powers, the Censorship of the Press, the Subjection of the Civil Population to Martial Law, the Aliens Restriction Act, the Special Constables Act, the Intoxicating Liquor Restriction Act, Army Supplies and Naval Billeting Act, Unreasonable Withholding of Food Supplies Act, and Articles of Commerce Act 71

II. The Revised Emergency Legislation.

The Defence of the Realm (Consolidation) Act, No. III., and the New Consolidated Regulations—The New Enacting Words—New Offences: Compulsion to furnish Information and to "Inform"—The Liberty of the Press—The Position of Newspaper Proprietors—The Question of Guilty Intent—The Death Penalty—Martial Law and Something More—Conclusion . 101

CONTENTS

CHAPTER IV

THE ARMED FORCES OF THE CROWN

The Prerogative of the Crown :—I. The United Kingdom—The Army Act, the King's Regulations, and the Articles of War—The Army Annual Act—The Contract of Enlistment—The Reserve Forces Act—The Militia Acts—The Territorial Forces Act—Commissions—Pensions—The Navy—The Naval Discipline Act—The Naval Reserve Acts 114

II. The Overseas Dominions and India—The Army Act in relation thereto—Dominion Defence Acts—The Colonial Naval Defence Act, 1865—Dominion Naval Forces Act, 1911—Dominion Naval Acts—The Committee of Imperial Defence—The Imperial General Staff 127

III. The Organisation and Control of the Forces—The Secretary of State and the Army Council—The First Lord and the Board of Admiralty . . . 135

CHAPTER V

MILITARY LAW AND COURTS-MARTIAL

Military Law—Persons normally Subject to it—The Code of Discipline—In Time of Peace—In Time of War—"Communicating Intelligence to the Enemy": Soldier's Letters, and Newspaper Correspondents—The Soldier's Dual Position—The Duty of Obedience in Peace and in War—Procedure of Courts-martial—The Control of the Civil Courts—Malice and Privilege—The Naval Discipline Act 142

PART II

THE CROWN AND THE ENEMY

CHAPTER I

THE LAWS OF WAR ON LAND

                                                                          PAGE

I. Sources and their Value—Views of German Military Writers—Views of German General Staff—The Civil Population in War—Combatants and Non-combatants—The *levée en masse*—Army "Followers" and Newspaper Correspondents — Chaplains, Nurses, and Medical Men – The "Red Cross"—"Undefended Places" and their Immunity from Bombardment . 165

II. Occupation by the Enemy—Rights and Duties of Inhabitants : (1) Can they be Compelled to Assist the Enemy? (2) Hostages and Vicarious Punishments ; (3) Forced Labour and Requisitions ; (4) Cash Contributions ; (5) War Treason . . . 180

III. The Conduct of Hostilities : Limitations — Aerial Warfare and Expanding Bullets—Treachery and Stratagems—Spies—Prisoners—The Wounded and Sick—Reprisals 190

IV. Rights and Duties of Neutrals 200

CHAPTER II

ANNEXATION AND ACTS OF STATE

Annexation—Status of New Territory—Status of Inhabitants—Power of Crown to cede Territory—Claims against New Government—Acts of State—Treaties as Sources of Right—Articles of Capitulation—Claims arising out of Property—Claims arising out of Contract—State Succession 202

CONTENTS

CHAPTER III

LAWS OF WAR AT SEA

Naval Warfare—Hague Conventions—Is Rescue "Unneutral"? — Internment — Bombardment — Mines— Signalling in Port — Mails and Mariners—Use of Neutral Ports—"Military" Areas . . . 212

PART III

THE CROWN AND ITS TREATY OBLIGATIONS

CHAPTER I

THE NEUTRALITY OF BELGIUM AND LUXEMBURG

Neutral States and Neutralised States—The Treaties— Right and Duty of Neutrals—Views of the German General Staff—Right and Duties of Neutralised States —The "Benevolent Neutrality" of the German Proposals—The Duty of the Contracting Parties to Interfere—"Collective Guarantee" and the Doctrine of Limited Liability—Joint and Several Liability— The Public Law of Europe — Retrospect and Prospect 229

CONTENTS

PART IV

THE SUBJECT AND THE ENEMY

CHAPTER I

ALIEN ENEMIES. CORPORATIONS AS ENEMIES

PAGE

Alien Enemy—Early Law—Safe-conducts—Declarations of Protection — Present Day — Protected, Tolerated, and Imprisoned Enemies—Corporations—Companies—*Salomon* v. *Salomon*—*S. P. G.* v. *Wheeler*—International Firms happening to be Registered in Germany—Place of Business — Non-trading Corporations—Nationality of Trusts—Receivers . . . 247

CHAPTER II

CONTRACTS WITH ALIEN ENEMIES

Early Law—Littleton—Coke—Later Doctrine—*Wells* v. *Williams* — *Alsenius* v. *Nygren* — Particularity of Pleading—Suits by Agents and Trustees—Prescription—Payment to Agents—Pre-war Contracts—Chancellor Kent—Bills of Exchange—Necessaries—Insurance—War pending Suit — Non-commercial Contracts—Enemy Defendants—Story—Attachment . . 267

CONTENTS

CHAPTER III

Trading with the Enemy

Origin and Nature of Prohibition—Traffic, not Contract, struck at—Bynkershoek—Kent—Scott—Story—Noncontractual Traffic—Increasing Importance attached to Financial Bearing—Penalty—Is Withdrawal Trade?—Continuous Voyage—Allies—Enemy Character . 294

CHAPTER IV

Person and Property of Enemies

I. On Land. Person—Property. II. At Sea. Enemy Character—Tests—Nationality—Domicile and House of Trade—Political Enemy never treated as Neutral or Friend, though Subject sometimes treated as Neutral—Domicile means Ordinary Civil Domicile, independent of Trade — Scott and Story quoted against Westlake and Dicey — House of Trade: Its Necessary Elements discussed — Mere Agency not Sufficient — Or Branch — There must be Trade *in* the Territory as well as *to* it—Case of Companies operating Abroad—Contracts and Captures — Confusion between Rules which (*a*) Invalidate Contracts — (*b*) Confiscate Traffic — Test of Enemy not the same in both—Admittedly, for the test of Innocence in the former case is not alleged to be Domicile but mere Tolerated Presence—Technical Rules as to Ownership disregarded—Transfers *in transitu* — Ships—Goods — Declaration of

London — Enemy Interests in Neutral Property—Neutral in Enemy Property—Charter-parties—Private Seizure—Conquest changes National Character—"At Sea" 304

CHAPTER V

THE PROCLAMATIONS OF AUGUST, SEPTEMBER, AND OCTOBER 1914

Failure to distinguish Contract from Trade—Successive Proclamations of 5th August, 12th August, 9th September—Circular of 21st August, and Statute—Retrospective—Analysis of these—Novel Criterion of Enemy Character for Proclamation Purposes—Branches—Agents 342

PART V

THE CROWN AND THE NEUTRAL

CHAPTER I

PRIZE-COURT PROCEDURE

Essentially different from Common-Law Trial—Not a Contest, but a Confession—An International Court, with an International Practice—Whether bound by Local Regulations—Cannot sit in Neutral Territory—Captor's Evidence only admitted if Flaws in Claimant's Evidence—"Further Proof"—Story—Scott—Lushington—Phillimore—Twiss—Claims and Evidence of Enemies 357

CONTENTS

CHAPTER II

CONTRABAND

Objective Warlike Test—Military Quality—Fluctuations —Test of Port of Destination in Doubtful Cases —" Occasional " Contraband—Pre-emption — Food, Naval Stores—Reversion in Nineteenth Century to Stricter Limit — Nullified by Chase's Doctrine of Intention — The Doctrine examined — Continuous Voyage—Kleen—Declaration of London—Proclamations of 1914—Declaration of Paris exploded—Penalty of Contraband Carriage 370

CHAPTER III

BLOCKADE

History—" Paper " Blockades—Modern Uselessness of Blockade—Notification—British and French Variance — Declaration of London — Continuous Voyage — Penalty of Blockade—Maintenance of Blockade— Impartiality — Spurious " Blockades " — (really instances of Contraband, Reprisals, etc.) — Infringement by Entry or Exit—Warships . . . 381

CHAPTER IV

UNNEUTRAL SERVICE

Four Cases : (1) Aiding Enemy's Warlike Operations— (2) Participating in Close Trade—(3) Carriage of Troops and High Officials—(4) Carriage of Despatches —Declaration of London—Dangers of its Wide Interpretation—Neutral Flag an Asylum for Isolated Individuals 387

PART VI

MISCELLANEOUS

CHAPTER I

COMMENCEMENT AND END OF WAR

Commencement—Acts of Hostility—"Conditional War" condemned by Balfour, Scarlett, Metternich—End—Treaty of Peace—Possible Saving for Subsequent Acts of Hostility—Effect of War on Treaties . . 395

CHAPTER II

THE MORATORIUM

History—Objects—Method—Proclamations of 2nd August, 6th August, 12th August, 1st September, 3rd September, 30th September—Analysis — Bills — Cheques — Contracts—No Moratorium for Delivery of Goods—Pre-moratorium Debts—Cases—Inclusion in Second Moratorium of Debts then first falling due—Interest—Bank Deposits and Notes—Foreign Debts—Current Accounts—Distraint—Cumulative Accounts—Courts Emergency Powers Act—Rules of 8th September 1914 401

CHAPTER III

FORCE MAJEURE, ETC.

Not recognised in England—Exceptions—Legal Impossibility, Continued Existence of Specific Things—No Freight when Voyage becomes Illegal — Unless

Delivery at Equivalent Port—War Dangers may excuse Deviation or Delay—Effect on Contract of Carriage—War Clauses—Foreign Act of State not an Excuse?—" Restraint of Princes "— Boulay-Paty—" War "—Insurance : may be affected by War Clauses—Neutrals can claim for Damage caused by British Seizure, if Traffic Lawful—And perhaps for Risk of *primâ facie* Innocent Articles being held Contraband—Agreements to carry Goods to the Enemy—to Run Blockades—to Contravene Foreign Enlistment Act—Meaning of " Equip " in Sec. 8 412

APPENDIX

A.—*Illustrating Part I., Chapter II.*

1. Notification of a State of War (Aug. 4, 1914) . . 429
2. Order under Aerial Navigation Act (Aug. 2, 1914) . 430
3. Proclamation authorising Lords of Admiralty to requisition British Ships (Aug. 3, 1914) . . 430
4. Order in Council taking over Control of Railroads (Aug. 4, 1914) 431
5. Proclamation calling out Army Reserve and Territorial Force (Aug. 4, 1914) 432
6. Proclamation regarding the Defence of the Realm (Aug. 4, 1914) 434
7. Proclamation extending Bank Holidays (Aug. 3, 1914) 435
8. Army Order as to Billeting (Aug. 4, 1914) . . 435
9. Army Order as to Billeting (Sept. 15, 1914) . . 437
10. Proclamation warning British Subjects against contributing to German Loan (Aug. 5, 1914) . . 437

B.—*Illustrating Part I., Chapter III.*

PAGE
1. An Act to consolidate and amend the Defence of the Realm Acts (Nov. 27, 1914) 438
2. Consolidated Regulations under Defence of the Realm Act (Nov. 28, 1914) 441
3. Special Constables Act (Aug. 28, 1914) . . . 464
4. Unreasonable Withholding of Food Supplies Act (Aug. 10, 1914) 466
5. Articles of Commerce (Returns) Act (Aug. 28, 1914) . 467
6. Army (Supply of Food, Forage, and Stores) Act (Aug. 7, 1914) 469
7. Aliens Restriction Act (Aug. 5, 1914) . . . 470
8. The Aliens Restriction (Consolidation) Order (Sept. 9, 1914) 473
9. Aliens Restriction (Change of Name) Order (Oct. 8, 1914) 487

C.—*Illustrating Part III.*

1. Despatch of Sir E. Grey as to Proposed Violation of Belgian Neutrality (Aug. 4, 1914) . . . 488
2. Ultimatum of Sir E. Grey to Germany (Aug. 4, 1914) . 489
3. Memorandum of Foreign Office (Dec. 7, 1914) . . 490

D.—*Illustrating Part IV., Chapter I.*

1. Extract from Declaration of War by William III. (May 7, 1689) 491
2. Extract from Naturalisation Act, 1870 . . . 492

CONTENTS

E.—*Illustrating Parts IV., V., and VI.*

	PAGE
1. Trading with the Enemy Act (Sept. 18, 1914)	492
2. Trading with the Enemy Proclamation (Aug. 5, 1914)	497
3. Proclamation regarding Banking Business (Aug. 10, 1914)	498
4. Treasury Circular (Aug. 21, 1914)	500
5. Board of Trade Notice (Dividends), (Aug. 31, 1914)	501
6. Trading with the Enemy Proclamation, No. 2 (Sept. 9, 1914)	501
7. Board of Trade Notices (Freight, Fees) (Sept. 25, 1914)	505
8. Trading with the Enemy Proclamation (Oct. 8, 1914)	506
9. Customs Order: Certificates of Origin (Oct. 9, 1914)	508
10. Trading with the Enemy Amendment Act (Nov. 27, 1914)	512
11. Postponement of Payments Act (Aug. 3, 1914)	523
12. Moratorium of Aug. 2, 1914	524
13. Moratorium of Aug. 6, 1914	525
14. Moratorium of Aug. 12, 1914	527
15. Moratorium of Sept. 1, 1914	528
16. Moratorium of Sept. 3, 1914	530
17. Moratorium of Sept. 30, 1914	531
18. Courts (Emergency Powers) Act (Aug. 31, 1914)	533
19. Proclamation regarding Contraband (Aug. 4, 1914)	535
20. Proclamation against British Carriage of Contraband (Aug. 5, 1914)	537
21. Order in Council as to Declaration of London (Aug. 20, 1914)	538

CONTENTS

	PAGE
22. Additions to List of Contraband (Sept. 21, 1914)	540
23. Revision of List of Contraband (Oct. 29 and Dec. 23, 1914)	541
24. Revised Treatment of Declaration of London (Oct. 29, 1914)	544
25. Notice as to Discounting Bills (Aug. 12, 1914)	546
26. Patents, Designs, and Trade Marks Rules (Aug. 21, 1914)	546
27. Patents, Designs, and Trade Marks Rules, Additional Rule (Sept. 7, 1914)	550
28. Prize Courts (Egypt, Zanzibar, and Cyprus) Act (Sept. 18, 1914)	550
29. Order in Council under Prize Courts Act (Sept. 30, 1914)	551

F.—*Authors' Notes.*

1. Continuous Voyage	553
2. Public Engagements towards Enemy Persons	554

LIST OF CASES	557
INDEX	569

PROFESSOR MORGAN'S chapters on the Defence of the Realm Acts and the Regulations thereunder were completed in the early part of December. At the moment of going to press (5th February) the Lord Chancellor has announced in the House of Lords that the Government contemplate introducing a bill to amend the second Act in so far as it deprives the subject of the right to be tried by jury. It is impossible to comment further on this aspect of the matter, as Professor Morgan is engaged on official duties in France with the British Expeditionary Force.

PART I
THE CROWN AND THE SUBJECT

CHAPTER I

A STATE OF WAR

The Prerogative to Declare War—War within the Realm—War and the Common Law—What is a "State of War"?—Emergency and "Public Danger"—What the Crown may or may not do—Trespass upon Land—Closing of the Ports—Stuart Doctrines of the Prerogative—Martial Law—Theories of Martial Law. Offences against the State—Treason—Treason in Time of War—Aliens and Treason—Sedition—Conspiracy—Espionage.

A State of War.—To what extent is a declaration of war by the sovereign binding upon English courts? Is its existence a matter for judicial determination at all, or must the courts take "judicial notice" of the act of the Executive in declaring it? Behind these questions lies another: How far are the courts, being once satisfied of its existence, as between England and a foreign state, bound to regard it as a plea of justification for acts of the Executive done within this country? In other words, does it invest the Executive with any extraordinary authority over British subjects?

To take the major question first. So far as the relations of England with the foreign country are concerned, the declaration of the Executive would appear to be conclusive. "By the law and constitution of this country, the sovereign alone has the power of declaring war and peace."[1] And such a declaration carries with it all the force of law. As such it is of equal authority with an Act of Parliament and is judicially noticed.[2] It is treated with the same respect as a declaration of the Executive as to the status of a foreign sovereign,[3] or as to the existence of any jurisdiction of His Majesty in a foreign country.[4] In this sense and to this extent it is properly described as "an Act of State," a term which, as we shall see, is constantly misused in legal controversy. The effect of such a declaration as regards aliens is beyond doubt—it puts them in the position of alien enemies with all its attendant disabilities. Its effect as regards British subjects is another matter and will require careful consideration. It may, however, easily happen that no declaration precedes the commencement of hostilities. But though no ultimatum be issued to the foreign power, it is inconceivable that this country could enter upon a war without some kind of official intimation to its own subjects. The Act governing the embodiment of the Territorial Force requires that Parliament be summoned within a fixed period, and some emergency legislation is always immediately necessary. The courts would regard statutes which thus "spoke of" war as entitled to judicial notice.[5] Failing

[1] The *Hoop*, 1 C. Rob. 196.
[2] *Esposito* v. *Bowden*, 7 E. & B. 763.
[3] *The Parlement Belge*, (1880) 5 P.D. 197.
[4] *R.* v. *Crewe*, L. T. Rep., vol. cii., p. 760.
[5] *R.* v. *de Berenger*, 3 M. & S. 67. Lord Ellenborough treated the contemporary statutes which "spoke of a war with France" as exacting judicial notice from the judges.

RUMOURS OF WARS

either a declaration or some such statute they might no doubt treat it as a question of fact. "Public notoriety" would in the opinion of Foster be sufficient.[1] But some act of the prerogative is clearly necessary. Subjects cannot commit the country to war[2] independently of the Crown; to attempt to do so would be an offence against the Foreign Enlistment Act. Foster's language about "actual hostility" being a question for the jury is, indeed, difficult to reconcile with that of Coke, who says precisely the opposite,[3] and the fact that the former is speaking of foreign war and the latter of a domestic state of war does not make Foster's position any stronger. The Court itself must decide this question as one of the admissibility of evidence, and it would certainly require some act of the Executive to establish the fact of war. It cannot go into questions of "strained relations."[4] Such matters are foreign to it in the most literal sense of the term. Wars and rumours of wars are not to be confounded. But once the Executive makes a declaration it is conclusive. And not only may it declare when war begins but also when it ends.[5]

---

[1] *Discourse of High Treason*, p. 219.

[2] *Cf.* Brooke's *Abridgement*, Tit. Denizen, pl. 20: "If all the people of England would make war with the King of Denmark, and our king will not consent to it, this is not war."

[3] Coke, *Inst.*, i. 249 *b*.

[4] *Janson* v. *Driefontein Consolidated Mines*, [1902] A.C. 484.

[5] *Cf.* the cases of the *Manilla* and the *Pelican* in Edward's *Adm. Rep.*, i., p. 4 and Appendix D, where it was held that His Majesty could decide at any time, and independently of a formal capitulation during the progress of a war with France,

War within the Realm. — This conclusion may appear difficult at first sight to reconcile with the statements of some writers,[1] that war is a fact which must be proved like any other fact. There certainly are a considerable number of cases which would appear to lend countenance to this view, but they are all concerned with the question of the existence of war *within* the British Dominions. In other words, they turn on the relation of sovereign and subject, and not of sovereign and alien, or of alien and subject. Whether a state of war exists within British territory is always a matter for judicial determination, and a mere proclamation to that effect has no authority. In the much-disputed *Marais* case it is plain that Lord Halsbury regarded the state of war as having been established to the satisfaction of the Court, and the Court below was clearly of the opinion that if the prisoner had been detained in the place where he was arrested, it would have been at liberty to inquire whether there was justification for the proclamation declaring a state of war to exist in that particular district.[2] And in a number of South African cases[3] the local courts have made it clear that a mere declaration by the military that a state of war exists is not a sufficient return to a writ of *Habeas Corpus*, or of *De homine libero exhibendo*.

whether the colony of St Domingo had ceased to be part of the French dominions, and thereby could determine whether it was an enemy country.

[1] *Cf.* Sir Frederick Pollock, *Law Quarterly Review*, xviii., p. 156.

[2] *Ex parte Marais*, [1902] A.C. 109.

[3] *The Queen* v. *Bekker*, [1900] 17 Juta. 348 ; *In re Tilonko*, [1906] Natal, L.R. (N.S.), xxvii., p. 570.

THE TEST OF WAR

It must be *shown* that there is a state of war.[1] As to what will suffice to constitute a state of war is a more doubtful question. The old test that the fact of the courts being able to sit is conclusive evidence that no state of war exists is, it is true, regarded by some writers (wrongly, as we hope to show) as definitely discarded since the *Marais* case. The South African courts have laid stress upon the control of the military as being the decisive factor, though with some difference of opinion as to whether the fact of the control being exercised or of the necessity for its exercise is to be regarded.[2] The fact however, of war being proved to exist in one part of the country, does not carry with it a presumption that it exists in other parts of the country.[3] If the North of Scotland were invaded by German troops, it would not follow that the South of England was in a state of war. The proof of the one proposition would not carry with it a proof of the other. This, however, is a question to which we shall return.

War and the Common Law. — We take it, therefore, as established, that the mere fact of England being at war with a foreign country does

---

[1] *Cf.* De Villiers, C.J., *In re Kok*, (1879) Buchanan's *Rep.* (S.C.) ix., p. 62 ; and *cf.* Maasdorp, J., *In re Fourie*, [1900] Buchanan, xvii., p. 173 : "There is abundant *proof* upon the documents that the military alone for the time being can enforce order."

[2] Contrast *R. v. Geldenhuys*, [1900] Shiel, x., p. 369 (military occupation and proclamation thereof regarded as conclusive), with *R. v. Bekker*, [1900] 17 Juta. 348 (proclamation disregarded and proof of necessity required).

[3] *Cf.* Cockburn in *Reg. v. Nelson and Brand*, and *cf.* Buchanan, J., in the Marais case.

not place English territory in a state of war—*i.e.*, it does not operate to subject it to martial law— reserving for later consideration what may be the scope of martial law when the seat of war is admittedly transferred to these islands. Does then the fact of our being at war with a foreign country invest the Executive with any power over the persons and property of British subjects which they would not possess in time of peace? The answer must, we think, be in the negative. The Executive will possess, in regard to British subjects, those powers and no more than those powers, of which it is already possessed at common law to deal with breaches of the law and disturbances of the peace. A mere declaration that the country is in danger will make no difference. Even those who are prepared to press the immunity of the Executive in the matter of martial law, once the fact of war is established, to its furthest conclusion, admit that, failing the establishment of the fact, the view here taken is sound. Sir Erle Richards, who takes high prerogative ground and argues against any rights of redress both during a state of war and after it, admits that "in times of emergency falling *short of war* the Court may decide whether there was sufficient necessity to justify any suspension of the ordinary law."[1] This, however, does not put it strongly enough. No necessity short of war itself will justify the suspension of the law in times of emergency. The Executive may at such times have very strong grounds for supposing that a British subject is actively assisting the enemy; but unless they can

[1] See the *Law Quarterly Review*, xviii., pp. 133-142.

produce such evidence as will justify a committal for trial for treason, or for an offence against the Official Secrets Act (to take two examples), they will not be able to plead "necessity" as a return to a writ of *Habeas Corpus* if the prisoner is arrested and detained without trial.

Let us consider this question more closely.

It is the prerogative of the Crown to provide for the defence of the realm. So much must be admitted. But what legal immunities, if any, this prerogative carries with it is a question on which a great confusion of thought seems to exist. This confusion is largely due to a vague idea that in a state of things intermediate between peace and war, a time of "emergency" or "imminent danger," some dormant prerogative is quickened into life at the expense of the common law rights of the subject. We believe that there is no foundation for this doctrine at all. It has been supported by the citation of passages from Coke and Hale which, if carefully examined, will be found to prove the very opposite. The passage in Coke is as follows:—

> "But when enemies come against the realm to the sea-coast it is lawful to come upon my land adjoining to the same coast, to make trenches or bulwarks for the defence of the realm, for every subject hath benefit by it. And for this by the common law, every man may come upon my land for the defence of the realm, as appears 8 Ed. IV. 23 A."[1]

It should be pointed out, in the first place, that this passage occurs in the report of a case in which the

---

[1] Coke, 12 Rep. 12, *The Case of Saltpetre*.

judges were discussing the right of the king to dig and take saltpetre to make gunpowder. The right was sustained on the ground of being a purveyance. Purveyance has now been abolished by statute, and much of the argument which supports it may therefore be taken to have lost its force. But there remains the categorical statement that the Crown may come upon my land for the defence of the realm. It seems to be pretty evident, however, from the context that Coke is considering a state of war, not an apprehension of war. Even then he is careful to stipulate that no more damage is to be done than is necessary, and that after the danger is over "the trenches and bulwarks ought to be removed." Moreover, he assimilates the right of the Crown to take these steps to the right to pull down neighbouring houses to arrest a fire. This alone serves to reduce the prerogative to the dimensions of that ordinary common law right of private citizens which justifies a trespass to abate a nuisance or to avoid a greater harm. Judged by these standards, the only right the Crown has is the right to meet not a nominal danger, nor even an apprehended one, but danger which is imminent and actually exists. There must be "necessity" for the act, and the test of that necessity is the objective test of the judgment which a "reasonable man" may be supposed to exercise at such a time.[1] If the person taking the precautions does not exercise such judgment, but acts unreasonably, no plea of apprehension will save him. True, the necessity will be

[1] See, for example, the case of *Cope* v. *Sharpe*, [1910] 1 K.B. 496, a case of precaution against fire.

judged by things as they were at the time and not as they afterwards turned out to be—a subsequent change in the wind or a subsidence of the gale may serve to show that the fire would not have spread to my neighbour's house, or that the shipper's cargo need not have been jettisoned after all. In such case I may plead that I could not reasonably have foreseen the turn of events, and any precautions, although not actually necessary as things turned out, will have been justified. But I must prove that. And we submit that the Crown is in just the same position as regards any measures it may take—it is in no better position, and no worse, than a private individual.

There is not the slightest authority for saying that the Crown enjoys any peculiar immunities from the law of trespass. No such prerogative was pleaded when an Admiralty officer entered on another's land to stake it out for purposes of defence.[1] . And a statement by a learned writer [2] that the Crown can expropriate land in virtue of its prerogative, for the defence of the realm, is not borne out by the only case he cites in support.[3] Indeed, the Defence Acts and the

---

[1] *Raleigh* v. *Goschen*, [1898] 1 Ch. 73.

[2] The late Mr W. F. Craies in the article "Lands Clauses Acts" in the *Encyclopædia of the Laws of England*," vol. viii., p. 1.

[3] *A. G.* v. *Tomline*, Ch. Div. 12, (1879) 214. The Crown was not suing directly in respect of any prerogative at all, but simply as owner of land which had been endangered by the defendant, a neighbouring landowner, removing shingle. There is an *obiter dictum* of Fry, J. (p. 230), about the duty of the Crown to protect all land from inundation as from foreign enemies, but there is nothing in it which bears out the claim put forward by Mr Craies.

Military Lands Acts, and the cases under them, are the strongest presumptive evidence to the contrary. The fact that the Crown has thought it necessary to go to Parliament for power to purchase land for the defence of the realm, and that such purchases when made, and the uses to which the purchased lands are put, are subject to the same rules[1] for determining what common law rights are injuriously affected as cases of compulsory purchase by railway companies and local authorities, goes far to negative the presumption. "Urgent public importance" makes no difference.

Similarly the contention is put forward that the "necessity arising from public danger or a state of war *might*, it is apprehended, justify the closing of the ports."[2] The sentence is ambiguous, and the references to Hale[3] do not strengthen it. What is quite certain is that the Crown has no such power, apart from statute, in time of peace.

---

[1] See, for example, *Blundell* v. *The King*, [1905] 1 K.B. 516, where it was held that the owner of land compulsorily taken for under the Defence Acts for the erection of a fort was entitled to compensation for loss of amenity to his adjoining land arising from the firing of guns. The contention of the Crown that the compensation should be differently estimated when the land was required for "purposes of urgent public importance" was not upheld. And cf. *in re Neds Point Battery*, Ir. Rep., [1903] 2 K.B. 198.

[2] Halsbury's *Encyclopædia of English Law*, vi. 460.

[3] Hale is much too cautious a writer to commit himself definitely. See his tract, *De Portibus Maris* (Hargreave's *Law Tracts*, vol. i.), "*Possibly* in time of hostility and public danger," p. 96. And see chapters viii. and ix. *passim* of the same tract.

It cannot prohibit imports or exports—to detain the subject's goods would entitle him to an action for trespass on the case.[1] To detain his person would entitle him to a writ of *Habeas Corpus*. The Crown can no longer prevent a subject from leaving[2] or entering the realm. Hale is clearly very doubtful about any prerogatives to the contrary, and he takes refuge in the reflection that restraints are possible "only where and when an Act of Parliament puts any restraint," which is to contradict much that he surmises elsewhere and to admit our case. We submit that the Crown's power as to the ports stands on the same footing as its power as to the land. Unless it can prove to the satisfaction of a court that there is actual danger, its own apprehension of it will not justify its officers in an action for trespass any more than it would justify the private citizen.

To take any other ground is to bring in the discredited notion of "Acts of State," a plea which,

---

[1] *Barrow* v. *Arnaud*, (1842) 8 Q.B. 595, and see Morgan, *The House of Lords and the Constitution*, p. 56. By *statute* the Crown has powers of detention under the Customs Consolidation Act.

[2] It is universally admitted that the old writ, *Ne exeat regno*, which at one time might be used to restrain subjects generally for reasons of state, is now entirely confined to judicial proceedings, being restricted to defendants in claims of a pecuniary character. No one would now contend with Jeffreys (*Sandys* v. *East India Co.*, 10 St. Tr. 520), that "surely the king may restrain his subjects from going beyond the sea, and is not bound to give any reason for his so doing." Hale, although writing in the seventeenth century, does not seem at all certain, even where it is a case of public danger.

as Stephen[1] rightly urges, has no meaning as between sovereign and subject. We do not know of a single case since the times of the Stuarts in which it has been successfully urged. It was put forward by the Attorney-General in a case before the Privy Council,[2] but their lordships did not think it necessary to pronounce upon such "grave questions." We think it fortunate for the law officers of that day that they did not.[3] Arguments of this kind are indistinguishable from those put forward on behalf of the most despotic claims of the Stuart kings. They are properly reprobated in the declaratory words of the Act against ship money.[4]

[1] *Hist. Crim. Law*, ii., p. 65. And cf. *Entick* v. *Carrington*, 19 St. Tr. 1030: "With respect to the argument of State necessity or a distinction that has been arrived at between State offences and others, the common law does not understand that kind of reasoning, nor do our books take notice of any such distinction."

[2] *Walker* v. *Baird*, [1892] A.C. 492 :—Lord Hobhouse : " Can the Crown, by treating with a foreign power, acquire new rights against its own subjects ? "

The Attorney-General (Sir R. Webster): "No, and it is not contended that the Crown can sanction an invasion by its officers of private rights in order to carry out any kind of treaty. It can only do so when the treaty is to put an end to war *or the present war*, and then the Crown has the power of compelling obedience to its provisions, on public grounds and for the public safety."

[3] It is difficult to see how any court could take note of the plea of apprehension of war as justifying preventive measures. In *Janson* v. *Driefontein Mines Co.*, [1902] A.C. 493, Lord Davey laid down in express words that the courts cannot decide whether war is imminent or not, nor can they recognise a state of affairs intermediate between war and peace.

[4] Denying the doctrine "that the king is the sole judge both

They rest on a train of reasoning now wholly discredited, according to which the king's right to control commerce and to limit the subject's freedom of movement was supposed to follow from his right to make peace and war. If he could make war, so, it was argued, he could take steps to prevent it, and an embargo on goods, or a commercial treaty, or a prohibition to leave the realm might be regarded as being steps of that character. But the life of the law, as has been truly said,[1] is not logic but experience, and the common law affords no ground for this kind of argument. The law presumes a state of peace until a state of war is proved; it has no room for something that is neither one thing nor the other.[2] Mere "disturbance" will never do as a return to a writ of *Habeas Corpus*.[3] There was considerable disturbance and even danger in the state of Ireland some months ago, but the Irish law officers knew better than

of the danger and when and how the same is to be presented and avoided," 17 Car. I. cap. 14.

[1] Holmes, *The Common Law*, p. 1.

[2] The position is well put by the learned authors of the *Manual of Military Law*, p. 4: "The law of most foreign countries recognises an intermediate state of war and peace, known by the name of the state of siege, under which the ordinary law is suspended for the time being by proclamation; but such a state of things cannot exist under English law, which never presupposes the possibility of civil war and makes no express provisions for such contingencies."

[3] *Cf.* De Villiers, C.J. (*In re Kok*, 9 Buchanan, S.C.R. 66): "The disturbed state of the country ought not, in my opinion, to influence the Court, for its first and most sacred duty is to administer justice to those who seek it, *and not to preserve the peace of the country*."

to urge it as an argument in favour of the validity of the proclamation forbidding the importation of arms. They rested their case, as they were bound to do, upon statute.[1]

There are signs in the reports of old cases that Stuart lawyers, with all their leniency to the prerogative, had a clearer conception of the true distinction than is sometimes exhibited to-day. Hakewill in his speech[2] on Bate's Case draws a distinction between "defensive" and "offensive" warfare which goes to the root of the matter. In case of actual invasion of the realm by foreign enemies there is, as he points out, a common law duty of the subject to assist in taking every available means to repel the enemy. But in case of "offensive" or foreign war, the king must come to Parliament. The fact that we are engaged in a foreign war does not operate to place us at the mercy of the Executive, or to suspend our common law rights. And even as regards measures of defence against an invading enemy, Oliver St John[3] and Mr Justice Berkeley[4] are to be found on the same side, the one in urging, the other in admitting, that unless the danger extends to the whole country, the common law subsists in all its integrity. Holborne, Hampden's counsel, insists[5] that unless the danger is "so imminent" that Parliament cannot be consulted, the Crown has no power to act. And this, we submit, approaches to

---

[1] *Hunter* v. *Coleman*, Ir. Rep., [1914] 372.
[2] See Parl. Debates in 1610, *Camd. Soc.*, and Prothero, *Select Documents*, p. 342.
[3] Rushworth, ii. 481.
[4] 3 St. Tr. p. 1090, *The Case of Ship Money*. [5] *Ibid.*

the true conclusion of the whole matter. It is indeed recognised in nearly every statute[1] that contemplates the exercise of unusual powers by the Crown to meet an "emergency." Parliament is to be summoned within so many days to approve the steps taken, even though it has already conceded them in general terms. Any powers which have not been so conceded are exercised by the Executive at its peril, and it must justify their exercise *in every case*. There can be no such thing as a general suspension, or even a partial modification, of the law.

"Martial Law."—The whole subject has been greatly confused by the importation into it of a term which was formerly restricted, and very properly restricted, to an entirely different subject. We refer to the term "martial law." Martial law formerly meant military law, the code of discipline applied to soldiers, and so the seventeenth-century writers undoubtedly understood it.[2] But modern writers have appropriated the term to the assumption of arbitrary power over civilians, and have then proceeded to read the earlier writers by the light of its rays. The result is to darken their counsel. It is a gross anachronism. Hale quite clearly meant by martial law, the law applied to an army *and nothing else*.[3] Meaning this, he was much too clear a thinker to fall into the error of assuming that it could mean some-

[1] *E.g.*, The Territorial Forces Act.
[2] It is in this sense that it is still used in the preamble to the Army Annual Act and the Army Act of 1881.
[3] *History of the Common Law*, pp. 36-42 : "The necessity of good order and discipline *in an army* is that *only* which can give these laws countenance."

thing else in time of war. It could not, he held, apply to civilians under any circumstances.[1] If this contemporary connotation of the term had been understood, modern lawyers could not have fallen into the error into which Lord Halsbury and many others have fallen of assuming that the Petition of Right, by forbidding martial law in time of peace, legalised it in time of war.[2] It did nothing of the kind. The contemporary debates in the House of Commons show that the men of those days did not contemplate its legality under any circumstances.[3] Even a rebel, they argued, taken with arms in his hand is entitled to be tried at common law.[4] If he cannot be

---

[1] *History of the Common Law*, p. 35 : "For others who were not listed under the army had no colour or reason to be bound by military constitutions applicable only to the army, whereof they were not parts ; but they were to be ordered and governed according to the laws to which they were subject *though it were time of war.*"

[2] Cockburn did not fall into this error (see *The Queen* v. *Nelson*, Finlason's edition, p. 66). He thought the Petition of Right condemned the exercise of martial law *against* the subject "under any circumstances," and even as against soldiers except in the case of armies in time of war. Blackburn (*Queen* v. *Eyre*, p. 73) was not so certain, but he was quite sure that no support for any inference in favour of martial law could be drawn from the Petition.

[3] *Cf.* Rolls, 3 Rushworth, App. 79, 80. Rolls insisted that martial law could only apply to soldiers, and even then only in war-time, and to aliens. And note the carefully guarded words of the court in *Barwis* v. *Keppel* (1766), 2 Wils. 314 : "And *flagrante bello* the common law has never interfered *with the army*."

[4] *Ibid.*, and to the same effect Stephen and James in Forsyth's *Opinions*, p. 551 ; so also Hargrave. *Cf.* also the Colonial Office Circular of 1862 (printed in Cd. 2905 of 1906) and the Jamaica Commission P.P., 1866, xxv., p. 18.

THE SUSPENSION OF LAW 19

so tried then law is altogether suspended. They did not trouble themselves with the question with which modern lawyers are so greatly vexed, as to whether there could exist a kind of qualified state of war under which the courts might still be sitting, but sitting under such circumstances of military indulgence as would bind them not to interfere. This modern view has helped to give a kind of colour of legality to martial "law" which would have been incomprehensible to them, denying as they did the very existence of the thing except within the determinate limits of purely military law. Consequently they escaped the ambush of ambiguity into which modern writers have fallen in trying to determine how far a state of war seals the lips of the judges. They would have said that if the courts sit at all they are free to examine every act of the military upon its merits. War was a suspension of law, and to talk of its giving the Crown power to "legislate," by proclamation or otherwise, would have been unintelligible to them. Coke's language is quite unequivocal.

"And therefore when the courts of justice be open and the judges and ministers of the same may by law protect men from wrong and violence, and distribute justice to all, it is said to be time of peace. So when by invasion, insurrection, or rebellion, or such like, the peaceable course of justice is disturbed and stopped so as the courts of justice be as it were shut up, *et silent leges inter arma*, then it is said to be time of war. And the trial hereof is by the records and judges of courts of justice; for by them it will appear Justice had her equal course of proceeding at that time or no, and this shall not be tried by jury."¹

Cockburn, like earlier writers, avoided the modern confusion of thought by adhering to the older definition of martial law as being simply military law.² So did Loughborough.³ Consequently they also were not troubled by questions how far the Crown could establish martial "law." They held that it could do nothing of the kind.⁴ There was no such thing as martial law. There might be anarchy as a fact, but a fact is triable. Cockburn doubted if martial "law" could apply to the subject "under any circumstances." Military law—that is to say, trial by military tribunals according to the procedure now laid down in the Army Act, Manual of Military Law, and the King's Regulations—might, he thought, possibly be extended to civilians; but he is here obviously pleading simply that rebels taken with arms in their hands shall be tried with some approach to regularity, if there are no civil courts in existence to try them, and not be incontinently put to death.⁵ He is trying to contract the sphere of martial law (or rather to mitigate the consequences of this denial of its existence) by extending that of military law. This is why he quarrels with Hale for describing martial, *i.e.* military, law as "in truth and reality not a law but something indulged rather than allowed as a law." Cockburn is anxious to show that even military law has its

---

¹ *Inst.*, i. 249 *b*.   ² *Cf.* Cockburn, pp. 104, 121.
³ In *Grant* v. *Gould*, 2 H.Bl. 69.
⁴ Cockburn, pp. 69-70 ; Blackburn, p. 77.
⁵ Cockburn, p. 108.

limits.[1] And so too Blackburn; if (and only if) the courts cannot sit there must be some kind of regular authority over the civil population, but let us try to regularise it as much as possible.[2] If the courts can sit at all, then (such· we take to be their attitude) *Cadit quaestio;* we will take no judicial notice of proclamations, every act must be justified on its merits, and the test will be the same test as we apply in times of peace (*i.e.*, in the case of force used to effect an arrest or to quell a riot), namely, the necessity of the case. Of such tests we shall have something to say later. Here it is enough to remark that Blackburn insists that the same tests should be applied in war as in peace. Indeed, he applies[3] exactly the same tests to justification for acts under the state of anarchy called martial law,

[1] Much the same line of reasoning can be traced in the Irish case of *Wright* v. *Fitzgerald*, 27 St. Tr. 765, where the court urged that even an Act of Indemnity could not cover purely arbitrary proceedings and that courts-martial upon civilians must at least pursue "a grave and serious examination ... the best the nature of the case and the exact circumstances would allow of." The authorities "*should not exceed the necessity* which gave them the power."

[2] We think this part of the arguments of these learned judges (or rather Cockburn's) misconceived. A trial by "martial law" is a purely executive act and cannot be the subject of an appeal. The memorandum of such proceedings cannot be treated as the record of a court of justice, and consequently the civil courts have no jurisdiction to review their judgments. Cf. *A. G.* v. *Van Reenen*, [1904] A.C. 117. The opinion of Fitzjames Stephen and Edward James (Forsyth, p. 551), seems to be better conceived—they urge that the so-called courts-martial under martial law cannot properly be described as courts-martial at all.

[3] Blackburn's Charge, p. 58.

as were applied in the case of a riot during time of peace—the classical case of *R. v. Pinney.* The right to use force is to be measured by the duty to use it. Good intentions will not avail; the force used must not be excessive. Even if the doing of an act illegal at common law "was the salvation of the country, that . . . would be no bar in law to a criminal prosecution."[1]

Martial "law" thus disappears altogether and with it the sophistries that have accommodated it. Every arbitrary act committed by the authorities is triable on its merits if the courts are there to try it. If they are not, it can be tried after the war is over, and the fact of war and the necessity for the act may be inquired into both during the war and after it. Hence the reason why English and colonial governments have always felt incumbent upon them to pass Acts of Indemnity at the end of war. Such Acts are not superfluous. Every one of them, as Cockburn put it, involves "a manifest violation of justice."[2] That is precisely why they were passed. It would be almost impossible to justify the things done in time of war by the plea of necessity which common law courts alone recognise. You cannot extend the test of *Proximus ardet ucalegon* from a house on fire to a country in conflagration. But just because the courts know no other test, the legislature has to be called in to indemnify the executive against mistakes.

If our proposition as to the persistence of the common law during a state of war be not sound, the

[1] Blackburn's Charge, p. 58.
[2] In *Phillips* v. *Eyre*, 4 Q.B. 242-3.

AN UNTENABLE THEORY

only alternative maintainable to our mind is its converse: namely, that the common law is altogether abrogated.[1] The view which takes refuge in an intermediate state of things, and argues that the common law is for the time being neither quick nor dead but merely passive, seems to us untenable. According to this view it cannot inquire into the acts of the military authorities, even though the courts are sitting, but may do so afterwards. The "necessity" is too overwhelming to permit of a contemporaneous inquiry, but not so overwhelming as to forbid a retrospective one. This appears to have been the view taken by the South African courts. In effect they "said we cannot intervene now, to do so would be to 'assume responsibility' for and lend countenance to the acts of the military authorities; but we reserve our right to do so afterwards."[2] This is very otiose, although it subsequently received the support of the Judicial Committee in the *Marais* case.[3] It

---

[1] This converse view is taken by Sir Erle Richards in a very able and instructive article in the *Law Quarterly Review*, vol. xviii. pp. 133-142. We think that there is no escape from his conclusion that "*if it be at once admitted* [as the Privy Council held in the Marais case] that the courts have no power to interfere at the time, it seems to us to follow that the right is gone altogether. . . . That the courts cannot take action at the time seems to be consistent only with the hypothesis that there is no right to redress."

[2] See the cases cited *supra*, p. 7, and especially *R.* v. *Geldenhuys;* also *In re Fourie.* "When the proper time comes to inquire into the conduct of the military authorities they may be rendered amenable."

[3] And see the remarks of Lord Halsbury on his own judgment in the Marais case, *Attorney-General of Natal* v. *Tilonko*, 95 L.T.R. 853.

would seem to make it possible for the military authorities to expand the geographical area of martial law at will. And, indeed, this was pretty much the conclusion at which the courts in these cases arrived. The older doctrine, which received strong countenance in American cases[1] (with one exception) and in the opinions of law officers of the Crown,[2] that nothing short of the complete supersession of civil authority and the closing of the courts—in other words, such overwhelming necessity as silences justice altogether —can establish martial "law," was rejected. But the view we are criticising seems to proceed, as in an isolated American case,[3] on the assumption that the judiciary exists by sufferance of the Executive. It goes very near to a repudiation of jurisdiction altogether, on the ground that the matters are "political." In that respect it is perilously like the discredited doctrine of acts of state.[4] And it seems to us that those who uphold it will find it difficult to escape the conclusions arrived at in the solitary American case which supports them, namely this : " If this right [of interference] does not reside in the courts when the conflict is raging—if the judicial power is, at that

[1] Cf. *ex parte Milligan*, (1866) 4 Wallace 2, and also the dissentient judgment of Mr Justice Woodberry in *Luther* v. *Borden*, (1849) 7 Howard 1. *Cf.* also *Mitchell* v. *Harnony*, 13 Howard 115.

[2] Forsyth, *Cases and Opinions*, p. 551.

[3] *Luther* v. *Borden*, (1848) 7 Howard 1.

[4] It is significant that the only case cited by their lordships in support of their opinion in the Marais case was one (*Elphinstone* v. *Bedreechund*, (1830) 2 St. Tr., N.S., 379) of the annexation of a conquered territory. In such a case, of course, the laws can be altered by the conqueror at his pleasure.

time, bound to follow the decision of the political, *it must equally be bound when the contest is over;* it cannot, when peace is restored, punish as offences and crimes the acts which it before recognised, and was bound to recognise, as lawful."[1]

The Use of Force in Time of Peace.—We are now in a position to consider, without being vexed by the distractions of martial law, what powers the Executive really does possess at common law to deal with disturbances. The common law arms it with the power to use force. How much force? The answer is that the degree of force which may be used is always strictly relative to the degree of force that has to be met. A riot, for example—understanding by a riot a disturbance of the peace by three persons at least who have actually entered on the executive of their purpose in such a violent manner as to alarm at least one person of reasonable firmness and courage[2]—is only a misdemeanour and cannot, as such, be suppressed with firearms.[3] It is only when the rioters use such violence—for example, commit or attempt to commit arson or murder—as

---

[1] *Luther* v. *Borden.* It may be remarked that the case, logical though its reasoning is, does not really support the position we are criticising, because the decisive factor was the presence of a federal power to whom under Act iv. sect. 4 of the American Constitution the "political" recognition of State governments was expressly entrusted.

[2] *Cf.* the definitions in *R.* v. *Grahame*, (1888) 16 Cox 427, and *Field* v. *Receiver of Metropolitan Police*, [1907] 2 K.B. 860.

[3] It has been held that in the case of an unlawful assembly not amounting to a riot, the magistrate must do his best to disperse it with the aid of the police; cf. *R.* v. *Neale,* 9 C.P. 431. It is not his duty, *at such a stage*, to call in the military.

to have been guilty of a felony that a greater degree of force, indeed any amount of force that may be necessary to suppress the riot, may be employed. And it is always for a court to decide if the force has been justified.[1] To use too little force is a breach of a public duty and indictable as a misdemeanour; to use too much may easily be a felony and punishable as such, and it may also be an actionable wrong.

The use of the military in times of "danger" or "emergency" is governed by the same considerations as the use of civilians. It is the duty of civilians to assist the police when called upon to do so.

In this respect a soldier is in exactly the same position as a civilian. "Red coats or white coats, it makes no difference."[2] A soldier from the point of view of the common law is "only a civilian armed in a particular manner,"[3] and he has no more right to use his arms than a civilian has. That right depends entirely on the circumstances of the case. A civilian cannot use arms to repress a mere breach of the peace, but he can do so to prevent a felony.[4] He

---

[1] For a discussion of the whole subject the reader may be referred to Professor Morgan's article, "The Army and the Civil Power," in the *Nineteenth Century*, May 1914.

[2] Cf. *R.* v. *Gilliam;* reported in Appendix to Clode's *Military Forces of the Crown.*

[3] *Cf.* Bowen, L.J., in Report on the Featherstone Riots, 1893 (c. 7234).

[4] Cf. *Handcock* v. *Baker*, 2 B. & P. 234: "There is a great difference between the right of a private person in the case of intended felony and of breach of the peace. It is lawful for a private person to do anything to prevent the perpetration of a felony." (This, however, is putting it rather too broadly.)

can, for example, use arms to repress a riot which, from being a misdemeanour, has, owing to the violence employed by the rioters, or to their refusal to disperse within an hour of the reading of the proclamation under the Riot Act, attained the proportions of a felony. But just because the military carry deadly weapons, and just because the soldiers are bound by military law to obey any commands their officers may give, even though they be unlawful at common law, the authorities have laid it down that the military should only be employed by the civil power when all other resources fail them. It is for this reason also that they have emphasised the necessity for a greater exercise of restraint on the part of officers in acting on their own initiative than would be expected of a civilian.¹ The position is well put by Tindal, C.J., in his charge to the Grand Jury at Bristol in 1832:

> "Every private person may lawfully endeavour, of his own authority, and without any warrant or sanction of the magistrates, to suppress a riot by every means in his power—and not only has he authority, but it is his bounden duty as a good subject of the King to perform this to the utmost of his ability. The law acknowledges no distinction in this respect between the private citizen

But in the case of a riot he would do well to act under the orders of the Justices or Sheriff. "It is the more discreet way for everyone in such a case to attend and be assistant to the Justices, Sheriffs, or other Ministers of the King in the doing of it." Opinion of the judges in "The Case of Arms," Popham's *Rep.* 121.

[1] *Cf.* The Memorandum of a Secretary at War, quoted in Clode's *Military Forces of the Crown*, ii. 636, when he speaks of the duty of the military to exercise "greater restraint."

and the individual. If the one is bound to attend the call of the civil magistrate, so is the other. If the one may interfere for that purpose, when the occasion demands it, without the requisition of the magistrates, so may the other too; if the one may employ arms for that purpose, when arms are necessary, the soldier may do the same. Undoubtedly the safe exercise of discretion to wait for the magistrate ought to operate in a still stronger degree upon a military force."

Thus the soldier does not put off the duties of the civilian, to assist in keeping the peace, when he puts on the uniform of the soldier; but the degree of discretion he is required to exercise in regard to the occasion of their performance would appear to be somewhat greater than that demanded of the civilian. This applies to the officer because he has men under his command who are bound to obey his orders; he is responsible not only, like the civilian, for the exercise of any force personally exerted by him, but also for the force he exercises through others.[1] He should therefore be the more disposed to await the summons of the magistrate. But, none the less, that summons once issued does not absolve him, as many have been inclined to believe,[2] from exercising his discretion as to whether he will comply with it.

[1] *Cf.* The Memorandum of Sir John Scott printed in Clode, ii. 645, where he says that the military, although they cannot be called in except under the same circumstances as would justify the magistrate in calling upon civilians, "still act as military" in giving their assistance. In other words, the bonds of discipline are not relaxed.

[2] There are several remarks in the case of *Redford* v. *Birley* which would seem to suggest this. Cf. *State Trials*, i. (N.S.),

So far we have confined this discussion to the case of disturbances of such a felonious character that the law recognises a justification for the use of deadly weapons to repress them. This, obviously, is the kind of case in which the employment of the military may be *primâ facie* justifiable. To employ them merely in keeping the peace, in executing warrants, in enforcing legal process generally, or in preventing the commission of crime is not a contingency contemplated by the King's Regulations at all. But as the King's Regulations do not exclude the law, neither do they exhaust it, and there can be no doubt that the military can be, and, indeed, in certain cases must be employed for these purposes also. This is simply because a soldier is also a civilian and has all the civilian's obligations—no less and no more—to assist in keeping the peace. It is a misdemeanour to refuse to assist a constable in effecting an arrest, and it matters not whether the person called upon by the constable be a soldier or a civilian. A soldier may also arrest, on his own initiative, in the same circumstances, and no others, in which a civilian may do so. But the use of soldiers as such, and acting together under a superior officer, in these minor contingencies is unusual, because as a rule it is unnecessary. The law is the same as it was a hundred years ago, but the situation is vastly different. There was then no organised police force,

pp. 1255, 1214, and (at 1220): "It appears to me that the military, being called in, are not answerable for the judgment of the magistrates." This is putting it much too broadly. Some of the War Office Memoranda printed in Clode's Appendices err on the same side.

and the military were frequently called out in cases where their use to-day would be regarded, morally speaking, as both unnecessary and provocative. The law, however, is the same now as it was then, and in recent years the military have been used — for example, in the Sidney Street case and in evictions in Ireland, whether actively or passively, either to shoot or to make an imposing display of contingent force—to assist in cases which fell far short of a riot. The law on the subject has been expressly put by Best, J., in *Redford* v. *Birley*.[1]

> "Can three hundred men [*i.e.* the Constabulary], whatever be their courage, execute a warrant on a man who has the supreme and absolute control over sixty thousand? ... If the constables could not execute the warrant or perform their duty, in what other way was it to be done but by interposing the soldiers? ... It appears to me that there is no foundation for saying that all this was a mere pretence to let loose the military authority and draw back the civil power."[2]

Much the same language was used by one of the law officers of the Crown, Sir John Scott, when asked for his opinion[3] as to whether His Majesty could give orders to the military to assist a constable in

---

[1] *State Trials* (N.S.), 1071.

[2] *Cf.* also the words of Mansfield, C.J., in *Burdett* v. *Abbott*, 4 Taunt. 449: "If it is necessary for the purposes of preventing mischief, or for the execution of the law, it is not only the right of the soldiers, but it is also their duty to exert themselves in assisting the execution of a legal process, or to prevent any crime or mischief being committed."

[3] Quoted in Clode's *Military Forces of the Crown*, vol. ii. Appendix, pp. 538 and 647.

executing a warrant of commitment, although he was, of course, careful to confine such cases to those where there existed a corresponding power to call for the assistance of civilians.

Treason.—So far we have dealt with public danger from the crowd rather than the individual. As regards the individual, the Government can, of course, always institute prosecutions for the use of seditious language as being calculated to excite disaffection or to provoke a breach of the peace; it can compel offenders to find sureties for keeping the peace; it can indict them for treason or treason-felony. And the mere agreement of two or more persons to effect a "public mischief" has been held to be a criminal conspiracy. The law of conspiracy is notoriously wide—no overt act is necessary to establish the crime, mere agreement is sufficient, and the crime itself may be presumed from a number of collateral proceedings of the remotest character.

What we have here to consider, as regards treason, is not those forms of domestic strife to which the concept of treason was extended by judicial construction, and most of which are now reduced to treason-felony by the Act of 1848. What we are concerned with is treason as originally defined in one of the clauses of the Statute of Treasons of 1351— the being "adherent to the king's enemies in his realm, giving to them aid and comfort in the realm *or elsewhere*," or as the "compassing the king's death." Entering into measures in concert with foreigners and others in order to aid invasion, or going or purposing to go into a foreign country to that end, was held to amount to treason as being a case of "compassing."[1] This is still the law, although such an offence may alternatively be the subject of an indictment for the lesser offence of treason-felony under the section of the Act of 1848, which includes under the definition of the new offence—

> "To move or to stir any foreigner or stranger with force to invade the United Kingdom, or any other of Her Majesty's dominions or countries under the obeisance of Her Majesty, her heirs or successors."

To compass, imagine, invent, devise, or intend such things is, therefore, indictable either as treason or as treason-felony. Such compassing or imagining must be manifested by some overt act. What constitutes an overt act is a question which has caused considerable controversy. Mere words spoken if purposeful and not idle, *i.e.* if they have reference to some design, are overt acts.[2] Written words stand on a somewhat different footing. If published they are punishable by the Acts of 1817 and 1848 as expressions of the compassing. If not published[3] something more must be shown—namely, that they are in direct contemplation of a treasonable design,

---

[1] Foster, *Crown Law: Discourse of High Treason*, p. 195. This judicial construction was in substance made statutory by the Treason Acts of 1795 and 1817, 36 Geo. III. c. 7, and 57 Geo. III. c. 6, the latter Act perpetuating the provisions of the former.

[2] Foster, *ibid.*, p. 200; and cf. *R.* v. *Charnock*, (1694) K.S.C. The words, if supplemented by meeting and consulting, are treasonable because there is "imagining and compassing."

[3] Peacham's case (an unpublished sermon) was certainly wrongly decided.

i.e., they are subject to do the same test as any other overt act alleged. The term overt act covers, however, many other things—in fact almost any act manifesting intention. The mere act of association is enough.[1] So too is the act of procuring arms.[2]

Treason in War Time.—If, however, the powers so incited are actually at war with us, the offence cannot be reduced to the statutory charge of treason-felony. It is clearly treason under the old law as a case of adhering to the king's enemies. And such adherence would include hostile acts against the king's allies. The term king's enemies as used in the Statute of Treasons means enemies in the international sense,[3] and the giving of aid and comfort is punishable as treason whether that aid and comfort be given within the realm or outside it. It is not necessary to show that war is *declared*. It is sufficient to prove that actual hostility exists, and this will be a question of fact for the jury. A British subject and an alien do not, of course, stand in the same position.

The allegiance which a British subject owes is natural and not local, and the duty is owed wherever he may be. He cannot repudiate it by withdrawal from British territory, still less by naturalisation in the enemy state. Such naturalisation is not recog-

---

[1] *Cf.* Whiteside, C.J., in *R.* v. *Mulcahy*, 7 I.R., 1 C.L. 12.

[2] *Reg.* v. *Davitt*, (1870) 11 Cox 676.

[3] In Y. B. 33 Hen. VI. 1 pl. 3 (1455), in an action of debt against the jailer of the King's Bench prison for an escape of a prisoner, the Court, commenting on the prisoner's defence that it was due to an act of "the king's enemies," held that the term could only be applied to alien enemies and not to subjects. If subjects of the king broke the prison they were not enemies but traitors.

nised by the law of this country in time of war, and the attempt to effect it is itself an act of treason.[1]

The allegiance of the alien is more circumscribed. It is local and depends on his residence here, and, according to the older writers, upon the protection which is extended to him during that residence. This basis may be said to be strengthened rather than weakened, in view of the tendency of modern law to extend that protection by removing the disabilities under which the resident alien formerly laboured. His disabilities are now almost purely political; as regards civil rights almost his only disability is that he cannot own a British ship.[2] His right to the same trial as a British subject would be entitled to in similar circumstances, which has long been admitted at common law, is now also secured by statute.[3] If, however, the alien chooses to leave the country, his allegiance terminates with the protection upon which it was based. Foster propounds the case of an alien who departs from this country during a state of war with his own country and adheres to the king's enemies, leaving his family and effects behind. Is he in such case guilty of treason? The author, supporting himself on an opinion of the judges in 1707, decides that if his departure was for "purposes of hostility,"

---

[1] *R.* v. *Lynch*, [1903] 1 K.B. 444.

[2] See British Nationality and Status of Aliens Act, 1914 (4 & 5 Geo. V. c. 17). On the other hand, an alien is usually exempted from the benefits of social legislation. He cannot qualify for an Old Age Pension, and although admitted to the benefits of the National Insurance Act, he is not placed in quite such a favourable position as British subjects.

[3] The Act of 1914, sec. 18: "An alien shall be triable in the same manner as if he were a British subject."

and he has left his family and effects here in our protection, he might be dealt with as a traitor.[1]

The question, however, arises as to how far war terminates this protection and with it the alien's duty of allegiance. It must be noted that in the case referred to Queen Anne had at the outbreak of war taken the resident aliens of the hostile country into her protection. It is submitted that the recent act of the Government in imprisoning resident aliens of German nationality is a withdrawal of protection, and that if any such contrive to avoid arrest or to effect an escape and then assist the enemy they are not guilty of treason. The point is, however, doubtful. Indeed the equation established by Foster between the privilege of protection and the duty of allegiance seems to disappear altogether in the judgment of Lord Loreburn in a recent case.[2] It was there held that although the enemy be in effective occupation of the territory, an alien resident in it still owes allegiance to the State to which the territory belongs. De Jager was a citizen of the Transvaal Republic, resident in Natal, and joined—under pressure, as he alleged—the burgher forces

---

[1] *Discourse of High Treason*, p. 183. This, however, is an exception to the general rule of English law, and might not receive countenance to-day. English law does not take notice of offences committed by aliens outside British territory, except in the case of Protectorates, and not always then. Cf. *R.* v. *Jameson*, [1896] 2 Q.B. 425 : "One other general canon of construction is this—that if any construction otherwise be possible, an Act will not be construed as applying to foreigners in respect of acts done by them outside the dominion of the sovereign power enacting."

[2] *De Jager* v. *Attorney-General of Natal*, [1907] A.C. 326.

when they entered into occupation. Lord Loreburn did, indeed, do lip-service to the doctrine of protection, contending that it persisted because it revived on the expulsion of the enemy forces. This is very like casuistry, and the real reason for the decision would appear to have been public policy.

> "The protection of the State does not cease merely because the State forces, for strategical or other reasons, are temporarily withdrawn. On the contrary, when such territory reverts to the control of its rightful sovereign, wrongs done during the foreign occupation are cognisable by the ordinary courts. The protection of the sovereign has not ceased. . . . Their lordships consider that the duty of a resident alien is so to act that the Crown shall not be harmed by reason of its having admitted him as a resident. He is not to take advantage of the hospitality extended to him against the sovereign who extended it. In modern times great numbers of aliens reside in this and most other countries, and in modern usage it is regarded as a hardship if they are compelled to quit, as they rarely are, even in the event of war between their own sovereign and the country where they so reside. It would be intolerable, and must inevitably end in a restriction of the international facilities now universally granted if, as soon as an enemy made good his military occupation of a particular district, those who had till then lived there peacefully as aliens could with impunity take up arms for the invaders (pp. 328 *et seq.*)."

The question of *force majeure* was not discussed. We shall consider it in connection with the duties of the subject in case of invasion. Here it need only be remarked that threats of death by the enemy would be a good defence in such a case to a charge of high treason.[1]

An accessory before the fact to a treason is treated as a principal.[2] The least degree of assent will suffice to constitute one a principal. And even purely passive omission to do one's duty when one is aware that treason is contemplated is an offence—it is misprision of treason and a felony.

A state of war probably tends to enlarge the category of overt acts. Subscribing to a loan raised by the enemy country may be regarded as an overt act of giving aid and comfort. Possibly trading with the enemy might be regarded as a treasonable correspondence. So too a state of war may conceivably enlarge the view taken by the courts of conspiracy, when it is a question of "public mischief." The doctrine of public mischief as a basis for a charge of conspiracy is not as obsolete[3] as it is sometimes thought to be, and while it is a question of law and not of fact, and as such determinable by the Court, it is possible that an enlarged view of it would be taken by a court in time of war. The test being an agreement to do something injurious to the public, it is obvious that the state of the realm at the time of the alleged offence may be an important ingredient in the determination of the question.

[1] Cf. *M'Growther's Case*, (1746) Foster's *Crown Cases*, p. 13.
[2] *Reg.* v. *Davitt*, supra.
[3] Cf. *Rex* v. *Brailsford and M'Culloch*, Cox, C.C., xxi., p. 16 —a case of conspiracy to make misrepresentations in procuring a passport.

Sedition.—The fact of this country being at war will not operate to extend the law. For example, criticism, however intemperate, of the policy of the Government in entering into war or in continuing to prosecute it will not amount to treason. It may be sedition, but to constitute it such the same tests must be applied as in time of peace. Its foreign aspect is irrelevant. Sedition is a purely domestic matter. If the language used is calculated to bring into hatred or contempt the person of His Majesty or the Government of the United Kingdom, it is seditious. Unlike treason,[1] the offence of sedition applies to words merely spoken, apart from any question of design, and the intent to excite disaffection or bring into hatred or contempt may be presumed from the character of the words used. But no court to-day would treat mere criticism of the Government as seditious. The modern test seems to be whether the language used is calculated to provoke a breach of the peace.[2] It may well be, however, that at a time when this country is at war people who do not share the speaker's opinions may be more easily excited to a breach of the peace by his language, and this is a fact which has to be taken into account. And to address words to persons in His Majesty's forces in order to seduce them from their duty is a statutory offence.[3]

[1] Cf. *Pine's Case*, (1628) 3 St. Tri. 363.

[2] Cf. *R.* v. *Aldred*, [1909] Cox, C.C., xxii., p. 1, and the words of Coleridge, J.: "Was the language calculated to promote public disorder or physical force or violence in a matter of state?"

[3] Under the Incitement to Mutiny Act, 1797, 37 Geo. III. c. 70. In *R.* v. *Bowman*, [1912] Cox, C.C., xxii. 729, it was held that the words need not be addressed to specific persons; they might be quite general.

Espionage.—Certain statutes have made it an offence to commit acts which might be of assistance to an enemy, independently of the question whether, at the time of their commission, we are at war or not. The Official Secrets Act, 1911, 1 & 2 Geo. V. c. 28, repealing and re-enacting with amendments the Official Secrets Act, 1889, makes it a felony punishable with a maximum sentence of penal servitude for seven years to approach or be in the neighbourhood of any prohibited "place," to make any sketch, plan, model, or note which is calculated to be, or might be, or is intended to be, directly or indirectly useful to "an enemy," for any purpose prejudicial to the safety or interests of the State. A prohibited place is defined by the Act as any work of defence, or office belonging to His Majesty.[1] This is extended to any place not belonging to His Majesty if it is being used for making, repairing, or storing any instruments for warlike use, or any plans or documents relating thereto, and it is clear that the definition extends to the premises of any printers or lithographers under contract with the Government. The Secretaries of State are empowered to extend this definition of a prohibited place if information relating thereto would be of use to an enemy, and it would appear that the Executive is the sole judge of the probability. It is further provided in express words that the prohibition may be so extended to any works for purposes of a public character, such as

---

[1] This includes arsenals, factories, dockyards, camps, ships, telegraph or signal stations, and any other places used for building, making, repairing or storing any ship, arms, or warlike material.

gas, water, or electricity works, and railways and other means of communication. Criminal intent as shown by particular acts need not be proved, it may be presumed from the circumstances or "character"; and it would appear that as in the case of an indictment for receiving or false pretences evidence tending to negative any accident or mistake may be called to prove bad character. Indeed, the onus of proof lies upon anyone accused of making, obtaining, or communicating any sketch or note, as to such prohibited place, to show that his purpose in so doing was not one prejudicial to the safety and interests of the State.

Under the same Act it is a misdemeanour for any person to be found in possession of sketches, notes, etc., relating to such places, and it is also a misdemeanour to communicate confidential documents to persons not authorised to receive them. It is also a misdemeanour knowingly to harbour any person whom one knows, or has reasonable grounds for supposing, to have committed or to be about to commit such an offence. It appears clear that as regards these misdemeanours the onus of proof is on the prosecution to prove *mens rea*. Mere possession of the notes or documents is not of itself unlawful. It may be innocent possession.

It is noteworthy that the Act makes considerable departures from the common law rules as to arrest and the use of search-warrants. At common law a person may not be arrested without a warrant for a misdemeanour not involving a breach of peace, nor may a search-warrant be issued except in respect of stolen goods.¹ The Official Secrets Act, however, authorises arrest without warrant whenever a person is reasonably suspected of having committed, or of having attempted to commit, or being about to commit any of the offences under the Act; and a justice or even a superintendent of police may grant a search-warrant to search premises for suspected papers. It is clear, therefore, that as regards the admission of evidence, arrest, and search, the Act places very exceptional powers in the hands of the authorities. But it is a case of *salus populi suprema lex*.²

Apart from the statute the Executive have no authority to seize and search for papers with or without a warrant. To attempt it is to commit a trespass.³ On the other hand, the power of a Secretary of State to issue warrants for opening the letters of persons suspected of practices dangerous to the State, although much questioned at one time,³ is undoubted and has, indeed, been recognised by statute.⁴

In somewhat the same category as espionage may be included attempts to forge public documents. Under the Forgery Act, 1913, 3 & 4 Geo. V. c. 27, it is a felony to forge any document made or issued

¹ *Entick* v. *Carrington*, 19 S.T. 1030: "If this point should be determined in favour of the jurisdiction, the secret cabinets and bureaus of every subject in this Kingdom will be thrown open."—Lord Camden.

² The Act, of course, applies to aliens within British territory. As regards British subjects it applies to them anywhere.

³ *Cf.* the case of Mazzini, Erskine May, *Const. Hist.*, ii. 154.

⁴ The Post Office Act, 1837, 1 Vict. c. 33, s. 25.

by an officer of State, or any document upon which by the law or usage at the time in force any officer[1] might act. To counterfeit a passport is clearly within the Act. And under present circumstances it is worthy of remark that by the Geneva Convention Act, 1911, 1 & 2 Geo. V. c. 20, it is a statutory offence, punishable on summary conviction by a fine not exceeding £10, to use the heraldic emblem of the "Red Cross," or the words "Red Cross," for any purpose whatsoever, if the person so using it has not the authority of the Army Council for doing so. It need hardly be said that any agreement to procure a public document, such as a passport, by misrepresentation, is an indictable conspiracy.[2]

[1] Presumably an officer would include an officer of His Majesty's forces. See *R.* v. *Whitaker*, *The Times*, Law Rep. 2nd July 1914, where it was held that such an officer is a public and ministerial officer. To forge any kind of military pass would therefore presumably come within the Act.

[2] Cf. *R.* v. *Brailsford*, supra.

CHAPTER II

THE DEFENCE OF THE REALM

Proclamations—Invasion—Duty of the Subject and Right of the Crown at Common Law—The Militia Ballot and Impressment—Police and Special Constables—Aliens—Precautionary Statutes — The Customs and Inland Revenue Acts—Defence Acts and Military Manœuvres Acts—Regulation of the Forces Act and Control of Railways—Aerial Navigation Acts and the Freedom of the Air—The Army Act (Billeting and Requisitions). Exercise of these statutory powers on the outbreak of war.

By The King.

A PROCLAMATION

Regarding the Defence of the Realm.

GEORGE R.I.

Whereas by the Law of Our Realm it is Our undoubted prerogative and the duty of all Our loyal subjects acting in Our behalf in times of imminent national danger to take all such measures as may be necessary for securing the public safety and the defence of Our Realm;

And whereas the present state of public affairs in Europe is such as to constitute an imminent national danger.

Now, therefore, We strictly command and enjoin Our subjects to obey and conform to all instructions and regulations which may be issued by Us or Our Admiralty or Army Council, or any officer of Our Navy or Army, or any other person acting in Our behalf for securing the objects aforesaid, and not to hinder or obstruct, but to afford all assistance in their power to, any person acting in accordance with any such instructions or regulations or otherwise in the execution of any measures duly taken for securing those objects.

> Given at Our Court at *Buckingham Palace*, this Fourth Day of August, in the year of Our Lord One thousand nine hundred and fourteen, and in the Fifth year of Our Reign.
> GOD SAVE THE KING.

We have seen that the Crown has no power except that which the common law allows it to meet an "emergency" or "imminent danger." A proclamation makes no difference. "The king hath no prerogative but that which the law of the land allows him."[1] A proclamation may advise, warn, admonish, but of itself it cannot compel. Its object is to publish the law, not to alter it.[2] We have now to consider further what "necessity" the law recognises as a plea of justification for any measures that the Crown may take. This will involve the examination of three things: (1) In common law, so far as it contemplates invasion or danger falling short of actual invasion; (2) The statute law to the extent to which it anticipates such danger and arms the Executive with powers to meet it; (3) the emergency legislation whereby Parliament has enabled the Crown to go beyond this, and to meet the particular exigencies of the situation created by the declaration of war with Germany.

[1] The Case of Proclamations, 12 Rep. 74.
[2] *Ex parte* Chavasse, *In re* Grazebrook, 4 De G.J. & S. 662.

Invasion.—Actual invasion of this country would, of course, create a state of war within the realm, or rather within a portion of it; and within that particular district it may be assumed that the common law would be suspended, for the simple reason that no courts would be able to administer it. Where the territorial line dividing such a district from the rest of the realm was to be drawn would be a question of fact for the courts sitting outside it to determine. So far as any general test can be laid down as to the delimitation of such a district at all, it is to be found in the fact of proximity.[1] When such an invasion takes place, the Crown may call upon all its subjects to assist in repelling the enemy,[2] on the same principle as the sheriff may call out the whole *posse comitatus* to assist in keeping the peace or in executing a writ.[3] Unjustifiable refusal to assist in such a case is punishable on indictment or criminal information as a misdemeanour. But in such a case the Crown is not confined to calling men

---

[1] Thus the earlier authorities. *Cf.* Coke, 12 Rep. 12, as to the land "adjoining" the coast where the enemy happens to be. And *cf.* the opinion of the judges cited in 1640 (cited in Clode, *Military Forces of the Crown*, ii. p. 440, Appendix VII.). "The lawyers and judges are all of opinion that martial law cannot be executed here in England, but where an enemy is *really near* to an army of the king's.

[2] *Cf.* Oliver St John: "The law . . . hath likewise, secondly, put the *armatam potestatem* and means of defence wholly in his (the king's) hands."—Rushworth, iii. 481.

[3] Cf. *Miller* v. *Knox*, H. of L. Rep. 4 Bing. N.C. 574, followed in the Irish case of *A. G.* v. *Kissane*, 32 Ir. L.R. And *cf.* the *Case of Arms* cited *supra*, p. 27.

out within their county.¹ Nor, we submit, is it confined to calling them out on the restricted scale prescribed by the various statutes dealing with the Militia.² These will be dealt with separately when we come to treat of the Armed Forces of the Crown. The king could not, indeed, compel his subjects to go outside the realm, and it may be that he could not compel them to go from a part of the country where the war is not to a part where the war is. But within the war area he can compel them to arm. It is a nice point. The Acts of Parliament, such as the Bill of Rights, the Mutiny Act, and the Army Annual Act say nothing of the prerogative in time of war; all they are concerned to deny is the claim of the Crown to maintain a standing army in time of peace. The Crown might therefore conceivably resort to conscription in time of war. Its right, however, to call upon all subjects within the war area is unquestioned. And it could certainly impress for the navy on any part of the coast, whether the enemy's fleet were adjacent or not. The law

---

[1] *Cf.* Foster, *Crown Law*, p. 177, citing the statutes of 16 & 17 Car. I c. 28, and 1 Edw. III. st. 2, c. 5: "That by law no man is compellable to go out of his county to serve as a soldier, except in case of necessity of sudden coming of strange enemies into the kingdom."

[2] It should be remembered that although the Militia is now by Orders in Council under the Territorial Forces Act (*cf.* the Army Order of 23rd December 1907) converted into the Special Reserve, the statutes relating to the Militia are not repealed, and the Militia Ballot for compulsory enlistment might be revived by the simple process of omitting to prolong the Militia (Ballot Suspension) Act of 1865, which is annually renewed by the Expiring Laws Continuance Act.

THE DUTY OF THE SUBJECT 47

regarding compulsory service in the navy is on quite a different footing from that which governs the army, as will be seen later. The common law has always recognised naval impressment.[1]

How far can and should the subject in case of invasion act in his own initiative? He has a right to carry arms in time of peace [2]—*a fortiori* in time of war. On the other hand, the training of persons without lawful authority to the use of arms [3] is forbidden by statute without any reservation as to time of peace. And illegal drilling will make any assembly unlawful, even though the drilling is not done at the assembly itself.[4] (But apparently (the Act is not clear) any two justices of the peace could authorise such drilling on their own responsibility.) And indeed an early case [5] lays it down that His Majesty's subjects, if "discreet," would wait on the justices, sheriffs, or other ministers of the king before they resort to armed force. This caution has peculiar force in the case of an invasion, because International Law, although increasingly tender to the claims of the civil population to take up arms in

[1] Cf. *Rex* v. *Broadfoot*, Foster, *Crown Cases*, p. 154. The power extends to the impressment of ships.

[2] *Cf.* The Bill of Rights: "That the subjects which are Protestants may have arms for their defence suitable to their condition and as allowed by law." Blackstone bases this claim on "the natural right of resistance and self-preservation." Under a temporary Act, now expired, this right was withdrawn from the inhabitants of Ireland.

[3] 60 Geo. III. and 1 Geo. IV. cap. 1. "An act to prevent the training of persons to the use of arms and to the practice of military evolutions and exercise."

[4] The *King* v. *Hunt*, 1 State Trials (N.S.), 171.

[5] The *Case of Arms*, Popham's Rep. 121.

48   THE DEFENCE OF THE REALM

case of invasion falling short of effective occupation, still requires some semblance of organisation and discipline.[1]

Can the Crown compel an alien to take up arms in the case of invasion? There is nothing to show that it may. It may, and does require him to contribute to the resources of the country by taxation, and it might require him to assist in keeping the peace.[2] It might even compel a resident alien enemy to do so, but there is some authority for saying that he would be justified in refusing to take up arms, having regard to the fact that he would be held guilty of treason by the laws of his own country.[3] On the other hand, he must not, as we have seen, lend assistance to the forces of his mother country, or he will be held guilty of treason by the law of his adopted country. His wisest course will be to do nothing at all. If, however, he joined the forces of the enemy under compulsion he would not be guilty of treason. Neither would a British subject. But the Court would require convincing evidence that the compulsion was both overwhelming and persistent.

> "The only force that doth excuse is a force upon the person, and present fear of death; and

---

[1] See Arts I. and II. of the Hague Regulations of 1907, which we discuss below in Part II., Chapter I.

[2] *Cf.* Hall, *Foreign Jurisdiction*, p. 73.

[3] *Cf.* Coleridge C.J., in *Isaacson* v. *Durant* 7, Q.B. 60: "If the Queen of these islands and the German Emperor were to go to war (*absit omen* as the judges said in *Calvin's Case*, but it has been and may be so again) any one of these resident non-naturalised Hanoverians, if serving in the British army, would . . . be liable to be shot by the Germans."

this force and fear must continue all the time the party remains with the rebels. It is incumbent for every man who makes force his defence to show an actual force and that he quitted the service as soon as he could."[1]

The subject who is called upon to assist the enemy is certainly in a perilous position. He may be shot if he refuses, and hanged if he consents. To serve the enemy is to betray his own country. If he sends supplies to the enemy in the next village with a view to propitiating him, he would certainly be guilty of treason. If, on the other hand, the enemies levy requisitions upon him, it is not treason for him to supply them.[2] We are now speaking of invasion. If the invasion results in effective occupation, the enemy is, of course, in a position to enforce his own law, and would in any case probably subject the population to "martial law."[3] In that case the presumption of duress is proportionately stronger. But we are here on the border line of International Law, and must reserve further discussion of these points for another chapter, reminding the reader at this stage that the Hague Conventions are no part of the municipal law of this country.

Private Citizens as Police.—Leaving the question of actual invasion resulting in a state of war within the realm or some portion of it, we may resume considera-

[1] Lee, C.J., in *M'Growther's Case* (1746), Foster's *Crown Cases*, p. 13.

[2] *Cf.* Foster, *Crown Law*.

[3] *Cf.* Hague Regulations Act, 43 : " L'autorité du pouvoir légal ayant passé de fait entre les mains de l'occupant."

tion of the subject treated in the first chapter, namely, the powers of the Crown to take steps to guard the public safety. Nothing exhibits so clearly the solicitude of the common law to provide within itself for all contingencies of danger than the law governing the exercise of police duties. The right and duty of the subject to assist in keeping the peace is indistinguishable historically from his right and duty to assist in defending the realm. Both stand on the same footing, and can be traced back to the old communal liability to raise the "Hue and Cry" in pursuit of the malefactor. In the eye of the law every man was, and indeed still may be, a constable. The line which separates the powers and duties of the police from those of the private citizen is even to-day somewhat indistinct; and in earlier times, before the establishment of police force paid and organised by the local authorities, or (in the case of London) by the Home Office, the office of constable was, like that of the overseer, unpaid and compulsory upon whomsoever the old local courts might elect or the justices appoint. His was the vicarious responsibility of the whole village, and in the Statute of Winchester, to which the office may be traced, his duties are the dual duties of militia and police. Under the Parish Constables Act of 1842,[1] which is still the law, every able-bodied man between twenty-five and fifty-five, with certain exemptions,[2] is

[1] 5 & 6 Vict. c. 109.
[2] The Secretary of State can at his pleasure suspend the exemptions. Refusal to serve as parish constable would, as in the case of the office of overseer, be punishable as a misdemeanour.

SPECIAL CONSTABLES

liable to be called upon by the justices at Quarter Sessions to serve as parish constable. And by another Act of 1831[1] the justices may, *if they apprehend riot or felony*, compel any number of men to serve as special constables.[2]

Persons appointed either as parish constables or as special constables will possess all the common law powers of a constable. It must be remembered that the powers of a constable to arrest are merely an enlargement of the power, or rather the duty, of the private citizen to arrest. The private citizen, the parish constable, the special constable, and the police constable may be regarded as so many species of the same genus. The private citizen can, and indeed should, arrest without warrant any person who in his presence commits a felony, or gives a dangerous wound,[3] or whom he reasonably suspects of having committed a felony, provided a felony has in fact been committed. So also he may perhaps[4] arrest in the case of a breach of the peace being actually committed in his presence. Certain statutes also empower him to arrest anyone whom he finds committing any of the offences which are the

---

[1] 1 & 2 Will. IV. c. 41.

[2] And by section 196 of the Municipal Corporations Act of 1882, *borough* justices are to appoint in October of each year special constables for the borough, who may be called on to act if and when the justices certify by their warrant that the police force of the borough is insufficient to maintain the police. Persons so appointed and called upon to act are to be paid at scheduled rates of pay.

[3] It is his *duty* to do so. *Cf.* 2 Hawkins, P.C., c. 12, s. 1.

[4] There appears to be some doubt on this point. See *Timothy* v. *Simpson*, (1835) 1 C.M. & R. 757.

subject of the statute.[1] A constable has all these powers and something more at common law. He can arrest anyone whom he suspects on reasonable grounds of having committed a felony, whether a felony has in fact been committed or not, and the fact that none has been committed will not, as it would in the case of a private person, expose him to an action for unlawful arrest and false imprisonment.[2] The *police* constable has also certain statutory powers likewise exceeding those conferred on private citizens. The question arises whether the parish constable and the special constable, in addition to the common law powers which they possess as constables, have also these statutory powers possessed by police constables. The Acts which confer these powers usually confer them on "a constable" or "peace officer,"[3] and it is submitted that these terms must include all classes of constables.[4]

The degree of force which may be employed by private citizens and constables in effecting an arrest depends partly on the nature of the offence and partly

---

[1] *E.g.*, The Larceny Act, 1861.

[2] It must be remembered that almost any kind of physical constraint of the person will constitute "imprisonment," and, indeed, mere detention is enough. So, too, any show or offer of violence is an assault, even though the attempt is not persisted in.

[3] *Cf.* 24 & 25 Vict. c. 100 (Offences against the Person Act), s. 38, where the words used are "any peace officer.'

[4] As regards any powers possessed by constables *at the date* of the Special Constables Act of 1831, it is provided by that Act that they shall extend to the special constables appointed under it. A *Metropolitan* special constable has by sec. 28 of the Police Act, 1890, all the powers of a constable.

on the status of the person attempting to effect it. A constable may use violence, when arresting on mere suspicion of a felony, when a private citizen would only do so at his peril.[1] If no felony had in fact been committed, the private citizen would be held responsible for the violence he used. On the other hand, resistance to a private citizen, if he is lawfully attempting to effect an arrest, is, as in the case of a "peace officer," not merely a common assault; it is a statutory offence.[2] But, subject to what has already been said as to their powers to arrest on reasonable suspicion of felony, constables, like private citizens, cannot plead mistake as an excuse for wrongful arrest; if they arrest the wrong person they are liable to an action in tort. The only exception is a statutory one, *i.e.*, where they act under a justice's warrant, regularly made out, and which on the face of it they are bound to obey.[3]

From all that has been said it will be apparent that no hard-and-fast line can be drawn between the rights and duties of the police and the public in the case of a breach of the peace from their rights

---

[1] Hale, ii. 78.

[2] 24 & 25 Vict. c. 100, s. 38 : To "assault, resist, or wilfully obstruct any Peace Officer in the due execution of his duty, or any persons acting in aid of such officer, . . . or assault *any person* with intention to resist lawful apprehension" is a statutory misdemeanour punishable with imprisonment not exceeding two years.

[3] These are the general principles. For a more detailed examination of the subject book the reader is referred to the text-books on Criminal Law and the Law of Torts. And see Stephen, *Digest of Criminal Procedure*, c. 12, and *History of the Criminal Law*, i. 193.

and duties in other and graver cases. Breach of the peace, riot, felony, rebellion, invasion—all these contingencies are contemplated and provided for by the common law. And in each and every case the Executive must show legal justification for any action it may take.

Aliens.—We have seen in the preceding chapter that the Crown cannot prevent a British subject from entering or leaving British territory, nor can it arbitrarily deprive him of his personal freedom.[1] It remains to consider the position of the alien. This is a subject which has excited a good deal of controversy. It may be taken as established that the Crown can prevent an alien from entering British territory or, what amounts to much the same thing, an alien has no right, enforceable by action, to enter.[2] Has he at common law a right to remain? Magna Carta is not conclusive. It seems to contemplate an exception, from the Crown's right to expel, in favour of such foreigners as happen to be merchants.

---

[1] We regard it as equally beyond dispute that it cannot under any circumstances expel a British subject from British dominions except under statutory powers. *Cf.* Hawkins, P.C., ii. c. 33, s. 17: "No power on earth except the authority of Parliament can send a subject of England, not even a criminal, out of the land against his will." Such powers are sometimes conferred on colonial governments under their Immigration Acts, and they are "common form" in the Orders in Council applied to protectorates under the Foreign Jurisdiction Acts. The common (Roman-Dutch) law of South Africa at one time recognised the right of the Executive to banish, but that is no longer the case. *Cf.* Rose Innes, C.J., in *Venter* v. *Rex*, [1907] T.S. p. 910.

[2] *Musgrove* v. *Ah Toy*, [1891] A.C. 272.

And it is not clear whether the Habeas Corpus Act, in forbidding the Crown to detain without trial or to deport beyond the seas the inhabitants of this realm, contemplates aliens as well as British subjects.[1] Blackstone, Chitty, and Ellenborough speak of a right inherent in the Crown to expel aliens. As against this must be set the law and practice of the Writ of Habeas Corpus, which is used not only to release aliens kept in confinement,[2] but also to test the legality of warrants for the extradition of foreigners who are fugitives from justice. Still it by no means follows that because a statute has regulated the use of the prerogative in a particular instance that the prerogative itself is thereby taken away. So far as we know the case has never been definitely decided in an English court of justice;[3] the nearest approach to an authoritative pronouncement is the extremely laconic "opinion" of Bethell and Cockburn as law officers of the Crown.[4] Still the weight of modern opinion would seem to be against any such claim. The Alien Immigration Act, 1905 (5 Edw. VII. c. 13), does not materially alter the law in this respect. All it does is to enable the Secretary of State to order the expulsion of alien if,

[1] The preamble speaks of "subjects." The sections generally speak of "persons."

[2] *Somerset's Case*, 20 St. Tr. 1 (Somersett was an alien). *Cf.* also the *case of the Hottentot Venus*, 13 East 195.

[3] There is a Privy Council case *In re Adam*, (1837) 1 Moo., P.C., 460, 477, supporting the right of the Crown in Mauritius to expel an alien. But that was decided on the basis of the local law, which was French.

[4] Forsyth, p. 468. The opinion is expressed in three lines, and no reasons are given in support.

and only if, he has been convicted by a court of felony or misdemeanour, or has been certified by a court of summary jurisdiction, within twelve months of his arrival, to be destitute or to be living under insanitary conditions. However objectionable the presence of an alien may be, and however dangerous he is to the safety of the State, he cannot be expelled unless he has already been convicted of some offence known to the criminal law. A spy in the service of a foreign power must be convicted of an offence under the Official Secrets Acts before the Executive can relieve the country of his attentions.[1]

Precautionary Statutes.—Although at common law the Crown has no power to prevent the importation or exportation of goods, it has been armed by statute with very considerable authority to prohibit both in an emergency. Of such emergency the Executive would appear to be the sole judge, but that is a point which will require careful consideration. The powers in question are given by the Customs Consolidation Act of 1876, the Customs and Inland Revenue Act, 1879, and the Exportation of Arms Act, 1900. As to importation, the Act of 1876 provides (sec. 43) that—

> "The importation of arms, ammunition, gunpowder, *or any other* goods may be prohibited by proclamation or Order in Council."

This is couched in very general terms. Nothing is said as to any emergency. It has been argued by Mr Justice Kenny with great persuasiveness in his

[1] *Cf.* Forsyth, p. 181, and the *Law Quarterly Review* (1890), p. 27.

dissenting judgment in the case of *Hunter* v. *Coleman*,[1] that such a prohibition must at least be general, *i.e.*, that the Crown could not restrict its operation to Ireland, while exempting England from the prohibition, because to do so would be to favour the trade of the latter at the expense of the former. The legislature, he urged, could never have contemplated the section being put to such a use. He admitted that the words of the section were sufficiently wide to cover the application of such a proclamation *to the whole country* even in time of tranquillity, because the Act was clearly concerned not with defence of the realm but with revenue—so far we may agree with him. What he denied was that a proclamation could discriminate between one part of the country and another. Such an exercise of the power, he urged, was not contemplated by the statute, and could only be justified by the prerogative on proof of emergency or public danger. We have seen, however, that the existence of such a prerogative is, to say the least, very doubtful. We think statute the greater must include the less, and that the Crown has power, whether in war or in peace, in danger or in security, to stop the import trade of the whole country. It is a tremendous power, but we do not see how otherwise the plain words of the statute can be construed.[2]

The power to prohibit exports is given by sec. 8 of the Customs and Inland Revenue Act, 1879, and sec. 1 of the Exportation of Arms Act. The difference between the two is that the former is the more general, both as to the articles which may be

[1] Ir. Rep., [1914] 372.
[2] *Cf.* the statute (sec. 39).

prohibited and as to the occasion of their prohibition. Not only arms and warlike material, but provisions and "any sort of victual which may be used as food for man." The terms are, indeed, not so wide as those of the Customs Consolidation Act; they do not extend to "any goods," and manufactures or raw material, unless they come within the words quoted above, are exempt. On the other hand, the occasion is left as completely to the discretion of the Executive as in the Customs Act. The Exportation of Arms Act is narrower: it is confined to arms and warlike stores, and the occasion is limited to cases where such articles are likely to be used "against our subjects" or our allies. It is, however, by no means certain, judging from the context, that the Executive is not the sole judge of such occasion. Nothing is said about a state of war.

The only remedy open to the subject whose goods are seized under proclamations issued in virtue of these Acts would appear to be to proceed by Petition of Right. This is the recognised procedure for the recovery of duty paid under protest[1] as to its legality, and the same procedure applies to the detention of the subject's goods by the Crown. Where goods are destroyed the owner may bring an action for their value, but no action in tort will lie against the Customs or Inland Revenue officer for their seizure.[2]

---

[1] See *In re Nathan*, (1887) 12 Q.B.D. 461. It was held by Mansfield, C.J., in *Whitbread* v. *Brooksbank*, (1774) 1 Cowp. 66, 69, that an action for money had and received would not lie against a Revenue officer to recover an over-payment.

[2] See the Inland Revenue Act of 1890, and to the same effect the Customs Consolidation Act, sec. 267.

EXPROPRIATION

Writers like Professor Dicey, in their eagerness to emphasise "the Rule of Law" governing the acts of the Executive, seem to lose sight of the immense immunity thus extended to such acts by statute. Moreover, these officers are given very large powers to effect the examination and seizure of goods, and resistance or evasion on the part of the subject is punishable by statutory penalties [1] which may extend to three years' imprisonment.

The Defence Acts and Expropriation.—We have seen in the preceding chapter that the Crown has no power at common law to enter upon the lands of a subject, or to expropriate them, or to seize his goods. Nor can it assemble troops upon the roads in such a manner as to obstruct their passage.[2] Hence Parliament has found it necessary to give the Crown power to do any or all of these things in order to provide for the defence of the realm. These powers are, however, carefully circumscribed, and the statutes conceding them are interpreted just as strictly as

---

[1] *Cf.* Customs Consolidation Act, secs. 48, 51, 143, 144, 168, 186, 189, 190, dealing with failure to report cargo, false entries, false declarations, evasion, landing or assisting to land prohibited goods. Fine or forfeiture is the usual penalty in such cases, but a sentence of three years' hard labour may be inflicted in cases where the evasion takes the form of using arms or disguises to land prohibited goods.

[2] *Cf.* Lord Haldane in his memorandum on the use of the troops in aid of the Civil Power (No. 236 of 1908). But regulations made by a *local* authority under the Locomotives Act, 1865, do not bind the Crown in the absence of express words to that effect, and therefore a driver on the public roads acting under the express instructions of the War Office cannot be fined for exceeding the limit of speed laid down in the regulations.—*Cooper* v. *Hawkin*, [1904] 2 K.B. 164.

would be the case with a railway company or a local authority enjoying similar franchises. For example, the Crown is given power by the Defence Acts and the Military Lands Act to acquire land compulsorily for military purposes by a procedure similar to that laid down in the Lands Clauses Consolidation Acts which represent a standardisation by Parliament of the conditions which it will impose on local authorities and public companies seeking powers of compulsory purchase. As a rule[1] the exercise of such powers, affecting as they do the right of the subject to the enjoyment of his property, is in each case brought under the review of Parliament, a special Act being necessary to confirm the Provisional Order issued in each case.[2] This is the procedure which Parliament has prescribed for cases when the War Office wishes to acquire land for the defence of the realm.[3] The subject whose lands are so taken has the same right to compensation, based upon the commercial value of his land, as he would have in the case of his lands being taken by a local authority under the Lands Clauses Act.[4] He is equally entitled to com-

[1] In social legislation of late years there has been a regrettable tendency to relax Parliamentary control, by making the orders of the Local Government Board final and conclusive. *Cf.* The Housing and Town Planning Act.

[2] A railway company would, of course, proceed by private bill, instead of provisional order, but here again the conditions are standardised by the Railway Clauses Acts.

[3] Such lands are vested in the Secretary of State for War in trust for the Crown.

[4] It must be noted that recent Acts such as the Development and Road Board Act, and the House and Town Planning Act, in adopting the Lands Clauses Acts, vary some of their

EXPROPRIATION

pensation if his lands are merely "injuriously affected." If the War Office puts the lands taken to a use not contemplated by the statute under which it acts, it could be restrained by injunction from so using them. The courts would claim the right to consider whether the use to which they were put was "reasonable."[1] Unless it can be shown that the legislation has contemplated that a thing "shall at all events be done," the courts will presume that it cannot be done in such a way as to take away or injuriously affect the common law rights of the subject.[2]

Similarly, the legislature has enabled the military authorities by statute to do what otherwise and at common law they could not do: to go upon private property, and to close public roads (but for not more than forty-eight hours) for the purpose of exercising troops and conducting manœuvres. The rights of local authorities and private owners are, however, carefully guarded and compensation for damage has to be paid.[3] The manœuvres must, however, not last more than three months, and the application of the powers to any particular lands or roads is to be determined by a Military Manœuvres on which the local authorities are in a majority. Under no circumstances may a private dwelling-house be entered.

---

provisions in the direction of according less generous treatment to the owner expropriated.

[1] *Cf.* Jessel, M.R., in *Hawley* v. *Steele*, (1877) 6 Ch.D. 526.

[2] Cf. *Metropolitan Asylums Board* v. *Hill*, (1881) L.R. A.C. 193, and *Hammersmith Railway Co.* v. *Brand*, (1868) L.R. H.L. 171.

[3] The Military Manœuvres Acts, 60 & 61 Vict. c. 43, and 1 & 2 Geo. V. c. 44.

Railways.—In the same way the legislature has authorised the military authorities in certain exigencies to take possession of the railroads, and even to billet troops and requisition animals and vehicles. The control of the railroads is provided for by sec. 16 of the Regulation of the Forces Act, 1871,[1] according to which, whenever "an emergency" has arisen in which it is "expedient for the public service" that His Majesty's Government should have such control, the Secretary of State may by warrant under his hand empower any persons named therein to take possession of any railroad (including tramways) and its plant, or of the plant alone. Compensation must, however, be paid to the companies—either by agreement or, failing agreement, by arbitration under the Lands Clauses Acts—and any contracts which would have been enforceable on behalf of the shareholders against other persons, or conversely, are to be equally enforceable by or against His Majesty's Government. Neither the shareholder nor the private trader is to suffer. Under the National Defence Act, 1888, the Crown is also empowered in times of emergency—in this case the emergency contemplated is obviously a state of war, either actual or imminent, as it is defined as being any occasion in which an order has been issued for the embodiment of the Militia[2]—to demand precedence for the carriage of naval and military troops and stores over ordinary traffic. Here again compensation is to be paid to the shareholders out of moneys provided by Parliament, and any private trader whose contracts have suffered

---

[1] 34 & 35 Vict. c. 86, s. 16.
[2] Now the Territorial Force.

AVIATION

by the delay may petition the authorities for compensation.[1]

Aerial Navigation.—Rights over land are well ascertained; the lawyer has his feet planted on the solid earth. Rights over air are not so easily ascertainable; they seem to partake of the volatile character of the element with which they are concerned. It is a doctrine of English law that the rights of private owners extend *usque ad coelum*. The public may have an aerial "right of way," but just as the soil of the highways or the bed of the river, unless it be "dedicated" to the public, belongs *ad medium filum* to the owner of the adjacent land, so the superincumbent air belongs to the owner of the land beneath. The question is further complicated by the international aspect—there is territorial air just as there are territorial waters, and there may be also "high air" just as there are high seas. The British view of the international aspect of these matters was enunciated in a resolution which was accepted by a majority of twenty-two votes to two at the conference of the International Law Association at Madrid in 1913.

> "(1) It is the right of every state to enact such prohibitions, restrictions, and regulations as it may think proper in regard to the passage of aircraft through the air space above its territories and territorial waters.

---

[1] In this case the petition is to be addressed to the Department, and it would appear to be a purely administrative proceeding. But under the Regulation of the Forces Act the proceedings contemplated are obviously judicial.

"(2) Subject to this right of subjacent states, liberty of passage of aircraft *ought* to be accorded freely to the aircraft of every nation."

The first clause is a legal proposition, the second merely a moral one.

The legislature has not regarded the air, and such rights over it as exist in law at all, with the same tenderness as it has treated the land. By the Aerial Navigation Act, 1911,[1] the Secretary of State may prohibit passage of the air over any specified place for the purpose of protecting the public from "danger," and under the Act of 1913[2] he may extend this prohibition to territorial waters, while the purposes of prohibition are made to include national defence and the safety of the realm. Disobedience to such orders is punishable by a fine or imprisonment, or both, and in order to enforce it officers (designated for the purpose by the Secretary of State) may fire at any aircraft disobeying it. All this is provided for by the Acts themselves, and the officers so acting are absolutely indemnified against all civil or criminal proceedings. There can therefore be no question of their having to justify their actions by the plea of "necessity," or of their being liable for mistake. The statutory powers are absolute, and, as such, they supersede the common law in such matters.

Billeting.—The claim of the Crown to billet troops upon the inhabitants of the realm, and to seize their goods for its own purposes was a subject of constant

---

[1] 1 & 2 Geo. V. c. 4.

[2] 2 & 3 Geo. V. c. 22, and see St R. & O., 1913, Nos. 228 and 243.

BILLETING

complaint in early times.[1] The first was prohibited by the Petition of Right,[2] the second by the Act abolishing purveyance.[3] Such powers as the Crown possesses to-day it derives from statute. They are carefully defined in Part III. of the Army Act, and sec. 102 of that Act expressly provides that the earlier Acts prohibiting billeting are not thereby repealed; they are merely suspended so long as the Army Act continues in force and so far, but only so far, as that Act provides. The Act authorises the billeting of soldiers, officers, and horses on the occupiers of victualling houses at the request of a constable acting on the demand of a commanding officer, who in his turn must produce an authorisation in the shape of a "route," issued by Secretary of State. The necessity of producing a route ensures that troops cannot be billeted except when actually on the march. It is no part of the duty of victualling houses to supply the deficiencies of barrack accommodation. Until lately it was always held that under no circumstances could the regular forces be billeted in private houses.[4] But it is provided by sec. 108 A of the Army Act (as amended) that in time of "emergency," *i.e.*, when the Territorial Force is embodied, troops may be billeted in private houses.

[1] *Cf.* Magna Carta, sec. 30.
[2] 3 Chas. I. c. 1 (1628), and again by 31 Chas. II. c. 1 (1679), and *cf.* the Bill of Rights, 1 Will. & Mary, c. 2. Billeting was first authorised by the Meeting Act, but with express prohibition of billeting in private houses, *i.e.*, in other than inns and victualling houses.
[3] In Chas. II. c. 24, s. 11.
[4] So in the Military Act with emphasis, and in sec. 104 of the Army Act.

66 THE DEFENCE OF THE REALM

Persons on whom a constable billets soldiers improperly may sue for damages.[1] Payment is to be made to victuallers in accordance with a schedule of prices fixed by Parliament in the Army Annual Act. These provisions have been extended to the Territorial Force, but here they are not confined to "routes."[2]

Impressment.—The "impressment" of carriages (since extended[3] to include aircraft and motor-cars, drivers and animals) is also unlawful except in so far as it is authorised by statute.[4] This power can only be exercised under a justice's warrant, issued on the demand of a commanding officer and executed by a constable. Its exercise appears to be confined to route marches. But if an "emergency" exist, the Secretary of State may issue a requisition independently of any route marches, requiring justices to issue warrants for the impressment of carriages and horses " of every description," and of vessels for transport. Refusal is punishable on summary conviction with a fine not exceeding ten pounds. If the emergency is such that the Army Reserve has been called out, or the Territorial Force embodied, the Secretary of State may authorise not only compulsory hire, but compulsory purchase, and refusal in such a case will result in seizure. "Due payment" is to be made, and in case of

[1] Cf. *Parker* v. *Flint*, 12 Mod. Rep. 255.
[2] Sec. 181, sub-sec. 4 of the Army Act, 1881 (44 & 45 Vict. c. 58), as amended by the Territorial Forces Act of 1907.
[3] The owner may be required to bring the motor-car to a place not exceeding one hundred miles from his place of abode.
[4] By secs. 112-121 of the Army Act.

dispute the amount is to be settled by a county court judge. A constable would be protected at common law from a mistake in the warrant under which he acted—impressment, unlike billeting, requires the intervention of a justice's warrant. It will be observed that these powers are only exercisable by the civil authorities—the military cannot act independently of them.

The Exercise of Statutory Powers on the Outbreak of War.—We are now in a position to consider how far the Crown has availed itself of the powers conferred by the statutes aforesaid by putting them into operation to meet the present emergency, and how far it has lately been empowered by Parliament by special legislation to go beyond them. The latter is a subject of immense importance, involving, as we shall see, the subjection of the civil population to military law. The former need not detain us long, as all that has been done is to issue proclamations and Orders in Council putting into force dormant statutory powers which may be unfamiliar but are certainly not new. We will therefore consider these first.[1]

Immediately on the outbreak of war, namely, on 4th August, an Order in Council was issued under the Regulation of the Forces Act, declaring that "an emergency has arisen," and His Majesty's Government accordingly took over the control of the

[1] The more important of these proclamations and Orders in Council are set out in the Appendix. The proclamations concerning the Armed Forces of the Crown are dealt with in the chapter below under that subject. Those on trading with the enemy are discussed in the corresponding chapter.

railways. On 16th September it was announced by the Board of Trade that an agreement had been concluded with the railway companies by which the terms of compensation were settled. Arbitration was therefore not resorted to. Two days earlier, on 2nd August, the Secretary of State, in pursuance of the powers conferred upon him by the Aerial Navigation Acts, made an order for "the safety and defence of the realm," whereby the navigation of aircraft of every class and description over the whole of the coast-line and territorial waters adjacent thereto is prohibited.

The drastic powers to restrict importation and exportation, under the statutes discussed in the preceding chapter, have also been put into force by proclamation. The exportation of warlike material was by specification prohibited as early as 3rd August, and two days later the prohibition was extended to forage and food for animals and victual of all sorts which might be used as "food for man."[1] These prohibitions of exportation were, however, issued in virtue of the Customs and Inland Revenue Act, which contemplate a total prohibition. On 5th August another proclamation was issued under the Exportation of Arms Act, which contemplates a partial prohibition, and this contained an independent list of articles[2] the prohibition of whose export was confined to foreign ports in

[1] It was found necessary to define "food for man" by particularising, and this was done by the Customs Proclamation (Statutory Rules and Orders, No. 1168, of 1914) of 10th August. This list was in turn revised on 20th August.

[2] Coal was first included in this list of prohibitions and then excluded.

VARYING AN ORDER 69

Europe and on the Mediterranean and Black Sea, the allied countries (together with Spain and Portugal) being exempt. Export of such articles to the enemy countries and to European neutrals (except Spain and Portugal) was thus prohibited. Belgium was subsequently (20th August) exempted from this prohibition.

It should be here remarked that there has always been some doubt[1] how far a statutory power to legislate by an Order in Council is exhausted by its exercise, and *functus officio*. In other words, it was uncertain whether a statutory rule or order once issued could be varied or extended by a subsequent order. It was presumably to remove such doubts that Parliament passed an emergency Act[2] empowering the Executive "whilst a state of war lasts" to vary or extend any proclamations or orders made under sec. 8 of the Customs and Inland Revenue Act of 1879. As we shall see when we come to consider the Emergency Legislation in general, a similar power has been expressly given in the case of the new statutes.[3]

We may here take note of the Proclamation issued on 5th August notifying that British subjects contributing to a loan raised on behalf of the

[1] This doubt does not appear to have been wholly removed by the Interpretation Act; sec. 32 of that Act authorises the revision of "rules, regulations, and bye-laws." Orders in Council do not appear to be included. See Craies, *Statute Law*, p. 258.

[2] The Customs Exportation Prohibition Act (1914), 4 & 5 Geo. V. c. 64.

[3] *E.g.*, The Aliens Restriction Act (1914), 4 & 5 Geo. V. c. 12, s. 1 (6).

German Government or contracting with the German Government would be guilty of high treason. We have already pointed out that the Crown cannot change the law by the prerogative alone, and this proclamation must be regarded as simply *quoad terrorem populi.* It reminds the king's subjects of what the law already is. To assist an enemy government is, as we have already seen, to "adhere" to the king's enemies within the meaning of the Statute of Treasons. "Persons resident or being in our dominions during the state of war" are, of course, included.

CHAPTER III

THE DEFENCE OF THE REALM (*continued*)

I. The New Emergency Legislation.

The Emergency Legislation: The Defence of the Realm Acts I. and II., Scope of the Regulations, Effect on Personal Liberty and on Rights of Property, A *Lex Regia*, Specified Statutory Powers, the Censorship of the Press, the Subjection of the Civil Population to Martial Law, the Aliens Restriction Act, the Special Constables Act, the Intoxicating Liquor Restriction Act, Army Supplies and Naval Billeting Act, Unreasonable Withholding of Food Supplies Act, and Articles of Commerce Act.

II. The Revised Emergency Legislation.

The Defence of the Realm (Consolidation) Act, No. III., and the New Consolidated Regulations—The New Enacting Words—New Offences: Compulsion to furnish Information and to "inform"—The Liberty of the Press—The Position of Newspaper Proprietors—the Question of Guilty intent—The Death Penalty—Martial Law and Something More—Conclusion.

"His Majesty in Council . . . may by such regulations authorise the trial by courts martial and punishment of persons contravening any of the provisions of such regulations . . . in like manner as if such persons were subject to military law and had on active service committed an offence under sec. 5 of the Army Act."

The Defence of the Realm Act,
4 & 5 Geo. V. c. 29, s. 1.

In the present emergency His Majesty's Government have abstained from taking the extreme step of declaring "martial law." To have done so would, in our opinion, have been illegal, for the reasons already advanced in our first chapter. The Government have adopted the much more prudent course of obtaining statutory powers (1) to prohibit certain acts likely to endanger the safety of the realm, and to punish by the summary jurisdiction of military law those who commit them, (2) to take certain precautions of a military character. Both classes of powers involve interference with common law rights. The first creates new offences and makes them punishable by a procedure unknown to the common law; the second enables the Executive to interfere with private rights of property and personal liberty. The reason for granting these large powers is obvious. There are many things the subject may do which are perfectly lawful but which, in time of war, may not be expedient—the illumination of his private dwelling, for example. There are many things which the Executive may wish to do, in the interests of public safety, which are undoubtedly unlawful but which, in time of war, are highly necessary—for example, to arrest and detain without trial suspected persons, to require persons to remain within doors, to prohibit their residence in a particular place, to stop roads, or to enter upon private land. To have to justify such acts in every case by proof of such "necessity" as would satisfy a court of common law would involve delay, uncertainty, litigation, such as would be highly prejudicial

EMERGENCY LEGISLATION

to the safety of the State. Parliament has met the situation by a series of emergency statutes of which by far the most important are two Acts known as the Defence of the Realm Acts.[1] These statutes and still more the Regulations which purport to be made under them will require very careful examination. They are unprecedented in character, and they raise some points upon which no court of law has ever yet decided. Moreover, they raise in a new form debatable[2] questions as to the limits of control exercisable by the civil courts over military jurisdiction where there may be reason to believe that that jurisdiction has been wantonly and oppressively exercised.

These Acts enact that His Majesty in Council "has power during the continuance of the present war" to issue regulations as to the powers and duties of the Admiralty and Army Council, and of the members of His Majesty's forces, and other persons acting in his behalf, "for securing the safety and defence of the realm." The Act does not define—beyond the use of these general words—what shall be the scope of these regulations, but it provides for the punishment of persons contravening such of the regulations as may deal with particular matters, to wit—

    (a) The prevention of persons from communicating with the enemy or from obtaining infor-

[1] The text of these Acts and of the Regulations made under the powers conferred by them will be found in the Appendix.

[2] *Sutton* v. *Johnstone*, 1 Term Rep. 509, when Lord Mansfield confessed to doubts as to the power of the civil courts in such courts—"There is no authority either way."

mation for that purpose, or any purpose likely to be prejudicial to our military operations or advantageous to those of the enemy.

(*b*) The prevention of persons from spreading reports "likely to cause disaffection or alarm."

(*c*) The securing of the safety of any means of communication, or of railways, docks, or harbours, or of "*any area*" which may be proclaimed to be an area which it is necessary to safeguard in the interests of the training or concentration of His Majesty's forces.

(*d*) The suspension of any restrictions on the acquisition or user of land under certain permanent statutes.

Scope of the Regulations.—Under these Acts statutory regulations of a very sweeping character have been issued. What, if any, limits can be imposed upon these regulations by a court of common law? The answer is that they must be read by the light of the Acts under which they purport to be made. If they deal with matters not contemplated by those Acts they are *ultra vires*. Parliament sometimes, but not often, provides that the validity of the exercise of such delegated powers shall not be questioned in any legal proceedings whatever, or that the rules so made "shall take effect as if contained in this Act, and shall be judicially noticed." When such words are used, the courts cannot go behind the rules and question their validity; all they can do is to interpret them.[1] But no such provision appears in the Defence of the Realm Acts, and we therefore

[1] *Institute of Patent Agents* v. *Lockwood*, [1894] A.C. 347.

submit that the new regulations made thereunder are subject to an enquiry by a court of law whether they are within the powers of those who made them. It would therefore, we think, be open to such a court to inquire whether the regulations really were designed "to secure the public safety and the defence of the realm," and as no provision in the shape of a direction that they be laid before the two Houses for forty days has been made for Parliamentary control of the regulations,[1] a court might scrutinise them with some particularity.

Indeed, we confess to some doubt as to whether the Act gives any more power than already exists at common law to make any regulations—although, as we shall see, such power has been assumed—other than those specified in (*a*), (*b*), (*c*), (*d*). The Act does not say "it shall be lawful for His Majesty in Council," but "His Majesty in Council *has power*" to issue regulations. And regulations for what purpose? The Act says "regulations *as to the powers and duties of the Admiralty and Army Council* . . . and other persons acting in his behalf for securing the safety and the defence of the realm." It would be legislation by innuendo, and a great perversion of the ordinary rules of interpretation, to assume that these words create new powers. Power to issue regulations as to the powers of a particular body—whether the Army Council or a tramway company—means, on the face of it, power to regulate existing powers, not to create new ones. It assumes existing powers the exercise of which it is desirable to subject to rules.

[1] *Ibid.*, Lord Herschell's remarks on the conclusiveness of such ratification by Parliament.

76 THE DEFENCE OF THE REALM

It is just possible that this loose and ambiguous wording was used in order to avoid the blunt enactment that the King in Council should have power to make any regulations it pleased for public safety. But such a course would be highly disingenuous; it would imply a power to suspend the whole of the common law at pleasure. We prefer to believe that no new powers were intended to be conferred, and that, indeed, none can be conferred by such words except within the specific terms of (*a*), (*b*), (*c*), (*d*). It has been held in a Canadian case that power to regulate traffic by bye-laws confers no power to prohibit it.[1]

Effect of the Regulations on Personal Liberty.—Now the Regulations issued are by no means confined to those specified in the Acts as carrying with them the sanction of punishment under military law. Article 13 of the Regulation of 12th August empowers *any person* authorised by the naval or military authorities to arrest *without warrant*[2] any person whose behaviour is of such a nature as to give reasonable grounds for suspecting that he has acted

[1] *Toronto Corporation* v. *Virgo*, [1896] A.C. 88. Unless the words (in the Defence of the Realm Act) "issue regulations for" mean something different from "regulate," the observations of Lord Davey in this case would seem to be conclusive against the Regulations we are criticising: "a power to 'regulate or govern' seems to imply the continued existence [here the independent existence] of that which is to be regulated or governed." And cf. *Ontario* v. *Canada*, [1896] A.C. 348, where "prohibition" legislation was held not to be within the powers to "regulate" trade and commerce.

[2] Similarly, Article 12 provides that any person authorised by the naval or military authority may enter, "if need be by force," any private house, and search it if there is reason to

or is about to act "in a manner prejudicial to the safety of the realm," and the article goes on to provide that he may be kept in custody until he can be dealt with by court martial if he has offended against any of the Regulations *specified* by the Acts, or until he can be dealt with in the ordinary course of the law if *otherwise*. Whilst so detained he is to be deemed to be in legal custody. This seems to us to be quite meaningless. Conduct "prejudicial to the safety of the realm" can only be an offence if it comes within the military offences as defined in (*a*), (*b*), (*c*). Such conduct is not of itself an offence at common law unless it comes within the recognised categories of treason, conspiracy, sedition, or is within the Official Secrets Act. The Defence of the Realm Acts in empowering the authorities to make *general* regulations say nothing as to the consequences which may attend a breach of such regulations when they do not fall within (*a*), (*b*), and (*c*), it prescribes no penalty, and it does not authorise arrest without warrant. As the Regulations must be read subject to the Act, Article 13 must therefore, we think, be regarded as *ultra vires*. Even if the Act does give new powers to make regulations (other than those specified in (*a*), (*b*), (*c*), (*d*)) changing the law, the only consequences that would, in the absence of an express penalty, attach to disobedience of them would be the penalties of a misdemeanour at common law. To disobey a statutory rule or order, *if (and only if) lawfully made*, is of course always a

suspect conduct "prejudicial to the public safety." No such power exists—how then can the authorities assume it? And *cf*. Article 12 A in the Regulations of 1st September.

misdemeanour.[1] But no one can be arrested for a mere misdemeanour without a warrant, and therefore the Regulation directing arrest without warrant for breach of the Regulations is wholly bad. Or are we to assume that the power to make regulations includes a power to abolish the common law as to arrest whenever convenient? If this can be read into the Act, when nothing is said therein to that effect, then anything can. In that case "any person authorised by the competent naval or military authority" may be authorised to do anything—to hang peaceful citizens on lamp-posts.

Effect of the Regulations on Private Rights of Property.—The same question arises as to the effect of the Regulations, outside the purposes categorically specified in the Act, upon actionable rights at common law. The Regulations prescribe (Article II.) that "it shall be lawful"[2] for the authorities to take possession of any buildings or other property, *even to the destruction of them*, and "to do any other act involving interference with private rights" which may be "necessary" to secure the defence of the realm. This raises very serious questions. Can a

---

[1] The leading case is *The King* v. *Harris*, (1791) 4 Term Rep. 202; and *cf.* the discussion of cases by Charles, J., in *The Queen* v. *Hall*, [1891] 1 Q.B. 767. The reader must bear in mind that it must always first be shown that the statute authorises the particular statutory order, before disobedience to it can be treated as a misdemeanour.

[2] As to the effect of such words, see Lord Cairns in *Julius* v. *the Bishop of Oxford*, (1880) 5 App. Cas. 214 H.L. In the Defence of the Realm Act itself the words are not used, and they seem to us entirely out of place in the Regulations, which cannot legalise anything except that which the statute legalises.

private house be destroyed without compensation? Now the question of whether or how far the imposition of a statutory duty or the grant of a statutory power takes away common law rights is a difficult one and much debated. Much will depend on the words of the statute if the duty imposed is imperative or the power granted is absolute, and the one could not be performed or the other exercised without some infringement of common law rights. The courts will assume that such infringement was contemplated by the legislation, and that consequently no action will lie. But the authorities will have to show that the acts performed may reasonably be considered necessary for the purpose authorised by Parliament, and that no negligence attended their performance. The Regulations must certainly be read subject to these rules of construction. That being so, these Regulations, which purport to give what the statute does not give, the power to destroy private property, are in our opinion wholly unwarranted. It is true that they speak of the exercise of such powers "where *necessary*" for the public safety. But merely precautionary steps—steps not taken in the face of imminent danger such as the actual presence of the enemy—are, as we have seen in our first chapter, not justifiable by the plea of necessity. And therefore the use of the words "where necessary" will not save these Regulations. If these particular articles are meant merely to declare the common law, and not to assume powers in excess of it, they are very lax in their wording. For example, Article III., omitting any qualification as to necessity, declares that—

The competent naval or military authority, and any person duly authorised by him, shall have right of access to any land or buildings or other property whatsoever.

No such arbitrary power exists at common law. None such is to be found in the Defence of the Realm Act. And therefore persons who act under this Regulation will, it seems, commit a trespass.

A "**Lex Regia.**"—The truth of the matter is that the Statute is brief without being terse, and the Regulations are voluble without being explicit. Had the Act said " it shall be lawful for His Majesty in Council to make any regulations he may deem expedient for the public safety and the defence of the realm, and such regulations shall not be questioned in any legal proceedings whatsoever," then the articles we have been criticising would have been unimpeachable. But the Act being what it is, we have never seen any statutory regulations which appeared to outrun so breathlessly the statutory powers actually conferred. For a parallel we should have to go back to the proclamations of Henry VIII., who could at least point to the *lex regia* on the statute-book (repealed in the reign of his successors) giving all his proclamations the force of law. We cannot admit that the Defence of the Realm Act is such a *lex regia*, and we are quite sure that our present Parliament has not contemplated anything of the kind. It may be said that the gravity of the occasion dispenses us from invoking the usual rules of construction. But if so we may as well dispense with the Rule of Law altogether and entrust the Cabinet with autocracy. And since we know on high authority that the conflict against destitution and disease is perpetual —*contra miseriam aeterna auctoritas*—we may soon be called upon to do so in time of "peace."

Specified Statutory Powers. — We may now proceed to consider those Regulations which deal with subjects (*a*), (*b*), (*c*) specified in the Act, and which therefore are expressly authorised. As such they are not open to the criticism which has been directed against the Regulations quoted above. As regards "communication with the enemy," it must be noted that what is contemplated is the *prevention* of such communication. Actually to communicate is already an offence at common law—it would, if intended to assist him, be indictable as treason. So too the spreading of reports likely to cause disaffection might constitute the offence of sedition or of incitement to mutiny, and it is conceivable that the propagation of reports likely to cause alarm might, where *two* or more persons are concerned, expose the authors to an indictment for conspiracy as being a "public mischief."[1] But all these are cases where there must be an actual attempt, manifested by *mens rea*, to commit a criminal offence. As such the common law provides for them. But it does not provide for anticipating them by the exercise of arbitrary measures on the part of the Executive. The law has done little to *prevent* crime,[2] except by punishing it when actually com-

[1] Cf. *R.* v. *De Berenger.*

[2] The Prevention of Crime Act, (1908), 8 Edw. VII. c. 59, is an exception which illustrates the rule. There are, of course, the powers of a constable to arrest *at night* a person whom he has good cause to suspect of being about to commit certain statutory felonies. But these powers are individual, not general.

mitted; it has done nothing at all to prevent acts which, without being criminal, are prejudicial to the safety of the State. The Defence of the Realm Acts are remarkable in that they do this very thing; they are stamped with a preventive character.

Their preventive character is most prominent in the special Regulations aimed at securing the safety of means of communication, railways, docks, harbours, and proclaimed "areas." Residence of undesirable persons, whether they be British subjects or aliens, within such areas may be prohibited by the authorities at their absolute discretion, and persons continuing to reside are subject to a kind of *état de siège* under which they may be ordered to extinguish lights and to keep within doors. Such regulations are clearly within the statute. Some of the others forbid acts such as sketching defences work and forging passes or permits which are already criminal under the Official Secrets Act and the Forgery Act, but they are made punishable by military law independently of ordinary law. In the words of the Regulations, they are made "war crimes." And the same may be said of tampering with telegraphic or telephonic messages.

The important question remains, however, whether the authorities could at their pleasure proclaim the whole of England as such an area, and thereby subject the entire civil population to military law? We think not. The Act says they may proclaim any area "to be an area which it is necessary to safeguard in the interests or concentration of any of His Majesty's forces." A court would, according to the ordinary rules of construction, be entitled to inquire whether the use of the power was a reasonable one and necessary for the purpose for which it was granted.

The Censorship of the Press.—Of these specified statutory powers, whereby regulations may be made, the infringement of which subjects the offender to military law, one calls for somewhat close examination as enabling the authorities to exercise a censorship over the Press. We refer to the power expressly given to make regulations

"designed to prevent the spread of reports likely to cause disaffection or alarm."

Now it is true nothing is explicitly said about the Press either in the Act or in the Regulations under it. The words quoted from the Act reproduce almost textually certain words in the Army Act, which make the spreading of such reports *by a soldier on active service* an offence punishable with penal servitude. To spread reports "likely to cause alarm" is no offence at common law, although as we have seen, if *two* or more persons agreed together to do it, it is possible that under the old law of conspiracy they might have been (we doubt if they still would be) indicted on a charge of conspiring to effect a "public mischief." The words in the Defence of the Realm Act do therefore create a new offence and, although the Press is not expressly mentioned, they do, of course, suffice to give to the military authorities very wide powers, indeed unlimited powers, over the proprietors and editors of newspapers. Here, if anywhere, we must seek for legal authority for the Press censorship, which otherwise has no foundation in law at all. Since the repeal in 1694 of the Licensing Act of 1662, there has been no such thing as a censorship of the Press; and indeed the term "liberty of the Press" has since then meant, and could only mean, exemption from the supervision of a censor. It was and is a negative conception. It never meant that the Press was immune from proceedings for libel when publication by a private person would be libellous. There has, indeed, grown up as the result of legislation in the nineteenth century[1] a "distinct law of the Press,"[2] which now invests it with some peculiar privileges, the result being that both the character of the wrong and the nature of the remedy differ materially, according as the libel does or does not appear in a "newspaper."[3] Subject to this qualification it may be said the law of the Press must be sought, not under any special rubric but in the law as to libel, seditious libel, and treason. Certainly there is no such thing as Press offences, and every man is free to publish what he likes, subject to the risk of being *subsequently* held guilty of an offence under one or other of these heads. We have no such thing as *preventive* legislation affecting the Press. In this

---

[1] Lord Campbell's Act (1843), the Newspaper Libel Act (1881), and the Law of Libel Amendment Act (1888).

[2] Fisher and Strahan, *Law of the Press*. Professor Dicey's fluent generalisation about there being "no special privilege on behalf of the Press" is decidedly inaccurate.

[3] The Act of 1881 provides us with a statutory definition of a newspaper as being "any paper containing public news, intelligence, or occurrences, or any remarks or observations thereon printed for sale and published in England or Ireland periodically, at intervals not exceeding twenty-six days." This is extended to include such publications although "containing only or principally advertisements."

respect, therefore, the Defence of the Realm Act makes an entirely new departure, and, although the Regulations under it do not set up any system of licensing, the words of the Act are wide enough to enable the authorities to do so. It must be remembered that as the law stood before the Defence of the Realm Act, criminal proceedings could only be taken against a newspaper where the words complained of were calculated to disturb the peace (this is the test of criminal libel), or were likely to excite disaffection (the test of seditious libel), or were in themselves treasonable. And it was always for a jury to decide these things.

The Defence of the Realm Act makes it an offence, triable without a jury and punishable with penal servitude, to publish reports "likely to cause alarm."[1] The fact that the report is *true* will be no defence any more than it is in the case of seditious libel. In "criminal libel" truth, since Lord Campbell's Act, is a good defence provided "public interest" is proved. And indeed the Regulations of 12th August (Article 14) under the Act expressly make it an offence to publish without lawful authority information (it may be true information) "with respect to the movements of any of His Majesty's forces" if the information is

[1] But see the third section of this chapter on the third (Consolidating) Defence of the Realm Act, which has since substituted for the words "reports likely to cause alarm" the words "false reports *or reports* likely to cause disaffection to His Majesty, or to interfere with the success of His Majesty's forces by land or sea, or to prejudice His Majesty's relations with foreign powers." These words are more definitive. It will be noticed that they are not confined to *false* reports. See next section.

such as might be directly or indirectly useful to the enemy.

The restrictions on the Press do not necessarily stop here. If the general Regulations criticised above, dealing with personal liberty, are authorised by the Act (we do not think they are), a newspaper proprietor or editor is, like any other person, liable to be arrested without warrant, or to have his premises searched for no better reason than that the military authorities suspect him of "conduct prejudicial to the public safety or defence of the realm."

The Subjection of the Civil Population to Military Law.—Persons contravening such of the Regulations as deal with the matters specified in the Act may be tried and sentenced by courts-martial "in like manner as if such persons were subject to military law and had on active service committed an offence under sec. 5 of the Army Act." The effect of this enactment is, for some purposes, to deprive the whole civil population of this country of the right to trial by jury, and to enable a court-martial, composed exclusively of military or naval officers, to sentence anyone contravening these Regulations to penal servitude for life.[1] The only exception to this power to inflict

---

[1] See Army Act, sec. 5: "Offences in relation to the enemy not punishable with death." This section provides that "every person subject to military law, who on active service commits any of the following offences"—such as leaving the ranks, etc.—"shall, on conviction, be liable to suffer penal servitude or such less punishment as is in this Act mentioned." Some of the lesser punishments could not be applied to civilians, *e.g.*, cashiering or dismissal from the service. "Active service" is defined in sec. 189 (1).

the severest sentence (short of capital punishment) is one made by the Regulations themselves, which provides that to be out of doors in a proclaimed area after the prohibited hours, or to show lights after such hours, shall not, unless the offence can be shown to be deliberately committed with a view to assisting the enemy, expose the offender to a sentence exceeding three months' hard labour.

Now what securities, if any, will the subject, tried and sentenced by such tribunals, have against an abuse of such jurisdiction? For example, he might be arrested and kept in custody indefinitely on a frivolous charge, at the instance of an officer acting maliciously and without reasonable or probable cause. Could he obtain a writ of Habeas Corpus to secure his release from custody? Would he on acquittal be able to sustain an action for malicious prosecution or for false imprisonment? Or again, he might be tried and sentenced under circumstances where the conviction was against the weight of evidence, or where evidence was improperly admitted or excluded. Could he in such case appeal against the conviction or the sentence? Or he might be sentenced for an offence which was not an offence under the Act. Could he get the conviction quashed? What remedy, if any, would he have against the members of the court-martial? These, it need hardly be said, are questions of immense importance.

Now it may be said at once that no *appeal*, strictly speaking, would lie to the Court of Criminal Law, which has no jurisdiction over military courts at all. Indeed, the civil courts are not, and never were,[1] courts of error over military courts. The old Court for Crown Cases Reserved and the disestablished writ of error never extended to the proceedings of such tribunals.

A general control is, indeed, exercised:—

> "The Court [a court-martial] being established in this country by positive [statute] law, the proceedings of it, and the relation in which it will stand to the courts of Westminster Hall, must depend on the same rules with all our courts which are constituted and have particular power given them, and whose acts therefore may become the subject of application to the courts of Westminster Hall for a prohibition. Naval Courts-martial, Military Courts-martial, Courts of Prize, are all liable to the controlling authority which the courts of Wesminster Hall have from time to time exercised for the purpose of preventing them from exceeding the jurisdiction given them, the general ground of prohibition being an excess of jurisdiction when they assume power to act in matters not within their cognisance ... that they have *decided wrong* ... is *not* a ground of prohibition."[2]

These are words of great latitude, but the most important of them are the words of qualification at the end. It is only when such tribunals presume to act in matters *outside* their jurisdiction that the courts will interfere. Once let that jurisdiction be established, once let it be proved that the persons over whom it is exercised are "military persons," and the control largely evaporates. The civil courts have

---
[1] *Cf.* Kenyon, C.J., in *R.* v. *Suddis*, 1 East 306.
[2] Lord Loughborough in *Grant* v. *Gould*, 2 H.Bl. 69.

MILITARY LAW AND CIVILIANS

held, for example, that they will not scrutinise the proceedings of military courts with the same strictness as those of civil courts. They will not discuss whether the conviction was against the weight of evidence. They have based their refusal to do so on the ground of the importance of preserving military discipline, and the inability of a civil court to "*feel* all the circumstances."[1] It is doubtful, however, whether the same considerations would influence the courts in the case of civilians tried under the new Act, for there is, of course, no military relationship between the military authorities and the civilian. But the case is not quite so simple where it is a case of an action for damages for wrongful arrest or malicious prosecution by a civilian against a military officer. Cases have occurred where an officer or soldier has been arrested and imprisoned, and perhaps prosecuted, by an officer for disobedience to a command, and has subsequently brought an action against the officer for damages on the ground that the command which the officer gave was one which it was either unlawful for the officer to give or impossible for the subordinate to obey. The attitude of the courts in such cases has wavered. In one case[2] they have laid down the doctrine that a subordinate must obey

---

[1] *Cf.* Lord Mansfield in *Sutton* v. *Johnstone*, p. 546, and Lord Loughborough in *Grant* v. *Gould*, supra. (The reasoning in *Sutton* v. *Johnstone* is anything but clear.) To the same effect Grose, J., in *R.* v. *Suddis:* "It is enough that we find such a sentence pronounced by a court of competent jurisdiction to inquire into the offence, and with power to inflict such a sentence; as to the rest, we must presume *omnia rite acta.*" This is going very far.

[2] *Sutton* v. *Johnstone*, 1 T.R. 509.

implicitly all commands, and that if he disobeys them and is arrested, imprisoned, and prosecuted, he has (even though he be acquitted) no remedy at law. This, however, was a case of a command in time of war. In another case, where the command was given in time of peace [1] and the soldier disobeyed it, he was awarded damages for wrongful arrest on the ground that the command was one which the officer had no right to give. In a third case,[2] also occurring in time of peace, the Court took the ground that they could not, in a civil action, take cognisance of questions of military discipline and duty at all. Now the question arises whether the considerations influencing the Court in the first and last of these cases can apply to the case of a civilian arrested, imprisoned, or prosecuted for contravening the new Regulations and subsequently released or acquitted. A civilian does not owe the duty of implicit obedience to military officers; he is not, by the new Act, deprived of the right to question the Regulations or the interpretation put upon them by an officer who commands him to do or refrain from doing a particular thing in virtue of them. The Defence of the Realm Act does not make him a soldier, or change his status. Arrest by military authorities of a soldier is always an act done under colour of that military discipline to which a soldier submits himself without reservation on enlistment. This

[1] *Warden* v. *Bailey*, 4 Taunt. 67—a decision which receives countenance from *Wall* v. *Macnamara*.

[2] *Dawkins* v. *Rokeby*, L.R. 8 Q.B. 255 and 7 H.L. 744; and to the same effect *Dawkins* v. *Paulet*, 5 Q.B. 108, but with a strongly dissentient judgment by Cockburn.

could not be said with the same assurance of the arrest of a civilian by the military under the Defence of the Realm Act. Nor could it be said of prosecution. According to the Court in *Sutton* v. *Johnstone*, if it is once established that a command is given by an officer to a subordinate and the command disobeyed, the mere fact of disobedience constitutes sufficient "probable cause" for putting him on his trial to negative a presumption of malice, even supposing (which he doubts) that a civil court could go into that question.[1] But this line of reasoning is entirely based on the military relationship between one member of the king's forces and another, and cannot apply to civilians. Nor has a civilian the remedy, which seemed to weigh so much with the Court in this case,[2] of lodging a complaint, as an officer may,[3] with the superior military authorities.

So far we have spoken of redress by an action in civil proceedings for unlawful arrest, imprisonment, or malicious prosecution. Supposing, however, a civilian desires to obtain release from arrest under the Defence Regulations. Would a writ of Habeas Corpus issue? As regards the custody of soldiers by the military authorities, it has been held[4] in an application for the writ, where indefinite detention without trial was alleged, that a return by the military authorities, to the effect that it was impossible to convene a court-martial, was conclusive.

[1] *Sutton* v. *Johnstone*.
[2] And also in *Dawkins* v. *Paulet*, C.R. 5 Q.B. 94.
[3] *Cf.* sec. 42 of the Army Act.
[4] *Blake's Case*, 2 M. & S. 428, and cf. *R.* v. *Suddis*, supra.

"We cannot lay down a general rule, but must, in a very great degree, give credence to people in high situations when they depose that all has been done which could conveniently and *according to the course of office* be done, and unless something be shown to the contrary."

Here again the line of argument seems to have been the military relationship. We doubt if it could apply to indefinite detention of a civilian.[1] And, for the reasons already advanced, we doubt if the Regulation [2] which professes to make such detention legal custody can diminish the rights of civilians in this respect. What the courts have always emphasised as necessary to satisfy them as to the legality of the detention is proof of military status.[3]

There can be no doubt that if the courts-martial were to try a civilian for an offence not within those defined in the Defence of the Realm Act, a writ of prohibition would issue to restrain them. And if our criticism of the general Regulations (issued, as we think, in excess of the powers conferred by the Act) be correct, then we think that the writ would issue to restrain the courts-martial from trying civilians for breaches of them. So too would a writ of certiorari in case of a conviction. The accused might apply to the Court of King's Bench for a rule calling on the Judge-Advocate-General to show cause why the writ should not issue to quash the conviction.

But when the case is admittedly within the

[1] A rule was recently refused where no unreasonable delay was shown.

[2] Article 13 of the Regulations of 12th August.

[3] *E.g.*, in *Hearson* v. *Churchill*, [1892] 2 Q.B. 144. And cf. *Q.* v. *Cumming* (*Ex parte* Hall), L.R. 19 Q.B. 13.

Defence of the Realm Act the only review to which a conviction and sentence will be subject will be the review by the Judge-Advocate-General, upon whose advice it will rest with the Secretary of State for War to confirm them.[1]

The Aliens Restriction Act.—In the first section of this chapter we have pointed out that the personal liberty of the alien resident in England in time of peace is protected by the common law, and that the Crown has no right, except in a very limited number of cases prescribed by the Alien Immigration Act, to expel him. It must, however, be remembered that war of itself changes the status of an alien, and by making him an alien enemy puts him outside the law. The extent to which it does this is discussed in Part IV. of this book. We think that while war outside the realm cannot invest the Crown with arbitrary power over British subjects within it, it does undoubtedly enable it to take such steps as it pleases in regard to alien enemies—*i.e.*, to arrest, detain, or deport them as it thinks fit. It was therefore, we think, unnecessary for the Crown to

---

[1] *Note.*—It would encumber the text with too much detail to enter into those of the Regulations which deal with the suspension of any restrictions imposed by the Military Lands Acts, etc., on the acquisition and user of land, and which enlarge the powers of the authorities under the Military Manœuvres Act. We have preferred to deal with these topics in the form of an explanatory footnote to the Regulations in the Appendix. It is sufficient to say here that the compulsory acquisition of land is made much more summary, and that the War Office in regulating the use of such land by bye-laws is no longer bound to respect public and private rights, *e.g.*, rights of common and of highway, etc.

secure statutory powers to deal with alien enemies resident in this country. The new Act, however, does more than this: it gives the Crown power to deal not merely with alien enemies but with aliens, and does not confine that power to the duration of war, but extends it to times of imminent national danger or great emergency. In this respect its duration, unlike that of the Defence of the Realm Acts, is unlimited, and it is not at all improbable that this emergency Act is destined to remain permanently on the Statute-book. It may well be, having regard to the freemasonry of espionage which has been discovered to exist in this country, that some permanent restrictions of the facilities hitherto so generously and so exceptionally extended to aliens by England, in comparison with other European countries, will appear desirable. The Act is, indeed, interesting in that it assimilates our law very closely to the laws of those countries, particularly by introducing the registration of aliens, and by enabling the Government to proclaim at any time of emergency an *état de siége* as regards such persons. Needless to say, it does not confer on the Executive any power to extend such a proclamation to British subjects. The full text of the Act and of the consolidated Regulations under it will be found in the Appendix, and the Act itself is so clear and explicit —presenting in this respect a marked contrast to the Defence of the Realm Act—that neither it nor the Regulations under it call for any legal criticism. The main features of it are that it enables the authorities to prohibit aliens from landing generally, and without qualification—in this respect it goes far beyond the Alien Immigration Act.[1] But what is much more important, it enables the Crown to deport aliens already resident in this country, to restrict their residence to particular places, and to compel them to remain there. The Regulations made under the Act are chiefly notable for prescribing the registration not only of alien enemies but also of friendly aliens, if the latter reside in an area from which the former are excluded.[2] And the duty is laid on every British householder of reporting the presence of any aliens in his household. The enforcement of these Regulations is not entrusted to the military authorities acting with the sanction of military law, as in the case of the Defence of the Realm Act; it rests with the police and the immigration officers, and the ordinary administration of justice is not superseded—the Courts of Summary Jurisdiction are to be employed.

The Special Constables Act.—We have seen that by an Act of 1831 the justices may, if (but only if) they apprehend riot or felony, compel any number of men to serve as special constables. By an emergency Act it is now provided that during the present war the justices may exercise these powers without restriction, *i.e.*, "although a tumult, riot, or felony has not taken place or is not immediately apprehended." We conclude that the Crown, acting through justices, might therefore now compel the whole adult population to act as special constables. The Act removes any doubt that may

---

[1] But, as we have seen, an alien has no right at common law to enter British territory at all.

[2] See Regulations, Part II., sec. 19 (1).

exist as to whether special constables have all the statutory powers of police constables, in addition to the powers of a constable at common law which they undoubtedly possess, by providing that they shall have *all* the powers, privileges, and duties of a police constable. The Act also enables His Majesty in Council to make regulations with respect to special constables appointed in boroughs under the Municipal Corporation Act.[1]

The Intoxicating Liquor (Temporary Restriction) Act.—The grant of a licence to sell intoxicating liquors by retail carries with it the right, during the term of the licence, to sell during hours and on days which are defined by statute.[2] These hours may be extended, but not diminished, at the discretion of the licensing justices. An emergency Act has been made, to take effect during the continuance of the war and for one month after its close, which enables the licensing justices, upon the recommendation of the chief officer of police, to direct the suspension of the sale of intoxicating liquor on licensed premises and registered clubs. There appears to be no restriction on the scope of such orders—provided they are approved by the Secretary of State—and it would seem that the sale by retail or consumption of intoxicating liquor could thus be totally prohibited

[1] Special constables appointed in boroughs are, by sec. 196 of the Municipal Corporations Act, 1882, entitled to receive remuneration at the rate of 3s. 6d. a day (see Schedule IV. to that Act). This must, of course, refer to special constables who are compelled to serve ; it cannot, we imagine, apply to those who voluntarily undertake part-time duty.

[2] This is putting it generally. But see the Licensing Acts of 1872 and 1874.

throughout the United Kingdom if the authorities saw fit. These orders may be made at the licensing meetings of the justices, and it is perhaps hardly necessary to say that no appeal to Quarter Sessions against such an order would lie.[1]

Army Supplies and Naval Billeting Acts.—The power, which as we have seen, is given to the Crown by the Army Annual Act to requisition means of transport has been extended by a special Act (The Army, Supply of Food, Forage, and Stores, Act) to include not only forage but stores "of all descriptions." Thus at a stroke of the draughtsman's pen is the ancient right of purveyance revived in all its amplitude. There would now appear to be nothing which the Crown may not demand from the private citizen for the needs of the army. This means compulsory purchase, and the same rules hold good as to its enforcement and the determination of the "due" price, as already govern the requisition of vehicles under the Army Act (see above on "Requisitions." Another Act has extended to sailors the provisions of the Army Act as to the billeting of soldiers.

Unreasonable Withholding of Food Supplies.—It only remains to notice a remarkable Act which recalls mediæval legislation against regrating and engrossing. Quite independently of statutes it was always held to be an offence at common law[2] to

---

[1] The justices will of course be acting in a purely administrative capacity, and in no sense could their action be regarded, as it must be in the case of the grant or refusal of a licence (*R.* v. *Woodhouse*, [1906] 2 K.B. 501), as judicial.

[2] See Coke, 3 Inst. 195.

"engross" or get into one's hands the necessaries of life with a view to taking an unfair advantage of the public. There were some differences of opinion as to what such necessaries were—hops and salt were debatable—but it was agreed that they included all "victual." Innumerable statutes[1] were passed from a very early till a very late time[2] prohibiting such engrossing, commanding provision dealers to sell at "a reasonable price," and authorising the justices in the case of certain articles to fix such a price.[3] The man who attempted to hold up food in this way might be proceeded against by indictment[4] or information, and convicted of a misdemeanour. There is a record of a conviction as late as 1800 where the common law doctrine was very forcibly laid down by Kenyon, C.J., in *The King* v. *Waddington*.[5] They have an immediate bearing on the state of affairs at the outbreak of the present war.

> "If a number of rich persons are to buy up the whole or a considerable part of the produce from which supply [of food] is desired in order to make their own private and exorbitant advantage of it to the public detriment . . . it

---

[1] They are set out in Hawkins' *Pleas of the Crown*, I., c. 80.
[2] *E.g.*, from 23 Edw. III. c. 6 to 31 Geo. II. c. 29.
[3] *E.g.*, the Assize of Bread in virtue of 31 Geo. II. c. 29.
[4] See the forms of indictment in Burn's *Justice of the Peace and Parish Officer*, 3rd ed. (1751), p. 290. Words about the evil example of such practices were part of the formula.
[5] 1 East 143, and *cf.* Grose, J., p. 164. Waddington was accused on an information the fourth count of which charged him with engrossing large quantities of hops "with intent to resell the same for an unreasonable profit, and thereby to inhance the price." He was convicted and fined £500.

is a most heinous offence against religion and against the established law of this country."

The offence, whether at common law or under statute, was, however, abolished in 1844.[1] The whole conception of public interest by which the doctrine was inspired had become discredited in the age of *laisser faire*, and the Individualists would have none of it. But while it thus disappeared from the criminal law it continues to maintain a place, although a somewhat uncertain place, in the law of contract and tort, under the conception of "restraint of trade." Agreements in restraint of trade are considered against public policy and unenforceable. But the tendency of late years is to take a very liberal view of what constitutes restraint of trade, especially as to restriction in point of space, if not of time.[2] The whole tendency of the common law in this country— the tendency is very different in America[3] and Australia — is to favour "liberty."[4] And so, too, in tort, an agreement in restraint of trade whereby a competing trader suffers loss will not enable him to sustain an action for conspiracy, unless he can prove that the agreement was both wrongful and malicious, and that the hurt of another rather than

[1] 7 & 8 Vict. c. 24. An Act of 12 Geo. III. c. 71 had already limited the scope of the offence by abolishing some of the earlier statutes on the ground that they "prevented a free trade."

[2] Cf. *Maxim-Nordenfelt, etc.,* v. *Nordenfelt,* [1894] A.C. 534.

[3] See the Northern Securities Case, U.S. Rep., No. 277 (October 1903).

[4] *Cf.* the judgment delivered by Sir G. Jessel in *Printing Co.* v. *Sampson,* (1875).

benefit to themselves was the immediate object of those who promoted it. "To draw a line between fair and unfair competition," as Lord Bowen put it in a memorable judgment, "between what is reasonable and unreasonable, passes the power of the courts."[1] Nor is it likely that the courts would to-day hold a combination in restraint of trade to be indictable as a criminal offence.

It will be observed, therefore, that to-day attempts either by one person, or by several persons acting in concert, to restrain competition and raise prices are quite beyond the reach of the law. When, therefore, on the outbreak of the present war it was apprehended that a grave economic crisis might arise owing to attempts to corner the market, the only way the situation could be met was by legislation. Hence an Act to enable the Board of Trade, so long as the war lasts, to take possession of foodstuffs unreasonably withheld. The Board is to pay "a reasonable price"—here is the *justum pretium* of mediæval economics—which price is, failing agreement, to be fixed by the arbitration of a judge of the High Court. A subsequent Act extends this power to "any article of commerce." This subsequent Act, which incorporates the Unreasonable Withholding of Food Supplies Act, is known as the Articles of Commerce (Returns) Act. Its effect is to facilitate the exercise of the powers granted to the Board of Trade by the earlier Act. It empowers the Board to call upon any person to make returns as to the quantity of "*any article* of commerce" in his possession, empowers an officer of the Board to search

---

[1] *Mogul Steamship Co.* v. *M'Gregor, Gow & Co.*, [1891] A.C.

DEFENCE OF THE REALM ACT 101

premises for this purpose, and makes refusal of information an offence punishable by fine or imprisonment at the discretion of a court of summary jurisdiction.

It is no part of our task to comment upon the profound changes in the theory of the functions of the State which such legislation implies, or to speculate how far that change is likely to outlast the circumstances which have occasioned it. The situation is an abnormal one, and calls for abnormal measures. It is, we think, a fair presumption that if the words in the Defence of the Realm Act authorising His Majesty in Council to issue regulations for the public safety and defence of the realm were really capable of the wide construction put upon them by the Regulations issued thereunder, all these collateral statutes dealing with the restriction of aliens and the requisitioning of food supplies and such matters would have been unnecessary. The fact that statutory powers were specifically sought and obtained in each of these cases—all of these cases of " public safety and defence of the realm "—goes to show that the Defence of the Realm Act could not confer the arbitrary power upon the Executive which it has assumed.

The Revised Legislation.—Since the foregoing was written and in type, a third Defence of the Realm Act has been placed on the Statute-book, and a fourth set of Regulations, consolidating and enlarging their predecessors, has been issued.[1] We

[1] This Act and the new Regulations thereunder were only published on 27th November. The full text will be found in the Appendix.

have therefore at the last moment to consider how far they necessitate a modification of what we have written in the preceding section of this chapter. We think that all that we have written by way of criticism and analysis of the earlier Act and Regulations was sound; indeed a remarkable change in the words of the new Act goes far to confirm our criticism and amounts to a confession of error. For four months we have been living under decrees of the military and naval authorities which were absolutely illegal.[1] We will proceed to examine the wording of the new Act, and to contrast it with that of the earlier Act.

The New Enacting Words.—We have to look at the enacting words of the new Act. Do they tend to remove the ambiguity which we have already criticised, as to the powers conferred on the Crown to make regulations? Are they less declaratory and more enacting? To some extent the Act does, indeed, improve upon the very lax drafting which we have criticised in the case of the earlier Act. Thus the first clause says—

> "His Majesty in Council has power during the continuance of the present war to issue regulations *for securing the public safety and defence of the realm,* and as to the powers and duties for that purpose of the Admiralty and Army Council and of the members of His Majesty's forces and other persons acting in his behalf; and may by such regulations authorise

---

[1] We refer, of course, to those decrees which were not confined to the exercise of the powers specifically conferred by the Act.

the trial by courts-martial, or in the case of minor offences by courts of summary jurisdiction, and punishment of persons committing offences [against the regulations and in particular] against any of the provisions of such regulations designed [etc.]."[1]

The words in italics are in the new Act transposed from the position they occupied in the first Act; in the earlier Act they came after, *and not before*, the words as to the powers and duties of the military and naval authorities. The words in brackets are altogether new.

What is the effect of this transposition of old words and insertion of new ones? Undoubtedly it makes a considerable change. His Majesty is now unequivocally given power (or rather it is declared he "has power") to make regulations not merely as to the powers of the military and naval authorities for the defence of the realm and the public safety, but to make regulations for such safety and defence independently of those powers. This is a very different thing. True, the term "has power" has a declaratory flavour as though it were merely declaring powers already possessed, and it is not altogether free from the objection of ambiguity, but doubtless

---

[1] *Cf.* the words in the original Act: "His Majesty in Council has power during the continuance of the present war to issue regulations as to the powers and duties of the Admiralty and Army Council, and of the members of His Majesty's forces, and other persons acting in his behalf, for securing the public safety and defence of the realm; and may by such regulations authorise the trial by courts-martial and punishment of persons contravening any of the provisions of such regulations designed" (these follow specified powers).

it means, and would probably be interpreted by a court to mean, that it shall be lawful for the Crown to exercise new powers. Furthermore the Act provides for the trial by court-martial of persons offending against any regulations issued under these general powers, and not merely of persons offending against the regulations issued under the specified powers.[1] The effect of all this is to give the Crown a *general* power to make regulations, and to subject all persons offending against those regulations to martial law. This meets nearly the whole of our criticism in the preceding section, and it is a remarkable confession of the illegality of the Regulations of the last four months. It is extraordinary, however, that no one, so far as we know, has during those four months pointed out these illegalities.

The earlier Regulations are not, like the Act under which they are made, repealed. It is provided that they are to continue in force and have effect as if made under the new Act.[2] On the other hand it is nowhere said that they are to have effect as if enacted in the Act, and therefore, although the empowering words of the Act itself are wider than those of its predecessor, it is still open to a court to consider whether any one of the Regulations is covered by those words, *i.e.*, whether it really is

[1] As to the distinction between general and specified powers, the reader is referred back to what we have already said in the preceding section of this chapter. See p. 77 *et seq*.

[2] The new (consolidated) Regulations of 27th November mainly consist of a consolidation of the earlier Regulations of 12th August, 1st September, 17th September, and 14th October.

designed to secure the safety and defence of the realm. If it were excessive, frivolous, or needlessly restrictive of the liberty of the subject the Court might hold it *ultra vires*. Now it is, as we have seen in the preceding section, a general rule of interpretation that a statute can only change the common law by express words or necessary intendment. And as these Regulations do, as we have seen and shall see, make very considerable exceptions to the common law, it is still a matter of some doubt how the courts would look at them.[1]

New Offences.—In the interstices of these consolidated Regulations are to be found some new articles which create new offences of a somewhat remarkable character. For example, Article 53 requires every person "to stop and answer any questions" and to furnish any information required by a constable or by an officer; and Article 49 requires him to inform against any persons whom "he knows" to have offended against the Regulations. These articles create two new offences entirely unknown to English law. They impose a very serious, it may be an intolerable, burden on the subject. Article 53 is so wide in its terms that it enables a constable or a military officer to compel a person to answer questions which may incriminate himself. That an officer or a constable should have the right to put any question he thinks fit to any person he

[1] It is worthy of note that one of the Regulations which we declared *ultra vires* in the preceding chapter, *i.e.*, that by which any person arrested without warrant was to be deemed to be in legal custody is quietly dropped in the new consolidated Regulations. It was, indeed, flagrantly illegal.

happens to meet, and that a military court[1] should have the power whether the question was "reasonable" and the answer satisfactory, seems to us to be going very far. Article 50 is also somewhat unsatisfactory. It provides that if a person does any act likely to be prejudicial to the public safety or defence of the realm, "and *not specifically provided for* in the foregoing Regulations, with the intention or for the purpose of assisting the enemy, he shall be deemed to be guilty of an offence against the Regulations." The law of treason and its wide interpretation of "overt acts" is quite strong enough to deal with any acts designed to assist the enemy, and the matter might well have been left to the common law courts. But this is a subject to which we shall return when we deal with the death penalty.

The Liberty of the Press.—The new Regulations which affect the liberty of the Press—it is significant that the Press is never once referred to by name—are much wider than their predecessors. The earlier Regulations made it an offence to publish any information with respect to the movement or disposition of any of the forces, etc., of His Majesty or his allies, or with respect to any plans of operations, if the information were such as might be directly or indirectly useful to the enemy. It will be noted that there is here no question of intent to assist the foe.

[1] It is a serious defect in these Regulations that while giving courts of summary jurisdiction a concurrent jurisdiction in "minor offences," the Regulations nowhere say what a minor offence is. Article 53 may by inference from Act 57 (*q.v.*) be one which deals with a minor offence, but the Regulations do not say so. And Article 49 is evidently meant to be exclusively interpreted by courts-martial.

It is sufficient that the information "might be" useful to the enemy. Practically, therefore, every newspaper proprietor or editor acts at his peril in publishing anything whatsoever.[1] The later Regulation goes further—even speculation is forbidden. Any publication of information as to "supposed plans" is made an offence. "Kriegspiel" by "our military expert" becomes a very dangerous game, and intelligent anticipation a perilous pastime. The earlier Regulations as to the spreading of "reports" are also enlarged. Originally the Regulations confined the offence to the spreading orally or in writing of reports "likely to create disaffection or alarm among any of His Majesty's forces or among the civilian population," and the offence was confined to the neighbourhood of a defended harbour. In the later Regulations this local restriction was removed. In the new Regulations there is a further extension. Not only is the spreading of "false" reports, irrespective of their effect, included (which is proper enough), but to publish any report or statement, even though it be true, is an offence, whether it excites alarm and disaffection be not, provided it is likely to interfere with the success of His Majesty's forces, or to prejudice His Majesty's relations with foreign powers. These are wide words and they make leader-writing a perilous pursuit. So also to spread reports or to make statements "likely to prejudice the *recruiting*, training, discipline, or administration" of any of His Majesty's forces is made an offence. To comment on insufficiency of accommodation on

[1] And it seems clear from a comparison of Article 18 and Article 57 that a court-martial alone is to decide.

Salisbury Plain is therefore quite clearly an offence, if the military authorities or [1] a court of summary jurisdiction choose to regard it as such.

From all of which it will be clear that although not a word is said about the liberty of the Press or the powers of the Press Bureau, that liberty is now in a precarious state—it hangs by a thread. Never since the days of the Licensing Act, not even under the Six Acts, was the Press in such peril.

The Position of Newspaper Proprietors.—What is the position of the newspaper proprietor whose newspaper publishes an unfriendly criticism on military administration, or speculates unfavourably about our military operations? Is he liable to be convicted for the new offence along with the journalist who wrote it and the editor who passed it? It is difficult to say. In proceedings for criminal libel the proprietor has, since Lord Campbell's Act was passed, been protected from prosecution if he can prove that such publication was made without his authority, knowledge, or consent, and was not due to want of proper care or caution on his part. This protection certainly does not extend to proceedings under the Defence of the Realm Act, any more than does the protection against vexatious prosecution provided by the Law of Libel Amendment Act of 1888. But the presumption of the common law has, with some exceptions such as the Law of Nuisance, always been that the master is not criminally liable, however

---

[1] Which? Here again the Regulations are regrettably laconic. Conceivably a newspaper editor might be tried by a court of summary jurisdiction instead of a court-martial, but he does not appear to have any right to claim such option.

much he may be civilly, for the acts of his servant, unless it can be shown that he expressly or impliedly authorised them.[1] There are statutory exceptions to this, as in the case of publicans under the Licensing Acts, but they are few; and before the master can be implicated in the offence of the servant, guilty intent on the part of the latter must be proved. Now, as we have seen, the Regulations make certain things punishable without proof of guilty knowledge. And the words are so wide that it is possible that any one who "publishes" may be convicted.

The Question of Guilty Intent.—The question of the culpability of the person who has the misfortune to offend against these Regulations calls for rather closer examination. It is a general presumption of our criminal law that a man cannot be convicted for an offence unless it can be proved that he knew what he was doing, that he intended to do it, and that he "directly" intended to do it. This mental state is what lawyers call *mens rea* or "guilty mind." If, in the case of a statutory offence, the statute is silent on the point, it will generally be presumed that proof of guilty mind is essential to a conviction for the offence.[2] But if it uses unequivocal words (as these new statutory Regulations under the Defence of the Realm Act frequently do) which look at the act from a purely objective point of view, then the courts may presume that the legislature intended to depart from the common law in this respect and to make the act punishable in any case. But the words in the

---

[1] *Rex* v. *Huggins*, 2 Raymond 1574.

[2] See *R.* v. *Tolson*, L.R. 23 Q.B.D. 168 and *Reg.* v. *Sleep*, L. & C. 44.

statute itself should be clear, and we doubt if a mere *regulation* under the Statute can make such a grave departure. For this reason we think that those words in the Regulations which affect to make a journalist guilty of an offence if he writes or publishes anything which may be inconvenient, irrespective of his *intention* in so doing, cannot be sustained in law, and that a conviction in such case would be bad. Parliament ought not to authorise, and we do not think it has authorised, the Executive to depart so freely from the common law. This is all the more true as the courts have laid it down that, to dispense with the necessity of *mens rea* in the case of a statutory offence, it should be shown that the danger to the public must be very great and the punishment very small.[1] In this case the danger is not always apparent, while the punishment is very severe.

The Death Penalty.—One very significant feature of the Act is that it extends the power of courts-martial, under the earlier Act, to sentence civilians to penal servitude for life by providing that where it is proved that an offence against the Regulations was committed "with the intention of assisting the enemy," the person convicted (by a court-martial) of such an offence shall be punishable with death. Thus, for the first time in England for at least two hundred and fifty years, a civilian may be sentenced to death without trial by jury. Is this justified? Is it necessary? It may be said (and we have said it) that the offence of assisting the enemy is already treason at common law and punishable as such with the death penalty. So it is and so it ought to be.

[1] *R.* v. *Tolson.*

CAPITAL PENALTIES

But it is one thing to try a man for an offence *defined* by the common law and by innumerable cases in the law reports and to try him with all the safeguards of a jury and with the right to appeal from their verdict, if it is one of "guilty" to the Court of Criminal Appeal; it is quite another thing to try him for an offence which is not so defined, and to try him by a court of officers ignorant of the common law,[1] who direct themselves, instead of directing a jury, both as to the law and the facts, and whose verdict and sentence in one are subject to no appeal but merely to the revision of a Ministerial officer—the Judge-Advocate. Considering that the king's courts are still sitting, that the king's writ runs throughout the realm, and that juries can be, and are being, empanelled every day, we think this subjection of the lives of private citizens to military law is entirely unjustified. The death penalty, once inflicted, is irrevocable. It is amazing that not a single member of the House of Commons criticised it during the progress of the bill.[2] We are bound to say that we think this clause of the Act a blot on the Statute-book.

Martial Law and Something More.— Martial law we can understand—it does not profess to be

[1] Indeed they are not bound to take any notice of the common law at all.

[2] It was reserved for the much maligned House of Lords to draw attention (but in vain) to these provisions. Lord Halsbury, Lord Loreburn, and Lord Bryce united in protest against it—great names and venerable. We know no stronger argument for a strong Second Chamber in this country than such an episode. It is as creditable to the Lords as it is discreditable to the Commons.

anything but what it is, *i.e.*, extra-legal and arbitrary, and as it originates in, so it is limited by, the necessities of the case. The moment the state of facts—the state of "war" within the realm—which gave rise to it ceases (and, as we have urged, even during the "war" itself if the courts are able to sit at all) the courts may restrain its exercise. But this Act silences the courts. It is more specious but far less restricted than martial law.

Certainly never in our history has the Executive assumed such arbitrary power over the life, liberty, and property of British subjects. The net of restriction is now so finely woven, so ingeniously designed, that it enmeshes every activity of the citizen. The military authorities can, by an ukase enlarging the definition of "specified areas," deport the whole population of any town or village from one part of the country to another. They could totally close all the public-houses throughout the United Kingdom for every hour of the day for the whole period of the war. They can, on mere suspicion and without proof of any offence having been committed, treat any private citizen as a ticket-of-leave man, and require him to reside where they please and to report himself whenever they think fit. They can, on mere suspicion, arrest anyone without warrant, and can equally without warrant enter any house by day or by night. They can punish with penal servitude for life any journalist who speculates as to the plan of campaign of the British or French forces, and with six months' imprisonment if he criticises the dietary or accommodation of the new recruits. They can stop any citizen in the streets, and compel himself to

EXTRAORDINARY POWERS 113

answer questions even though they incriminate himself. They can compel the whole population of England to keep indoors by day as well as by night. They can stop up any road or arrest any vehicle. The private citizen is placed under the absolute orders of any major holding His Majesty's commission. The military authority issues these orders, and the military authority decides whether the citizen has offended against them. To challenge these Regulations in a court of law will, as we have seen, be often difficult and sometimes impossible. To "appeal" against the sentence of a court-martial to a civil court may be attempted by a writ of *certiorari*, but precedents are not encouraging. We must leave the reader to judge for himself whether this "Parliamentary despotism," which recalls nothing so much as the kind of legislation hitherto exclusively reserved for uncivilised Protectorates,[1] is either necessary or wise.

[1] *Cf.* the remarks of Farwell, L.J., on the administration of British Bechuanaland in *R.* v. *Crewe*, L.T. Rep., vol. cii., p. 780.

That a single afternoon, or rather part of it, should have been thought sufficient for the committee stage of the bill is a curious commentary on the vigilance of the House of Commons.

CHAPTER IV

THE ARMED FORCES OF THE CROWN

The Prerogative of the Crown :—I. The United Kingdom—The Army Act, the King's Regulations, and the Articles of War—The Army Annual Act—The Contract of Enlistment—The Reserve Forces Act—The Militia Acts—The Territorial Forces Act—Commissions—Pensions—The Navy—The Naval Discipline Act—The Naval Reserve Acts.

II. The Overseas Dominions and India—The Army Act in relation thereto—Dominion Defence Acts—The Colonial Naval Defence Act, 1865—Dominion Naval Forces Act, 1911—Dominion Naval Acts—The Committee of Imperial Defence—The Imperial General Staff.

III. The Organisation and Control of the Forces — The Secretary of State and the Army Council—The First Lord and the Board of Admiralty.

"WHEREAS the raising or keeping of a standing army within the United Kingdom of Great Britain and Ireland in time of peace, unless it be with the consent of Parliament, is against law; and Whereas it is adjudged by His Majesty and the present Parliament that a body of forces shall be continued for the safety of the United Kingdom. . . ."—Preamble to the Army Annual Act.

"WHEREAS it is expedient to amend the law relating to the government of the Navy, whereon under the good Providence of God, the wealth, safety, and strength of the kingdom chiefly depend."—Preamble to the Naval Discipline Act.

The Prerogative.—It is the sole prerogative of the Crown to raise armed forces. If a private citizen attempted to raise troops and drill them on his own account he would commit a statutory offence.[1] So, too, the sole government, command, and disposition of all forces by sea and land is "the undoubted right" of His Majesty.[2] It matters not whether the forces be raised in this country or in the dominions overseas. A soldier in the service of a colonial government is just as much the king's soldier[3] as a member of the home forces.

But the prerogative has been regulated by statute, and is subject to constitutional limitations. The doctrine laid down in the Bill of Rights, that the maintenance of a standing army by the Crown in time of peace without the consent of Parliament is now consecrated in the preamble to the Army Annual Act which, with some slight variation, repeats the words of the original Mutiny Act. And not only is the maintenance of a standing army therefore dependent on the consent of Parliament, but so is its discipline and pay. Most military

---

[1] Unauthorised drilling is illegal by the Act of 1820, and unauthorised recruiting is made punishable by sec. 98 of the Army Act, with a fine of not more than £20 on summary conviction.

[2] *Cf.* the recitals of 13 Chas. II. c. vi.

[3] Cf. *Williams* v. *Howarth*, [1905] A.C. 55, where a soldier of the New South Wales contingent sued the Colonial Government (represented by a nominal dependant) for arrears of pay—"whether the money by which he was to be paid was to be found by the colony or the mother country was not a matter which could in any way affect his relations to his employer the Crown. . . . The government in relation to this contract is the king himself. The soldier is his soldier, and the supplies granted to His Majesty for the purpose of paying his soldiers, whether they be granted by the Imperial or the Colonial legislature, are money granted to the king."

offences are not offences at common law at all, and both the procedure by which they are tried and the punishment with which they are attended would, in the absence of statutory authority, be illegal. A soldier who disobeys a lawful command in such a manner as to show "a wilful defiance of authority" is under the military code liable even in time of peace to be sentenced to death by court-martial. Such "exemplary and speedy punishments" can only be authorised by the consent of Parliament. And the pay of the troops, no less than their discipline and numbers, is dependent upon the supplies annually voted by Parliament in the Army estimates.

The government of the army so authorised does, it is true, remain solely in the hands of the king. But here he is limited by the etiquette of the constitution in virtue of which some minister must always be found who will assume responsibility for the acts of the sovereign. The king cannot act alone. The officer receives his commission from the king, but it is countersigned by the Secretary of State. Without such counter-signature it would be as inoperative as an order under the sign-manual of the king for the issue of money out of His Majesty's Treasury without the counter-signature of a minister. So, too, the attestation form for the enlistment of a soldier must be authorised by the Secretary of State. And as we shall see when we come to consider the position of the Secretary of State, statute law has not been altogether silent on this point. Anyone who studies the Regulation of the Forces Act of 1881, the Reserve Forces Act of 1882, or the Territorial and Reserve Forces Act of 1907, will be struck by the pains which Parliament has taken to subdue the prerogative. It is very rarely that Parliament omits to qualify the words "it shall be lawful for His Majesty" with the addition "through his Secretary of State." The Territorial Force cannot be embodied if an address to His Majesty by both Houses is presented against their embodiment, and if Parliament is prorogued a proclamation is to be issued to enable it to meet such an eventuality.[1] It would seem as if Parliament had watched with more jealousy the exercise of the royal authority over the Army than over any other department of government.

I. THE UNITED KINGDOM.

The Army Act.—The Army Act of 1881[2] consolidates the law relating to the discipline of the Army. This aspect of it will be considered more closely in the chapter which follows. It provides for discipline in war—"on active service"—as well as in peace, by embodying the old Articles of War. But sec. 69 empowers the Crown to make new "Articles of War," and no doubt it could in time of war do this in virtue of the prerogative alone.[3] The Army Act is supplemented by the

[1] Sec. 17. If Parliament is not sitting it must be summoned within ten days.

[2] 44 & 45 Vict. c. 58. The Act is, however, continually being amended by subsequent Acts. Considerable changes were made by the Army Annual Act of 1909, consequent on the creation of the Army Council. Changes were also made by the Territorial Forces Act of 1907.

[3] The question of how far an Act regulating the exercise of an undoubted prerogative thereby precludes the Crown from

King's Regulations, issued with the approval of the Secretary of State, which form a code of instructions to officers as to the discharge of their normal duties— for example, their duties in aid of the civil power. These are sometimes supplemented by special Army orders. These may be said to constitute for the soldier a "Whole Duty of Man."

The Army Act is re-enacted annually by the Army Annual Act, which authorises the continuance of the Regular Forces and prescribes their numbers.

Enlistment.—The forces raised under the Act are raised by voluntary enlistment. The Crown has no power, even as regards the forces so prescribed, to compel men in *time of peace* to serve *outside the realm*. What it can do in time of war is another matter. The question of its power to compel men to serve *within* the realm in time of peace will be considered when we come to treat of the Militia Acts. The period of voluntary enlistment in the Regular Forces is fixed at twelve years, and although the Crown may by Regulations shorten this period, it cannot lengthen it. This term may be served wholly in the Army or partly in the Army and partly in the Army Reserve —the Secretary of State may regulate its distribution. At the end of nine years' service the soldier may re-engage for another period not exceeding a total term of twenty-one years. In case of imminent national danger or great emergency soldiers entitled under the terms of their enlistment to be transferred to the Reserve may be retained in their army service.

exercising it in any other way may be considered as an open one. See *Rutter* v. *Chapman*, 8 M. & W. 67, and *Bacon's Abridgment*, (1832) Title Prerogative (E) 5 f. 462.

The contract of enlistment is set out in the attestation paper which every recruit receives on offering himself, and enlistment is complete when the recruit has given his answers to the attestation paper, made and signed a declaration as to their truth, and taken the oath of allegiance before a justice of the peace, or an officer authorised to act as such by the Secretary of State. "Infants" are not disabled from entering into this contract. Once the recruit has enlisted, he undergoes a kind of *capitis deminutio*—he is unable to enter into any other contract of service. The Crown may terminate this "contract" by discharging the soldier when it pleases, but it need hardly be said that the soldier is absolutely bound. The law is quite clear as to the absolute power of the Crown to dismiss any of its servants, whether civil or military, at pleasure. The rule is founded upon considerations of public policy, and will be read into every contract of service concluded by the Crown.[1] We shall consider its applications in detail when we come to consider the subject of commissions.

The Reserve Forces.—The Reserve Forces consist of men who have already served either in the Regular Army or in the old Militia. They are governed by the Reserve Forces Act of 1882.[2] Reservists comprise (1) men whose term of enlistment is uncompleted and who have been transferred from the Regular Army Forces to the Reserve.

---

[1] *Cf.* Lord Watson in *De Dohse* v. *Reg.*, (1886) H.L. 66; also *Dunn* v. *the Queen*, [1896] 1 Q.B. 117, and the case of *Mitchell* v. *the Queen* in the footnote, p. 121.

[2] 45 & 46 Vict. c. 48.

(2) Special Reservists, consisting of men specially engaged as such, or of the Militia Forces, which in virtue of Orders in Council under the Territorial Forces Act have been now entirely transferred into the Army Reserve.[1] The Reserve Forces may be called out for annual training not exceeding twelve days in any one year. In imminent national danger or great emergency they may be called out on permanent service by proclamation. This step cannot be taken without the authorisation, prospective or retrospective, of Parliament, which, if not sitting, must be summoned to meet within ten days of the proclamation. It will thus be seen that the numbers of the Standing Army provided for by the Army Annual Act cannot be expanded without the approval of Parliament. When so called out they are subject to military law; when not called out they are governed by the Army Reserve Regulations.

The Militia Acts.—Although the Militia by its transformation into the Special Reserve has practically ceased to exist, the statutes relating to it are not repealed, and new militia forces might at any time be raised compulsorily by ballot under the Militia Act of 1757[2] were it not for the temporary suspension of the ballot every year under the Expiring Laws Continuance Act, which continues the Militia Ballot Suspension Act of 1865.[3] The Militia therefore, although in a state of suspended animation, cannot

---

[1] But no member of the Militia can on transfer have his existing conditions of service varied without his own consent. He therefore cannot be compelled to serve out of the United Kingdom

[2] 30 Geo. II.   [3] 28 & 29 Vict.

MILITIA

be wholly left out of account in a survey of the armed forces of the Crown. As we have already seen in the first part of the preceding chapter, the basis of the Militia is the old communal duty of the inhabitants of the county to assist in preserving the king's peace. The Militia never were, and are not now,[1] bound to serve outside the realm in any circumstances. They were raised by counties,[2] and the control was, until 1871,[3] in the hands of the lords-lieutenant. Since that year it has been revested in His Majesty, and is exercisable through the Secretary of the State. The Act of 1757 first introduced the Militia ballot, by which a fixed number or "quota," reapportioned among parishes according to their population, was to be chosen by ballot, under the supervision of the Lord-Lieutenant, from all men between the ages of eighteen and fifty. Men so chosen had to serve for three years or provide a substitute. These provisions of the Act of 1757 have never been repealed, and should Parliament at any time omit to renew for the year the Act of 1865 which suspended the operation of the ballot, the Crown might, by Order in Council, put it into operation. The ballot fell into disuse in 1815, and has never been revived, except during the years 1830-1832. Voluntary enlistment was substituted in 1852, and until its absorption in

---

[1] The Militia Act of 1882 (45 & 46 Vict.), sec. 12 (1): "No part of the Militia shall be carried or ordered to go out of the United Kingdom."

[2] *Ibid.*, sec. 8 (1): "Every militiaman shall be enlisted as a militiaman for some county."

[3] The Regulation of the Forces Act, 34 & 35 Vict. c. 86, s. 6.

the Special Reserve in 1908 the Militia was recruited in this manner.

The Territorial Forces Act.[1]—The auxiliary forces are now governed by the Territorial and Reserve Forces Act of 1907. This Act adopted the county as the basis of the new force, which was to consist of such number of men as might be prescribed from time to time by Parliament. The force was to consist of recruits enlisting for a period, which might be doubled by re-engagement, not exceeding four years. Except when actually embodied, the Territorial may discharge himself, subject to three months' notice and the payment of a small fine. He is bound to attend a certain number of drills and a training which may not exceed thirty days. When the Army Reserve has been called out, he may be required to prolong his service for twelve months. He may be compelled to serve in any part of the United Kingdom, but he cannot be compelled to serve outside it. He may, however, volunteer to serve outside or to be called out for defence, even though the force is not actually embodied. Any man who, without leave or reasonable excuse, fails to appear on embodiment will be held guilty of "deserting" or of "absenting himself without leave" within the Army Act, and may be arrested and tried by court-martial. The Territorial is not subject to military law, except when being trained or exercised, attached to the Regular Forces, or embodied. But he is liable to be fined £5 by a court of summary jurisdiction if without leave or reasonable excuse

[1] There is an admirable study of the Act in *The Law of the Territorial Force*, by Mr H. T. Baker, M.P.

he fails to attend his preliminary or annual training, or the prescribed number of drills. He cannot be transferred from one corps to another without his own consent. The old Volunteer and Yeomanry Forces have now been transferred to the Territorial Force.

Commissions.—A commission is held during His Majesty's pleasure, and may be terminated when His Majesty thinks fit. This has been often laid down, and when the sentence inflicted by a court-martial takes the form of cashiering or dismissal from His Majesty's service, then, however defective the procedure of the military tribunal or whatever circumstances of malice may attend its proceedings, the civil courts absolutely decline to interfere. They will not go into any question of injury where it is an injury affecting the military status of the accused [1] —this is "a thing which depends entirely on the Crown, seeing that every person who enters into military services engages to be entirely at the will and pleasure of the sovereign."[1] The position is equally well put in another case.

> "What the king had power to do independently of any inquiry, he plainly may do though the inquiry should not be satisfactory to a court of law, or even though the court which conducted it had no legal jurisdiction."[2]

The unrestricted scope of this power has an important bearing on the right given by sec. 42 of the Army Act to an officer, who thinks himself wronged, to complain to the Commander-in-Chief and his successor the Army Council. That section

---

[1] *Mansergh's Case*, (1861) 1 B. & S. 400.
[2] *In re Poe*, (1833) 5 B. & A. 688.

prescribes that the Army Council is to examine and report through the Secretary of State to His Majesty on such complaints. The right can be rendered quite inoperative if the Crown chooses to dismiss the officer. He is then estopped from vindicating his reputation.[1]

The converse does not hold good. An officer cannot choose the occasion of his resignation, and unless and until it is accepted he remains subject to military law.[2] In an early case[3] it was argued that an officer's commission is a reciprocal contract, and that if one party may determine it at pleasure so may the other, and Lord Mansfield allowed that the right to resign might exist, subject to some qualifications as to notice and circumstances. But the plaintiff in this case was in the service not of the Crown but of the East India Company, and it has never been regarded as a precedent in subsequent

---

[1] See *Woods* v. *Lyttleton*, T.L.R. vol. 25, p. 665 (June 1909).

[2] [I regret to be obliged to dissent in this particular. In the absence of authority, the inequitable nature of an engagement under which one side alone is bound to continued performance induces me to regard the acceptance of a commission (like the receipt of the seals of office) as the undertaking of an honourable employment, which can be resigned at any time except in the midst of the execution of a particular service: which I think was the case in the two naval instances cited on p. 125. I am fortified in this conclusion by the fact that when it was desired to introduce the system of one-sided engagement in the United States, this was effected by legislation (Act of Congress, 1861 ; *cf.* the 49th Article of War, and *U.S.* v. *Mimmack*, 97 U.S. 426); and further, by the analogy of the other professions ; in particular, of the Bar.—T.B.]

[3] *Parker* v. *Lord Clive* and *Vertue* v. *Lord Clive*, 4 Burrows 2419 and 2475. Actions for assault and false imprisonment by two captains who had been arrested by Lord Clive for throwing up their commissions. The plaintiffs were unsuccessful.

cases where the Crown itself was concerned; indeed, it has been laid down in the most unequivocal language that an officer in His Majesty's forces cannot at will and pleasure resign his appointment.

> "If this were so, every officer of the Queen's ships might with impunity abandon the ship whenever he pleased."[1]

So long as a naval officer's name is borne on the books of any one of His Majesty's ships in commission he is deemed to be in the service, and he may be arrested and confined as a deserter if he takes his leave.[2] So, too, the King's Regulations lay it down that until an army officer's resignation has been accepted and notified in the *Gazette*, he remains a member of His Majesty's forces.[3]

Pensions.—A pension is an act of grace, and the courts will not enforce a claim for the payment of one. The right to dismiss at pleasure carries with it the right to determine what conditions shall attend on the termination of service.[4] A petition of right, therefore, will not lie to enforce a claim to arrears of pension,[5] and if the sentence of a court-martial, however defective the proceedings, involves a loss of pension, the civil courts will not regard it as a loss

---

[1] *The Queen* v. *Cumming* (*Ex parte Hall*), (1887) 19 Q.B.D. 13.

[2] *Hearson* v. *Churchill*, [1892] 2 Q.B. 144.

[3] The King's Regulations (1912), Par. 254.

[4] *Re Tufnell*, L.R. 3 Ch.D. 164.

[5] Cf. *Gidley* v. *Palmerston*, (1822) 3 Brod. & B. 275—a civil pension, and *Mitchell* v. *the Queen*, (1890) cited in the notes to *Dunn* v. *the Queen*, [1896] 1 Q.B. 121, Mitchell being a military officer.

of civil rights which they can protect.[1] Nor will a mandamus lie against the Secretary of State for War to compel him to carry out the terms of a royal warrant regulating the pay and retiring allowances of soldiers of the Army, as no legal duty in relation to such officers is imposed upon the Secretary of State either by statute or by common law.[2]

The Navy.—It is a remarkable fact that the prerogative in relation to the Navy has never undergone that subjugation at the hands of Parliament which is so characteristic of the Crown's relations to the Army. The Crown is not precluded by statute from raising a standing navy in time of peace, nor from enforcing a permanent discipline. We have, in the words of the authors of the official manual, "an enduring code for a standing navy."[3] Not only so, but the Crown may, as we have seen, even compel the subject, if he come within the seafaring class, to impressment to serve in the Navy.[4] The pay, however, of the naval forces is entirely dependent on the annual grant of supplies by Parliament in the Naval Estimates. Their discipline is regulated by

---

[1] *Roberts's Case, Times*, 11th June 1879.

[2] *The Queen* v. *the Secretary of State for War*, [1891] 2 Q.B. 326. And cf. *Queen* v. *Lords Commissioners of the Treasury*, (1872) L.R. 7 Q.B. 387, and *R.* v. *Treasury*, [1909] 2 K.B. 191.

[3] *The Manual of Naval Law*, 4th ed., 1912.

[4] Cf. *Rex* v. *Broadfoot*, supra, and *R.* v. *Tubbs*, (1776) Cowp. 512, where Lord Mansfield said: "the power of pressing is founded upon immemorial usage." Also the words of Lord Kenyon in *Ex parte Fox*, (1793) 5 T.R. 276: "the right of pressing is founded on the common law, and extends to all seafaring men."

the Naval Discipline Act as amended by the Acts of 1884 and 1909, and by the Admiralty Instructions. The term of enlistment is regulated by the Naval Enlistment Acts of 1835 and 1884. By the Royal Naval Reserve Act of 1859, amended by Acts of 1896 and 1902, a reserve force of volunteers, now unrestricted in number, may be raised, to consist of men who serve for five years and are liable to twenty-eight days' training or exercise. They may be called out on active service by proclamation, and when so summoned may be required to serve in any waters. The Naval Forces Act of 1903 empowers the Admiralty to raise another force known as the Royal Naval Volunteer Reserve.

II. THE OVERSEAS DOMINIONS AND INDIA.

The Dominions.—As we have seen, the power of the Crown to raise armed forces also holds good in the dominions. But it is subject to the same constitutional limitations (with the exception of India) there as here. It may be taken as certain that the Bill of Rights is part of the common law of the settled colonies.[1] And there can be no doubt that where a conquered colony has received representative institutions, the Crown could not raise troops without the consent of the legislature. Up till about the middle of the last century the Crown maintained Imperial garrisons in the colonies at the expense of

---

[1] *Cf.* Cockburn on the application of the Petition of Right to Jamaica in *The Queen* v. *Nelson*, where he held that it was a statute declaratory of the common law and therefore applied. There has been some conflict of opinion as to whether Jamaica was a settled colony or conquered.

the mother country. Of late years the self-governing dominions have begun to provide for their own defence on land.

Australia, Canada, South Africa, and New Zealand have, within the last seven years, each of them passed local Defence Acts, all of which, with some variations, adopt the principle of compulsory service. In Australia and South Africa the compulsion extends to training in peace; in Canada, which has a militia, the compulsion is limited to service in war. The scope of this compulsion to serve in war is, in point of age, decidedly large—every citizen from seventeen to eighteen years of age is liable to serve right up to his sixtieth year. In each case these Defence Forces, as they are called, are divided into a Permanent Force and a Citizen Force, corresponding roughly to our Regular and Territorial Forces respectively, but with this important difference, that service in the Citizen Forces is not, as here, voluntary, but compulsory. The chief exemption in South Africa is significant—persons not of European descent cannot be members of the force.[1] But in no case can a member of the dominion forces be compelled to serve outside the particular dominion,[2] though he may volunteer to do so.[2] But that does not mean that co-operation with the Imperial forces is necessarily confined to the territory of each dominion. What it does mean is that the co-operation which is now being so

---

[1] South African Statutes, No. 13, of 1912 (Defence Act), sec. 7.
[2] Commonwealth Defence Act (No. 20, of 1903, as amended in 1909), sec. 49; and *cf.* sec. 1 of the South African Act, which, however, requires service *in* South Africa even outside the Union.

splendidly given is voluntary—it is the expression of a spontaneous loyalty, unbought and unforced.

Such Imperial contingencies are provided for. The Governor-General is empowered in time of war to place the Defence Forces or any part thereof under the orders of the commander of any portion of the king's Regular Forces. That express provision was necessary, because, in the absence of it, the king's commission issued to officers in England gives them no legal authority over dominion forces. In virtue of it the colonial troops can now be brigaded with our own men without impairing the unity of command. What is hardly less important than unity of command is uniformity of discipline. Here there was a legal difficulty. A colonial legislature could enact a code of discipline for enforcement within its own territory, but, in accordance with a well-known rule of law, it could not make that code enforceable outside it. Unlike the Imperial legislature, colonial parliaments cannot legislate ex-territorially. To what code of military law, then, are Canadian and Australian troops serving in Europe subject? Sec. 177 of our own Army Act has solved the difficulty: the colonial code is to apply in virtue of the Imperial legislation; failing such a code, our own code, as enacted in the Army Act, is to be extended to the colonial troops serving by our side. As a matter of fact, Australia has adopted our own Army Act, the provisions of which are common form in the Defence Acts of the dominions.

India.—The Indian Army consists of two forces—the English army in India and the native troops, corresponding in some respects to the legions and the auxiliaries of the Roman Empire. There is one aspect of the Indian Army which is of great constitutional importance. The Army Annual Act, by which Parliament annually fixes the number of His Majesty's troops, and thereby restricts the Crown to raise no more men than are therein granted, contains the words " exclusive of the numbers actually serving within His Majesty's Indian possessions." In other words, the numbers of the Indian Army are unlimited by statute. Here it would seem is an instrument of despotism : the Crown might intimidate its English subjects by the presence of an Indian army whose members are subject to no Parliamentary control. Troops sent to India are placed on the Indian establishment; they cease to come under the annual review of the Army Estimates. But the draughtsman of the Government of India Act was careful to guard against such an attempt to outflank the constitutional securities of the Bill of Rights. The Act provides that—

> "Except for preventing or repelling actual invasion of His Majesty's Indian possessions, or under other sudden and urgent necessity, the revenues of India are not, without the consent of both Houses of Parliament, applicable to defraying the expenses of any military operation carried on beyond the external frontiers of those possessions by His Majesty's forces charged upon those revenues."

The English troops in India and the English officers of the native troops are, like their comrades at home, subject to the disciplinary code of the Army Act. The native troops are governed by a different law—the Indian Articles of War—and by secs. 177 and 180 of the Army Act those Articles continue to govern the discipline of the Indian troops now serving in Europe.

Dominion Navies.—The recent policy of concentrating the Imperial Fleet in home waters has stimulated the colonies to something like a naval policy. As early as 1865 Parliament passed a Colonial Naval Defence Act to extend the Naval Discipline Act to colonial ships of war, and to enable His Majesty to accept offers of ships and men from colonial governments. Australia began in 1884 to provide for a system of naval defence, and entered into an agreement with the Imperial Government by which she undertook to contribute an annual subsidy to the maintenance of an auxiliary squadron in Australian waters. She stipulated, however, that those vessels were not to be employed outside the Australian waters, even in time of war, without the consent of the colonial governments. "Cash contributions without control," said one of her representatives, "are not in harmony with colonial nationalism." This was to raise profound questions of constitutional law, foreign policy, and naval strategy. When Australia began to substitute a contribution of men for a subsidy of money, and not only to maintain ships but to provide them, the question became imperative. Sir Wilfrid Laurier went further and declared that, as regarded Canada, "it was for the Parliament of Canada, if she created a Canadian navy, to say not only where but *when* it should go to war." Happily that extreme doctrine of a kind of colonial neutrality found little countenance. The modern conditions of naval strategy make unity of control absolutely imperative in time of war, and the fate of the dominions may be decided by a battle in the waters of the North Sea. In a remarkably powerful Memorandum of October 1911—one of the most important documents that has ever issued from Whitehall—the Admiralty, in reply to a request from Mr Borden, laid down the principles of Imperial strategy and pointed out that it is the *general* naval supremacy of Great Britain which is the primary safeguard of the security and interests of the great dominions. Once that is destroyed in home waters nothing could save them. Canada and Australia, while pursuing different policies of contribution, eventually united in support of this cardinal truth, and the Naval Defence Acts of the two dominions provide that in case of emergency the Governor in Council may place at the disposal of His Majesty for general service in the Royal Navy the ships and crews of the dominions. Such ships were already subject to the code of discipline laid down in our own Naval Discipline Act, which by an enabling Act known as the Colonial Naval Defence Act can be adopted, subject to such adaptation as they think fit, by the dominion governments. By a recent Act (1911), the ships when placed at the disposal of the Admiralty are subject to our Naval Discipline Act, the King's Regulations, and the Admiralty Instructions, without any modification at all.

We cannot here enter into the profoundly interesting questions raised in the debates on the Canadian

Naval Aid Bill, whose fate is still uncertain. They resolve themselves into a single question: which is the better policy? to contribute ships which shall become, whether in peace or in war, an integral and permanent constituent of the Imperial Fleet, as New Zealand has done, or to raise local navies which, except in emergency, shall remain exclusively under colonial control—which is the policy pursued by Australia? The Admiralty very properly has left the question to each dominion to decide for itself.

The Committee of Imperial Defence.—An extremely important departure in the direction of the co-ordination of the problems of Imperial Defence was taken a few years ago by the creation of a committee to deal with such problems. The constitution of this committee is an informal one, almost as informal as that of the Cabinet itself, and it has never been defined either by prerogative or statute. It normally consists of the ministers responsible for the Army and Navy respectively, together with the Prime Minister, the Secretary of State for Foreign Affairs, and the Secretary for India. It is, however, a very elastic body, and whenever matters affecting their departments are under consideration, other ministers may be summoned, and not only they but the permanent officials. The presence of officials thus discriminates this body from the Cabinet, from which it also differs in having a permanent secretariat with a permanent record of its deliberations for the use of successive administrations. In that respect it has done much to neutralise problems of defence, so far as political parties are concerned, and to secure continuity of policy. Indeed, a member of the Opposition, Mr Balfour, is summoned to its deliberations. Not only so, but representatives of the colonies may and, when present in London do attend. The Prime Ministers of the dominions present at the periodical Colonial Conference invariably take advantage of their presence in this country to attend the meetings of the Committee. And lately the Imperial Government have invited the dominions to participate regularly in its deliberations by providing for the permanent presence in London of one of their ministers, though nothing has, we believe, yet been done to carry this proposal into effect. There are, of course, limits set to the power of a body of this kind, owing to the necessity of preserving the supremacy of the Cabinet and its complete responsibility to Parliament. Hence the Committee has no independent initiative and no executive authority. It is a purely consultative body. But its importance in providing for a common policy of defence throughout the Empire cannot be overestimated, and in it probably lies the germ of all future developments in the direction of the closer unity of the Empire.

Mention may here be made of the Colonial Conference. This is a body which meets every four years to discuss Imperial problems, and is attended by the Prime Ministers and others of the self-governing dominions. It also is an informal body, but, likewise, keeps a record of its proceedings and has a permanent secretariat. The same limits to its powers are set by constitutional considerations as in the case of the Committee of Imperial Defence, and there remains the further consideration of the autonomy of the dominions. Their governments are extremely jealous of their political independence, and their representatives at the meetings of the Conference are rather mandatory delegates, limited by the instructions from their governments, than plenipotentiaries. Special conferences are sometimes held to discuss problems of defence and the like, and here the same considerations govern. They were well expressed by Mr Asquith in the House of Commons on 26th August 1909.

> "All resolutions come to and proposals approved by the conference which has now been held must be taken, so far as the delegates of the dominions are concerned, to be *ad referendum*, and of no binding force unless and until submitted to their various parliaments."

The Imperial General Staff.—It is not within the province of the book to discuss questions of Imperial strategy, but notice should be taken of the recently created Imperial General Staff instituted to provide for common study of Imperial strategy by the Staffs of the War Office and of the dominions. Its relation to the Committee of Imperial Defence is that of an executive body to a deliberative one. A member of the War Office staff is attached to the staff of each dominion, and conversely each dominion is represented by an officer at the War Office.

III. THE ORGANISATION AND CONTROL OF THE FORCES.

The Army.—The control of the Army is vested in the Secretary of State for War and the Army

Council. There are faint shadows of the king's former pre-eminence as Commander-in-Chief of the Army, but statutory changes have put the king in commission. Until quite lately the Army was subject to the dual control of the Secretary of State for War and a commander-in-chief, and the position of the latter and his relations to the former were not a little peculiar. The Commander-in-Chief was in such direct relations with the King as to confuse, if not to impair, the Minister's sole responsibility for the Army to Parliament. Palmerston had strongly contended for such responsibility.[1] But so long as the office of Commander-in-Chief existed it was difficult to establish. In 1904, however, the office of Commander-in-Chief was abolished and by letters patent an Army Council was appointed, among whom the duties of the defunct office were distributed. It consists of seven members, four of whom are military and three civil. They are—

> The Secretary of State.
> The first military member—the Chief of the General Staff.
> The second military member—the Adjutant-General to the Forces.
> The third military member—the Quartermaster-General.

---

[1] "That to him [the Secretary at War] alone Parliament and the country looked for the execution of the law, and that even the royal authority could not release him from an obligation which it had concurred with the other two branches of the legislature to impose. The Secretary at War seems indeed to be the officer who stands peculiarly between the people and the Army to protect the former from the latter."—Palmerston (cited in Clode's *Military Forces of the Crown*, i. 201).

ARMY COUNCIL

The fourth military member—the Master-General of the Ordnance.
The Parliamentary Under-Secretary.
The Financial Secretary.

The War Office was itself divided into departments corresponding to this personal distribution of duties. An Order in Council of 10th August 1904 subsequently provided that the responsibility, both to the Crown and to the Parliament, for all the business of the Council was to be borne by the Secretary of State, and that he might specially reserve to himself any business which he pleased.

The creation of this Army Council was a pure exercise of the prerogative, but five years later it was placed on a statutory basis by the Army Act of 1909.[1] The proposed transformation gave rise to an important constitutional question. Some minister is always responsible for the exercise of the prerogative, and so long as the control of the Army rested on the prerogative no doubt could arise. But the creation of a statutory body and the assignment to it of statutory duties might enable a future secretary of state to disclaim all responsibility for the discharge of such duties.[2] As the result of Parliamentary

---

[1] Schedule II. of the Act provides by enumeration for the transfer to the Army Council of certain duties and powers hitherto imposed by the Army Act on the Secretary of State.

[2] The same point has arisen in connection with the creation of the statutory body known as the India Council, and the assignment to it of statutory duties under the Government of India Act. *Cf.* Hansard (1869), vol. cxcv., col. 1828, etc., and the words of James, L.J., in *Kinloch* v. *Secretary of State for India*, (1880) L.R. 15 Ch.D.: "There really is, in point of law,

criticism of these provisions of the Army Bill of 1909 the following clause was inserted:—

> "The Secretary of State may, however, reserve to himself any part of such business.
> "Nothing in this Act shall affect the responsibility of the Secretary of State to his Majesty and to Parliament."[1]

This is a unique instance of the translation into express statutory words of the constitutional convention that a minister is responsible to Parliament for the exercise of the prerogative. Lord Haldane, in the course of these debates, laid down the supremacy of the Secretary of State over the Army Council in very explicit language.

> "He is responsible to Parliament for everything done by the Army Council collectively, or by any member of it; he has power to apportion business or to withdraw any business."[2]

It need hardly be said that the appointment of a soldier like Lord Kitchener to the office of Secretary of State for War in no way diminishes this responsibility to Parliament.

It will then be seen that Parliamentary control is absolute. A writer of authority[3] declared some fifty

no such person or body politic whatever as the Secretary of State for India *in Council*. . . . The Secretary of State is the agent of the Crown, bound, no doubt, under his responsibility to Parliament."

[1] 9 Ed. VII. c. 3, s. 4.
[2] Hansard, *Parl. Deb.*, 1909, Fifth Series, vol. iii., p. 934.
[3] Clode, *The Military Forces of the Crown*, ii. 73.

ADMIRALTY

years ago that it was "a dogma of military administration that the king has an absolute power of preferring and cashiering officers." We doubt if this could be said to-day, if it is read as meaning a personal power. The commissions of officers have to be countersigned by the Secretary of State, and no officer can be reduced to the ranks or cashiered without his authority. His is the control, and his the responsibility. This was recognised in the report of the Esher Committee.

> "The complete responsibility to Parliament and the country *for the discipline as well as the administration* of the Army must now be accepted as definitely established."[1]

The Navy.—This new conciliar organisation of the War Office had long been the constitution of the Admiralty. The ancient office of Lord High Admiral had been put in commission as early as 1708, and a Board of Admiralty appointed to discharge his duties. This Board is constituted, and from time to time reconstituted, by letters patent. It consists of—

> The First Lord.
> Four Naval Lords.
> A Civil Lord.
> A Financial (Parliamentary) Secretary.

It has never been put on a statutory basis. But an Order in Council of 14th January 1869 expressly

[1] War Office (Reconstitution) Committee Report, part i., sec. ii., p. 8, citing paragraph 82 of the Hartington Commission's Report.

lays it down that the First Lord is solely responsible to Parliament, and that the other lords are responsible to him. This has never been seriously doubted, but some controversy has arisen as to the position of the First Sea Lord and his relation to the other three naval lords. Is he merely *primus inter pares*, or is he a kind of commander-in-chief to whom his naval colleagues are subordinate? The personal ascendancy of Lord Fisher obscured this point, nor was it made any clearer by an Admiralty Minute of 20th October 1904, which provided that in matters of great importance the First Sea Lord was always to be consulted by the other naval lords. This, however, could not, we think, impair the collective responsibility of the Board, or the deliberative equality of its members, and, indeed, the Minute provided that the other naval lords might have direct access to the First Lord, *i.e.* the Minister, if they so desired. The Board is, in fact, a real deliberative body, and not a dummy like the Local Government "Board" and the "Board" of Trade, with their purely ornamental members. Indeed, the Naval Estimates require the approval and signature of all the members before they are submitted to Parliament. On the other hand, the ascendancy of the Minister is undoubted, and if he finds himself in the presence of intractable colleagues he can always overcome their opposition by the simple expedient of securing authority from the Cabinet for the reconstitution of the Board by the issue of new letters patent. The Esher Committee in recommending the reconstitution of the War Office on the model of the Admiralty clearly recognised this.

"We consider that as a first step in the reconstitution of the War Office the position of the Secretary of State should be placed on precisely the same footing as that of the First Lord of the Admiralty, and that all submission to the Crown in regard to military questions should be made by *him alone*."[1]

[1] Report, part i., sec. ii., p. 8.

CHAPTER V

MILITARY LAW AND COURTS-MARTIAL

Military Law—Persons normally Subject to it—The Code of Discipline—In Time of Peace—In Time of War—"Communicating Intelligence to the Enemy": Soldier's Letters, and Newspaper Correspondents—The Soldier's Dual Position—The Duty of Obedience in Peace and in War—Procedure of Courts-martial—The Control of the Civil Courts—Malice and Privilege—The Naval Discipline Act.

Military Law.—We have had occasion in discussing the Defence of the Realm Act to say something of military law in connection with its partial extension to civilians under the terms of that Act. Here we have to deal with it in its normal sense, and with the persons to whom it normally applies. A soldier occupies a dual position—he is subject to the common law, like any other citizen, but he is also subject to military law. He is in somewhat the same position as a clerk in holy orders who besides being subject to the common law is also subject to the ecclesiastical law administered by the Courts Christian. But there are considerable differences in the scope of ecclesiastical law and of military law. The worst that can happen to a clergyman is excommunication, admonition, suspension, deprivation, or degradation; the ecclesiastical courts cannot inflict sentences of imprisonment[1] or capital punishment. Soldiers,[2] on the other hand, may be sentenced by courts-martial to penal servitude or even to death, and this for offences which at common law are not offences at all. The reason for this is that what may be venial in a civilian is often unpardonable in a soldier. The use of insulting language—unless it amounts to that kind of defamation which is known as slander and requires proof of special damage, or unless it is calculated to provoke a breach of peace—is not an offence at common law. It is an offence, and a serious offence, under military law. So, too, a common assault, punishable only with a fine or a short sentence of imprisonment at common law, may under military law be punishable with penal servitude, or even in certain cases[3] with death. Now just because these offences and punishments, and the courts by which they are tried, are unknown to the common law, they require statutory authority. The law is stated in the preamble to the Army Act.

> "And whereas no man may be forejudged of life or limb, or subjected in time of peace to any kind of punishment within this realm by martial law or in any other manner than the judgment

[1] Indirectly they can imprison, through the writ *de contumace capiendo*.

[2] The term "soldier" is here used in its widest sense to include officers. But in the Army Act it is restricted to privates and non-commissioned officers.

[3] Thus to strike an officer with a weapon (or merely to lift it up), even though no grievous bodily harm ensue, is punishable under the Naval Discipline Act with death. And to "offer any violence" to a superior officer, being in the execution of his office, is punishable with death by sec. 8 (1) of the Army Act.

of his peers, and according to the known and established laws of this realm : yet, nevertheless, it being requisite that an exact discipline be observed, and that persons belonging to the said forces who mutiny or stir up sedition or are guilty of crimes and offences to the prejudice of good order and military discipline be brought to a more exemplary and speedy punishment than the usual forms of law will allow." . . .

The Code of Discipline.—It is therefore enacted that certain enumerated offences shall be visited with certain punishments, which vary in severity according as the offence is committed in peace or in war, or is wilful or not. Thus disobedience may assume any one of several forms and be punished accordingly. If it amounts to "a wilful defiance of authority," it is punishable, under sec. 9 (1), with death even in time of peace. Mere disobedience without the imputation of "wilful defiance" is provided for by sec. 9 (2) with a sentence not exceeding imprisonment for two years, with hard labour, in the case of a soldier, and with cashiering in the case of an officer. If this latter offence be committed on active service, a sentence of penal servitude may be inflicted. But conduct may fall short of actual disobedience and yet be punishable. It may take the form (1) of "the use of insubordinate language" (sec. 8 (2)); or, more vaguely, (2) of conduct "prejudicial to good order and discipline" (sec. 40); or (3) it may hesitate dislike to future orders—in other words, it may be disobedience of a contemplative character. The authors of the official *Manual of Military Law*, in the chapter on "Offences and Scales of Punishment," put the situation thus (p. 17):

> "If the command be a lawful command, and demands an immediate and prompt compliance, hesitation or unnecessary delay in obeying it may constitute disobedience fully as much as a positive refusal to obey (under sec. 9 (2)). . . . If the soldier, on receiving the command, makes a reply implying an intention to refuse . . . he may be charged under sec. 8 with using insubordinate language; or under sec. 40 with conduct in prejudice of good order and military discipline. . . ."

And the annotator of sec. 9 of the Act writes on p. 276:

> "A man who, when ordered to do a duty at a future time, says 'I will not do it,' does not thereby commit an offence under this section, though he may be liable under sec. 8."

In every one of these three cases (under sec. 9 (2), sec. 8 (2), and sec. 40) the rule is the same, and it is this:

> "Shall on conviction be liable, if an officer, to be cashiered, or to suffer such less punishment as is in this Act mentioned, and, if a soldier, to suffer imprisonment, or such less punishment as is in this Act mentioned."

We shall have occasion to consider presently what may or may not be "a lawful command," and the dilemma in which a soldier may be placed in case of an apparent conflict between his military duty to obey a command and his common law duty to disregard it if it appears to him unlawful.

Offences in Time of War.—It will have been observed that military offences which are lightly punished in time of peace are much more seriously regarded in time of war. This is common-sense. But it does not meet the whole situation. There are some things which may not be offences at all in time of peace but which are very serious offences in time of war.[1] Hence the Army Act contains a category of offences peculiar to a time of war, such as cowardice. These are set out in (4), (5), and (6). They do not call for detailed treatment here. The chief distinction made is that between offences punishable by death[2] and offences punishable by penal servitude,[3] imprisonment, or cashiering.[4] In the case of offences punishable by death, no distinction is made between the officer and the soldier. It is worth remarking that a soldier on active service is bound to be scrupulously careful in his correspondence with friends or with newspapers (if, indeed, the latter be permissible at all). For example, the offence of "giving intelligence to the enemy" (which is

[1] For example, the cases provided for under sec. 5 (dealing with offences on active service)—"uses words calculated to create alarm or despondency."

[2] These are principally (1) "shameful" abandonment or surrender of any garrison, place, post, or guard; (2) treacherous or cowardly correspondence with the enemy; (3) acts "calculated to imperil the success of His Majesty's forces"; and (4) cowardice.

[3] The second class of offences includes (1) leaving the ranks without leave; (2) damage to property without leave; (3) spreading alarming reports.

[4] The third class includes (1) plundering and housebreaking in search of plunder; (2) being asleep or drunk at one's post during sentry-duty.

punishable with penal servitude) is held[1] to include such indirect and even unintentional communication of intelligence as "sending letters, or sketches, or plans, to friends or newspapers, if the probable result would be their communication to the enemy." It must be remembered that newspaper correspondents attached to the forces in the field are, for the time being, "military persons" so far as subjection to military law is concerned, and could therefore be dealt with by court-martial under this section. And in view of the current controversy as to the limits of the censorship, the following official caution is worth noting :—

> "Every one present with an army should bear in mind that the publication of letters from the army containing facts and opinions, often entirely erroneous, relating to the operations or prospects of the campaign, can scarcely fail to have mischievous results; and it is well known that both during the Peninsular and Crimean Wars the enemy were indebted for information to English newspapers."[2]

In all these cases the officer or soldier, whether on active service or not, must be tried by court-martial before any of these offences can be visited with punishment. The extent to which the proceedings of court-martial are subject to control by the War Office and the civil courts respectively will be considered later.

The Soldier's Dual Position: the Duty of Obedience.—It is the duty of the soldier to obey the

[1] By the editors of the *Manual* (1914), p. 380 *note.*
[2] *Ibid.*

orders of his superior. But if he obeys orders which are unlawful at common law—for example, an order to fire on a crowd whose conduct did not amount to a felony—such obedience might result in both him and the officer above him being indicted for manslaughter. What will then be their position? If he or the soldiers acting under him use more force than is necessary, then everything will depend upon whether he acted in good faith.[1] If he did, then even though a coroner's jury returned a verdict of manslaughter, the Crown would probably enter a *nolle prosequi*. The position of the soldiers under him is in some ways more difficult, because though they are bound to do nothing "unlawful" at common law, they are also bound to obey all the commands of their military superiors. Their dilemma has been put in its sharpest form in the statement that they may be liable to be hanged if they obey an order, and to be shot if they disobey it.[2] But it is very unlikely that they would be put on their trial by the civil authorities for obeying an order to fire for which there was no justification, unless it was clearly one which could not conceivably be lawful (such as an order to fire on a perfectly peaceful crowd of spectators). It is the officer who, if anyone, in such a case, would be put on his trial.

It seems to us, however, that too much stress has

[1] *Cf.* the words of Abbott, C.J. : "The question has always been not whether the act done might upon full and mature investigation be found strictly right, but from what motive it has proceeded."

[2] Thus Professor Dicey, following somewhat too precisely Stephen in his *History of the Criminal Law*, i. 205-6.

MILITARY AND CIVIL DUTY 149

been laid on the poignancy of the difficulty in which an officer or a soldier is placed by being subject to two jurisdictions—military and civil—which may result in his being punished whichever of two alternatives he adopts, *i.e.*, action or inaction. A soldier is no doubt regarded at common law as being just as much liable for the consequences of his acts as a civilian, but to establish guilt it is always necessary to prove the existence of that "guilty mind," known to lawyers as *mens rea*, and the *catena* of acts and intents necessary to establish it would rarely co-exist in the same way in the case of a civilian and of a soldier. The military duty of the soldier to obey orders implicitly would probably be taken into account in a court of common law in the case of a soldier obeying them. As regards the officer giving the order, the words of Lord Mansfield in the case of *Wall* v. *Macnamara*[1] are worth quoting:

> "In trying the legality of acts done by military officers in the exercise of their duty, particularly beyond the seas, great latitude ought to be allowed, and they ought not to suffer for a slip of form if their intention appears by the evidence to have been upright; it is the same as when complaints are brought against inferior civil magistrates, such as J.P.'s, for acts done by them in the exercise of their civil duty. Then the principal inquiry to be made by a court of justice is *how the heart stood*. And if there appears to be nothing wrong there, great latitude will be allowed for misapprehension or mistake. But on the other hand, if the heart

[1] Cited in *Sutton* v. *Johnstone, supra.*

is wrong, if cruelty, malice, and oppression appear, they shall not cover themselves with the thin veil of legal forms."

This was, it is true, a case of tort, and one cannot argue from motive (in the sense of moral reasons for action) in tort—even supposing, which is doubtful, that Mansfield is right—to intent in crime. In criminal law a man's motives are immaterial; the test is not what was the state of his "heart" but what was the state of his mind—his actions are to be judged by the facts as he *bona fide* believed them to be, provided also that he had also reasonable grounds for his belief.[1] In tort the general rule, despite Lord Mansfield, is that a man acts at his peril; criminal law is more lenient—its test is: did he mean to do wrong? understanding by "wrong" the objective test of what is in fact a breach of the law.

As regards the soldier, as distinct from the officer, mere obedience to orders is doubtless no excuse,[2] but the fact that orders were given which he was bound by military law implicitly to obey has been taken into account in the courts in estimating the culpability of the soldier. It would appear that, unless the orders are manifestly illegal, the presumption of absence of guilty mind will be stronger in his case than in that of a civilian.[3]

[1] *The Queen* v. *Tolson*, 23 Q.B.D. 168, and cf. *Dickinson* v. *Lade* in *Times* Law Report, 25th April 1914.

[2] This is always the rule when it is a case of *malum in se*. In such a case the orders of a master will not protect a servant. Cf. *Reg.* v. *James*, (1837) 8 C. & P. 131.

[3] There are cases on both sides of the line. Cf. *Rex* v. *Thomas* in Russell on *Crimes*, iii. 94, and, on the other side, *Reg.* v. *Smith*, 17 C.G. H. Rep. 561, where the Court said,

So far we have confined our consideration of the soldier's position to his liability before a court of common law. When we turn to his position before a military tribunal the matter is not so clear. How far can he, in his anxiety to keep within the common law by refusing to obey an order which he deems unlawful, plead such an excuse before a court-martial, or, rather, raise it in proceedings consequent upon the decision of such a court? The dicta of the judges on this point have been largely, but not uniformly, in the direction of insisting that there are in military law no limits to the obedience which he owes. The high-water mark of this doctrine was reached in the case of *Sutton* v. *Johnstone*, in the course of which Lord Mansfield declared:

> "A subordinate officer must not, even to save the lives of others or his own life, judge of the danger, propriety, expediency, or consequence of the order he receives; he must obey. Nothing but a physical impossibility can excuse him. . . . The first, second, and third part of a soldier is obedience."[1]

This is putting it very strongly, but it must be remembered that this was a case of a refusal to obey orders, however unreasonable, to engage the enemy, and obedience in such a case would not have involved the commission of an offence at common law. We know of no case of military punishment for dis-

"That he is responsible whenever he obeys an order not strictly legal, is a proposition which the Court cannot accept." See below for discussion of this case.

[1] 1 East 548, also 1 T.R. 493.

obedience which raised such an issue. If such a case occurred it is not impossible that the courts would grant redress in the shape of damages for false imprisonment, if a soldier had been imprisoned for a refusal to obey orders which were unlawful or *ultra vires*,[1] and might, indeed, grant a rule for a Habeas Corpus to release him from confinement. They might inquire whether there was reasonable and probable cause for the imprisonment. To that extent the words of Mansfield and Loughborough in *Sutton* v. *Johnstone* about the finality of the decisions of military tribunals need qualification. Their lordships laid stress on the fact that the military code provided its own corrective, pointing out that every reason which requires the original charge to be tried by a military jurisdiction equally holds to try the " probable cause " (for its exercise) by that jurisdiction.

This is, of course, true; military sentences are reviewed by the Judge Advocate, and, in the case of officers, there is a statutory right, given by sec. 42 of the Army Act, to make complaints to the "Commander-in-Chief." So, too, by sec. 27 of the Army Act to make a false accusation against an officer or soldier, whether before a court-martial or otherwise, is itself an offence punishable by court-martial.[2] But these remedies may not always be adequate, and,

[1] So it would seem from the remarks of the Court in the case of *Warden* v. *Bailey*, (1811) 4 Taunt. 67.

[2] A soldier, as distinct from an officer, is given the right, by sec. 43, if he thinks himself wronged in any matter by any officer than his captain, or by any soldier, to complain thereof to his captain. If he thinks himself wronged by his captain he may complain to his commanding officer; if by his commanding officer, then to a general officer.

in the case of officers at any rate, when the punishment takes the form, as with officers it usually does, of cashiering, the Crown can always shelter itself behind the prerogative to determine an officer's commission at its pleasure.[1] The soldier, in whatever capacity he serves, is "the king's soldier."[2]

It was argued, in support of the extreme view of an officer's right to require, and a soldier's duty to give, implicit obedience to any commands that the former might issue, that otherwise an officer would be embarrassed in the exercise of his functions by the fear of vexatious actions from subordinates whom he had punished or proceeded against for refusal to obey such commands. Unless the officer was absolutely protected from civil proceedings by such subordinates whom he had thus punished, he was (so ran the argument) placed in an impossible position. But as to this the words of Cockburn in his dissenting judgment in *Dawkins* v. *Paulet* seem to us an adequate reply.

> "I cannot believe that officers in command would hesitate to give orders, which a sense of duty required, from any idle apprehension of being harassed by vexatious actions: men worthy to command would do their duty, and would trust to the firmness of judges and to the

[1] Cf. *Woods* v. *Lyttleton* and others, T.L.R. 25, p. 665, and *cf.* the significant words of Lord Denman, *In re Poe*, 5 B. & A. 818, "what the king had power to do independently of any inquiry he plainly may do though the inquiry should not be satisfactory to a court of law, or even though the court which conducted it had no legal jurisdiction."

[2] Cf. *Williams* v. *Howarth*, [1905] A.C. 551, and *Queen* v. *Secretary of State for War*, [1891] 2 Q.B. 326.

honesty and good sense of juries to protect them in respect of acts honestly, though possibly erroneously, done under a sense of duty."[1]

The question has, however, never been authoritatively settled.

Obedience in Time of War.—So far we have been mainly concerned with the consequences of obedience or disobedience to orders in time of peace. Different considerations arise in time of war. As we have seen, the strong words of the Court in *Sutton v. Johnstone* as to the unqualified duty of unquestioning obedience referred to an order given in time of war, the question being whether a prosecution subsequently instituted in time of peace before a court-martial for disobedience to the said order was "malicious and without reasonable and probable cause," and therefore a tort entitling the captain to damages against his superior officer, who had had him arrested and put on trial. He was acquitted by the court-martial, but on subsequently bringing an action for damages in a civil court the latter decided that no action lay. No doubt the atmosphere of war surrounding the circumstances of the order enveloped in the eyes of the civil court the subsequent proceedings before the court-martial[2] and accounted for their decision. The words of their lordships clearly contemplate a command given in time of war.

[1] 5 Q.B. 108.
[2] Only on this supposition is it possible to reconcile the decision with the subsequent case of *Warden* v. *Bailey*, 4 Taunt. 67, where a soldier disobeying *in time of peace* a command, which the officer had no right to give, obtained damages for unlawful arrest.

"Nothing less than a physical impossibility to obey could be a justification. A subordinate officer must not judge of the danger, propriety, expediency, or consequence of the order he receives; he must obey. Nothing can excuse him but a physical impossibility. A forlorn hope is devoted, many gallant officers have been devoted, fleets have been saved, and victories obtained, by ordering particular ships upon desperate services, with almost a certainty of death or capture."

And hence the Court held, without scrutinising the order, that the mere fact that an order, however impossible of compliance, was given at all, and that it was disobeyed, constituted a "probable cause" for bringing the plaintiff to trial.

This was a case of disobedience in time of war raising a question of tort. We only know of one case—in this case of obedience—in time of war having come before the courts, and the case in question was not a civil action but a criminal prosecution.[1] The circumstances were peculiar. A soldier, acting under the orders of his officer, shot a servant for delay in producing a bridle that was requisitioned at a farm in a district in which martial law had been proclaimed during the South African War. The soldier was tried for murder by a special court under a special Act[2]—it was not a military court but a civil court empowered to try offences during the period of the war, whether committed by soldiers or civilians. There was thus a kind of *état*

[1] *The Queen* v. *Smith*, 17 Cape Reports, [1900] 561.
[2] "The Indemnity and Special Tribunals Act" (Cape Statutes, No. 6, of 1900).

de siège, but the Court was to administer not military law but the common law. The Court would accept neither of the two extreme propositions put forward by the prosecution and the defence respectively. It refused to hold that a soldier was bound to obey, and was therefore protected in obeying, every order, however unlawful; it equally declined to accept the proposition that a soldier was responsible at common law whenever he obeyed a command that was unlawful. It assumed the order was unlawful, but acquitted the soldier on the ground—

> "That a soldier is only bound to obey lawful orders, and is responsible if he obeys an order not strictly legal, is an extreme proposition which the Court cannot accept for its guidance. . . . The order is not so *plainly illegal* that Smith would have been justified under the circumstances in refusing to obey it. Although he is only bound to obey lawful orders, he is protected in obeying some orders not strictly legal. If in any doubtful case a soldier was entitled to judge for himself, to consider the circumstances of the case, and to hesitate in obeying the orders given him, that would be subversive of all military discipline. One must remember that *especially in time of war* immediate obedience to orders is required for a private soldier, and therefore it is not desirable that a soldier should be encouraged to question the orders given him by his superior in cases where there is some doubt whether the order is lawful or not."

Control of Courts-martial by Civil Courts.—Returning to the question raised in *Sutton* v. *Johnstone* as to the control by the civil courts of court-martial proceedings in cases arising directly out of disobedience to orders given in time of war, it should be remarked that the courts will not interfere either at the time or subsequently with the proceeding of courts-martial held on active service. This was laid down in *Bauvis* v. *Keppel*.[1] This was an action upon the case against an officer by a sergeant of the Guards whom he had reduced to the ranks when on active service in Germany. It alleged that the officer had acted "wrongly, unlawfully, maliciously, and without any reasonable cause." As the sergeant had been tried by court-martial, the action was in the nature of an action for malicious prosecution. The Court decided that no action lay.

> "By an Act of Parliament to punish mutiny and desertion the King's power to make articles of war is confined to His own dominions;[2] when His army is out of His dominions He acts by virtue of this prerogative and without the statute or articles of war; and therefore you cannot argue upon either of them, for they are both to be laid out of this case, and *flagrante bello* the common law has never interfered with the army. *Inter arma silent leges;* we think (as at present advised) we have no jurisdiction at all in this case."

Judgment was given for the defendant, and the

[1] (1766) 2 Wilson's Rep. 314.
[2] This is no longer true. The old Articles of War are incorporated in that part of the Army Act which deals with offences on active service, and by sec. 189 "active service" is extended to include military operations in a foreign country. And by sec. 69 of the Act His Majesty is empowered to make further articles of war, rules of procedure, but subject to the limitations of the Act.

verdict of the jury giving damages to the plaintiff was set aside.

As regards the control of the civil courts over the proceedings of courts-martial in time of peace, a good deal has already been said in Chap. III. of this book, when dealing with the extension of military law to civilians under the Defence of the Realm Act. We do not propose to enter here at length into the procedure of courts-martial. The subject is fully dealt with in the Rules of Procedure[1] issued by the Secretary of State in 1907, in virtue of the powers given to him under sec. 70 of the Army Act. Trial takes place, of course, without a jury, the court being composed of officers whose number and rank vary according as the court is a general court-martial, a district court-martial, or a regimental court-martial.[2] And the power of these courts are regulated according to the character of the offence. The Court is to proceed according to the rules of evidence at common law.[3] It cannot, of course, apart from special and temporary Acts like the Defence of the Realm Act, or except in the case of "army followers" on active service, try civilians, but it can summon them before it to give evidence, and if they are contumacious may certify the fact to a court of common law which, on being satisfied, may commit the offender for contempt.

Malice and Privilege.—After what has been said in Chap. II. of the control of the civil courts little remains to be said here, except as to the question of

---

[1] See *Manual of Military Law* (1914), pp. 571-727.
[2] See secs. 47-50.
[3] Secs. 127 and 128.

Malice and Privilege. Proceedings before a court-martial, *i.e.* statements made in the conduct of the proceedings, are, as in the case of any other court, absolutely privileged.[1] So, too, the report of such a court would appear to be absolutely privileged. So also communications made by a person not necessarily acting as a judge or a witness, but in the course of his military duty—*e.g.*, a report to the Army Council by a commanding officer—are, judging by the decision in *Dawkins* v. *Paulet*,[2] absolutely privileged. But that case is not conclusive, and if such a report is *published*, it is by no means certain that the publication would be regarded as privileged, even though made by the orders of a superior and in the discharge of a public duty, unless the matter was one which it was "proper for the public to know."[3] In such case the orders of his superior, even though it be the Army Council itself, would not protect the officer.

As regards malicious prosecution, the situation is by no means clear, but it would appear that an officer acting within the limits of his authority,[4] but maliciously and without probable cause, is

---

[1] *Dawkins* v. *Lord Rokeby*, L.R. 8 Q.B. 255 ; 7 H.L. 744.

[2] *Dawkins* v. *Paulet*, L.R. 5 Q.B. 94. It is difficult to see why military persons, not actually acting as judges or witnesses, should have more than the qualified privilege of persons making a communication *bona fide* upon a subject-matter in which they have, or honestly believe that they have, an interest or duty, such communication being made by one with a corresponding interest or duty.

[3] See the questions put to the jury in the case of *Adams* v. *Ward*, *Times* (Law Report), 20th Feb. 1914.

[4] Actions for things done outside the course of duty would always lie.

160 MILITARY LAW AND COURTS-MARTIAL

protected from an action in a civil court by a person subject to military law, the argument being that, as we have seen, there are statutory remedies provided under the Army Act itself.[1]

If a court-martial so abuses its power as to act without jurisdiction or to inflict a sentence which it has no power to inflict, its members will not only be liable civilly, but may also be guilty of a criminal offence.[2] To sentence a soldier to death without trial, and to cause the sentence to be executed, would no doubt subject the officer or officers to indictment for murder.[3]

The Naval Discipline Act.—When embarked on any of His Majesty's ships as passengers, officers and soldiers of the Army are subject to the Naval Discipline Act and the Orders in Council made thereunder.[4] Unlike the Army Act,[5] the Naval Discipline Act is a permanent Act. The persons normally subject to it are defined as anyone in or belonging to His Majesty's Navy, and borne on the books of any of His Majesty's ships in commis-

---

[1] See *Sutton* v. *Johnstone*, and *Dawkins* v. *Paulet*, cited *supra*. And see the article by Dr Holdsworth in the *Law Quarterly Review*.

[2] False imprisonment is a misdemeanour, though generally the subject of an action in tort. See *R.* v. *Lesley*.

[3] Cf. *Governor Wall's Case*, 28 St. Tr. 176, for the discussion of malice aforethought.

[4] See the Naval Discipline Act, 1866, 29 & 30 Vict. c. 109, s. 88, and the Order in Council of 30th June 1890.

[5] "This Act shall continue in force only for such time and subject to such provisions as may be specified in an *annual* Act of Parliament, bringing into force, or continuing the same." (Army Act (1881), sec. 2).

sion.¹ But it contains some peculiar provisions not to be found in the Army Act. Thus by Article 6 "all spies for the enemy shall be deemed subject to this Act." And even in time of peace civilians on board are subject to the Act if they attempt to seduce the sailors from their duty. It is worthy of remark that there is a statutory provision—not to be found in the Army Act—providing for the observance of Divine Service on board His Majesty's ships. Beyond this the Act does not call for comment. The same rules govern the control by the civil courts of naval courts-martial as is the case with the Army.

[1] Article 87. For full text of the Act and of the Admiralty Instructions, see the *Manual of Naval Law* (Stephens, Gilford, and Smith), 1912.

PART II
THE CROWN AND THE ENEMY

CHAPTER I

THE LAWS OF WAR ON LAND

I. Sources and their Value—Views of German Military Writers—Views of German General Staff—The Civil Population in War—Combatants and Non-combatants—The *levée en masse*—Army "Followers" and Newspaper Correspondents—Chaplains, Nurses, and Medical Men—The "Red Cross"—"Undefended Places" and their Immunity from Bombardment.

II. Occupation by the Enemy—Rights and Duties of Inhabitants: (1) Can they be Compelled to Assist the Enemy? (2) Hostages and Vicarious Punishments; (3) Forced Labour and Requisitions; (4) Cash Contributions; (5) War Treason.

III. The Conduct of Hostilities: Limitations—Aerial Warfare and Expanding Bullets—Treachery and Stratagems—Spies—Prisoners—The Wounded and Sick—Reprisals.

IV. Rights and Duties of Neutrals.

I. SOURCES AND THEIR VALUE.

THE "laws" of war may be described as the qualifications introduced by theory and practice into the original rule, that as soon as two sovereigns are at war all the subjects of the one become the enemies of all the subjects of the other. This, involving as it does a distinction between combatants and non-combatants, is certainly the most important principle, though not, indeed, the only one embodied in these laws. Their sources are partly "written," partly unwritten. The written law is to be found in such international agreements as the Hague Conventions,[1] and perhaps the consensus of juristic opinion;[2] the unwritten is the practice uniformly followed by armies in the field.[3] Now opinions as to the relative value of these two sources may sometimes differ, especially as between jurists and soldiers. The former regard such written laws as the Hague Conventions as the most authoritative of the two—they may almost be described as laws of perfect obligation. Diplomatists would no doubt take the same view.[4] But soldiers—or rather the soldiers of the Prussian General Staff—are inclined to hold exactly the opposite. By *kriegsrecht* they understand "not a *lex scripta* introduced by international law, but only a reciprocity

[1] Professor Holland (*The Laws of War on Land*, p. 2) would include in the written law the instructions issued by national governments to their respective armies. But it is difficult to regard these as "international."

[2] Of course, the opinions of jurists are not *responsa prudentium* any more than the opinions of English writers of authority on the common law, and if "written law" is used in the sense of statute law the opinions of jurists must be relegated to the second class of sources.

[3] Professor Oppenheim (*Manual of Military Law*, ch. xiv.) treats the usages of war as "not legally binding." But it seems to us difficult to detach them from customary law or to define at what point a "usage" is or is not a "custom."

[4] *Cf.* Baron Marschall von Bieberstein at the Hague Conference of 1907: "The international (maritime) law which we wish to create should contain only those clauses the execution of which is possible from a military point of view, *even in exceptional circumstances*" (*Actes et Documents*, i., p. 282). He would appear, therefore, to regard the *lex scripta* of the Hague Conventions as inviolable and subject to no casuistry.

of mutual agreement, a limitation of arbitrary action, which usage and convention, good-nature and a calculating egoism have erected, but for whose observance no express sanction exists, except a deciding 'fear of Reprisals.'"[1] These writers not only ascribe superior authority to such usages, but frankly insist that the *lex scripta* is to be read subject to them. Indeed, the Prussian General Staff pointedly refer to the Hague Convention of 1899 and such agreements as waves of "sentiment and flabby emotion" (*Sentimentalität und weichlicher Gefühlsschwarmerei*) which "are in fundamental contradiction with the nature and object of war itself." It is important to bear this in mind when we come to consider the cogency of the Hague Conventions. We are far from approving this view, still less do we imply that it is the view taken by the other contracting Powers towards these solemn agreements. It is, indeed, a peculiarly Prussian view. Even as regards those " usages " which they do admit, they always apply a casuistry of war (*kriegsraison*), according to which every such usage must be regarded as subject to the exigencies of " Necessity." The young officer is warned by the Staff against the contamination of "the intellectual influences" (*den geistigen Strömungen*) of his time—the more educated he is, the greater will be his danger.

The truth is that German military tradition is still inspired by Clausewitz—Clausewitz, who is the true

[1] *Kriegsbrauch im Landkriege*, p. 2. This is the official book of the Prussian General Staff. It should be noted, however, that our own War Office in their official manual treat the Hague Regulations as of paramount obligation.

ancestor of Treitschke[1] and von der Goltz,[2] and who in his classical treatise on war, *Vom Kriege*, a brilliant and profoundly interesting work, dismisses the laws of war in a sentence.

> "Laws of war are self-imposed restrictions, almost imperceptible and hardly worth mentioning, termed 'usages of war.' Now philanthropists may easily imagine that there is a skilful method of disarming and overcoming an enemy without causing great bloodshed, and that this is the proper tendency of the art of war. However plausible this may appear, still it is an error which must be extirpated, for in such dangerous things as war the errors which proceed from the spirit of benevolence are the worst. . . . To introduce into the philosophy of war itself a principle of moderation would be an absurdity. . . . War is an act of violence which in its application knows no bounds."[3]

The War-book (as we will in future term it) of the German General Staff enforces exactly the same teaching. Let the young officer study history, it urges, and he will then learn that certain severities (*gewisse Härten*) are indispensable in war, that, in fact, "very frequently the only true humanity lies in a reckless application of them."[4]

---

[1] See his *Historische und Politische Aufsätze*, passim. For illustrative extracts the reader may be referred to Professor Morgan's article on Treitschke in the *Nineteenth Century* for October 1914.

[2] The debt of von der Goltz to Clausewitz is visible on every page of his *Nation in Arms*. His thought is nearly always the same and so sometimes is his expression.

[3] *Vom Kriege*, i., kap. 1 (2).

[4] *Kriegsbrauch im Landkriege*, p. 3.

This school of thought, representing as it does the greatest military academy of Europe, must therefore be carefully regarded in our discussion of the principles of the laws of war. It must, however, be understood that by regard we do not mean respect. If, indeed, we were to admit these doctrines, we might as well cease to discuss the laws of war at all. But they have a profound, and indeed a tragic significance when we come to consider the position of the civil population in a war to which Germany is a party. German writers have freely predicted that its lot would not be enviable.[1]

Before entering on a categorical discussion of the laws of war, it may be as well to define, quite independently of the reservations peculiar to the Prussian General Staff, the limitations to which the Hague Conventions[2] are generally subject. They do not exclude the unwritten rules, but neither do they exhaust them. Where they are silent the rules speak;[3] where they are eloquent, the rules interpret.

[1] *Cf.* von der Goltz, sec. vi.: "the next war will be one of inconceivable violence. It will be the exodus of two peoples . . . and no longer the struggle of two armies."

[2] The principal of these conventions (referred to in future as H. C.) are No. IV., dealing with the Laws and Customs of War on Land, with its annexed Regulations (referred to as H. R.); No. III., dealing with the Commencement of Hostilities; and No. V., dealing with the Rights and Duties of Neutrals. In addition to these there are the Hague Declarations (referred to as H. D.), respecting the discharge of projectiles from balloons, the use of asphyxiating gases, and the employment of expanding bullets.

[3] *Cf.* H. C., IV. In cases not provided for, "the principles of the law of nations, as they result from the usages established among civilised peoples, the laws of humanity, and the exigencies of the public conscience" remain.

It would no more be possible to exclude those rules in construing the Conventions than it would be possible to interpret an English statute without the aid of the common law. So much is common ground. But the Regulations which are annexed to the Conventions may be interpreted not only according to common principles of international law, but according to the construction which each country chooses to put upon them. The Powers did not bind themselves to promulgate the Regulations as they stood, but only to issue instructions "in conformity" with them.[1] The Convention is a treaty which binds the signataries as it stands; it is possible to view the ancillary Regulations with greater latitude. Moreover, some of the most important articles in the Regulations are the subject of "reservations" by certain Powers whereby they decline to be bound by them.[2] Moreover, the view taken of the moral efficacy of these international agreements by different Powers—the difference is most marked in a comparison between the attitudes of Britain and Germany respectively—exhibits some curious divergences. The representatives of the two countries agreed in admitting that it did not follow that because the Conventions had not prohibited a certain act they thereby sanctioned it. But whereas the English representative regarded this as a reason why we could never be too explicit,[3] the

[1] H. C., IV., Article 1. But Great Britain has adopted the Regulations literally by issuing them officially to the Army.

[2] *E.g.*, Germany (also Austria, Russia, and Japan) declined to subscribe to Article 44 of H. R. prohibiting the application of compulsion to a civil population to furnish information.

[3] *Cf.* Sir Ernest Satow, *Actes et Documents*, i., p. 281.

spokesman of Germany urged it as a reason why they could never be too laconic.[1] In the view of the latter not international law but "conscience, good sense, and the sentiment of duties imposed by the principles of humanity will be the surest guides" for the conduct of soldiers and sailors, and "the most efficacious guarantees against abuse."[2] To particularise would be to "enfeeble humane and civilising thoughts."[3] If the latter view be correct, it is difficult to see why there should be any written agreements at all. The only rule which results from such an Economy of Truth would seem to be: All things are lawful, but all things are not expedient.

It will be obvious, then, that the scope and authority of the Hague Conventions is somewhat precarious. None the less, however, we are entitled to regard those of them, and those articles of them, which have received the assent of all the contracting Powers as an approximation to a general code of the laws of war,[4] and by them the acts of the contracting parties will by humane and civilised people surely be judged.

Combatants and Non-combatants.—No distinction is more vital to the conduct of war and the amelioration of its horrors than that which separates

[1] Baron Marschall von Bieberstein, *ibid.*, p. 282.
[2] *Ibid.*, p. 282.
[3] *Ibid.*, p. 81.
[4] *Cf.* Dr Lueder in Holtzendorff (iv., 268), whose doctrine presents in some respects a refreshing contrast to the views advanced by diplomatists and soldiers among his fellow-countrymen. "International law can only advance by codification. . . . The humanising and the codification of it go hand in hand. . . . Codification should not merely express the law, but advance it."

combatants from non-combatants. The recognition of this distinction marks, indeed, the principal advance made by international law in treating war primarily as an act of hostility between states rather than individuals.[1] In earlier times non-combatants were exposed to the fate of combatants, or if any distinction was made it was to their prejudice. There has probably always been a certain freemasonry of arms in virtue of which combatants accorded one another certain privileges, but non-combatants were outside it, and sack, devastation, pillage, and killing in cold blood were not regarded as dishonourable to the profession of arms. To-day it is generally recognised that those who take no part in hostilities are entitled, where discrimination is possible at all, to immunity from them.[2] Each class has its privileges—the combatant must, of course, expect to be killed in combat, but he is entitled to "quarter" if he throws down his arms, and, if captured, he can claim to be treated as a prisoner of war. The non-combatant may not be killed, but if he assumes a combative attitude he not only runs, like the combatant, the risk of being killed, but, unlike him, exposes himself to the certainty of it—he cannot claim "quarter" or the status of a prisoner of war. This is common-sense. A man cannot have it both ways. He cannot put on and put off a combatant character as he pleases.

[1] We agree, however, with Dr Pearce Higgins (*War and the Private Citizen*, p. 12) that the general proposition cannot be accepted unreservedly.

[2] This is admitted, as a general principle, by the German Staff (*Kriegsbrauch im Landkriege*, p. 45).

CLASSES OF COMBATANTS

But how is the distinction to be made? Four classes of belligerents have to be considered: (1) the regular armies; (2) auxiliary forces; (3) organised civilians, whether specifically authorised or not; (4) individuals. Now it is universally admitted that the first and second classes are lawful belligerents. Every state may properly act on the maxim, "He that is not with us is against us." Every state is at liberty to decide what shall be the composition of its forces; this is a. domestic[1] matter. Territorials, Militia, Reservists are as fully entitled to the denomination of army as Regulars. So is a civil guard.[2] And it matters not whether such service is compulsory or voluntary. It is also admitted to-day that a State may decree, even after the outbreak of hostilities, a general levy of the whole population, and that when so called up they are all entitled to the privileges of combatants.[3] But what constitutes authorisation was long a disputed question. At one time emphasis was laid on authorisation by the State, coupled with the wearing of some distinctive uniform. This was the test applied by Germany in 1870, and, admittedly,[4] with excessive severity, as she demanded that every irregular should produce proof of individual authorisation, at the same time demanding, with more reason, that something more distinctive than the national civilian costume of the

[1] *Cf.* Dr Lueder in Holtzendorff, who says, this is entirely an *innerstaatliche* (domestic) matter.

[2] Holtzendorff, iv., 374. This admission, in view of what has happened in Belgium, is worth noting.

[3] Dr Lueder goes so far as to say that a State could lawfully arm even women and young persons (*ibid.*, p. 376).

[4] *Ibid.*, p. 378.

blouse should be worn. To-day emphasis is laid rather on the test of responsible leadership than of State authorisation. The Hague Regulations of 1907, following out certain recommendations of the Brussels Conference of 1874, have laid down the following requirements as the conditions of recognition :—[1]

(1) That of being commanded by a person responsible for his subordinates.
(2) That of having a distinctive mark, fixed and recognisable at a distance.[2]
(3) That of carrying arms openly ; and
(4) That of conforming in their operations to the laws and customs of war.

This test is approved by the Prussian General Staff,[3] with the qualification that there is an onus of proof on isolated individuals, who claim combatant privileges, to show that they belong to such an organised band. Indeed, the "sniper" or isolated combatant puts himself in a position of great peril.[4]

The Levée en masse.—It may happen that without either State authorisation or improvised organisation a whole population rises spontaneously

[1] H.R., Article 1.
[2] Recognisable "within musket-shot" (*auf Flintenschussweite*) is the way it is put in Holtzendorff, p. 382, to which the writer adds that it must not be something which can be easily and surreptitiously put on or put off. Nor must the claimant to combatant rights carry arms "in his pocket."
[3] *Kriegsbrauch*, p. 6.
[4] *Cf.* Holtzendorff, p. 377 : "The individual, be he native or be he alien, who with his own fist (*auf eigene Faust*) exercises force against the enemy" is not to be regarded as "a lawful belligerent."

in the defence of hearth and home. This is particularly probable and no less justifiable, when a small country without a standing army, or with only a very small one, finds itself suddenly invaded. Even the Prussian War-book admits that "smaller and less powerful States" can only find protection in such a resource,[1] and Dr Lueder declares,[2] almost with emotion, that "there exists no ground for denying to the masses of a country the natural right to defend their Fatherland." The Hague Regulations have, in fact, provided that—

> "The population of a territory not yet occupied[3] who on the approach of the enemy spontaneously take up arms in order to resist the invaders, without having had time to organise themselves in accordance with Article 1 [see *supra*], shall be regarded as belligerents provided they carry their arms openly and respect the laws and customs of war."[4]

How far this Regulation commands the assent of German military authorities it would be difficult to say. We have already noticed the disparaging terms in which the Prussian War-book refers to the Hague Convention of 1899, in which this provision occurs in the same terms as in that of 1907. Despite the obeisance done to the principle of "defence of the Fatherland," in one sentence the Prussian War-book goes on in the next to dispute the provisions of the Hague Regulation just quoted,

---

[1] *Kriegsbrauch*, p. 7.
[2] Holtzendorff, iv., 385.
[3] What constitutes "occupation" will be discussed later.
[4] H.R., Article 2.

and insists on the necessity of an organisation being elaborated by the population, however sudden the invasion, and contends that in default of it they should be given no quarter.[1] There can, unfortunately, be little doubt, judging the passage as a whole, that the German military authorities will not recognise the *levée en masse*. And the German jurists, though less blunt, are not more favourable.[2] Indeed, between them and the military there is not very much to choose, for after arguing in favour of a generous recognition of combatant status, if only to avoid "embitterment," they go on to qualify this in a melancholy parenthesis with the words, "unless *the Terrorism so often necessary in war* does not demand the contrary."[3]

Army Followers and Newspaper Correspondents. — The Hague Regulations provide that individuals who follow an army without directly belonging to it, such as newspaper correspondents, reporters, sutlers, and contractors, who fall into the power of the enemy, and whom the latter thinks fit to detain, are to be treated as prisoners of war, provided they can produce a certificate from the military authorities of the army they were accom-

---

[1] *Kriegsbrauch*, p. 7.
[2] Holtzendorff, iv., 386.
[3] *Ibid.*, p. 378. With this it is pleasant to contrast the ungrudging and unqualified statement of Professor Oppenheim in a manual officially issued by our own War Office: "The rules which affect a *levée en masse* should be generously interpreted. The first duty of a citizen is to defend his country, and provided he does so loyally he should not be treated as a marauder or criminal" (*Land Warfare*, p. 21, paragraph 30).

panying.[1] Our own Army Act in the same way identifies with the Army, for purposes of discipline,[2] the persons who accompany it by permission. Thus secs. 175 (8) and 176 (10) in defining "persons subject to military law" includes thereunder, firstly, as "officers"—

> "Every person not otherwise subject to military law accompanying a force on active service who shall hold from the commanding officer of such force a pass revocable at the pleasure of such commanding officer entitling such person to be treated on the footing of an officer" (sec. 175 (8));

and secondly, as "soldiers," *i.e.*, in the ranks—

> "All persons not otherwise subject to military law who are followers of or accompany His Majesty's troops, or any portion thereof, when employed in active service."

Chaplains, Nurses, and Medical Men.—Chaplains and "the personnel engaged *exclusively* in the collection, transport, and treatment of the wounded and the sick, as well as in the administration of medical units and establishments,"[3] are placed in a quite exceptional position. Not only are they entitled to immunity from attack[4] (so far as discrimination is possible), but also from capture. They are not to be

[1] H.R., Article 13.

[2] Special rules as to their trial by court-martial are to be found in sec. 184 of the Act.

[3] Geneva Convention, Article 9.

[4] *Cf.* the Geneva Convention, Article 6: "Mobile medical units (that is to say, those which are intended to accompany armies into the field) and the fixed establishments of the medical service shall be respected and protected by the belligerents."

treated as prisoners of war, and, if they do happen to get captured, they are to be sent back to their army or their country as soon as is compatible with military exigencies.[1] In the meantime, during their detention, they are to carry on their duties under the direction of their captors. If due notice of authorisation is given by one belligerent to the other, voluntary aid societies, properly authorised, are entitled to participate in these privileges. But all such persons must, in order to claim them, wear, fixed to the left arm, an armlet (*brassard*) with a red cross on a white ground (a device adopted, by reversing the federal colours, as a compliment to Switzerland), delivered and stamped by the competent military authority and, if no military uniform is worn, accompanied by a certificate of identity.[2] These privileges, however, do not extend to persons who are temporarily employed in such ministrations, *e.g.*, soldiers who volunteer to do ambulance duty for the time being.

Bombardment and Siege.—With the immunities of non-combatants may be classed the privileges of undefended places. Such places are, by the Hague Regulations, declared to be exempt "from bombardment or attack by any means whatsoever" (*par quelque moyen que ce soit*).[3] Therefore, to attack

[1] The Geneva Convention, Articles 9 and 12.

[2] *Ibid.*, Article 20. It will be remembered that England, by the Geneva Convention Act, 1911 (1 & 2 Geo. V. c. 20), has made it a statutory offence to use the *heraldic* emblem of the "Red Cross," or the words "Red Cross," for any purpose whatsoever if the person so using it has not the authority of the Army Council for such use.

[3] H. R., Article 25. As to the discharge of projectiles from balloons and aeroplanes, see below.

BOMBARDMENT

such a place by dropping bombs from balloons or aeroplanes, whatever may be said about the use of such projectiles over *defended* towns, is clearly a breach of international law. Nor does a refusal of the inhabitants to pay ransom justify a bombardment of such a place.[1] What, then, is an "undefended place"? The Regulations do not define the term. An *enceinte* of forts would, no doubt, serve to bring a town within the definition, but so, according to a writer of high authority,[2] would the mere fact of the presence of troops, even if they are only marching through it. Some light may be thrown on the matter by the Hague Convention dealing with naval bombardment, according to which "military works, military or naval establishments, depôts of arms or war material, workshops or plant[3] which could be used for the needs of the hostile fleet or army" may be destroyed by bombardment in spite of the locality being "undefended." Certain counsels of perfection are embodied in the Hague Regulations[4] as to the desirability of the commander of the attacking force taking steps to warn the inhabitants of the impending bombardment.[5] But he need not do so.

---

[1] Hague Convention, No. IX., of 1907, respecting bombardments by naval forces in time of war.

[2] Professor Oppenheim in *Land Warfare*, p. 34 (paragraph 119).

[3] Presumably, therefore, the presence of railway rolling-stock would put the place outside the category of "undefended places."

[4] H. R., Article 26.

[5] The Prussian War-book (p. 19) roundly denounces the recommendation of such notification as "not according to war" (*unkriegs gemäss*). It would, the book argues, involve a loss of precious time.

Nor need he give notice to non-combatants to leave.[1] Nor again is he required to spare the residential quarters; such discrimination would probably be impossible. But the Regulations are very explicit as to the duty of taking all necessary steps (*toutes les mesures nécessaires doivent être prises*)[2] to spare churches, museums, colleges, charitable institutions, hospitals, and places where the sick and wounded are collected.[3] Such discrimination is, as a rule, perfectly possible, especially when, as the Regulations recommend, and as is usually the case, they are distinguished by special visible signs. Of course, such buildings must not be put to alien, *i.e.* to military, uses.

II. OCCUPATION.

Occupation.—The question of the rights and duties of an enemy in occupation of hostile territory raise in the most comprehensive form the whole problem of the treatment of non-combatants. Before considering all that it involves, it may be as well to set out the German military view of the responsibilities of the occupant. On the face of it the German War-book would seem to indicate a considerable advance on the ruthless doctrines laid down by Clausewitz a

---

[1] The Prussian War-book likewise denounces the teachers of international law who argue for granting such days of grace to enable "women, children, sick, and wounded" to leave. Their very presence is, say the German Staff, to be desired by the besiegers, as it enables the latter to terrorise the town into an early surrender (p. 21).

[2] H. R., Article 27.

[3] The Prussian War-book endorses this rule.

century ago. Clausewitz knows no mercy. Writing on requisitions he extols "the modern method of providing for troops, that is to say, seizing everything which is to be found in the country without regard to *meum* and *tuum*," and proceeds to argue that requisitions should be enforced not so much by the use of the local functionaries as

> by the fear of responsibility, punishment, and ill-treatment which in such cases presses like a general weight on the whole population. . . . This resource has no limits except those of the exhaustion, impoverishment, and devastation of the country.[1]

With this may be contrasted the apparent humanitarianism of the German War-book.

> "It follows, then, as a matter of law that as regards the personal position of the inhabitants of the occupied land, they are not to be injured either in life or in limb, in honour or in freedom, and that every unlawful killing, every malicious or careless bodily injury, every insult, every disturbance of domestic peace, every attack on the family, honour, and morality: to sum up—every unlawful and outrageous attack or violence is just as much punishable as are similar practices when committed against the inhabitants of one's own fatherland."[2]

Nothing could be more admirable. Unfortunately, as we shall see later, the War-book goes on to qualify this correct doctrine in every direction, with the result that the standard set for German officers is far below that reached by international law. What

[1] *Vom Kriege*, v., kap. 14, pt. 3.
[2] *Kriegsbrauch*, pp. 46-7.

the latter, *i.e.*, the legal standard is we will now proceed to consider.

What is "Occupation."—The occupation contemplated by the laws of war is similar to the occupation which establishes a title to the acquisition of sovereignty over lands in time of peace. It is similar, but it is not the same. The latter kind of occupation gives complete sovereignty, the former does not. A belligerent does not in virtue of warlike "occupation" become the sovereign of the occupied territories. Lordship is not in such a case united with ownership. The inhabitants do not become his subjects, nor is the territory to be regarded as *res nullius*. At the same time, although the results attending occupation are different in the two cases, the conditions necessary to establish it are much the same. There must be an absence of State authority on the one side and the ability to furnish a substitute on the other. A territory liable to be "occupied" by the enemy is in much the same position as a territory which is uninhabited or inhabited only by uncivilised tribes, and is therefore [1] open to acquisition. And the occupying Power must, in both cases, be in a position to make its authority felt and its protection effective.[2]

[1] *Cf.* Westlake, i., ch. v.; Hall, ch. ii.; Oppenheim, sec. 221. But the modern tendency is to base acquisition of sovereignty over inhabited lands, even though uncivilised, upon some form of treaty or conquest. And *cf.* the test laid down in *Freeman* v. *Fairlie*, 1 Moo. Ind. App. 324, where it was held that a settled country corresponds to one without a *lex loci*.

[2] As to the acquisition of title (in time of peace) over uninhabited or uncivilised countries, *cf.* the rules laid down in Articles 34 and 35 of the Berlin (African Conference) Act, and Westlake's comment, i., 107—a "regular government must be established."

FLYING COLUMNS

Beyond this it is impossible to go in the way of definition. The Hague Regulation [1] is laconic—

> " A territory is considered as occupied when it is placed under the authority of the hostile army.
> " Occupation extends only to the territories where this authority is established and is capable of being exercised."

This at least implies that the national forces are defeated or withdrawn, and that the national government is not in a position to exercise its authority. Some authorities [2] consider that the occupation can be established by flying columns, and that the presence of garrisons is immaterial. This, however, seems to open the door to dangerous latitude, and to enable the enemy to say that a patrol of Uhlans could establish an occupation and with it the claim to treat the inhabitants as guilty of "war treason" if they resisted, together with all the other penalties that attach to contumacious behaviour on the part of inhabitants of "occupied" territory. The German War-book admits that "fictitious occupation" by means of a mere declaration will not do.[3] But what will do it is difficult to say.

The effect of occupation is to substitute temporarily the authority of the enemy for that of the national government. It rests, however, very much with the belligerent to decide the limits of this vicarious function. "So far as possible" he is to respect the

---

[1] H. R., Article 42.
[2] *E.g.*, Professor Holland, p. 52, and Professor Oppenheim, p. 76.
[3] *Kriegsbrauch*, p. 67.

laws of the country,[1] but his occupation necessarily entails some kind of martial law. He is required[2] to respect the actionable rights of the inhabitants so far as the national courts are able to adjudicate upon them. He may continue to collect the national taxes,[3] but he may not impose new ones, or rather he may only levy such "contributions as are necessary for the needs of the army or of the administration of the territory."[4] The question of "contributions" will be considered presently.

Rights and Duties of the Inhabitants. (1) *Compulsion to Assist the Enemy.*—It seems to be generally admitted that the belligerent may not compel the inhabitants to take part in operations of war directed against their own country.[5] This, however, is simply a general statement of principle, and attempts to define it more closely have not been conspicuously successful. Nothing is said about the vexed question of compulsory service as guides, and the general proposition, embodied in Article 44—

> "Any compulsion by a belligerent on the population of occupied territory to give information as to the army of the other belligerent, or as to his means of defence, is prohibited,"

---

[1] H. R., Article 43.
[2] *Ibid.*, Article 23 (*h*). We cannot think that the subsection (which in terms is general) was intended to apply to suits brought by subjects of one belligerent in the courts of another. See Professor Oppenheim's pamphlet on the Interpretation of Article 23 (*h*.)
[3] *Ibid.*, Article 48.
[4] *Ibid.*, Article 49.
[5] *Ibid.*, Article 23.

failed to command the assent of several Powers.[1] The German War-book will not admit it for a moment—

> "A yet sharper measure appears in the compulsion of the inhabitants to furnish particulars as to their own army, its strategy, resources, and military secrets. The majority of writers of all nations are united in condemning such a measure. None the less, one cannot always dispense with this—doubtless one will always practise it with regret—but the argument of war will frequently necessitate it."[2]

This makes anything possible. And the German Staff do not hesitate to insist on the impressment by the enemy of the inhabitants as guides—

> "However repugnant it may be to humane feeling to compel a man to do harm to his own fatherland and to facilitate the defeat of his own country's forces, no army operating in a hostile territory will renounce this resource."[3]

(2) *Hostages and Vicarious Punishments.* — The taking of hostages is unusual in modern warfare and has been frequently condemned, but the Hague Regulations are silent on the point. German writers, legal[4] as well as military, defend the practice even in

---

[1] Germany, Austria, Japan, Russia, all refused to subscribe to it. The reasons given by the German representative, Baron von Bieberstein, are not very satisfying, as we have already seen (*supra*, p. 171). To forbid one thing, he argued, would be to imply the permission of others, and, besides, specification was both undesirable and impossible (*Actes et Documents*, i., 86).

[2] *Kriegsbrauch*, p. 48.

[3] *Ibid.*, p. 48.

[4] *Cf.* Holtzendorff, iv., 475-8, which contain an uneasy justification.

its harshest form, for no better reason than that it has generally been successful.[1] But more enlightened opinion is against them.[2] And if the Hague Regulations are silent on this question of punishing individuals for the acts of a whole population, they are very explicit on the question of punishing a whole population for the acts of individuals.

> "No general penalty, pecuniary or otherwise, can be inflicted on the population on account of isolated acts for which it cannot be regarded as collectively responsible."[3]

(3) *Forced Labour and Requisitions.*—It seems to be admitted that the belligerent may compel the inhabitants to work for him. But as the Regulations have laid it down that they cannot be compelled to assist in operations against their national forces, it follows that the work must not be of a military character. For example, the inhabitants cannot be compelled to dig trenches. The Prussian War-book,[4] however, argues that such distinctions are impossible, and that *kriegsraison* alone can decide. Requisitions of private property, on the other hand, *must* be of a military character. To take private property which can serve no such purpose is indistinguishable from plundering. The Hague Regulations (Article 53) lay it down that means of transport and war

---

[1] Cf. *Kriegsbrauch*, p. 50, where the writers defend the exposure of innocent inhabitants to the enemy's fire by placing them on military trains with the argument that its real justification is that it is successful.

[2] *E.g.*, Professor Oppenheim in *Land Warfare*, p. 99.

[3] H. R., Article 50. But see below as to reprisals.

[4] P. 48.

material may be so taken, but compensation should be paid for them on the conclusion of peace. But supplies generally may also be requisitioned, but only for "the needs of the army of occupation." To amass booty is clearly forbidden. The Regulations provide that these supplies shall be " in proportion to the resources of the country,"[1] shall be authorised by a responsible officer, and, if possible, paid for in cash (*au comptant*); if cash payment is impossible, receipts shall be given and payment made as soon as possible. The term "the needs of the army of occupation" is very liberally interpreted in the German War-book.[2] Nor does that magisterial authority show much tenderness for the principle of proportion.[3]

Contributions.—The Hague Regulations (Article 49) deprecate cash contributions unless they be necessary for the maintenance of the army or the administration of the territory. They are, of course, liable to great abuse, and may easily be a cloak for mere plundering. The German War-book admits this, and, in view of recent practices in Belgium, its words are worth recalling. They cannot, the writers point out, be justified as requisitions may, by necessity, and therefore should rarely be resorted to.

---

[1] The British Requisitioning Instructions recommend leaving from three days' to a week's supply of food in the possession of each household (*cf.* Oppenheim, p. 90, note *e*).

[2] P. 53. "In this case every sequestration, every temporary or permanent appropriation, every use, every injury, and all destruction are permissible."

[3] P. 62. "That they [requisitions] should be proportioned to the resources of the district is all very well in theory, but it would rarely be observed in practice." And the writers add grimly, payment is not necessary, but receipts may be given !

They are never, adds the War-book, to be used as a form of ransom from pillage or incendiarism, nor is the victor entitled to take advantage of them to recoup himself for the cost of the war. And the provisional government should never demand anything which could be construed as directly or indirectly compulsory participation in the war.[1] Pillage is directly prohibited in the Hague Regulations;[2] nor is the German War-book any less explicit.

> "Movable private property which in earlier times was the incontestable booty of the victor, is held by modern opinion to be inviolable. The carrying off of gold, watches, rings, trinkets, or other objects of value is therefore to be regarded as simple robbery, and correspondingly punishable."[3]

And equally significant in the light of recent events are the words about plundering as "the worst kind of annexation of a stranger's property," understanding by plundering the taking of another man's goods "under the compulsion of military terror or abuse of a military opportunity." And to take goods from empty houses—

> "No plundering but downright burglary is it for a man to take away things out of an unoccupied house, or at a time when the occupant happens to be absent."[4]

These are excellent sentiments.

[1] *Kriegsbrauch*, pp. 62-3.
[2] H. R., Articles 22 (*g*) and 47.
[3] *Kriegsbrauch*, p. 58.
[4] *Ibid.*, p. 59.

War Treason.—The term "war treason" is very misleading. Treason, as we have seen in our first chapter, is essentially a breach of the duty of allegiance, whether it be a breach by the subject of his natural allegiance or by the resident alien of his local and temporary allegiance. "War treason" has really nothing to do with this. It refers to the relation between the inhabitants of an occupied country and the enemy occupant, and it cannot be said that between these parties any relationship of allegiance exists. What the term really means is acts by non-combatants calculated to endanger the army of occupation. In this sense the term "war treason" (*kriegsverrat*) is used in the German Warbook.

> "By it is to be understood injury to or endangering of the enemy's forces by deceit or by the communication to one's own army of information as to the position, movement, intentions, and the like of the occupying army, and it matters not whether the person concerned has used legitimate methods or illegitimate (*e.g.*, espionage) in obtaining such information."[1]

Within this category would also come doing damage to the occupying enemy's lines of communication or their war material. So also would intentional misleading of his troops. Where an inhabitant has volunteered to guide them the "treason" is clear. But supposing he is compelled to act as guide? As we have seen, the Hague Regulations regard the exercise of such compulsion as illegitimate, and it should follow that, if it *is* exercised, the pressed

[1] *Kriegsbrauch*, p. 50.

guide should not be regarded as guilty of treason because he fails to perform or deliberately misperforms a duty which he does not owe. But the German Government (who refused to subscribe to the Regulations) do not admit this, and their War-book declares[1] that the guide who, being forced to act as guide, intentionally leads the enemy troops astray should be punished with death. This seems hard measure.

III. THE CONDUCT OF HOSTILITIES.

Limitations.—War is an act of violence, but not of unlimited violence. As early as 1868 the Declaration of St Petersburg laid it down that "the only legitimate object which states should endeavour to accomplish during war is to weaken the military forces of the enemy," and that this object is accomplished by their disablement and not by their unlimited destruction or the needless aggravation of their sufferings. This principle is consecrated in the twenty-second article of the Hague Regulations, declaring that the right of belligerent to adopt means of injuring the enemy is not unlimited.[2] Independently of these Regulations "Declarations" prohibiting the use of certain instruments of warfare had already been agreed to by some (not always all) of the great Powers. There have been four such Declarations, and they provide for—

(1) The renunciation of the use of explosive or incendiary projectiles below a certain weight (14 oz.).[2]

[1] *Kriegsbrauch*, p. 51.
[2] Declaration of St Petersburg, 1868.

(2) The renunciation of the use of "explosive bullets"—*i.e.*, bullets "with a hard envelope which does not entirely cover the core, or is pierced with incisions.[1]

(3) The abstention from the use of projectiles the sole object of which is the diffusion of asphyxiating or deleterious gases.[2]

These three Declarations were signed by all the great European Powers. The fourth—

"To prohibit, for a period extending to the close of the Third Peace Conference, the discharge of projectiles and explosives from balloons or by other new methods of a similar nature,"[3]

was less fortunate. The only great Powers who signed it were the United States and Great Britain. It may be regarded as a dead letter. But it must be remembered that the use of such projectiles upon undefended places is expressly forbidden by Article 25 of the Hague Regulations, to which article Germany was a party.

Expanding Bullets.—As regards the first and second of the Declarations, dealing with the use of explosive projectiles and expanding bullets, there has been a good deal of military controversy as to what constitutes an expanding bullet. In a highly important Memorandum issued by the British War Office on 17th November 1914, the whole matter is dispassionately discussed, and the opinion of Sir Victor Horsley as to the character of the bullets

---

[1] Hague Declaration, 1899.
[2] *Ibid.*, 1899.
[3] *Ibid.*, 1907.

used by the British forces is cited. The British bullet is described as

> "a pointed one with an envelope of cupronickel which completely covers the core, except, of course, at the base through which the core is inserted."

Sir Victor Horsley gives it as his carefully considered opinion that this bullet is "probably the most humane projectile yet devised." Such bullets have a long, solid point consisting mainly of a hard nickel sheath, the strength of which prevents the bullet breaking up into fragments. It makes a singularly clean and incisive wound.[1] On the other hand, a bullet whose point is not so protected, *i.e.* is "soft-nosed," expands and flattens in the body and creates a terribly devastating wound. As such it violates not only the Hague Declaration but also the Hague Regulation which forbids the use of projectiles such as cause unnecessary suffering (*des maux superflus*).[2]

Treachery.—The Hague Regulations specify certain other limitations which had long been recognised

---

[1] [During a recent visit (October) to France I have frequently had occasion to examine the wounds caused by bullets of this kind. They look exactly like a neat puncture or incision. On the other hand, I have seen a French soldier who had been wounded in the hand by an expanding bullet, and the wound was a ghastly circular hole, quite an inch in diameter, with a periphery of shattered flesh.—J. H. M.]

[2] H. R., Article 23 (*e*). The War Office Memorandum quoted above declares that there is "clear evidence that Germany has not confined herself" to the use of "unobjectionable ammunition."

TREACHERY

as part of the unwritten laws of war. It is forbidden—

(1) To declare that no quarter will be given.
(2) To kill or wound *treacherously* (*par trahison*) individuals belonging to the hostile nation or army.
(3) To wound or kill an enemy who, having laid down his arms, or having no longer any means of defence, has surrendered at discretion.

The word "treachery" raises the whole question of the legitimacy of "ruses" or "stratagems" in war.[1] This is much more a matter of military etiquette and national honour than of law. The Hague Regulations are very laconic on the point. There are things which a nation with a high standard of honour will not stoop to do—things which its officers would regard as unbecoming to a gentleman. Indeed the practice of an army in this matter is a pretty good indication of the morals of a nation. Frederick the Great put the matter with characteristic cynicism—

"One uses alternatively in war the skin of the lion and the skin of the fox; cunning frequently succeeds where force would fail."[2]

The Hague Regulations confine themselves to forbidding improper use of (*d'user indûment*) a flag of truce.[3] This may be regarded as the one unpardon-

[1] Professor Oppenheim (p. 37, note *b*) cites as an example of killing or wounding by "treachery" calling out, "Do not fire, we are friends," and then firing a volley, or shamming disablement or death and then using arms.
[2] Quoted in *Kriegsbrauch*, p. 23.
[3] H. R., Article 23 (*f*), and *cf.* H. R., Article 34.

able sin about which all are agreed. To raise the flag of truce in order to cover an attack is the meanest of military misdemeanours. The German War-book declares:

> "Apparent surrender in order to kill the unsuspicious enemy as he approaches, misuse of the flag of truce or of the Red Cross in order to get to closer quarters, or for the purposes of an attack"[1]

—such conduct, it declares, is contrary to the most elementary notions of chivalry and honour. It is worthy of remark that on this question the military authors of the War-book profess to take a higher standard than that adopted by jurists—

> "The putting on of the enemy's uniforms, the use of enemy or neutral banners, flags, and insignia for purposes of deceit, is generally declared permissible[2] by writers on the laws of war, but military writers have unanimously spoken out against such things (*Kriegsbrauch*, p. 24)."

As, however, the passage is immediately followed by extensive quotations (without any further expression

---

[1] *Kriegsbrauch*, p. 23.

[2] This is not altogether true. For example, in the military manual (*Land Warfare*) issued by the War Office, Prof. Oppenheim, writing in conjunction with Colonel Edmonds, says: "Theory and practice are unanimous in forbidding their employment during combat, that is, the opening of fire whilst in the guise of the enemy" (p. 39); and Professor Holland (*The Laws of War on Land*, p. 45) would appear to regard the use of false uniforms as quite illegitimate. The connection of these two eminent jurists with the British War Office gives their views considerable official significance.

of disapproval) from German legal writers, in favour of a complete disregard of chivalry and honour when "necessary," it is difficult to attach much importance to such a passage. It is a misfortune of the German War-book that when it advocates "frightfulness" it is never ambiguous, while when it recommends tenderness it is always so.[1]

Ambushes, false messages, feigned advances and feigned retreats, surprises, etc., are, of course, always legitimate, and it is the business of the other party, by its Intelligence service, to read such cipher and be ready for it.

Spies.—A spy is defined in the Hague Regulations[2] as one who, "acting clandestinely or on false pretences, obtains, or seeks to obtain, information in the zone of operations of a belligerent, with the intention of communicating it to the enemy." Deceit is the hall-mark of espionage. For a soldier *without disguise* to penetrate the enemy's lines with a view to obtaining information is not espionage. Simulation and dissimulation are the methods of the spy; to pretend to be what he is not, or to pretend not to be what he is. Spying is practised by all nations and defended by none. No attempt has been made to protect him by international law; on the contrary, the Hague Regulations (although they require some form of trial) expressly declare that the spy is not entitled to be treated as a prisoner of war. To put it

---

[1] On the other hand, the manual issued by the British War Office is distinguished by an explicit condemnation of dishonourable practices and an entire absence of casuistry which cannot be too highly praised.

[2] H. R., Article 29.

bluntly, he is to be shot. He has neither the rights of a combatant nor the privileges of a non-combatant.

Prisoners.—On no subject are the Hague Regulations so explicit as on the treatment of prisoners of war. This is obviously a matter in which nations have a reciprocity of interest, and, if only from fear of reprisals, they usually pursue a certain uniformity. Every member of the armed forces of the enemy, including the extensions of that term to organised irregulars, and to the *levée en masse*, is entitled, when disabled or when he has surrendered, to be treated as a prisoner of war. He must not be killed, nor must his captivity be of a punitive character. He is not to be treated as a criminal, nor is he, unless absolutely necessary, to be kept in close confinement. If he is set to work he is to be paid for his labour on the same scale as a soldier of the national army employed on similar work, but the work must not partake of the nature of military operations. He is not to be deprived of his private property, and this is to include his military uniform, clothing, and kit.[1] His captors — by which must be understood the enemy government (he is not to be regarded as the captive of his actual captor) — are bound to maintain him, and, in default of special agreement between the belligerents, he is entitled to the same food, quarters, and clothing as the soldiers of the enemy government receive. He can be shot if he attempts to escape, and he can be punished for offences against discipline. Much has been done by the Hague Regulations to humanise the treatment of prisoners, particularly by the direction that a Prisoners of War Information

[1] *The British Manual of Military Law*, ch. xiv.

Bureau be established on the outbreak of war in each of the belligerent countries, whose duty it shall be "to answer all inquiries about prisoners of war." Through such bureaux letters, money - orders, valuables, and postal parcels are to be forwarded to prisoners of war free of all charges for postage, carriage, or customs duties. Prisoners are to be enabled to make their wills, and the dead are to be treated with the respect due to their rank. A prisoner has no claim to be repatriated during the continuance of the war, but as soon as peace is concluded he is to be restored to his own country with all possible expedition.[1] It is questionable whether these Regulations apply to interned civilians as they do to soldiers.

The Wounded and Sick.—The treatment of the wounded and sick was the first, as it is perhaps the most imperative, object of solicitude on the part of the comity of nations. As early as 1864 a Convention was signed at Geneva for the regulation of their treatment, and this has been supplemented by the Geneva Convention of 1906. Their cardinal principle is that no distinction of nationality shall be made by the belligerent between the treatment of his own wounded and of those of the enemy. If he is encumbered with the enemy's wounded, and is compelled to abandon them, he must leave with them, so far as military exigencies allow, a portion of his medical personnel and material to provide for their care and sustenance. After an engagement the commander in possession of the field of battle should take measures to search for both the enemy's wounded

[1] H. R., Articles 4 to 20.

and his own, and should protect both the quick and the dead against pillage and maltreatment. It is enjoined that there shall be mutual provision of information by one belligerent to the other as to the identity of the dead and wounded who have come into his possession. Molestation of the wounded can be punished as a "war crime." "Persons who rob, mishandle, or kill the wounded lying defenceless on the field of battle are 'hyenas of the battlefield' (*Hyänen des schlachtfelds*)," and deserve, and will receive, no mercy.[1]

Reprisals.—Reprisals are not laws of war so much as primitive sanctions to secure respect for them. They resemble the mediæval principle of an eye for an eye and a tooth for a tooth. They have never been authoritatively defined, and indeed by their very nature they defy definition. As Professor Holland puts it: "the permissibility of such measures is a painful exception to the rule that a belligerent must observe the laws of war even without reciprocity on the part of the enemy."[2] This is a case where if it needs be that evil shall come, woe unto him through whom it cometh. Their object should, however, be not vindictive but deterrent, and there are certain breaches of the laws of war, such as the killing of the wounded, upon which no self-respecting belligerent would retaliate in kind. He might, however, with some justification notify the enemy that no quarter would be given. All writers are agreed that reprisals should be very sparingly exercised. But very little is to be found in the books. The authors of the

[1] *Kriegsbrauch*, p. 24.
[2] *The Laws of War on Land*, p. 60.

Handbuch des Völkerrechts deal with the matter under the head of *kriegsraison*, a term which we have rendered by the words " the casuistry of war." They argue with some justification that reprisals are the kind of the exception which proves the rule, and declare that the relation of *Kriegsraison* to *Kriegsrecht*, of reprisals in war to the laws of war, is analogous to that of Necessity to Criminal Law.[1] This is a fair statement of the case. The analogy suggests the relation of justifiable homicide to murder. The matter has never been regulated, and the disinclination to do so is intelligible enough, for this is certainly a case where regulation might seem to suggest recognition. Professor Holland, who writes with unrivalled authority on these matters, summarises[2] prevalent authoritative opinion upon this subject in the form of four restrictions.

(1) The offence in question must have been carefully inquired into.

(2) Redress for the wrong, or punishment of the real offender, must be unattainable.

(3) The reprisals must be authorised, unless under very special circumstances, by the commander-in-chief.

(4) They must not be disproportioned to the offence, and must in no case be of a barbarous character.

That is as far as it is possible to go.

[1] Holtzendorff, iv., 255-7 : " Die Kriegsraison verhält sich zum Kriegsrecht wie der Nothstand zum Strafrecht."
[2] *The Laws of War on Land*, p. 61.

IV. RIGHTS AND DUTIES OF NEUTRALS.[1]

Neutrality is a negative conception. It denotes a "passive"[2] or "impartial"[3] attitude towards the two or more combatants on the part of a third party. The neutral state continues, of course, to maintain diplomatic relations with the combatant states, but it carefully refrains from giving countenance or support to either of them. The rights and duties of neutrals are defined in a Hague Convention (No. V. of 1907) devoted to that subject. They may be briefly summarised as follows:—(1) The neutral Power has a right to forbid, and a duty to prevent, the passage of belligerent troops across its territory, the establishment of belligerent communications, or the recruitment of belligerent troops.[4] If belligerent troops enter or take refuge in its territory, it must intern them for the rest of the war. But it is under no obligation to detain escaped prisoners of war. A neutral Power may permit, if it thinks fit, to a belligerent the passage of *his own* sick and wounded through its territory, but if it accords this privilege to one belligerent it must equally accord it to the others. A neutral Power is not bound to prevent its subjects, resident within its own territory, from supplying either of the belligerents with arms,

---

[1] This subject is partially dealt with in the chapter on the Neutrality of Belgium, and also in Part III.

[2] Holtzendorff, iv., 605.   [3] *Kriegsbrauch*, p. 68.

[4] Under English law the recruiting of troops by a British subject or resident alien to serve against a friendly Power is an offence under our municipal law—by the terms of the Foreign Enlistment Act.

ammunition, and stores. Neutral persons are the subjects of neutral states. Their position is only doubtful when they are present or resident in the territory of either belligerent. English law tends to identify them with their place of residence ; German opinion is the other way and favours discrimination. But Germany stood almost alone in this attitude at the Hague Conferences.[1]

[1] For further discussion of the position of neutrals the reader is referred to the chapters on Contraband and Unneutral Service, and Enemy Property. The subject of Declaration and End of War is dealt with in Part IV.

CHAPTER II

ANNEXATION AND ACTS OF STATE

Annexation—Status of New Territory—Status of Inhabitants—Power of Crown to cede Territory—Claims against New Government—Acts of State—Treaties as Sources of Right—Articles of Capitulation—Claims arising out of Property—Claims arising out of Contract—State Succession.

Annexation and Status of New Territory.—The Crown may acquire territory, apart from settlement by its subjects, either by conquest or cession. This, however, is putting the proposition in a somewhat too disjunctive form, as it may well, and usually does, happen that the conquest is recognised by a treaty of cession or in the form of articles of capitulation. There is usually, therefore, a treaty of some kind. How far can it, and the rights arising under it, be subject to interpretation in a court of law? And, independently of any such treaty, what is the legal status and what are the legal rights of the inhabitants? Now so far as the status of the new territory is concerned, *i.e.*, whether it is, and, if it is, how much of it is, British territory—this is what American courts would call a " political " question which appears to be considered incapable of judicial determination. It is a question involving the larger question of the relations between our own state and another state; one of those " transactions of independent states between each other [which] are governed by other laws than those which municipal courts administer." [1] It would seem that the status of territory is viewed by the courts in the same light as the status of another sovereign, and that judicial notice will be taken of a declaration by the Executive as conclusive on the point.

> "When once there is the authoritative certificate of the Queen through her Minister of State as to the status of another sovereign, that, in the courts of this country, is conclusive." [2]

Certain it is that judges have declared that they cannot decide what is or is not a part of the realm,[3] and if the matter has not been settled by statute a certificate of the Secretary of State for Foreign Affairs would probably be regarded as decisive.[4]

Status of Inhabitants.—Admitting the fact of annexation, what is the position of the inhabitants who were subjects of the former sovereign? Are they aliens or British subjects? The answer is that conquest [5] probably and cession [6] certainly operates

[1] *Secretary of State for India in Council* v. *Kamachee*, (1859) 13 Moo. P.C. 75.

[2] *Mighell* v. *Sultan of Johore*, [1894] 1 Q.B. 149.

[3] *The Franconia*, (1876) 2 Ex. Div. 126.

[4] The Foreign Jurisdiction Act of 1891 (sec. 4) provides that in questions of foreign jurisdiction the certificate of the Secretary of State shall be decisive. Cf. *R.* v. *Crewe*, L.T. Rep., vol. cii., p. 760.

[5] *Campbell* v. *Hall*, (1774) 1 Cowp. 204, and *Mayor of Lyons*, 1 Moo Ind. A.C. 175. This was the older view, but at that date the theory of international law was that mere occupation of territory substituted the full sovereignty of the occupant for that of the previous sovereign.

[6] Westlake, *Private International Law*, p. 355; and cf. *Isaacson* v. *Durant*.

as naturalisation. The conquered inhabitants, still present in the territory, become, in the words of Mansfield, " subjects, not enemies or aliens." If they object to this compulsory naturalisation, their only course is to leave the territory and, if it be a dependency, return to their mother-country. The Articles of Capitulation may make provision by giving a period of grace or by enabling the inhabitants to opt as to whether they will acquire the new nationality or retain the old.[1] The question is in some ways of less importance than it was in earlier times, because the status of alien no longer carries with it in English law the disabilities as to the acquisition of real property and other rights which formerly attended it.

Cession of Territory by Crown. — Conversely cession of territory by the British Crown operates to convert the inhabitants of the territory ceded from British subjects into aliens. This converse proposition was, however, at one time the subject of considerable dispute. It was admitted that the Crown, and only the Crown, can acquire territory—even a self-governing colony, much less an individual British subject, cannot acquire territory except in the name of the Crown.[2] At the same time it was equally undeniable that as the king in acquiring territory

---

[1] *Cf.* the cases of Dominica and Mauritius in Forsyth, *Cases and Opinions*, pp. 255 and 326.

[2] *Cf.* the recitals of the India Act of 1793. If newly conquered lands are to be incorporated in the territory of any particular colony, the proper procedure would seem to be for His Majesty by letters patent to authorise the colonial government to annex, and for the colonial legislature subsequently to pass an Act incorporating the said territory.

acquired it "in right of his crown," Parliament might at any time step in and legislate for it, till which time the king might legislate for it in virtue of his prerogative.¹ But what of the converse case? Can the king cede British territory in virtue of his prerogative alone, and, if he may, does such cession operate to transform British subjects into aliens? The two parts of this question were regarded as inseparable from the decision of either of them. Those who denied that the king could alienate British territory without the consent of Parliament based their argument on the supposition that such cession operated to make aliens of British subjects, and that as nationality was (so they argued) indelible only Parliament could authorise an act which divested British subjects of their nationality against their will. In other words, the king could not force his subjects to change their allegiance. Those who insisted, on the other hand, that the king *could* alienate British territory in virtue of his prerogative met this argument by the contention that such cession did not operate to transform British subjects (i.e. *antenati*) into aliens.² Neither side was wholly right. The latter school were right in their conclusion and wrong in their premises; the former were right in their premises and wrong in their conclusion. Cession does operate as alienage,³ *and* the Crown has the right to alienate. That is to say, it can

¹ Lord Mansfield in *Campbell* v. *Hall*, op. cit.
² See the arguments on both sides (Chalmers's Opinion, p. 265, and Reeves's Opinion, p. 303) in Forsyth's *Cases and Opinions*.
³ Cf. *Isaacson* v. *Durant*, op. cit.

alienate British territory under a treaty of peace as incident to the conclusion of war.¹ Whether it could alienate it *in time of peace*, and independently of its prerogative to make war and peace, is more doubtful. The question was hotly debated when the ministry of the day introduced into Parliament a bill to give effect to that part of the Anglo-German treaty which provided for the cession of Heligoland to Germany. It cannot be said to be decided, but a ministry would no doubt in such cases seek to protect itself by statutory authority.² And treaties of cession usually work a tacit change of allegiance by providing the terms on which such a change can be escaped.

Legal Rights of New Subjects—Acts of State.— Returning to the status of the inhabitants of territories newly annexed by the Crown, we have to consider what are their legal rights. Now while there can be no doubt that they become British subjects, with all the legal rights of such subjects under the *lex loci*, as fully and as impartially as any Englishman resorting to the new dependency (the sovereign must not discriminate between his old and his new subjects[3]), there is considerable uncertainty as to how far the Articles of Capitulation or treaties of cession give them rights enforceable in a court of

---

[1] Even this was denied by Lord Loughborough in the debate on the cession of the American colonies. But the weight of opinion was, and is, against him.

[2] *Cf.* the *obiter dictum* of Brett, L.J., in the *Franconia*, (1876) 2 Ex Div. 126: "What are the limits of the realm should in general be declared by Parliament."

[3] *Campbell* v. *Hall*, 1 Cowp. 204.

ACTS OF STATE

law, and, more particularly, how far they can claim redress for anything done by the Crown incidental to the conclusion of peace. For acts done during the war no alien can sue. They are "Acts of State" —a term which, as we have seen in an earlier chapter, means an act done or ratified by the authority of the Crown in respect of an alien, who is thereby excluded from suing the officer who did it. Such authority or ratification deprives an alien of any redress, even in time of peace, for an act done outside the dominions,[1] although it would only deprive him within the dominions if he were not received into protection, which he invariably is. Now war of itself makes any official act done to an alien enemy an Act of State. What then is to be said of acts arising out of the conclusion of war? The question was considered in the case of *Elphinstone* v. *Bedreechund*,[2] where it was held by the Privy Council that the seizure of property in connection with the conquest of Indian territory was an Act of State and—

> " in the nature of hostile seizure, made if not *flagrante bello* yet *mondum cessante bello*, regard being had to the time, the place, and the person."

The qualifications must be noted. That of *time* raises the question as to when annexation is deemed to be perfected. Its perfection, converting, as it does, aliens into British subjects, or receiving aliens of other nationality than that of the conquered sovereign into British protection, should exclude any further excuse for arbitrary acts by the Executive

[1] *Buron* v. *Denman*, (1842) 2 Ex. 167.
[2] St. Tr. N.S. 379.

under plea of Act of State. That of *place* raises the question as to what are the territorial limits of the annexation. The question of the *person* may raise the problem of the immunity of military officers in regard to acts arising out of a military relationship.[1] Now the first two of these qualifications were subsequently considered in two cases arising out of the annexation of Pondoland in South Africa. In the one case, *Sprigg* v. *Sigcau*,[2] it was held by the Privy Council that the arbitrary arrest and detention by the Governor, *after* annexation, of a native chief of Pondoland, which was defended as an " Act of State," was illegal as being " an invasion of the individual rights and liberties of a British subject." In the other case, *Cook* v. *Sprigg*,[3] it was held by the Privy Council that no action lay against the new, *i.e.* the Cape, Government to enforce certain concessions of land granted to the appellant by the paramount chiefs of Pondoland, to whose sovereignty the Cape Government had succeeded. It was held that the acquisition of Pondoland being itself " an Act of State "—in other words an " international " question—a question of this character could not be entertained. Now the repudiation by the Cape Government of the grant took place *after* annexation, and it is difficult not to regard the decision as a denial of those rights of

---

[1] Cf. *Barwis* v. *Keppel* in Part I. Chapter IV.

[2] [1897] A.C. 238. With this case it is interesting to compare that of *R.* v. *Crewe* (*Ex parte Sekgome*) cited earlier, in which the fact of Bechuanaland being a protectorate and not British territory was held, in virtue of the Foreign Jurisdiction Acts, to establish " a Parliamentary despotism."

[3] [1899] A.C. 572.

private property which a new government is presumed to respect equally with the rights of personal liberty. It is difficult to reconcile the second case with the first; it is still more difficult to reconcile it with the classical utterances of Lord Mansfield in *Campbell* v. *Hall* as to the rights of new British subjects who have become such in virtue of annexation. It is difficult to see how the shadow of annexation can project itself so long after the act of annexation is accomplished as to make such repudiation Acts of State.

Treaties and Capitulations as Sources of Right.—The Privy Council went out of its way to deliver an *obiter dictum* on the obligation of treaties and articles of capitulation, which is also in contradiction with the views of Lord Mansfield in *Campbell* v. *Hall*. In that case he declared—

> "The articles of capitulation upon which the country is surrendered, and the articles of peace by which it is ceded, are sacred and inviolable, according to their true intent and meaning."[1]

With this it is difficult to reconcile the words of their lordships in *Cook* v. *Sprigg*.

> "If there is either an express or a well-understood bargain between the ceding potentate and the Government, to which the cession is made that private property shall be respected, that is only a bargain which can be enforced by sovereign against sovereign by diplomatic pressure."

[1] *Campbell* v. *Hall*, 1 Cowp. 204; and cf. *Cameron* v. *Kyte*, (1835) 3 Knapp. 342.

Obiter dicta are always dangerous and sometimes confusing. This one seems to go much too far. The respect for private property does not depend on there being treaties to that effect. It depends partly on international law—in particular, that part of the laws of war which declares private property inviolate—partly on the rule of English common law laid down by Lord Mansfield that the inhabitants acquire the rights of British subjects. Those rights are determined with reference to the *lex loci*, which continues till it is altered by the conqueror,[1] but such alteration cannot take the form of arbitrary exemptions or privileges which are not law at all; all that the sovereign can do is to introduce a new system of law.

Claims of Property and Claims of Contract.— If, however, the case is regarded not so much as a question of the right to undisturbed possession of private property as a contractual claim against the new government, to enforce liabilities contracted by the old one,[2] the decision is more intelligible although the *obiter dicta* become more irrelevant. The courts did, indeed, make this distinction in a subsequent case—*West Rand Central Gold Mining Co.* v. *the King*[3]—and it is a perfectly intelligible one.

"It must not be forgotten that the obligations of conquering states with regard to private

[1] Cf. *Freeman* v. *Fairlie*, 1 Moo. Ind. App. 305, and *Campbell* v. *Hall*; also *Smith* v. *Brown*, 2 Salkeld 666; also *R.* v. *Vaughan*, 4 Burrows 2494.

[2] This is how it is regarded by Mr Harrison Moore in his *Act of State in English Law*, p. 89.

[3] [1905] 2 K.B. 391—a claim arising out of the South African War.

property of private individuals, particularly land as to which the title had already been perfected before the conquest or annexation, are altogether different from the obligations which arise in respect of personal rights of contract."

It would appear to be well established that where the claim is clearly of this contractual character, it cannot be enforced by Petition of Right against the new government, even though it would have been enforceable against the old.[1] It seems unfortunate that the Court having decided the case on this admitted principle should also in its turn have been betrayed into an *obiter dictum* quite unnecessary to the discussion of the case, and no less questionable, namely, that while "a change of sovereignty ought not to affect private property," none the less "no municipal tribunal has authority to enforce such an obligation." True, the Court limited this denial of rights to cases where the territory was acquired by conquest as distinct from peaceable cession, basing it apparently on the absolute power of the conqueror. But this leaves the matter in a very unsatisfactory state.

[1] Cf. *Doss* v. *Secretary of State for India*, (1875) L.R. 19 Eq. 509.

CHAPTER III

LAWS OF WAR AT SEA

Naval Warfare — Hague Conventions — Is Rescue "Unneutral"?—Internment—Bombardment—Mines—Signalling in Port—Mails and Mariners—Use of Neutral Ports —" Military " Areas.

MARINE warfare is sharply differentiated from land warfare. It is carried on on the common highway of nations. Combatants and civilians are neatly separated. The cameraderie of the sea unites friend and foe. Both are in presence of a common danger: the inscrutable forces of nature.

Sea warfare has never been as brutal as land war; the instances of slaughter of prisoners appear only to be found in the exasperated days of the Spanish-Dutch wars,[1] when soldier-prisoners were drowned and killed with little compunction. That private property is safe on land, and unsafe at sea, is an academic proposition which is almost devoid of meaning.

It was perhaps for these reasons that the formal regulation of sea warfare was not made until long after the Geneva Convention of 1864 for the conduct of war on land. Isolated rules, such as the curious one which permits chasing, but not firing, under false colours, had, of course, existed long before.

Hague Conventions.—The Hague Conference of 1899 took up the subject and produced a Con-

[1] Grotius, *Hist.*, xiv.

vention (III.) according certain immunities to hospital ships corresponding with those which are supposed to be accorded to medical corps on land, and these provisions were further improved in 1907 (No. X.). Article 8 of 1899 (10 of 1907) provides generally for the safety and care of sick or wounded "taken on board" (but it may only apply to hospital ships, and not to sick or wounded prisoners generally). Neutrals, in order to obtain the full immunities of hospital ships, have to secure a belligerent authorisation, and, since 1907, they must be put under belligerent control. What is the position of an unofficial, but neutral, angel of mercy? She is graciously considered not to have forfeited her neutral character, but the un-English and unfortunate provision[1] is made compelling her to give up (it may be weeks or months after an engagement) any "wounded, sick, or shipwrecked" who may be on board. This shocking article speaks of demanding *la remise:* and it may be possible, therefore, to read it in a satisfactory way as applying solely to a request for the "return" of the belligerent's *own* sick and wounded. When the *Alabama* was sunk, the Federals claimed the men whom the *Deerhound* had picked up. Lord Russell replied that British seamen were not accustomed to give up those whom they had rescued to their enemies. When a Russian squadron was destroyed by the Japanese, the British, French, and Italian commanders on the station received and retained the survivors. The position of a British sailor who is forced to give up men whom he has rescued at his own life's risk to perhaps

[1] Article 12 of 1907.

unscrupulous enemies, or enemies who may be compelled by circumstances to starve or drown them, is not an enviable one, nor one in accordance with our traditions. Again, men may be wrecked by tempest. If they are belligerents, their rescuers are bound to hold them at the disposition of the other belligerent![1]

Rescue "Un-neutral."—Internment—The platonic provisions for the immunity of hospital ships are as dust in the balance compared with this positive enactment on the side of inhumanity. We can never admit that the rescue of drowning men is an "un-neutral service." And in historic fact it has never been so considered. That many would like to consider it such is irrelevant.

The practice of internment had not, previously to 1899, been introduced at sea. It was novel, even on land, and rather a startling duty for a neutral. To entertain an organised force within its territory was clearly impossible. But it might well have been considered sufficient to disarm and disperse it. Why should its members be imprisoned? In the case of a ship, or a body of sailors, the case is a great deal stronger. An army is out of place in a friend's territory; a ship is not. Resort to friendly ports is the commonest thing in the world for a man-of-war. An armed body of soldiers is capable of immediate action. A body of shipwrecked sailors is not: they have lost their warlike machine. Yet these Conventions, pervaded by a militaristic spirit, and ignoring maritime considerations, proceed to assimilate ships and sailors to defeated troops. Convention XIII. of 1907 (Article

[1] Great Britain understands the article as applying solely to rescue "during or after a naval engagement." But a ship may be wrecked long after she has been in action.

RESCUE AND INTERNMENT 215

24) permits the internment of every ship, with its personnel, which does not leave when it should. And it must leave within twenty-four hours "or the time prescribed by the law of the place,"[1] even if it sails to certain destruction. The continued presence of the *Goeben* and *Breslau* in Constantinople has been considered obnoxious to this article. But it cannot apply to a ship which has ceased to be the ship of a belligerent, and has been taken into the neutral's own navy.[2] It is entirely facultative. It only provides a means whereby the neutral can more readily do its duty of not affording a "base of operations" to the belligerent. "La puissance neutre a le droit," to prevent the ship from leaving port. But the neutral power is not bound to adopt this measure. It alone (subject to remonstrance in a proper case) is the judge of how long it will allow a belligerent to remain. Its law may vary the rule of twenty-four hours established by the Convention (Arts. 12, 13, not accepted by Germany). And if it chooses to purchase or to destroy rather than to intern, it is free to do so, so far as the Convention is concerned.

So far, there is no objection to the Article. But it is probable that the express mention of twenty-four hours, and of internment, will bring

[1] This saving offers a wide loophole for complaisance.

[2] It has also been urged that the transfer of these ships was contrary to the Declaration of London, Article 56. But, from its mention of "presumptions"—which imply a trial—it is certain that this article applies only to the transfer of merchantmen. The motives of a sovereign state in buying a ship for its navy cannot be impeached. In the *Minerva* (*Knuttel*) (1807 6 C.R. 396) the purchaser was a sovereign; but the intention was to employ the ship in trade—the trade of France.

about a feeling that it is the duty of a neutral to intern every belligerent ship with its people after twenty-four hours, even if a hostile squadron is waiting for it outside. This is really to put a premium on superior power; a warship is at home in a friendly harbour, and so long as she does not make it a regular offensive base, we cannot see that her immediate internment is just or politic. It is certainly not called for by the precedents of history, which are the only sure guide.

Article 13 of Convention X. of 1907 goes further. If it is a man-of-war that picks up wounded, sick, or shipwrecked sailors, they *must* be interned. By Article 15 distressed mariners landed at a neutral port are to be similarly treated. Holland has held (on Renault's authority[1]) this inapplicable in the case of the survivors of the *Aboukir* and her consorts. She regards it as applying solely to the case of a belligerent vessel discharging her sick, wounded, or shipwrecked men there.[2] And in this case it was a Dutch ship that brought them. A German might have stopped them *en route:* but they were safe on landing. The article is as badly drafted as any in the Convention, which is saying much; but it is general in terms.[3] Argentina interned the survivors of the *Cap Trafalgar*, who were landed by German boats. Would sailors have to be interned who were

[1] See Pearce Higgins, *The Hague Peace Conventions*, p. 391.

[2] Does she *débarquer des naufragés* when it is she herself that is stranded, and they swim ashore?

[3] Norway was reported to have interned naval and military passengers found on board a stranded British ship, the *Warsaw*. So strong a step to take in the opposite direction from that taken by the Dutch was at once abandoned, if ever contemplated.

landed by their enemies? It would be a *reductio ad absurdum* to allow the latter to turn neutral countries into convenient prisons. An extraordinary provision in Article 9 of 1899[1] allows a captor permanently to neutralise his prisoners by sending them to a port of their own country. As it might be the only thing to do with them, short of drowning them, we have here again a premium for captors.

Can a captor, under extreme exigencies of warfare, kill his prisoners? It is not so expressed, nor are reprisals expressly admitted. But it is scarcely to be doubted that such possibilities are tacitly understood.

Naval Bombardment.—By H. C. 1907 (No. 9), the bombardment by naval forces of towns and buildings which are not "defended" is prohibited. But workshops and "installations" calculated to be useful to the hostile army or navy may (*inter alia*) be bombarded, and the commander is not to be blamed if he accidentally hits something else. Military and naval establishments and *matériel* he can of course destroy. Whether a town is "defended" because a warship is present is problematical. It would seem not: otherwise the express permission to fire on ships of war in harbour would be superfluous. Whether it is "defended" when anchored contact mines are used off the harbour is a still more difficult question. Britain, France, Japan, and Germany refused to sign the Article affirming the contrary. Nevertheless, it seems difficult to justify an objectless bombardment, even of such places, when their occupation is not contemplated.

Mines.—The locale of maritime warfare is generally the high seas—the common highway of nations.

[1] 14 of 1907.

Prescription admits of the engagement by one naval force of another on this highway. But it certainly does not admit more. A new usage cannot be recognised as valid merely because there is no authority against it. Lamb's schoolboy who justified a highly startling procedure on the naïve ground that "he did not know the thing had been forewarned" has many grave imitators to-day. Never was it more necessary to see that each innovation in international law shall be justified by better arguments than that.

The first extension of danger came with the torpedo. Torpedoes were not exempt from the chances of being lost, and fishermen could thenceforward, as was humorously remarked, "earn considerable sums by not interfering with them." The possibility had to be envisaged that explosive objects might be found floating about. Then, ten years ago, there came the laying of mines at sea in the Far East. Chinese junks, completely neutral and innocent, and completely uninteresting to the Western world, were duly blown up; but no emphatic condemnation of this danger to the general safety was enunciated. The Conference of 1907 ended in covering it with a qualified sanction. Britain opposed it as entirely unlawful and improper —which no doubt it was—but she entered into a regularisation of it in certain events, when she should have refused to touch the question unless and until the freedom of the high seas had been accepted as a *sine qua non*. It would have been better—much better—to break up the Conference.

The Regulations regarded the use of automatic

contact mines. They recited themselves to be inspired by the principle of the freedom of the seas as the common highway of all nations. And they proceeded to provide for the use of mines, using the approved cloaks of aspirations for humane behaviour seasoned with exceptions and provisos of the "as far as possible" order, which are so familiar to students of these instruments. Take Article 3 as a sample. "When automatic contact mines are employed, all *possible* precautions *ought* to be taken for the safety of peaceable navigation. The belligerents undertake to arrange, *as far as possible*, that such mines shall become innocuous in a limited time, and, in case they are not kept under observation, to give notice of the danger zone *as soon as military*[1] *exigencies shall permit*, by a notice to mariners and also to governments through diplomatic channels."

The loopholes are obvious. In fact, the bucket is a sieve.

We may dismiss Article 2, which prevents the maintenance of a commercial blockade by mines of this kind. Article 1 interdicts (1) the use of torpedoes which do not become innocuous at the end of their run ; (2) the use of automatic anchored mines which do not become innocuous on breaking loose; (3) the use of floating automatic mines which do not become innocuous in an hour.

It will be observed that the second of these is the important thing. If mines are anchored they may be put anywhere. The provisions are merely designed to minimise the existence of mines as to which neither the belligerent nor anyone else knows

[1] *I.e.*, naval.

precisely where they are. Mine-fields are legalised on the high seas, and neutrals are not entitled to know about them, nor to complain of their inconvenience if they do. The legalisation is only by inference, but it is a plain inference: though Satow emphatically declared that "the legitimacy of a given act cannot be presumed for the mere reason that the Conference has not forbidden it." It is even said that Article 6 legalises mines which do not become harmless within an hour, or on breaking loose; for it contains an undertaking by the Powers to convert their existing mines "as soon as possible"—and that halcyon time might be long in arriving.

Mr Perez Triana (Colombia) recently has advocated in the *Times* his proposal made at the Conference to prohibit mine-fields altogether, except as a means of defence (*i.e.*, not to protect transports, but only to protect the coast within cannon range).[1] The criticism passed on this proposal, that it is difficult to distinguish attack from defence, is met by its concrete definition.

However, Marschall von Bieberstein's view prevailed. Germany placed mines in the armoury of Europe, and involved neutrals in the direst violence of war. We may quote his words to the Conference:—"Military acts are not governed solely by principles of international law." That we know. "There are other factors; conscience, good sense, and the sentiment of duty imposed by principles of humanity," which the officers of the German Navy would ever fulfil in the strictest fashion. This he observed with the utmost emphasis. Dutch, Danish,

[1] See Pearce Higgins, *Hague Peace Conferences*, p. 338.

Swedish, and Italian seamen are now in a position to see precisely what he meant. He would blow up their ships and throw them some coin as compensation. "As to the sentiments of humanity and civilisation — I cannot admit that there is any government or country which is superior in these sentiments to that which I have the honour to represent." That, also, we have often been informed.

Britain has been driven to counter-mine. We will frankly say that we should have been better pleased if she had not. As in the case of the Orders in Councils directed against the Berlin and Milan decrees, "illegality is met with illegality." That Germany has damaged neutral commerce is no reason for repeating the process. But it may well be that so long as neutrals made no effort to clear the sea of the German mines, they could not expect Britain to remain exposed to dangers from which she could only satisfactorily protect herself by similar means. Neutrality which submits to illegality from one party alone is not a complete neutrality. A neutral league to clear the seas of British and German mines alike would be fulfilling a plain duty. Had an American liner, with a full complement of passengers, been sunk in these waters, this is a phenomenon which we might have seen.

Signalling in Neutral Ports.—With the general duties of neutrality (discussed in the XIII. Hague Convention of 1907) we cannot deal in the limits of space at our disposal. The history of the topic is well known. Neutral duties had been brought to so high a pitch in theory, that the Japanese War of 1904-5 showed that practice must fall considerably short of it. Witness the voyage of the Second Russian Fleet to the East, when French ports were visited for days at a time. We will only observe here that belligerents are bound to refrain from setting up in neutral ports and harbours (*N.B.*, not inland) wireless telegraphy installations or any apparatus intended to serve as a means of communication with belligerent forces, whether on land or at sea (Article 5, end). Is the neutral bound to prevent them from doing so? The Convention does not say so. Nor does it seem to interdict private individuals from setting up installations or from signalling. If a station is set up as a general source of information, it cannot come within the article simply because it is used, incidentally, to transmit news to a belligerent vessel or fleet.

Merchant Sailors and Mails.—It was the usage in former days, when every ship was potentially a warship and every sailor a potential man-of-war's-man, to make prisoners of the crews of captured merchantmen. This is forbidden by Convention XI. of 1907, if the crew will give their parole (not required in the case of its neutral members). The same convention extends the protection of coastal fishermen and small coasters,[1] and introduces a new protection to the mails (whether neutral or belligerent, and whether found on a neutral or an enemy ship)—except in case of correspondence for a blockaded port. This cannot mean that the mail is exempt from examination and delay; yet it would be very easy, if it were

---

[1] Such, we presume, as the boats of the Aran islanders of Galway. *Cf.* the *Berlin*, L. J. Newsp., 14th Nov. 1914, 626 (deep-sea fishery).

once admitted that the mail could be overhauled, to suppress inconvenient letters for good. To open the mail-bags at all involves considerable straining of the Convention, which evidently contemplated an absolute inviolability. This convention has not been signed by Russia, and therefore does not apply to the present war (Art. 9).

Generally.—A neutral port, it must suffice to add, must not be used by belligerent men-of-war as a "base of operations," nor to increase their fighting efficiency (though they may repair). Russian torpedo-boats were, rather unnecessarily, expelled from Malta in 1904, though under repair at the time. Only enough fuel may be supplied to a ship to enable her to reach her nearest home port; and she may not have any more for three months.[1] It is very difficult to see how these provisions can be applied to the present war. Art. 28 of H. C. XIII. makes it applicable only when all the belligerents are parties to the Convention. In fact, they are all parties, but have excluded different Articles. It would seem that an Article excluded by any one belligerent is inoperative. For example, the first part of the proposition regarding fuel is excluded by Germany, and the second by Great Britain. But all these Articles are more or less interdependent, and it may be that no signatory is bound to accept the Convention with subtractions made by its enemy.

"Military Areas."—Another quite novel institution, adverse to the freedom of the seas, has been put forward under the name of "military areas." Its

[1] Convention XIII., *passim. Cf.* T. Baty, 14 *Journ. Soc. Comp. Leg.* 200.

very name shows it to be permeated by military, as distinct from naval, conceptions.[1] It first arose in connection with the Japan-Russian War of 1904-5. War correspondents chartered a vessel fitted with wireless telegraphy, and they were threatened with the treatment of spies if they ventured within the area of Russian operations. It may be very inconvenient for an admiral to have his movements known; but if one chooses to fight on the world's highway, one must take that risk. It is impossible to appropriate sections of the high seas as an arena, and warn off neutrals from their own legitimate resorts. Much was done, and more was threatened, in the war of 1904-5, which would not have been tolerated for an instant—as the Doggerbank incident showed—in home waters. The "arena" theory found a certain footing in the minds of publicists; and it has, as was to be expected, been viewed with respect by war colleges and some Admiralties, while even the Institute of International Law in 1906 expressed themselves against the transmission of wireless messages by neutrals within the sphere of action of the military operations: a limited opinion which was nevertheless strongly combated by Sir E. Fry.

Can an incident in the Far East, and the views of war colleges and navy boards deprive neutrals of the primary right to navigate the high seas in safety when and where they please? We do not think so; and we attach no special importance to

---

[1] We are well aware that the word "military" has acquired a technical sense, in which "military" operations include naval ones. The very fact shows how entirely, with this school of thought, the conception of land warfare is dominant.

the declaration issued by the British Admiralty, affecting to make the North Sea "a military area." All that such a declaration can effect is to put neutrals on guard: to inform them that their presence in such waters will be regarded as suspicious, and that, when navigating there, they will be more than ordinarily liable to charges of contraband trading or of un-neutral service. Probably no more is meant.

Napoleon, in 1805, ordered Allemand to sink vessels which might give information of the whereabouts of his fleet. The order was worthy of the law-breaker who framed the Berlin and Milan decrees, and who raided neutral territory to seize and shoot the Duke of Enghien. But even the fear of Napoleon was not sufficient to induce the admiral —himself a *mauvais sujet*—to sink the Swedish and American ships with which he met. Only a few Portuguese coasting shallops seem to have fallen victims; and Portugal was then virtually in alliance with France. Even over these proceedings a veil of secrecy was thrown, which was only penetrated within the last few years by the publication of the French Admiralty archives.[1]

"You could hardly expect," said Lord Macnaghten once, "to find in any judicial utterance a note of warning against an experiment which no one even

[1] *Cf.* E. Desbrières, *Projets et Tentatifs*, Paris, 1900-2. It is a marked feature of modern international law enormously to extend the powers of belligerents. They reached their low-water mark in 1856. Since then, their continuous growth to a pitch almost pre-Grotian has been oddly inconsistent with the simultaneous growth of pacific humanitarianism. We can only chronicle the fact, leaving it to others to explain the enigma.

P

thought of trying!"[1] And we regard with considerable jealousy these attempts, by mines and threats, to postpone the interests of the neutral pacific world to those of belligerents.[2]

With the subject of capture of enemy merchantmen we deal in the next part, as it is in theory competent to all members of a belligerent state.

[1] *Carritt* v. *Bradley*, [1903] A.C. 233.
[2] It was reported (*Times*, 29th December 1914) that Norway had lost at least 6, Sweden (outside the Baltic) 5, Denmark 4, and Holland 2 (besides many trawlers). No money can compensate for the loss of life, the great insecurity, and the interruption of trade.

PART III

THE CROWN AND ITS TREATY OBLIGATIONS

CHAPTER I

THE NEUTRALITY OF BELGIUM AND LUXEMBURG[1]

Neutral States and Neutralised States—The Treaties—Right and Duty of Neutrals—Views of the German General Staff—Right and Duties of Neutralised States—The "Benevolent Neutrality" of the German Proposals—The Duty of the Contracting Parties to Interfere—"Collective Guarantee" and the Doctrine of Limited Liability — Joint and Several Liability — The Public Law of Europe—Retrospect and Prospect.

"Such guarantees of lasting neutrality are therefore to be regarded as a landmark of Progress in the formation of a European polity; by means of them one withdrew the territories concerned, which by their situation were particularly threatened with being the battlefield in a struggle between great neighbour states, by means of a common provision against such an eventuality, and up till now no Power has dared to violate a guarantee of this kind. . . . He who injures a right does injury to the cause of right itself, and in the guarantees lies the express obligation to prevent such things. . . . Nothing could make the situation of Europe more insecure than an egotistical repudiation by the great states of these duties of international fellowship."[2]

---

[1] Three paragraphs of this chapter are reprinted from an article by Professor Morgan which appeared in the *Westminster Gazette* of Monday, 4th August. The rest is new.

[2] Holtzendorff, *Handbuch des Völkerrechts*, iii. (Part 16), pp. 93, 108, 109. This is a book of unrivalled authority in

We have placed at the head of this chapter a quotation which, for cogency of statement, it would be difficult to equal and impossible to surpass. Not that it stands alone—far from it. Were a symposium of the jurists of all nations invited, their opinions would reveal a complete unanimity of subscription to the words quoted above.[1] But it has been reserved for a German writer of high authority, in a publication which may be regarded as the most complete and weighty thing of its kind in the literature of German jurisprudence, to express with peculiar felicity and force the nature of the obligation which the German Government have now violated. We shall have occasion to drive home this self-condemnation by citations from quarters where we should least expect to find materials for it—namely, the official "War-book" of the Prussian General Staff.

Neutralised States.—Let us first consider exactly what the position of Belgium was. She was, in virtue of treaties to which Prussia was a party—they

---

Germany. The whole passage is a most powerful argument for the inviolability of such guarantees, and insists on the duty of the parties to them, *whether jointly or severally*, whether invited or uninvited, to intervene by force of arms whenever any one of them, or any other, disregards the guarantee. The original of the last sentence is: "Nichts könnte den Zustand Europas unsicherer machen als ein egoistisches sichzuruckzichen der grossen staaten von den Pflichten internationaler Gemeinschaft."

[1] One quotation from English jurists will suffice—it is typical of all the rest: "Such treaties are to be regarded as a part of the permanent system of Europe, only liable to be affected by one of those great revolutions which disturb that system at long intervals."—Westlake.

will be discussed hereafter—placed in the position of a "neutralised" state. Now a neutralised state is something very different from a neutral state. In international law a state has normally neither the "right" (in the sense of a protected right) nor the duty to remain neutral. Any state may attack her or she may attack any state. But a neutralised state undertakes the duty of remaining neutral, and in return she acquires the right to have her neutrality respected. She becomes, as it were, the ward of Europe. She is placed in a state of perpetual nonage, and the great Powers become her guardians, with fiduciary duties towards her and her estate. This position was assured to Belgium by the Treaty of London in 1831, Article VII. of which provides—

> "Belgium, within the limits specified, shall form an independent and perpetually neutral state. She will be bound to observe this same neutrality towards all other states."

By Article XXV. the five great powers—Great Britain, France, Prussia, Austria, and Russia—pledged themselves to guarantee this status. The effect of that pledge—*i.e.*, whether it be merely joint or both joint and several—we shall consider later. In 1839 another treaty was concluded which *inter alia* incorporated Article VII., and bound Holland and the five great Powers to respect (though not to guarantee) it. Holland at the same time concluded an independent treaty with Belgium to the same effect, and the corresponding article of this treaty was with others incorporated in a treaty of guarantee between the five

Powers and Belgium.[1] This treaty remains part of the permanent law of Europe, but in August 1870 the English Government concluded ancillary treaties, for the duration of the Franco-Prussian War and twelve months thereafter, with France and Germany, by which these Powers individually pledged themselves to respect the inviolability of Belgium.[2] These treaties did not reflect upon the inviolability of the original treaty. Rather they affirmed it. Prussia, in particular, showed "extreme eagerness"[3] to sign one as enabling her to clear herself of any suspicion as to her attitude to the parent treaty.

Right and Duty of Neutral States.—We may now consider with more particularity firstly, the duty of Belgium towards the contracting Powers; and secondly, their duty towards her. She acquired the right to be left alone, and she had imposed upon herself a corresponding duty. It was her duty to forbid, nay to resist, any attempt to use her territory as a basis for operations against any Power, or to use it as a means of passage for a belligerent force. For any state, neutralised or not, to connive at such attempts on the part of one belligerent would be an act of hostility towards the other. Let us quote an authority which the German Government regards as more conclusive than all the law and the

[1] For texts, see Hertslet, *Map of Europe by Treaty*, vol. ii., pp. 858-71, 909-12, 979-93, 994-5, and 996-8, and Martens, *Nouvelle Recueil Générale*, t. xvi., p. 790.

[2] For an excellent account of the negotiations, see Lord Fitzmaurice's *Life of Lord Granville*, ii., ch. ii., pp. 39 et seq.

[3] Fitzmaurice, *op. cit.*, p. 41.

prophets—the War-book of the German General Staff.

"The territory of neutral states is available for neither of the belligerent parties in regard to the conduct of the war. The Government of the neutral state must therefore, once war is declared, forbid passage to the subjects of both parties."[1]

It must, proceeds this authority, guard with the utmost jealousy against the troops of either belligerent putting a single foot over the lines of its frontiers. This is one of the few rules of war to which the military casuistry (*kriegsraison*) of the German Staff will admit no exception.[2] And as it cannot equally assist both belligerents, it must assist neither.[3]

So much so that if either belligerent violates a neutral state that state can resist such violation.[4]

Right and Duty of Neutralised States.—Now if all this be true of a neutral state it is doubly true of

[1] *Kriegsbrauch im Landkriege* (issued by the Prussian General Staff in 1905), p. 69; and *cf.* the Hague Convention, No. V., of 1907, on the duties of neutrals in war on land.

"The territory of neutral powers is inviolable.
"Belligerents are forbidden to move troops or convoys of either munitions of war or supplies across the territory of a neutral Power."

[2] *Kriegsbrauch*, p. 74. The sovereignty of the neutral must be respected "even though the necessity of war might seem to make such [a departure from it] desirable" ("auch wenn das Bedürfnis des krieges einen solchen verlangen sollte").

[3] Holtzendorff, iv., p. 658; and Vattel, iii., ch. 7, sec. 104.

[4] *Kriegsbrauch*, p. 74. In such case the neutral state "has the right to step in against such violation with all the means in its power."

a *neutralised* state. A neutral state can resist; a neutralised state *must* resist. It is not only its right to do so but its duty. For her to allow one belligerent to pass through her territory is to disregard her duty towards the other. So true is this that such a violation is regarded as the one case in which a neutralised state can depart from its duty of perpetual abstention from war. As a rule she can never make war—it was in virtue of this rule that Belgium could not be a party to the collective guarantees of the inviolability of Luxemburg.[1] But so paramount is her duty to remain at peace that she may make war against those who would disregard it. Nay, to do so is not regarded as a departure on her part from her duty of neutrality—rather it is the supreme expression of it. This, true of a neutral state, is doubly true of a neutralised one.

> "The fact of a neutral Power resisting, even by force, attempts to violate its territory cannot be regarded as a hostile act."[2]

Germany's Proposal of "Benevolent" Neutrality.—We may now proceed to consider the action of Germany in the light of these principles. On August 2nd, at 7 P.M., the German Minister in Brussels handed a note to the Belgian Minister for Foreign Affairs, in which he demanded a free passage for

---

[1] *Cf.* Article III. of 1867 : "Ce principe est et demeure placé sous la sanction de le garantie collective des puissances signataires du présent traité, *à l'exception de la Belgique, qui est elle-même un état neutre.*"

[2] H.

German troops through Belgium. It was accompanied by the following remarks :—

"Germany intends no kind of hostility towards Belgium. If Belgium is willing to take up an attitude, in the existing war, towards Germany of *benevolent Neutrality* (*eine wohlwollende Neutralität*) the German Government will bind itself to guarantee on the conclusion of peace the ownership and independence of the kingdom to its fullest extent.

"Should Belgium take up a hostile attitude against the German troops — in particular, place difficulties in the way of their passage by opposition from the fortresses of the Meuse or by destruction of railways, etc.—then Germany will be regretfully compelled to treat the kingdom *as an enemy* (das Königreich *als Feind* zu betrachten). In this event Germany will be unable to undertake any obligations towards the kingdom, but must leave over the later regulation of the mutual relations of the two states to the arbitrament of war."[1]

Germany, it will be observed, demanded the "benevolent" *i.e.*, the friendly "neutrality" of Belgium, and promised in return the "ownership" (*Besitzstand*), *i.e.* the maintenance, and "independence" of Belgium at the end of the war. This was to demand what Germany had not the right to ask and to offer what she had not the power, even supposing she had the will, to give. There is no such thing as "friendly" or "benevolent"[2] or partial neutrality ; the

[1] Belgian Grey-book, No. 20 (2nd August 1914).
[2] This curious phrase is a German invention, and is first encountered in 1870, when Count Bernstorff, the German

whole tendency of international law is to reject all such qualifications of the meaning of neutrality. Nay, more, Belgium could not accord "benevolent" neutrality to any one Power without destroying the very basis on which her neutralisation rests. The moment she favoured one Power she, by that very act, would have destroyed the guarantee secured to her by all the others. Not only so, but she would have committed an offence against at least one of them—namely, France. The "independence," therefore, which Germany offered her in return was so compromising to her as to be worthless. All it could mean would be that she exchanged the protection of Europe for the suzerainty of Germany.

The Vindication of the broken Treaty.—It remains to consider what, in the case of such an infraction of the treaty, is the duty of the other contracting Powers. Their duty is twofold: to refrain from violation of the neutrality themselves, and to prevent others from violating it.[1] They owe both a passive duty and an active one. It is the duty of the neutralised state to resist violation; it is equally the duty of the contracting Powers to support her in her resistance. It is also their interest. Such neutralised states are invariably by their position between the territories of great Powers "buffer-states," and by imposing on them a perpetual "close

Ambassador in London, calmly informed the British Government that it ought to have displayed "benevolent neutrality" towards Germany. As Lord Westbury remarked: "Benevolent neutrality is an absurd contradiction in terms."—See Fitzmaurice's *Granville*, ii., 67.

[1] And *cf.* Oppenheim, *Int. Law (Peace)*, p. 148; and Westlake, *Int. Law (Peace)*, p. 30, etc.

GUARANTEE 237

season" these Powers are thereby protected against one another. The security of these small states diminishes the risk of collisions between the great states.[1] The guarantors are "both justified and obliged"[2] to step in to the help of their injured ward if summoned by her. They are also justified even if not so summoned.[3] No one is so emphatic on this duty of perfect obligation as Holtzendorff and his collaborators.

But it has been argued that the guarantee is only a collective one, that there is only a "limited liability," and that no one of the contracting Powers is bound to interfere unless the others are also prepared to do so. This view was once put forward, we regret to say, by an English statesman, Lord Stanley,[4] in speaking of the "collective guarantee" of the neutrality of Luxemburg. But no one, we believe, has ever ventured to apply it in so many words to Belgium. Lord Stanley expressed himself as follows:—

> "No one of those Powers is called upon to act singly or separately. It is a case, so to speak, of limited liability. We are bound in honour—you cannot put a legal construction upon it—to see in concert with others that these arrangements are maintained. ... If they, situated exactly as we are, decline to join, we are not bound single-handed to make up the deficiencies of the rest. Such a guarantee has obviously rather the character of a moral sanction to the arrangement which it defends than that of a contingent liability to make war."

[1] Westlake, *op. cit.;* Holtzendorff, p. 109.
[2] Holtzendorff, p. 90.   [3] Holtzendorff, p. 90.
[4] Hansard, *Debates*, vol. 187, p. 1916, etc.

To the same effect Lord Derby. But the interesting thing is that in repudiating a joint and several liability in the case of Luxemburg, Lord Derby fully admitted the existence of such an unlimited liability in the case of Belgium.[1] In her case the words used in the treaty were, "the annexed articles . . . are thus placed under the guarantee of their said Majesties";[2] in the case of Luxemburg they are, "this principle is and remains placed under the sanction of the collective guarantee of the signatory Powers." The individual liability towards Belgium may therefore be said to be more explicit than in the case of Luxemburg. The whole argument as to Luxemburg, however, leads to a *reductio ad absurdum*. The violation of the neutrality by one of the contracting parties would, on such an argument, absolve the rest of all responsibility.[3] The Powers are clearly bound, severally as well as jointly, to protect Belgium. Whatever be said about Luxemburg, no one has ever denied this as to Belgium, and it seems to have escaped notice recently that in 1832 *two* of the five Powers (France and England) acting independently of the other three, who hung back, interfered to protect Belgium, at the invitation of her king, against Holland, on the express ground that it was their individual duty, under the general

---

[1] Hansard, vol. 183, p. 150.
[2] Martens, *Nouv. Rec.*, xvi., p. 790.
[3] See the scathing criticism of the argument by Lord Houghton (Hansard, vol. 183, p. 964). Professor Oppenheim (p. 602), we notice, says the duty is incumbent on the *majority*. But he is referring to a clearly collective guarantee. He admits that a joint and several liability may exist.

guarantee, so to do.[1] We think their duties towards Luxemburg are not less incumbent on each as well as all of them. It is obvious from Article III. of the Luxemburg Treaty of 1867 that the "contingent liability to make war" was clearly present to the minds of the contracting parties, and that they did not regard it as a mere "moral sanction." As our German jurist (who has no word too strong to say against this repudiation of solemn obligations) pointedly remarks: "One doesn't conclude international treaties merely in order to display 'moral sanctions' or duties of honour."[2] Lords Stanley and Derby, he points out, confounded collectivity with unanimity, and thereby would have destroyed the guarantee, for unanimity would always be impossible.[3] As for Belgium, the ancillary treaties of 1870 by which Prussia and France pledged themselves to observe their undertakings towards Belgium under the main treaty, so far from admitting that it implied a limited liability on the part of individual guarantors, admit the very opposite.[4]

In short, the contracting Powers cannot thus shuffle off their obligations by the evasive question, "Am I my brother's keeper?" They are bound not merely to one another but to Belgium herself. This is a fact which is too frequently overlooked. It should be remembered that the contracting Powers not only made a treaty with one another, but that each and all of them made a treaty with Belgium. They have not always waited on each other in this pusillanimous

[1] See the Convention of 1832 in Hertslet, ii., 909-12.
[2] Dr Gessner in Holtzendorff, iii., 101.
[3] *Ibid.*, p. 102.   [4] Thus Gessner in Holtzendorff.

way. When Germany applied to Belgium after the fall of Sedan for permission to transport her wounded through Belgian territory, Great Britain took it upon herself to advise Belgium to refuse the application. It was refused, and Germany acquiesced.[1]

Views of German Jurists.—England's actions—particularly in 1870—have spoken better than her words. There have been times—in the case of Luxemburg—when, as we have seen, some of her ministers equivocated. Even Mr Gladstone on one occasion spoke of the enforcement of treaties being conditioned by circumstances.[2] But the significant thing is that no one has criticised these equivocations so severely as the German authorities. To say such things about treaties is, they insist, to go perilously near making them inoperative; if a Power does not intend to fulfil a treaty, it should not make it. They have no words too severe for what they call such "sophistries." They point out that Bismarck attached the utmost importance to the neutralisation of Luxemburg. They warn us against the fatal consequences of treating lightly such insurances:

> "The dissolution of these protective treaties would produce the result that at the next opportunity countries such as Switzerland,

[1] Hall, *Int. Law*, p. 595.

[2] This, however, was exceptional. In a debate in the House of Commons on 12th April 1872, he strenuously opposed a motion for an address to the Crown "to take the needful steps for withdrawing from all treaties *binding this country to intervene by force of arms in the affairs of other nations*"—a motion which was overwhelmingly defeated. He insisted on the inviolability of such engagements as covenants of indefinite duration.

Belgium, and Luxemburg would be annexed and divided by their powerful neighbours, among whom again friction would then be more acute and war more frequent."

They remind Englishmen of the glorious words of Canning about the solemnity of "the positive stipulations of treaties." And thus we arrive at this singular result that the sternest condemnation of the violation of Belgian neutrality has been pronounced by the country which was the first, as it will be the last, to violate it. And by a strange irony the offender has pronounced beforehand the sentence on his own misdeeds.

Retrospect and Prospect.—We have thought it wise to go into this matter in some detail, because it is a solemn one—none more solemn ever troubled the conscience of a nation. Ever since the Treaty of Vienna placed it on record[1] that the neutralisation of Switzerland was in the true interests of European policy, the hopes of men have been fixed on the extension of these Truces of God to all the small nations of Europe. They seemed to hold within them the fair promise of that Eternal Peace which was the dream of the great philosopher of Königsberg. The Angel of Death might be abroad in Europe, but the lintel and the door-posts of these small nations would always be passed by. Friendly to all and partial to none, they neither pursued the

---

[1] "La neutralité et l'inviolabilité de la Suisse, ainsi que son indépendance de toute influence étrangère, est conforme aux véritables intérêts de la politique Européenne."

cupidities of their neighbours nor attracted them. They were the sanctuaries of peace, and for nearly a century they had been inviolate.

To-day one of them lies desecrated—her people wandering on the face of the earth, her hearths cold and desolate, her churches polluted, the grass growing in her streets. A once busy and thriving community begs its bread in alien lands or prowls famishingly among the blackened ruins of its homes. Some are caught up amid a cloud of enveloping cavalry and borne off into an impenetrable exile; husbands torn from wives, parents from children, peasants from their crofts. Others remain as the menials of the conqueror, earning a precarious immunity from outrage by the sweat of their brow. Her towns are held to ransom, her magistracy are hostages, her treasures are in pawn. All this anguish has fallen upon Belgium because she resisted the overtures of the seducer. It may well be that she will rise from her ashes purified and ennobled by her suffering, for the price of liberty, we have been told, is eternal vigilance.

> "Nur der verdient sich Freiheit wie das leben
> Der täglich sie erobern muss."[1]

It may be so. But behind all this lies an even greater issue—the good faith and public law of Europe. Had the great Powers failed to vindicate it, Europe would have been condemned to a dishonoured dotage, and of her it would have had again to be said what a great historian once said of her complicity in the Partition of Poland—*la*

[1] Goethe.

INTIMATING GOOD FAITH

vieille Europe finit par une banqueroute cynique.[1] Happily, other counsels prevailed, and she has vindicated her honour against betrayal. Europe is doubtless destined to go, in Burke's memorable phrase, through great varieties of untried being, and the future no man can foresee. But we venture to think that good faith, plain dealing, public law, being tried in this furnace of affliction, will stand higher than they have ever done before, and that it will again be the proud boast of our own country in particular that—

> "The great resource of Europe was in England; not in a sort of England detached from the rest of the world, and amusing herself with the puppet show of a naval power (it can be no better, whilst all the sources of that power, and of every sort of power, are precarious), but in that sort of England who considered herself as embodied with Europe; in that sort of England who, sympathetic with the adversity or the happiness of mankind, felt that nothing in human affairs was foreign to her."

---

[1] *Cf.* Sir Edward Grey's solemn warning: "If it is a case that Belgium's neutrality is gone, no matter what might have been offered her in return, then her independence is gone; *and the moment her independence goes, that of Holland will follow*" (House of Commons, 3rd August). And see the Appendix to this book, in which we reproduce the Memorandum issued by the Foreign Office on 7th December 1914, as to a conversation of Sir Edward Grey with the Belgian Minister on 7th April 1913.

PART IV

THE SUBJECT AND THE ENEMY

CHAPTER I

ALIEN ENEMIES. CORPORATIONS AS ENEMIES

Alien Enemy—Early Law—Safe-conducts—Declarations of Protection—Present Day—Protected, Tolerated, and Imprisoned Enemies — Corporations — Companies— Salomon v. Salomon—S. P. G. v. Wheeler—International Firms happening to be registered in Germany—Place of Business—Non-trading Corporations—Nationality of Trusts—Receivers.

Alien Enemy.—Who is an alien enemy?

The answer is very plain and simple. Everyone born within the allegiance of the King is a British subject. Everyone born within the allegiance of the hostile Power is an alien enemy. The principal qualifications of this statement arise from (1) statutory nationality, and (2) naturalisation. By well-known statutes of Anne, George II., and George III.,[1] the character of a British subject was conferred, whether with or against his desire, on every child of a British father, though born abroad, and, again, on all the children of his sons. It is doubted whether this capacity of conferring British citizenship on two foreign-born generations was enjoyed by naturalised British subjects. Piggott and Westlake[2] incline for the affirmative—the latter very decidedly, while Dicey[3] seems to think otherwise. Possibly if the child was born while the naturalised father was at the

---

[1] 7 Anne c. 5 ; 4 Geo. II. c. 21 ; 13 Geo. III. c. 21.
[2] Piggott, *Nationality*, 126, 302 ; Westlake, *Int. Law*, i. 228.
[3] *Law Quarterly Review*, vol. v., p. 438.

moment within the country of his old allegiance, the very words of the Naturalisation Act, 1870, prevented the possibility of his conferring British nationality on his offspring. Now, by 4 & 5 Geo. V. c. 17, operative from 1st Jan. 1915, the naturalised subject is put on the same footing with the natural-born, but the privilege always extends to one generation only. In this respect the Act is not retrospective.

Naturalisation, on the other hand, may, to a certain extent, make a British subject an alien and *vice versa*. This is not the place to treat in detail the various methods by which the operation may be effected. It is, however, supposed to be competent to naturalise an enemy, *flagrante bello;* though the converse assumption of enemy nationality at such a time is not allowed (*R.* v. *Lynch*[1]). By the Act of 1870, whilst a British subject was permitted to repudiate entirely his allegiance to the British crown, a foreigner would only be adopted *sub modo*. His duties towards his original state were recognised; and unless it had given him up completely, on naturalisation, he would not be regarded by us, "when within the limits of that state," as a British subject. Endless controversy has centred round the precise meaning of this phrase.[2] The position of the wife and children, remaining in the United Kingdom, of such a naturalised foreigner who visits his former country, in particular, was extremely uncertain. Here, we need only advert to the awkward position of a naturalised foreigner when invasion brings him within the lines of an army belonging to his former state.[3]

[1] [1903] 1 K.B. 444. [2] *Cf.* Piggott, *Nationality*, p. 113 *et passim*.
[3] Cf. *A. G.* v. *de Jager*, [1907] A.C. 329.

It would be an awkward position in any case: and now that an invading army is held to acquire no sovereignty in invaded territory, such a person would still be entitled, in English law, to the character of a British subject, and be bound by its obligations. For he is not "within the territory" of his former sovereign, though within his power. But now, by the British Nationality, etc., Act, 1914, a British naturalisation is complete and unqualified: secs. 3, 27.

One other qualification of the general doctrine ought to be noted. Is a person born within the territory of a foreign sovereign to be considered his subject when that sovereign repudiates him? We think not. The general statement that a person born within a foreign allegiance is a subject of the local sovereign, rests on the universal presumption that the law of that state is the same as the law of England. If it is shown not to be so, the law will not fix on an individual an allegiance which no one claims. Many countries (including Austria and Germany) test nationality by descent. Mere birth in Germany does not make a person a German. It is confidently submitted that English law will not consider such a person to owe a German sovereign an allegiance which he does not exact. The analogy of domicile does not hold. Allegiance is a political conception, in which the attitude of the sovereign in question is all-important. Domicile is a conception of practical convenience, as to which the attitude of the law of the place, in recognising it or not, is comparatively unimportant.

Earlier Law.—There is no trace in the earlier authorities of any theory that it is the place where a person dwells or trades, or dwells and trades, that makes him a friend or an enemy. The very conception of "domicile" had not then arisen. Had the case been otherwise, all discussion of whether and how far private violence against an alien enemy was lawful, could never have had any practical meaning. For if everyone living in England was entitled to the privileges of an Englishman, there could seldom or never have been any question about the matter. Nor could the burning question of the confiscation of their goods often have arisen.

Coke reminds us that to be born within the ligeance is not quite the same thing as to be born within the realm. *Calvin's Case* is on this point the great authority.[1]

In that case, as is common learning, all the elements of allegiance are thoroughly discussed. Alien forces, though within the territory of a sovereign and under his meridian, are not within his allegiance, for they are not under his protection. And so Perkin Warbeck (a Fleming) was tried as an enemy in arms. And the allegiance is personal, not political, so that no one who is born owing allegiance to an English king can be an alien. Thus, when the electoral prince of Hanover became king, Hanoverians born after that date were not aliens in England. The "treason hatched in their hearts," by the Spencers under Edward II., led them to invent "this damnable and damned opinion," that homage was due rather to the king's political office than to his person; but parliament duly condemned these tenets, and Coke seems to have hoped to hear no more of them. For

[1] 4 Co. Rep. 1.

an office—not having a soul—cannot execute judgment and do equity.

It is clear, therefore, that the alien enemy is determined to be such by his nationality, so far as Coke is concerned. And until we arrive at a very much later date, there is no hint of any general doctrine of determining the capacity of parties or their legal rights by the place of their establishment rather than by their simple national character, derived (in English estimation) from the locality of their birth. The only qualification to which Coke alludes is the possibility of an *inimicus permissus*—the holder of an express and individual safe-conduct.[1] He dismisses him in three lines and a half.

Generous Declarations of War.—But just as the original rightlessness of all aliens, as proclaimed by Littleton (*cf.* p. 268 *infra*), had given way under the exigencies of commerce to the rightlessness of enemies, so that newer principle suffered inroads under the same influence.

By the eighteenth century, we find a certain *temperamentum* introduced. It became customary, in the Declaration of War itself, for the sovereign to promise formal and ample protection to alien enemies being in the realm and demeaning themselves peaceably. To deny them rights after such a promise would have been contrary to good faith. Consequently we find Sir M. Foster[2] observing that in such a case they enjoy full protection for their persons and property in as ample a manner as the

---

[1] 4 Co. Rep. 1, 31.
[2] *Discourse of High Treason*, p. 185. *Cf.* Phillimore, *Int. Law*, iii., secs. 194, 195.

native subject. Foster's object was to estimate their liability to be tried for treason, and he grounds that liability on the correlative protection they enjoy.

So, if they are given an individual license or safe-conduct, they enjoy civil rights within the terms of the instrument.[1]

But it does not follow that if, in the absence of such a guarantee of full royal protection, and of any individual license implying the same, they are in anything like the same privileged position. If they are merely permitted to remain, all that the sovereign can certainly be said to guarantee to them is personal safety.[2] The Crown guarantees neither their possessions nor their contracts. It may, and it generally did, confiscate the former. And no right of action was or is allowed on the latter.

Present Cautious Position.—This tolerated, but by no means favoured, position, appears to be that of alien enemies in the war of 1914. By no clause in the Declaration of War has the King taken them into his formal protection. By no proclamation has His Majesty expressly or tacitly done more than to permit their presence subject to various arbitrary regulations. This cannot be considered as a general license to live on the footing of Englishmen, and it certainly does not amount to an individual license. The utmost that can be said is that it is equivalent to a revocable license to remain at the alien's own risk (except as regards his personal safety): and perhaps to carry on a strictly limited commerce. It is true that the Aliens Restriction Rules (21 (c))

---

[1] Foster, *ubi supra*, sec. 3.
[2] *Ibid.*, p. 186, sec. 4.

refer to the enemy aliens travelling to "business"; and an argument has been founded on this expression, in favour of the theory that alien enemies have been granted a tacit license to enter into valid contracts. But it is perfectly possible to have to travel to business without having power to contract. Minors do, not to speak of bankrupts. A license must be clear and specific, and a casual expression in a hurriedly drafted set of rules is altogether insufficient to establish it.[1]

The judges, tem. Anne (12th Jan. 1707), laid it down that an alien enemy might be a traitor, if with a hostile intent he quitted the country to join his own sovereign, leaving his family and effects under the Queen's protection. In this decision (questionable as it may be) they laid stress, according to Foster, "on the Queen's declaration of war against France and Spain, whereby she took into her protection the persons and estates of the subjects of those crowns residing here and demeaning themselves dutifully and not corresponding with the enemy." William and Mary, he proceeds, did the same in their declaration of war against France, and so did King George II. (Foster, *Crown Cases*, xxxi.). The case of *Wells* v. *Williams*, 1 L. Raym. 282, was decided in 9 Will. III. "These declarations," says Foster, "did in fact put Frenchmen residing here and demeaning themselves dutifully, even in time of war, upon the foot of aliens coming hither by license or safe-conduct. They enabled them to acquire personal chattels, and to maintain actions for the

[1] *Thurn & Taxis* (P.) v. *Moffitt* (*Times*, 17th Oct. 1914) was a case of tort ; *cf.* p. 305 *infra*.

recovery of their personal rights, in as full a manner as aliens *amy* may."

Coke observes that on a plea of alien enemy, "it shall be tried by the record if he be in amity or not, viz., a proclamation of war"—adding that a mere prohibition of commerce (without war) "as anciently between the emperor and the queen, doth not disable a German in a personal action." Hargrave's note is to the effect (as in Foster) that the king usually qualifies his proclamation of war by permitting the subjects of the enemy resident here to continue so long as they peaceably demean themselves; "and without doubt, such persons are to be deemed alien friends in effect." Such proclamations have become useless and dangerous, in the modern conditions of intermingling populations. The Crown now reserves full liberty to act, and does not tie its hands by any such qualification of the declaration of war; moreover, declarations themselves for some time went out of use. Accordingly, the present practice is simply to tolerate the presence of enemies, without leading them to expect any legal status. They may be required to obtain certificates or to register, but this is not regarded as a license.[1] On the present occasion, the "emergency" legislation passed for an extraordinary state of things has armed the Government with express statutory power to deal with aliens. It has availed itself of that power to restrict their movements, by penal sanctions. But the Crown has issued no word which would necessarily

[1] *Alciator* v. *Smith*, (1812) 3 Camp. 244: not cited, apparently, in *Alien Enemy Cases, Times*, 20th Jan. 1914, treating registration as license.

lead an alien enemy to believe that he is taken under the ægis of the state in as full a manner as any British subject. Can its permission to remain—itself tacit and implied, rather than express—be taken as an equivalent to the old proclamations of assurance? It would be difficult indeed to say so.

Alleged Rival Principle. — The suggestion has indeed been made, that apart from any such license or proclamation, the national character of, at any rate, a merchant, for civil purposes in time of war is ascertained, not by his allegiance, but by the place where he is carrying on business.[1] We believe the foundation for this theory to reside in a misunderstanding of a doctrine which is of a very special and peculiar character—the admiralty doctrine of forfeiture of goods at sea in transit to or from the enemy. This topic will be better dealt with when we discuss the subject of trading with the enemy (Pt. IV. c. III., *infra*, pp. 297, 306). At present, it is sufficient to remark that there is no trace of any such theory in any other connection.

Companies and Corporations.—We have seen that a political office had no soul or energy, in the eyes of Coke. Can a fictitious—(or, if one prefers, ideal)—person have a national character? Can it be said of a company whose shareholders and directors are all alien enemies, that it is of British nationality?

An ambiguity lurks in the question. That the organisation is "British," in the sense that it is subject to the ordinary rules of British company law, instead of to the peculiar rules which have quite recently been imposed upon the management of

---

[1] Cf. *Jansen* v. *Driefontein Consolidated Mines*, [1902] A.C. 484.

companies incorporated abroad, tells us nothing with regard to the propriety or otherwise of assimilating it to ordinary British subjects. The mere fact that those who carry it on must do certain things, and that their liabilities will be measured in certain ways, does not give us any guide as to its position in war. The fact that a motor-car is registered in England, especially if that is its only place of registration, may loosely be said to make it a "British" car. But, if it is the property of a Frenchman, it would be much more truly stated to be a French car. The fact is, the term "nationality" is in these cases used in a loose and popular sense. It would be extremely dangerous to draw legal conclusions from such ambiguous language. Suppose, again, that the company is first incorporated in England, or the car built there. Such an interesting event does not make the car or the company "British" in any sense comparable to that in which a British subject is British. We are told that an English incorporated company, being a pure creation of English law, must necessarily be British by nationality. There is no abstract reason why it should. English law may manufacture a conception. But it does not necessarily mean to invest it with any national virtue.

Moreover, supposing for the sake of argument that we admit that it does entertain that benevolent intention—what really happens when a trading company is incorporated? Is some ideal institution launched upon an expectant world—some imaginary-real entity which embodies the aspirations of thinkers, philanthropists, or else some abstract conception independent of any particular person's interests?

We know it is not so. The interests of the company are simply the interests of the shareholders. Incorporation is nothing more than a device to enable them to avoid paying their debts in full.

In maintaining the necessity of inquiring into the actual composition of a company, one is of course faced by the case of *Salomon* v. *Salomon*.[1] That case if it may so be said, was perfectly rightly decided. The legislature having enacted that Frankensteins might create monsters, we must put up with the consequences, and not complain if these enable persons to do by this means what they could not lawfully do otherwise. But the rule against contracting with an alien enemy does not rest on any unlawfulness of dealings with individual enemies, but on the hard fact that it is impossible to have litigation with them. They have no *persona standi in judicio*. Therefore it is that they cannot contract, or enforce or be held to their contracts. Bynkershoek[2] pointed this out centuries ago. It is difficult, if not impossible, for them to appear among the enemy. If, therefore, a company is managed by enemy directors, or if it is composed of enemy shareholders, the rule *eadem ratio, eadem lex* applies. The persons who are really and substantially interested in the concern cannot practically control its management and supervise the litigation by which alone it can enforce its rights. It would appear that the right course in such a case is to treat the company as an alien enemy; to sequestrate its assets, and to refuse it a hearing in the courts. Any other course would expose the

---

[1] [1897] A.C. 22. Cf. *Munkittrick* v. *Perryman*, 74 L.T. 149.
[2] *Quaestiones Juris Publici*, iii.

enemy shareholders to the dissipation of the assets by the managers and agents. In proper cases, of course, a license could be issued. And such a course appears to have the countenance of Judge Story. In *Society for the Propagation of the Gospel* v. *Wheeler*, His Honour says[1]:—"The corporation, as such, might perhaps have no authority[2] to maintain an action here. But in the character of its members, as aliens, we have incontestable authority to enforce the corporate rights. And it has been solemnly settled by the Supreme Court, that for this purpose the Court will go behind the corporate name and see who are the parties really interested. And if, for this purpose, the Court will ascertain who the corporators are, it seems to follow, that the character of the corporators may be averred, *not only to sustain, but also to bar* an action brought in the name of the corporation. It might therefore have been pleaded in this case, even if the corporation had been established in a neutral country, that all its members were alien enemies; and upon such a plea it would have deserved great consideration whether it was not, *pendente bello*, an effectual bar." Judge Story adds:—"Where the corporation is established in the enemy's country, the plea would *a fortiori* apply." He does not in terms deal with the case where the "establishment" is in the home country; but there is no reason why it should not apply there also. It is a little difficult to say what precisely he means by "establishment"—incorporation or operation—but in all probability he never imagined the possibility of a body of enemies continuing to operate under

[1] (1814) 8 Cranch 133.   [2] Not being incorporated in the U.S.

a New York charter. In the particular case he held that a corporation created and chartered for an ideal and special object by the British Government must, if it is considered in America as a corporation at all, be considered as a hostile British one. He found nothing on the pleadings, however, to negative the existence of a license or safe-conduct conferring a *persona standi in judicio*.

Enormous difficulty is created by the existence of companies whose character is more ambiguous than in the extreme case just discussed. So many elements enter into the affairs of a company—its shareholders, its management, its operations may all be under such varying and complex national influences —that it is impossible to lay down any fixed rule, and to say that in any particular case a company has a hostile character. What may with some confidence be affirmed is, that the company which contains members of warring nationalities ought to be wound up. A partnership between enemies cannot continue, because the communication which ought to be open between partners is interrupted. It is certainly impossible for persons who cannot communicate to carry on the affairs of a company, and it would be equally improper to treat any of them as bound by what the rest do in their absence. Presumably, therefore, the rough test of the place of incorporation will here be held decisive. The enemy owner or part owner of a car which happens to be in England must leave it to the mercies of the British Crown; and the enemy shareholder in companies incorporated in London, Edinburgh, or Dublin must on principle retire from their membership. It would be unfair to them to allow their capital to remain to be exploited by their late co-shareholders: and probably the ideal course in such circumstances would be for the Crown to confiscate the shares and realise their value. Lord Lindley thinks that *Exp. Boussmaker*, 13 Vesey 71, suggests that an alien enemy does not cease to be a member of a company incorporated by the law of England. But that was a case in which no continuing contractual relation was involved.

It was the case of hostile creditors in an English bankruptcy, and it is difficult to see how it could have been decided otherwise than it was. To have ignored the hostile creditors would have amounted to confiscating their rights, not for the benefit of the Crown, but for that of individuals, their fellow-creditors. To have paid them would have involved impolitic, and indeed impossible, communication. The proper course was taken, of setting aside their shares. It would be entirely in accordance with *Exp. Boussmaker*, if the interest of enemies in companies held to be impressed with a British national character were treated similarly. Merely to intercept the dividends is to leave the property at risk, and to put the hostile shareholders in the position of having their capital played with by the British ones. Ethically, that may or may not be defensible; but it is quite inconsistent with the general principle of security for enemy property within the realm.

The analogy of an insured person (who might conceivably be entitled to bonuses like a shareholder) in a life insurance company is not inappropriate. The decision of the Supreme Court of the United States in

COMPANIES INCORPORATED ABROAD 261

Stathem's Case[1] shows what is the right course in such a case, namely, to set aside the alien's interest, and treat him as discharged from all future liabilities and entitled to no future benefits under the policy.

The converse case arises of the position of companies incorporated in Germany, Austria and Hungary. If such a company has anything of a specifically govermental character, no doubt (in accordance with the dictum of Story regarding the East India Company in *S. P. G.* v. *Wheeler*, just cited) it would be regarded as hostile, whatever the nationality of its shareholders. But should the mere fact of incorporation in the enemy country have the same effect? Should the fact that A, B, and C, British subjects, have taken steps to be permitted to trade in the German Empire with limited liability under a fancy name, be held sufficient to make it no longer possible to deal with them on those terms in England, and to justify the sequestration of their property here in England? It would appear somewhat pedantic to take such a view. A more complicated case arises if there are enemy shareholders in such a company. There might then be sufficient to justify a finding that the company bore a hostile character. But upon the whole, we think that the existence of a few hostile shareholders need not necessarily have this effect, and that the true rule to be followed in such a case is to regard the company as incapable of carrying on business, and to administer its assets on the principle of *In re Boussmaker;* and perhaps this might be the proper course, however numerous and influential the hostile

[1] *Infra,* pp. 279, 285.

shareholders are. Any other would be extremely unfair to neutral members of the company.[1]

Tax Cases.—The cases which have been decided in this country on the liability of a trading corporation to taxation—mainly income-tax—do not afford much assistance. The term "domicile" is used in the legislative enactments bearing on the subject, and is only appropriate to an individual. It was necessary for the courts to say what it meant in the case of corporations. There is no such necessity, in the present case, to interpret an inappropriate word.

The argument that there is some fundamental difference between a partnership and a company derives most of its strength from the fact that it is not the shareholders, but the directors who do in fact meet and consult. But is the case altogether unknown of a block of foreign shareholders combining to change the *personnel* of the directorate?

Place of Business.—So far, we have refrained from introducing the question of the place of the company's management and operations. If it is right to say that the legal position of a trader does not depend on what his allegiance or abode is, but on where he carries on his business, that might often be decisive of the company's national character. For a trading company is only created to carry on business. We shall recur to this suggestion later.[2]

---

[1] It has been said in America that there is a presumption that the corporators are of the nationality of the state where the company is (? first) incorporated. Unless this is a presumption *de jure* it is of no value. See *O. & M. Ry. Co.* v. *Wheeler*, 1 Black 286; *Merrick* v. *Van Santrood*, (1866) 34 N.Y. 208, 8 Barbour 574; *N.Y.* v. *Cent. Ry. of N.J.*, (1876) 48 Barbour 478. [2] *Infra*, p. 325.

It will be sufficient to say here that there is no real ground for it. National character as it affects trade is no such singular and artificial modification of national character as it affects personal duty.

Non-trading Corporations. — Corporations established as a mere device for enabling persons to trade without paying their debts are comparatively easy to discuss. The ideal corporations which stand for the accomplishment of interests not exclusively private are in a much more difficult position. If, as we have said, they subserve any governmental aim, there is no doubt of their national character.[1] This covers municipalities, colonising companies, etc., etc. But the mere fact of incorporation in the hostile country ought not to have this effect. In fact, there is this dilemma before the advocates of such a theory. Either the foreign corporation has no legal existence in the United Kingdom [2]—in which case, as Story remarks, the Court will have to consider who are the individual members of the corporation—or else it exists in the eye of the law as a corporation, in which case it is incorporated by British law, and is entitled to be considered a British company. Owing its existence in England to a provision of British law as much as any ordinary British company does, it is immaterial whether the conditions of that existence are (as in the ordinary case) the filing of a memorandum, or the grant of a charter, or (as in this special case) the performance of certain acts abroad.

[1] *Per* Story, J., in *S. P. G.* v. *Wheeler*.
[2] Cf. *Stevens* v. *Phœnix Insce. Co.*, (1869) 41 N.Y. 150, *per* Mason, J. :—"A corporation can have no existence out of the bounds of the sovereignty by which it was created."

We may dismiss, therefore, the suggestion that the mere fact of incorporation in the hostile country is sufficient to brand a corporation with the character of an enemy. If the *personnel*, management, and operations of the corporation are in the hostile territory, the hostile character will attach. And in Story's opinion, it is the place of management, rather than that of immediate activity, that seems to be the decisive feature. *The Society for the Propagation of the Gospel* v. *Wheeler* was the case of a body chartered for religious purposes in England and composed solely of British subjects. Its operations were at that date (1813) mainly limited to British territory—but it must have operated in American territory, or it would not have required to occupy property in the state of New York. The fact that its operations extended to the territory of that state was not held to divest it in any degree of its British character: and Story, J., declared it without hesitation to be an alien hostile corporation.

In short, we believe the question to be one of fact. Are the foreign elements, duly weighed—the act and place of incorporation, the place of management, the nationality and civil domicile of the corporators, and particularly of the directorate, the objects of the corporation, and the regions of its activity—such as to impress it with a distinctively national character? It would be too much to say, "such as to make some one national character on the whole preponderate." There must be a distinct and overwhelming preponderance of the hostile element—and such existed in the case before Story.

This is consistent with the case of the English

Roman Catholic colleges and the Irish Roman Catholic colleges in France.[1] These were voluntary associations incorporated, if at all, by the law of the States of the Church.[2] All their operations were carried on in France, and their members were British subjects. They were held to be foreign corporations, and not entitled to the compensation provided by a treaty for "British subjects." Counsel for the respondent commissioners in the *English Colleges* case lay stress on the actual or presumed French charters. But in Lord Gifford's delivery of the opinion[3] of the Privy Council no reference is made to this. Stress is solely laid on the fact of the establishments and their revenues being under the control of the French government, although contributed by and administered by British subjects. In the *Irish Colleges* case, Leach, M.R., in a characteristically confused opinion, substantially adopts Lord Gifford's view. Though he speaks of the associations as being formed under the authority of the king, what he means is (as he goes on to say) that the French government in fact controlled these establishments.

Could a trust be said to have a nationality? or a *fidei-commissum* jointly created by several persons of different nationalities and undertaken jointly by several persons of the like description? To put the question is to answer it. Ideal conceptions have no

---

[1] 2 Knapp, 23, 51.
[2] Except as to St Omer, and the seminary at Paris, in which cases Louis XV. seems to have granted a charter.
[3] Expressly stated to be concurred in by the Lord Chancellor and the Chief Justice of the K.B. (Brougham and Denman).

nationality unless they are identified substantially with one particular state.

So far as the particular objects of the Proclamation of 9th September on Trading with the Enemy (whatever they may be) are concerned, "enemy character" attaches only to companies incorporated in an enemy country. Apparently a British company can obtain money from England *in Germany*, even though its shareholders are all Germans!

Under the Trading with the Enemy Act, 1914, the Court has power to appoint a receiver of *any* firm or company to carry it on in the public interest, in cases where its management is prejudicially affected by the war, at the request of the Board of Trade. This power has been exercised (*Times*, 21st October 1914). It was intimated that such applications might be made summarily on motion. We cannot think that such a receiver as was here appointed could bind his absent enemy principals if they were a firm. As they were a company incorporated and operating in England, this difficulty scarcely arose. The Court can give him leave to borrow money, and to create charges—even in priority to existing ones. But presumably property abroad cannot be affected.

In *Continental, etc., Ltd.* v. *Tilling, Ltd.* (*Times*, 24th November 1914, affirmed, diss. Buckley, L.J., *ib.*, 20th January 1914), Lush, J., held that a corporation created here was in the position of a British subject for purposes of suit. Subsequently (27th November), an Act was passed restricting the incorporation of new companies, and requiring the immediate disclosure of hostile interests in old ones.

CHAPTER II

CONTRACTS WITH ALIEN ENEMIES

Early Law — Littleton — Coke — Later Doctrine — *Wells v. Williams* — *Alsenius v. Nygren* — Particularity of Pleading — Suits by Agents and Trustees — Prescription — Payment to Agents — Pre-war Contracts — Chancellor Kent — Bills of Exchange — Necessaries — Insurance — War pending Suit — Non-commercial Contracts — Enemy Defendants — Story — Attachment.

THE subject of contracts with enemies has a long and interesting history. It would take us too far afield to recount it at length; but something must be said concerning it.

The origin of the invalidity of contracts made with enemies must be sought in the fact that it is impossible for alien enemies to sue. As we shall see, the doctrine originally extended to all aliens; but that was in days when executory contracts were still undeveloped. In those times the alien was something of a *rara avis*. He was under the direct protection of the king, and we can scarcely doubt that he was protected with the strong hand and not by personal actions.

Such an alien enemy had no *persona standi in judicio*.

Brian, J., says in 19 Edw. IV. (Bro. Ab. tit. *Denizen and Alien*, p. 20), that an obligation made to the enemy of the king is void. The plea in the Year Book is that the plaintiff was born in the allegiance of the

King of Denmark, who and all his subjects had been enemies since the eighth year of the king. "Perhaps," said Brian, " the obligation would be void against the party, but the king should have it": which Brooke queries.

Coke's opinion of the rights of aliens comes under the curious head of villenage.[1] There are six kinds of persons who cannot sue. One is a villein. Another is an alien. Littleton had said, probably with truth, that an alien might not sue.[2] Coke boldly, and probably without historical warrant,[3] construes this as meaning an "alien enemy." "In this case the law doth distinguish betweene an alien that is a subject to one that is an enemy to the King, and one that is subject to one that is in league with the King. And true it is that an alien enemie shall maintaine neither reall nor personall action, *donec terræ fuerint communes*,[4] that is, untill both nations

[1] Inst. sec. 129 (*b*). Cf. *Thorington* v. *Smith*, 9 Wall. 1 (both parties enemies).

[2] And in fact it was questioned as late as *Pisani* v. *Lawson*, (1839) 6 Bi. N.C. 90, whether an alien friend could sue on a libel published in England. It is somewhat difficult to reconcile Littleton's view (bk. 2, ch. 11, secs. 196, 198) with the provisions of the Statute of the Staple.

[3] *Cf.* Pollock and Maitland, *Hist. Eng. Law*, II., p. 445 ; and note the then generally recognised propriety of a defendant being sued in the court of his feudal lord. *Cf.* also *Douglas* v. *Molford*, cited in Calvin's Case, where a Scots earl (tem. 20, Edw. IV.) sued like an enemy under a safe-conduct.

[4] Coke takes this expression (drawn from Bracton) to mean, "until the two realms be at peace." But it almost certainly refers to the expectation, always present in Bracton's day, that the crowns of France and England might come into one hand, and the parties thus be under the same allegiance,

be in peace. But an alien that is in league may maintain personal actions."

We have already traced the development by which in a limited class of cases, a power of suit was conferred.[1] Commencing with enemies with a safe-conduct, we saw an instance of such a case in *Wells* v. *Williams*,[2] where there had been an express invitation to alien enemies to remain.[3] We have instances to the contrary in *Alsenius* v. *Nygren*[4] and *Alciator's Case*, where there had been no such invitation. It is only necessary further to say a few words on other English cases—to explain the position of contracts made before war supervened—and to deal shortly with an American theory that it is only commercial contracts that are affected by war.

Particularity.—(1) By a series of cases it has been established that the defence of alien enemy must be established by the greatest particularity of pleading. Every avenue of escape must be stopped up, and not left to be pleaded in replication by the alien party.

The form of the plea was carefully considered in *Casseres* v. *Bell*, (1799) 8 T.R. 166, where it was stated that it should expressly negative the plaintiff's being here under safe-conduct. As long ago as 2 Geo. II., in *Oppenheimer* v. *Levy*, 2 Str. 1082, it was settled that it was not sufficient to plead that the plaintiff was an alien born at Vienna under the

---

[1] *Supra*, pp. 254, 271.   [2] (9 Gul. III.), 1 L. Raym. 282.
[3] Probably the motive of this indulgence was the desire to harbour the numerous and industrious Protestant subjects of King Louis XIV. Hall seems ignorant of it (*I. L.* ed. vi. 387).
[4] (1854) 4 El. & Bl. 217 ; 1 Jur. (N.S.) 16 ; 24 L.R., Q.B. 19 ; 3 W.R. 25.

dominion of the King of the Romans—" As by law an alien friend may maintain a personal action, as being allowed to traffic (1 And. 25 : Dy. 2 (b): Broke, *Denizen;* Yelverton, 198), it is necessary in order to abate the writ that he should be shown to be alien enemy . . . and all the precedents are *inimici dni regis*." Further back, in 38 Eliz. (*Watford* v. *Masham*, Moore 431), it was even adjudged, " Que alien nee south obedience del enemy la Roigne, poit aver accon de debt pur obligation and pur psonal choses." Kenyon, C.J., considering the defence an odious one, and relying on *Derrier* v. *Arnaud*, 7 Gul. III. 4 Mod. 405, held that it ought to have expressly negatived a safe-conduct. The case cited hardly bears him out: it was then a question not of substance but of mere nomenclature, whether *oriundus* could supply the place of *natus;* and in fact it was held that it could. A more conclusive precedent is to be found in *Hoppin* v. *Leppett*, (1737) Andr. 76, where a plea that the plaintiff was an alien born in Germany out of the king's allegiance was held insufficient: it should have expressly alleged him to be an enemy.

The same view as Lord Kenyon's was taken in America in *Clarke* v. *Morey*.[1] It is remarkable that James Kent, whose judgment in *Griswold* v. *Waddington* was so strongly against the continuance of contracts with enemies, should here have used such sweeping expressions about the continuance of commercial relations, and "the moderation which the influence of commerce inspires—*emollit mores, nec sinit esse feros.*" The Court held that the mere omission on the part of the U.S. executive to order

[1] (1813) 10 Johns. (Amer.) 69.

the aliens away, implied a tacit safe-conduct. Kent relied on *Wells* v. *Williams* for this proposition. As we have seen, there had there been an express safe-conduct, embodied in the Declaration of War by King William III.

A limit was put to this extreme severity of Kent and Kenyon in *Alsenius* v. *Nygren*,[1] where it was held unnecessary expressly to negative the qualified naturalisation, which could at that period be conferred by the certificate of a secretary of state. The general statement that the plaintiff was not here by license implicitly included it. A check was thus imposed on the tendency introduced by Kenyon to put artificial difficulties in the way of the defence. In fact, Kenyon's doctrine does not seem to have been received in the Court of Chancery, where a plea of alien enemy was upheld, without requiring it to negative a safe-conduct, in *Albrecht* v. *Sussman*[2] and in *Daubigny* v. *Davallon*,[3] where Plumer observed in argument that the same technical expressions as were usual at law had never been expected in equity.

Bacon (*Abr.*, *Tit. Alien, D.*) thinks that "if an alien friend comes here in time of peace, *per licentiam domini regis*, as the French Protestants did, and lives here *sub protectione*, and a war afterwards happens between the two nations, he may maintain an action, for suing is but a consequential right of protection." But he adds that the specific protection relied on must be pleaded. The instance he gives is one of a

---

[1] P. 269 *supra*. Cf. *Alciator* v. *Smith*, p. 254.
[2] *Infra*, p. 292, (1813) 2 V. & B. 323.   [3] (1794) 2 Anstruther 467.

definite and express invitation, and not a tacit one. And in any case, "the compiler," as the editor (Sir H. Guillim) of the fifth edition of Bacon observes, "seemed to have as little inclination to supply the deficiencies of his author [Gilbert, C.B.] as he had sagacity to mark or correct his errors." Guillim is "sensible that too many erroneous passages have been suffered to pass without observation." (But *cf.* p. 254.)

Suits by Agents and Trustees.—(2) As a British trustee or agent has a *persona standi in judicio*, there seems to be no reason why he should not sue in his own name. The historical grounds of the rule regarding alien enemies had, however, become obscure, and the practical convenience of not enriching them had become evident, by the close of the eighteenth century. Communications had become so much improved, that it was easy and common for the alien's acquisitions to be transmitted home to the enemy country. Consequently the rule was extended to suits by British agents and trustees.

In *Brandon* v. *Nesbit*, (1794) 6 T.R. 23, it was argued that the object of preventing an enemy from suing was to prevent the enrichment of the hostile power. In this case the nominal plaintiff was a British trustee, and it was urged that it was his own affair if he let the goods leave the country; but Lord Kenyon held that judgment must be for the defendant. In *Bristowe* v. *Towers* (*ibid.*, p. 35), no plea of alien enemy was put in, or the decision would clearly have been to the same effect. In a note to the former case, Lord Kenyon is reported to have observed that the Court was greatly confirmed in their opinion after hearing the latter one.

Both these cases were of policies of insurance on alleged French goods. But the opinion of the Court is quite general. In *Daubuz* v. *Morshead*, (1815) 6 Taunt. 332, a person was allowed to recover as trustee for an alien enemy. The defendant had, however, drawn the bill sued upon, as a prisoner of war (cf. *Antoine* v. *Morshead, infra*), and the bill thus stood in a peculiarly privileged position.

In *Flindt* v. *Waters*, (1812) 15 East 260, the British agent of foreign insurers was allowed to sue for a sum which had become due before the insurers became hostile. The underwriters, however, as in *Bristowe* v. *Towers*, had failed to plead specially the defence of alien enemy. *Harman* v. *Kingston*, 3 Camp. 152, shows that it is not a defence *under the general issue*, even if the foreigners are suing themselves, that they have become enemies before action. As we have seen, it must not only be specially pleaded, but replies must be anticipated with particularity.

Performance in Favour of Agents.—There is some American authority for the position that an enemy's agent established in the home country is entitled to sue for performance due to his principal. The difficulty occurs *in limine*, of whether he can be considered an agent at all. If partnerships are cancelled between subject and enemy, so must agencies be. And if the agency is at an end, the agent's authority is determined. But, conceding for the moment that it continues, can the agent enforce his hostile principal's rights? And are voluntary payments to him on account of his principal valid?

Questions such as those were discussed in *Denniston*

S

v. *Imbrie*,[1] where it was said: "We think that if the alien enemy has an agent in the U.S., or if the plaintiff himself was in the U.S. [to the debtor's knowledge], interest ought not to abate. . . . The debtor might have paid his debt *either* to the creditor or his agent, in this country, without the danger of violating his duty or the laws of the land." The Court adds that an enemy creditor may always secure his stipulated interest, during the war, by having an agent on the spot to receive it. It may be admitted that if the debtor chooses to pay in such circumstances, he may violate no law. But the question is whether he can be compelled to pay.

And the authority of the dictum, even to this limited extent, is weakened by *U.S.* v. *Grossmeyer*,[2] in which the Supreme Court laid down that—

(1) Intercourse during war with an enemy is unlawful to parties standing in the relation of debtor and creditor as much as to those who do not so stand.

(2) Conceding that a creditor may have an agent in an enemy's country to whom his debtor there may pay a debt contracted before the war, yet the agent must be one who was appointed before the war. He cannot be one appointed during it.

(3) A transaction originally unlawful—such as a person's unlawful trading on behalf of another with an enemy—cannot be made lawful by any ratification.

A Georgian (Einstein) was indebted to Grossmeyer, a New Yorker, for goods sold and money lent. Correspondence passed between them during the Civil War,

---

[1] (1818) 3 Wash. 396. Followed in *Ward* v. *Smith*, (1868) 7 Wall. 447. Cf. *Conn* v. *Penn*, 1 Peter C.C. 496.
[2] (1869) 9 Wall. 72. Cf. *U.S.* v. *Lane*, 8 *ibid.* 195.

and in consequence an intermediary bought cotton from Einstein and kept it in the South for Grossmeyer, who ultimately claimed it as his property. The government claimed it as having been dealt with in violation of the War Intercourse Acts. They succeeded.

"It was natural that Grossmeyer should desire to be paid, and creditable to Einstein to wish to discharge his obligation to him, but the same thing can be said of very many persons . . . and if all persons in this condition had been allowed to do what was done in this case, it would have produced great embarrassment and obstructed very materially the operations of the army." Admitting that an agent may receive payments for an enemy principal, the necessity for communications with the enemy territory, which existed in the present case, made it impossible for such an agency to be validly created.[1] For our own part we consider that they prevent such an agency from being properly supervised and performed. We therefore are constrained to prefer the doctrine of the English cases.

On general considerations it would seem that to allow an agent to sue, or to permit payment to be validly made to him, is improper.[2] If the rule that contracts with an enemy are cancelled is to be upheld at all, on grounds of national policy, it is surely as unwise to permit an enemy or his agent to get cash in England from his customers, as it is to permit him to do so abroad. True, the rule against trade with the enemy (*vide* Chapters III., V.) will

[1] Cf. *Don* v. *Lippmann, infra,* p. 291.
[2] This is now confirmed by *Maxwell* v. *Grunhut,* 24th Nov. 1914 (C.A.).

make it possible to intercept the cash, whether it is himself or his agent who is sending it to the enemy's territory. But this is a very insufficient protection, since it is only in a minority of cases that such interception will be physically possible. Through neutral countries, the conveyance can be readily and safely effectuated. Our opinion consequently is that the American cases which (as Mr Bentwich remarks) were civil war cases and not cases arising in international war, are misconceived, and that the interposition of an agent can make no difference. In fact, we hold strongly that the agency is cancelled, and that the question can therefore hardly arise, except in the one case where the agent is established in a neutral country, when of course the agency would still subsist.

Performance by Agents.—We are unable, however, to see that there can be any harm in the mere receipt of goods or cash from an enemy through whatever channel in England. This seems to be prohibited [1] by the Proclamation of 9th September 1914; but more dangerous things have been allowed. "If an enemy orders his agent in the North to pay a debt contracted before the war, I am not aware of anything wrong in this according to the public law of war. Goods might be seized in passing, but the appropriation of property or money already here is not prohibited." [2]

On the other hand, it is clear that a contract cannot be validly made, during war, simply by the interposition of a neutral or friendly agent, even though appointed with full powers prior to the out-

[1] When the enemy is residing or carrying on business in the hostile territory. [2] *Allen* v. *Russell*, 3 Am. Law Register.

break of hostilities. Where such an agent appointed by a Floridan had taken a lease of land in Key West, within the Federal lines, the lease was held invalid. "The transaction was conducted by [an attorney here], but it was none the less a contract between enemies, and so an offence against the law of nations."[1]

Pre-war Contracts.—(3). If a contract has been made prior to the outbreak of war, the hostile alien is none the less an alien and unable to sue. The remedy is therefore suspended, in principle, until he can do so. If a contract has been completely performed, or if a *quantum meruit* is due upon it, there is no difficulty about this, except for a doubt as to whether the Statute of Limitations runs against the hostile creditor.[2] But in other cases, where there still remains something more complicated than payment to be done under the contract, it would be going too far to assert broadly that all further execution is suspended. All performance which involves intercourse with the enemy territory certainly is so: and since it would usually be unfair to postpone performance indefinitely, such contracts are necessarily cancelled. But there seems no reason to suppose that in other cases the outbreak of war of itself interposes an absolute release. In the great majority it does, but for a further reason. In that majority of cases, performance is not only suspended, but the contract is again cancelled. These cases include—

(1) Those in which the continued existence of

[1] Loring, J., in *Filor's Case*, (1867) 3 Court of Claims, 36.
[2] Westlake, *Int. Law*, ii. 49, citing *Hanger* v. *Abbott*, 6 Wall. 532; *De Wahl* v. *Braune*, 25 L.J., N.S. Ex. 343. *Cf.* p. 293 *infra*

the contract is against public policy—*e.g.*, the insurance of enemy ships.[1]

(2) Those in which performance cannot be suspended without unfairness or inconsistency with the terms of the contract express or implied (including practically all trading contracts).

There are other contracts which may, though executory, remain in force. Thus, a German in Hamburg has paid for a series of architectural plans, to be prepared and handed to a specified builder in Newcastle. There is no reason why the contract should be cancelled, or even suspended, since it involves no communication with the enemy, no benefit to the enemy, and no injustice to anyone. The remedy is no doubt suspended until the close of hostilities: but it is dubious whether the delay in performance could then be defended. The case is of course different where the British party has not enjoyed the benefit of the contract. He cannot be expected to perform his part in expectation of a return at some indefinite date. Such a contract would be cancelled by the outbreak of war. Scott, in the *Juffrow Catharine*,[2] shows himself somewhat lenient to such engagements. Orders for lace, he says, take a long time to execute, and the manufacturers must have advances. Although the demand on that account would be suspended during hostilities, yet "it might be difficult to relieve the British merchant from the demand when the foreign corre-

---

[1] It is true that payments might be suspended till the end of war; but as Ellenborough remarked in *Gamba's Case*, (1803) 4 East 409, the enemy obtains credit from this accumulation of arrears.   [2] (1804) 5 C.R. 140.

spondent was rehabilitated, and restored to his right of action by the return of peace." He also observes that "during the present hostilities there has been a more than ordinary difficulty in carrying on any correspondence with the enemy's countries," and remarks that the Court has thought it not unreasonable to make some allowance for this." Under modern conditions of trade, when time is generally an essential feature, such cases must be few and far between.[1] Whether a contract would be considered cancelled out of consideration for an enemy who has paid his money or performed his undertaking, and finds himself obliged to wait indefinitely for performance, on account of the necessary interruption of communication, may be doubtful.

The doctrine of the suspension and revival of contracts cannot be invoked to revive a contract whose revival would be unjust. Instancing contracts where time is of the essence, or the parties cannot be made equal, the U.S.A. Supreme Court (*N.Y. Life Insurance Co.* v. *Stathem*, (1876) 93 U.S. 24) declined to treat a life insurance contract as merely suspended, though in *Kershaw* v. *Kelsey*[2] a less celebrated authority (the Supreme Judicial Court of Massachusetts) treated a lease as remaining valid. The latter case may be explained on the footing that a lease is a *jus in rem*, and (unless confiscated) a subsisting interest apart from contract. Kelsey of Massachusetts, in Mississippi, during the civil war took a lease from the plaintiff of a cotton plantation there, at a rent of $10,000, half in cash, and half out

---

[1] Cf. *N.Y.L.I. Co.* v. *Clopton, infra*, p. 286.
[2] (1868) 100 Mass. 561.

of the cotton crop. The Court brush aside Kent and Story and Johnson, as inconsiderate dealers in *obiter dicta*, and they rely on *Coolidge* v. *Inglee* (*infra*, p. 285). The contract involved no necessary transmission of property or cash from South to North, and thus did not necessitate any trading between hostile territories.

In fact, the whole doctrine of the suspension of contracts has little practical application beyond the single case where the contract has before war been completely performed on the one side, and nothing but cash payment is due on the other.

In the celebrated case of *Griswold* v. *Waddington*,[1] Kent lays down the substantial grounds of convenience, which lie at the root of the proposition that contracts between enemies are as a rule cancelled. His reasoning has been belittled, as unnecessary for the decision of the case, by those who would restrict the proposition to commercial contracts, or to such as contemplate the transit of goods from one belligerent country to another. They have, however, been generally treated as embodying correct views. The dissolution of contracts rests, indeed, on the same principle as prohibits the transit of merchandise : namely, the danger of allowing intimate communication between the belligerent countries. But it constitutes a different branch of that principle, not another aspect of the same branch. Communication may be independently involved in export, or in contract. It is not in contracts for export alone that it becomes dangerous.

[1] (1818) 15 Johnson (Amer.) 57, and the more valuable judgment of Chancellor Kent on appeal, (1819) 16 *ibid*. 438.

"The law has put the sting of disability into every kind of voluntary communication and contract with an enemy which is made without the special permission of the government. There is wisdom and policy, patriotism and safety, in this principle, and every relaxation of it tends to corrupt the allegiance of the subject, and prolong the calamities of war" (p. 482).

"It appears to me," concludes Kent, after a long examination of the continental and English authorities, "that the declaration of war did, of itself, work a dissolution of all commercial partnerships existing at the time between British subjects and American citizens. By dealing with either party, no third person could require a legal right against the other, because one alien enemy cannot, in that capacity, make a private contract binding upon the other. . . . If one alien enemy can go on and bind his hostile partner by contracts in time of war, when the other can have no agency, consultation, or control concerning them, the law would be as unjust as it would be extravagant. . . . Suppose that H. and J. W. had entered into a contract before the war, which was to continue until 1814, by which one of them was to ship, half-yearly, to London, consigned to the other, a cargo of provisions, and the other in return to ship to New York a cargo of goods. The war which broke out in 1812 would surely have put an end to the further operation of this contract, lawful and innocent as it was when made. No person could raise a doubt on this point" (p. 488).

"Shall we say that the partnership continues, during the war, in a quiescent state? . . . It would be most unjust. . . ." The power of the partners to control each other would be gone. "If the law continues the connection after it has destroyed the check, the law is then cruel and unjust" (p. 491).

The unfairness, on which Kent lays stress, would of course occur in many other cases, where the conditions would or might be totally different after the lapse of time covered by the war.[1]

The absolute inability of enemies to sue was affirmed in *Whelan* v. *Cook*, (1867) 29 Maryland 1. It was argued that as the plaintiff's rights were only suspended, it was error to dismiss his bill: but the Court held otherwise.

Bills of Exchange.—The general doctrine covers, of course, the drawing and indorsement of bills of exchange (*Willison* v. *Patteson*, 7 Taunt. 439). "It follows[2] as a necessary consequence of the doctrine of the illegality of all intercourse or traffic, without express permission, that all contracts with the enemy made during war are utterly void. . . . The drawing of a bill of exchange by an alien enemy on a subject of the adverse country is an illegal and void contract, because it is a communication and a contract. The purchase of bills on the enemy's country, or the remission and deposit of funds there, is a dangerous and illegal act. . . . The remission of funds in money or bills to subjects of the enemy is unlawful. The inhibition extends in every communication, direct or circuitous. All endeavours [at interposing third parties] have failed, and no artifice has succeeded to legalise the trade." The only difficulty arises when the bill has been indorsed for value to a person with whom the holder is competent to deal. *E.g.*,

[1] *Cf.* Hall, *Int. Law*, p. 388.   [2] Kent, *Comm.* i, 67.

a German draws a bill in favour of a British subject, who indorses it for value to another. It would seem that the original imbecility of the bill cannot be cured by such a transfer: although no doubt a suit for money had and received might lie for the return of the value on account of which the bill was indorsed.

Necessaries.—Contracts for their necessary subsistence made by prisoners of war are in a peculiar position. They are not invalid, but cannot be sued upon until the return of peace (*Antoine* v. *Morshead*, 6 Taunt. 237). Possibly the contracts for necessaries of tolerated aliens are in the same or an analogous situation. But—" If all the *détenus* were liable to be starved, it would be a ground for the legislature to legalise their contracts, but it would not make their bills legal"—*per* Lens, S., in *Willison* v. *Patteson*, (1817) 7 Taunt. 445.

Insurance.—In the great debate which took place in the House of Commons in 1747,[1] Lord Mansfield (then the Hon. Wm. Murray) made short work of the contention that it was of any particular damage to the enemy to refuse to insure his trade. Insurance is a paying business; and Britain would receive more in war premiums than she would lose in payments on policies. He alludes to the fact that the personal interest of the underwriter to save the ships and cargoes insured is put into conflict with his national duty to secure their capture, and repudiates the insinuation—" For my Part, I never heard that any such Thing was suspected: but on the contrary I

[1] *Debates and Proceedings* (Lond., 1770), p. 122. *Cf.* Bynk., *Q. J. P.* i. 21. See also *L. Q. R.*, Jan. 1915, "Intercourse with Alien Enemies."

have learned that some of the richest Prizes taken in this war fell into our Hands by intelligence communicated by those employed to get insurances upon them" (p. 129). The instinct of the nation declined to accept his eloquent plea. Since *Furtado* v. *Rogers*[1] insurance of enemy goods and ships has been regarded as an impossible contract, and has not infrequently been penalised by imprisonment.[2] In the debate alluded to, it was even alleged to amount to treason.

War Pending Suit.—If an alien becomes an enemy during the progress of the suit, it is suspended (*Le Bret* v. *Papillon*, (1844) 4 East 503).[3]

But in *Vanbrynen* v. *Wilson*, 9 East 321, the Court refused to stay judgment and execution where the alien had become an enemy after verdict.

In *Hutchinson* v. *Brock*, 11 Mass. 119, the alien had only become an enemy after suit commenced, and it was held that the remedy in such a case was only suspended, and that a plea claiming judgment for the defendant was misconceived.

"**Non-commercial**" **Contracts.**—(4). There are certain American cases, already alluded to, which proceed on the supposed principle that "non-commercial" contracts are unaffected by war. This principle rests on the assumption which, as we shall see, distinguishes a certain school of thought in the treatment of the question of trading with the enemy—namely, that the sole or principal object of the invalidation of enemy contracts is to prevent the commercial enrichment of the enemy. It was pointed out long ago by Lord Mansfield and

---

[1] (1802) 3 Bos. & P. 191.
[2] *Cf.* 21 Geo. II. c. 4; 33 Geo. III. c. 27.   [3] *Cf.* p. 290 *infra.*

NON-COMMERCIAL CONTRACTS   285

others, that, since trade is reciprocal, traffic can never do more good to the enemy than to the home country. The true reason of the rule in both cases alike is, that communication between the subjects of belligerents is risky, both to the individuals who undertake it and to the state which permits it. The foundation of the rule cancelling or suspending contracts is simply that it would be unfair to hold a person to a contract when he cannot appear and defend himself.

Nevertheless, on a defective appreciation of the rule and its reasons, American courts have upheld some transactions of a very extraordinary nature. The most remarkable of these decisions was that of the Louisiana court in *Moosseaux* v. *Urquhart*,[1] where an agent managing an estate in New Orleans for a Northerner was held to bind his principal and continue his agency during the war.

Coolidge v. *Inglee*, (1816) 13 Mass. 26,[2] is perhaps the earliest case in which this ground is taken. Jackson, J., held, " dismissing the idea of something mysteriously noxious and criminal in every kind of intercourse with an enemy," that only commercial (*i.e.*, enriching) intercourse was prohibited, and that other contracts might be allowable. And he held valid a contract for the purchase of a British license from a person who, it was alleged, was acting for a British subject—(one of those licenses which were so much reflected on by Kent, C., in the *Julia*[3])—as it did not directly tend to enrich the enemy.

[1] (1867) 19 La. An. 482.
[2] Over-ruled in *Patton* v. *Nicholson*, (1818) 3 Wheat. 204.
[3] *Infra*, p. 298. *Cf.* the *Ariadne*, 2 Wheat. 143.

N.Y. Life Insurance Co. v. *Stathem*, (1868) 93 U.S. 29, is a strong authority in the opposite sense. A policy of life insurance is not a "commercial transaction," any more than the lease of an office.

It was not a commercial contract that was held invalid when made by the attorney of a Confederate in *Filor's Case*.[1] It was a contract for the sale of land within the friendly lines. "The authorities have placed a construction on the extent of the meaning of the term *all commercial intercourse*.[2] It extends to *all contracts*, all pacific dealings."[3] Nor was it a commercial contract, but a mortgage, that was held invalid in *Hyatt* v. *James*.[4] It is said by Lawrence that "a power of attorney executed in N.Y. to transfer stock in a N.O. bank was declared by the Louisiana Attorney-General to be illegal and void."[5] So, in *N.Y. Life Insurance Co.* v. *Clopton*,[6] the distinction is taken, not between commercial and non-commercial contracts, but between contracts where there is no necessity (as there is in partnership and charter-party) for "amicable and incessant" performance. The insurance (in 1858) of a non-combatant Virginian cleric's life was here upheld, and the failure to pay premiums during the Civil War excused. This seems a mistaken application, by the way, of the Court's own principle. An insurance company is entitled to satisfy itself as to the observance by the insured of the conditions of the policy: and this

---

[1] (1867) 3 Court of Claims, 25.
[2] In the U.S. Acts and Proclamations.
[3] *Ibid.* p. 30.   [4] (1867) 2 Bush (Ky.) 463.
[5] Wheaton's *Int. Law*, note 176.
[6] (1870) 7 Bush (Ky.) 185.

cannot be done when communications are interrupted.

The Louisiana reports themselves contain an assertion of the invalidity of all contracts with enemy subjects, in *Hennen* v. *Gilman*,[1] by Ilsley, J. This was a case of a bill of sale given by Mr and Mrs Gilman, who were domiciled at St Helena, within the Confederate lines, to one Gregory, who was domiciled in New Orleans, occupied by the Federal forces.

"Contracts entered into between belligerent enemies are absolutely null, because they affect eminently the public order. . . . It would be dangerous for any nation in a state of civil war to permit that degree of intercourse to be carried on, which must necessarily result from trading and commerce. It would certainly interfere with the secrecy, certainty, and dispatch of military operations, without which every war could not be successfully carried on." Although trade and commerce are particularly adverted to, the reason for invalidating contracts—the danger of intercourse—applies to all contracts equally.

In *Philip* v. *Hatch*[2] the contract was embodied in a promissory note made in Texas, and drawn by an Iowa citizen and resident in favour of a Texan. The Iowan was not in Texas, but signed by an attorney. The note was given in discharge of a contract of purchase by the defendant's attorney. The Court does not limit its denial of validity to contracts entered into during war to commercial transactions. "All commercial intercourse, and *all* contracts, between the subjects or citizens of opposing belligerents are

[1] (1868) 20 La. An. 241.   [2] (1871) 1 Dillon 571.

wholly invalid"[1]: and Kent's "masterly reasoning" and research are expressly approved.

In *Brown* v. *U.S.*,[2] Story observed that "no principle was better settled than that all contracts made with an enemy during war were utterly void."[3]

That great authority, Nelson, J.,[4] observes that on a state of war supervening—"The people of the two countries immediately become the enemies of each other: all intercourse, commercial or otherwise, unlawful."[5]

In the American Civil War, a proclamation of 31st March 1863 declared "commercial" intercourse with the enemy illegal. But it was ultimately seen that this was not enough, and on 3rd July 1863 it was declared to be the purpose of the executive to allow no intercourse with the enemy, except that of a character exclusively military.

Suits against Enemies.—It is perfectly inconsistent with the whole doctrine of the suspension and cancellation of contracts, as well as with the substantial reason for non-intercourse (namely, the danger of permitting communication) and the historical reason (namely, the want of a *persona standi in judicio*), that an alien enemy should be capable of being sued during war. How can he properly defend himself? His position would be

[1] The stress on "commercial *intercourse*" is probably due to its having been prohibited, *eo nomine*, by the Act of 13th July 1861. See p. 286, note 2 *supra*.

[2] *Infra*, p. 296.

[3] And see particularly the opinion quoted and adopted by him in the *Julia*, 8 Cranch 181, *infra*, p. 298.

[4] *Cf.* Hall, *Int. Law*, p. 669 (5th ed.).

[5] *The Prize Cases*, *infra*, p. 299.

most unfortunate and most unjust. The case of *Dorsey* v. *Kyle*[1] may be adduced in support of the contrary assertion. But cases occurring in civil war, as this did, are not valuable precedents. The subject of the revolted states remains a subject of the central authority. Two consequences follow. The central authority need consider no restraints of International Law. On the other hand, it will be inclined to refrain from pressing hardly on returned prodigals. Prof. Bentwich, in his work on *War and Private Property*, though recognising this peculiarity, scarcely appreciates its full consequences.

It is on this ground that *M'Veigh* v. *U.S.*,[2] cited by Westlake (*Int. Law*, ii. 51), is to be explained. The resident (Virginian) Confederate owner of property did not cease to be in contemplation of law a citizen of the United States: he could not be deprived of his constitutional right to be heard on a claim for forfeiture of his property under an Act[3] of Congress. The Court, in a short judgment, expressed the opinion that an alien enemy could be sued, but the opinion was *obiter*, because, as was argued, "persons like M'Veigh, though rebels, were not alien enemies: they were enemies for the purpose of having war made on them, and of having their property confiscated if Congress took proper measures: still, they were citizens of the U.S., and they are not to be kept out of the courts of the U.S. . . ."[4]

So, in *U.S.* v. *1756 Shares*,[5] a Confederate was

[1] (1869) 30 Maryland 512, followed by Bailhache, J., in *Robinson* v. *C. 1. C. of Mannheim* (*Times*, 17th October 1914.
[2] (1870) 11 Wall. 259.   [3] 17th July 1862.
[4] *Ibid.*, p. 264.   [5] 44, (1865) 5 Blatch. 231.

conceded the right, under the Forfeiture Act, 17th July 1862, of disputing that he came within its terms.

Dorsey v. *Kyle*, moreover, was a suit grounded on foreign attachment, and was decided on the words of the statute authorising such process. "Every person who doth not reside in this state" is liable to have his property attached. The case falls a long way short of the general proposition that an alien enemy may be sued.

Support to our opinion is afforded by Story's note to sec. 53, *Equity Pleadings*. Discussing the right of an enemy to file a bill of discovery, he desires to distinguish two cases, in one of which a bill was allowed, and in the other refused, to an alien enemy. In the former case it seems, he says, to have been a bill filed by an alien enemy who was the original defendant to a suit at law. "Now, if the original plaintiff could proceed in the suit at law against the original defendant (*which it seems difficult on principle to maintain*), it seems just and reasonable" to allow the defendant's auxiliary bill. "If a country will suffer an alien enemy to be sued in its courts, it is against common justice to disable him from the use of proper means to defend himself against a dishonest or unfounded claim."

According to *Dean* v. *Nelson*,[1] a decree of foreclosure is inoperative against a person who has been compelled to remain in the enemy territory. The reasoning of this civil war case would apply to an alien enemy, though it was held[2] not to extend to a person who voluntarily departs and engages

[1] (1869) 10 Wall. 158.
[2] *Ludlow* v. *Ramsay*, (1870) 11 Wall. 581.

in rebellion. "The defendants were within the Confederate lines, and it was unlawful for them to cross those lines. A notice directed to them and published in a newspaper was a mere idle form. They could not lawfully see and obey it. As to them, the proceedings were wholly void and inoperative."[1]

"The proceedings," says Sir W. Follett in *Don* v. *Lippmann*,[2] "were altogether such as neither the Scots nor the English law would recognise. They were taken in the absence of Sir Alexander Don in the courts of a country where he was at the time an alien enemy, where he would not have been permitted by the law of that country to appear and claim any civil rights, and where he had neither property to be attached, nor an appointed agent to be answerable for him.

"All the cases in which the decrees of foreign courts have been treated as *primâ facie* evidence of the existence of a debt, have been those where the party did appear, or had full opportunity of appearing ... or where they had property situate or agents residing within the jurisdiction" (*Goddard* v. *Swinton*,[3] *Edwards* v. *Parcott*,[4] *Sinclair* v. *Fraser*).[5]

It will be noted that he speaks of property which could be attached, and of the representation by an agent, as elements which might have weakened the case. But to have an agent with whom one cannot communicate and over whom one can exercise no control is not very helpful. Nor is the process of attachment meant to do more than to secure the appearance of a defendant. If he cannot appear, it is devoid of purpose.

---

[1] *Per* Bradley, J.   [2] (1837) 5 Cl. & F. 6.
[3] Morr. 4533.   [4] *Ibid.* 4535.   [5] *Ibid.* 4542.

292 CONTRACTS WITH ALIEN ENEMIES

Albrecht v. *Sussman*[1] is the common case of a neutral domiciled and trading in hostile territory. Of course he was held to be an enemy. The only peculiarity of the case was that the consular character did not save him.[2] The illegitimacy of arguing that, conversely, an alien enemy resident and domiciled in a neutral country must be considered as a neutral, is well shown by Dana in his notes to Wheaton. It was, however, alleged in the plaintiff's bill that the defendant had attached goods of theirs in the city of London: and on this circumstance an argument has been founded in support of process against enemies. But the plausibility of the argument vanishes when it is noted that the goods were sent to London under license. *Quoad hoc*, the aliens were not enemies.

The American decisions, in the absence of much authority on those points, are tempting precedents. But the temptation to regard them as applicable to a case of international war must be resisted.[3] It is singular that Prof. Bentwich, regarding it as possible (mainly on this American authority) to sue an alien enemy, nevertheless also approves of the American rule suspending the operation during war of the Statute of Limitations. It is difficult to see why the creditor should have it both ways—why the statute should be suspended whilst the creditor is able to sue.[4]

---

[1] (1813) 2 V. & B. 323 (Plumer and Eldon).

[2] The same was decided in the *Baltica*, (1854) Spink 264, and *Coppell* v. *Hall*, (1868) 7 Wall. 542.

[3] *Cf.* now the *Alien Enemy Cases, Times,* 20th Jan. 1914.

[4] In *De Wahl* v. *Braune*, (1856) 25 L.J., N.S. Ex. 343, the mere fact that the statute would bar the remedy was considered by Bramwell insufficient to enable a British subject, who could not sue without joining an alien enemy (her husband) to do so.

It is unsatisfactory to undertake, with Bailhache, J., and the Court of Appeal[1] the protection of the absent enemy's interests. The safe course is to adhere the principle that he has no *locus standi*. Any other decision would deprive the Crown of its inchoate right to the enemy's property,[2] by leaving it to be appropriated by the private creditor.

In *Ludlow* v. *Ramsay*[3] this contingency actually occurred, but the government's claim was abandoned.

Prescription Period.—According to *Brown* v. *Hiatt*, (1870) 2 Dillon 372, the period of limitation is suspended during the currency of the war, even if it has already begun to run. And so in *Levy* v. *Stewart*, (1870) 11 Wall. 244.[4]

Confiscation for Subjects' Benefit.—The Crown had power to confiscate debts due to an enemy, and formerly regularly did so; but the practice has for many years been discontinued. Probably it can confiscate other *choses in action* as well: and in this case the contract would not be cancelled or suspended, if capable of performance in favour of the Crown.[5] It was suggested (in *De Wahl* v. *Braune*, p. 277 *supra*) that when a wife, prior to 1871, was a subject married to an enemy, the Crown might well seize the husband's rights under her contracts and enforce them for her benefit.[6] The marriage subsisted, for "An alien enemy is perfectly alive though subjected to disabilities."[7]

[1] *Alien Enemy Cases, Times*, 20th Jan. 1914.
[2] See Part IV., Chap. I., *infra*.   [3] (1870) 11 Wall. 581.
[4] *Cf.* p. 277 *supra* and Troplong, t. ii., *De le Préscription*, pp. 258 *sq.*
[5] *A. G.* v. *Weedon*, Parker 267.
[6] *Per* Pollock, C.B. 344.   [7] *Per* Martin, B.

CHAPTER III

TRADING WITH THE ENEMY

Origin and Nature of Prohibition — Traffic, not Contract, struck at—Bynkershoek — Kent — Scott—Story — Non-contractual Traffic—Increasing Importance attached to Financial Bearing—Penalty—Is Withdrawal Trade?—Continuous Voyage—Allies—Enemy Character.

Origin of Prohibition.—It is scarcely to be doubted that the origin of the rule prohibiting trade with the enemy was neither the abstract notion of the impossibility of any jural relation between enemies, nor the modern notion of the injury which can be inflicted upon a country by declining to trade with it. Examination of the cases discloses the fact that the origin of the rule lay in the danger of permitting unauthorised communication with the enemy. Besides the obvious danger of facilitating sheer treason, there is the further danger of leakage of information and honest unwariness. When dealing with business intimates, political caution takes a second place, and is relaxed.

According to the Black Book of the Admiralty, direction is made that—" inquisition be taken of all those who intercommunicate, buy, or sell, with any of the enemies of the lord king, without special license of the king or of his admiral."

Traffic not Contract.—This doctrine of prohibiting trade with the enemy is quite distinct from the rule which dissolves or suspends contracts with the enemy,[1] and appears to be more modern. We have a clear intimation of it from Bynkershoek (*Quæstiones Juris Publici*, 1709, I. iii.). Of course in the sixteenth and earlier centuries, an attempt at total prohibition of trade with the enemy had frequently been made. Thus, Queen Elizabeth, in 1586, proclaimed an absolute veto[2] against trade with the Dutch on the part of any nation—what would now be called a "paper blockade." Such pretensions subsided during the seventeenth century into the qualified institutions of blockade and contraband. Neutrals would not submit to the wholesale interruption of their commerce with a customer. But as regards the subjects of belligerents, they had to submit to the ordinances of their own sovereigns. And it became generally recognised that trade between belligerent countries was impossible. Bynkershoek gives as the principal reason the great danger and difficulty which foreign merchants ran in a hostile country.

"Quid valebunt commercia, si, ut constat, bona hostium, quæ apud nos inveniuntur, vel ad nos adferuntur, fisco cedunt? et an quis, quamdiu jus occidendi hostis obtinuit, cum mercibus ad hostem accesserit, et inter commercia hostis eum trucidaverit? id diceres recte factum? sed omnino cessant commercia" (Bynkershoek, *Q. J. P.*, I. iii.).

In the cases decided by the great masters of prize

---

[1] *Cf.* the *Rapid*, 8 Cranch, p. 163.
[2] A proclamation by Lord Leicester in April 1586 denounced the penalty of confiscation against all who traded with Spain: Bynkershoek, (1709) *Q. J. P.*, I. iii., *exteri vero tantum navium erciumque publicatione*.

law, the benefit to us of destroying our own trade is never explicitly urged as the ground of the rule. It is always put on the ground of the danger of allowing intimate intercourse.

Thus Chancellor Kent says:[1] "It facilitates the means of conveying intelligence, and carrying on a traitorous correspondence with the enemy.

"It is difficult to conceive of a point of doctrine more deeply or extensively rooted in the general maritime law of Europe, and in the universal and immemorial usage of the whole community of the civilised world.

"To suffer individuals to carry on a friendly or commercial intercourse while the two governments were at war, would be playing the act of government and the act of individuals in contradiction to each other. It would counteract the operations of war, and throw obstacles in the way of the public efforts and lead to disorder, imbecility, and treason.

"The idea that any commercial intercourse or pacific dealing can lawfully subsist between the people of the powers at war . . . is utterly inconsistent with the new class of duties growing out of a state of war."

And so Halleck (*Int. Law*, ii. 143): "This rule is not founded on any peculiar criminality in the intention of the party, or on any direct loss or injury resulting to the state, but is the necessary consequence of a state of war . . . especially [in the case of] the merchant or trader, who, under the temptations of an unlimited intercourse with the enemy, by artifice or fraud, or from motives of cupidity, might be led to sacrifice those interests."

Non-contractual Traffic.—As in the case of

[1] *Commentaries*, i. 66. *Cf.* Northey, A.G., in Forsyth, *Cases*, 252.

contracts, an attempt has been made in America to limit the application of the principle to commercial traffic, on the false theory that it is the enrichment of the enemy state that is sought to be prohibited. Such an argument was presented with much force to the Supreme Court in the *Rapid*,[1] and decisively rejected. A native American's agent had hired the *Rapid* in Boston to proceed to Indian Island, a British station on the borders of Nova Scotia, to bring away goods which his principal had purchased and stored there. She was captured on the high seas by the *Jefferson*. "Trade," said Harper, for the claimant to the goods, "is a commercial contract, or a series of contracts, of sale. Contract is of the essence of trading. Here was merely a case of removal by H. of his own property from the enemies' country to this." Pinckney, *contra*, argued that all intercourse was prohibited.

And Johnson, J., held that: "The universal sense of nations has acknowledged the demoralising effects that would result from the admission of individual intercourse. The whole nation are embarked in one common bottom, and must be reconciled to submit to one common fate.... If by trading, in prize law, was meant that signification of the term which consists in negotiation or contract, this case would certainly not come under the penalties of the rule. But the object, policy, and spirit of the rule is to cut off all communication or actual locomotive intercourse between individuals of the belligerent states. Negotiation or contract has, therefore, no necessary connection with the offence. *Intercourse*

[1] (1814) 8 Cranch 155.

inconsistent with *actual hostility* is the offence against which the operation of the rule is directed."

The Court admitted that it was a hard case. "But it is the unenvied province of this Court to be directed by the head, and not the heart." Marshall, Livingston, and Story were members of the Court, and presumably concurred in the decision.

Accordingly, in that extremely hard case, ship and cargo were condemned on account of a voyage which was being made from hostile British territory, to bring away the goods of a United States subject. There could be no question here of any commercial advantage, or of any exchange. It was all pure gain to the Americans. But the disadvantages of allowing any such communication outweighed such gain, in the opinion of the Court.

Sir W. Scott asserts precisely the same doctrine, in general terms, in the *Cosmopolite*[1]: "It is perfectly well known that by war *all communication* between subjects of the belligerent countries must be suspended, and that no intercourse can legally be carried on between the subjects of the hostile states." And in the better-known case of the *Hoop*,[2] he puts the interdiction of commercial intercourse on the ground of its giving colour for other intercourse.

In the *Julia*[3] (a case of identification with the enemy[4]) there are some valuable observations of the Massachusetts Circuit Court Judge, adopted by Story. "I lay it down as a fundamental proposition, that, strictly speaking, in war all intercourse between the subjects and citizens of the belligerent countries

---

[1] 4 C.R. 10.
[2] 1 *ibid.* 165; *infra*, p. 345.
[3] 8 Cranch 181.
[4] *Cf.* p. 390 *infra.*

is illegal, unless sanctioned by the authority of the government, or in the exercise of the rights of humanity. I am aware that the proposition is usually laid down in more restricted terms by elementary writers, and is confined to commercial intercourse. . . . Independent of all authority, it would seem a necessary result of a state of war, to suspend all negotiations and intercourse between the subjects of the belligerent nations. By the war, every subject is placed in hostility to the adverse party. He is bound by every effort of his own to assist his own government, and to counteract the measures of its enemy. . . . No contract is considered as valid between enemies, at least so far as to give them a remedy in the courts of either government; and they have, in the language of the civil law, no *persona standi in judicio.* The ground upon which any trading with the enemy is prohibited, is not the criminal intentions of the parties, or the direct and immediate injury to the state. The principle is extracted from a more enlarged policy, which looks to the general interests of the nations, which may be sacrificed under the temptation of unlimited intercourse, or sold by the cupidity of corrupted avarice. . . . It is argued that the cases of trading with the enemy are not applicable, because there is no evidence of actual commerce. . . . If I am right in the position, that all intercourse which humanity or necessity does not require is prohibited, it will not be very material to decide whether there be a technical commerce or not."

That high authority, Nelson, J.,[1] observes that

[1] *The Prize Cases,* (1862) 2 Black 635, 687.

on war—"The people of the two countries immediately become the enemies of each other; all intercourse, commercial *or otherwise,* unlawful; *all* contracts existing at the commencement of the war suspended, and all made during its existence utterly void."

The first occasion on which the doctrine of the military benefit to a belligerent of cutting off the enemy's trade with it was explicitly urged, appears to have been the case of *Brandon* v. *Nesbit,*[1] in which the Crown counsel put it strongly forward. It does not appear, however, to have weighed with the Court.

It is not until we get to *Esposito* v. *Bowden*[2] that we find much stress being laid on the importance of damaging our trade with the enemy. In that case, the question was whether the performance of a contract to load a cargo of corn in a neutral Neapolitan ship at Odessa for Falmouth was rendered illegal by the outbreak of war with Russia. It was rightly held that it was: but language was used by the Exchequer Chamber laying stress on the mercantile dealings with Russians in Russia which the performance of the contract would necessitate. "The payment of export duties would have supplied (the enemy) directly with the means of carrying on the war." Stress was thus laid, not on the broad fact of transit from Russian territory to English, but (1) on the assumed illegality of Englishmen having dealings with Russians in Russia, and (2) on the advantage to Russia accruing from the payment of export duties and stevedores' charges.

So, in *Kershaw* v. *Kelsey,* the Court holds prohibited

---

[1] *Supra,* p. 272.
[2] (1857) 7 E. & B. 764. Cf. *Barrick* v. *Buba,* 2 C.B. (N.S.) 563.

only such intercourse as involves submission to, or protection by, the enemy, or tends to increase his resources (including all commercial intercourse). It is submitted that these isolated dicta, not enunciated by prize judges, are founded on a misapprehension: and that it is clear from the case of the *Rapid*, and the language of Scott, Marshall, Story, and Johnson, that the trade is prohibited without the slightest regard to whether it is in itself a benefit to the enemy or not.

Penalty.—The penalty of such trade is confiscation of ship and illicit cargo, and of any cargo belonging to the same owner. Neutral cargo embarked in such an adventure must in general be released, whether the ship be British or not. The extremely fine and important point may be raised, whether British goods can safely be sent to enemy territory in a neutral ship. (*Cf.* p. 303.) The Declaration of Paris protects enemy goods on a neutral ship. But it says nothing about a country's own goods in that situation. On the other hand, it may be doubtful whether, by general law, a nation was ever entitled to supervise the behaviour of its subjects by overhauling neutral vessels. The *Jonge Pieter, infra,* p. 303, was presumably a neutral Prussian, and we take it that a Dutchman bound for Amsterdam could be obliged to give up British goods which were destined for Germany, and that any inference would be admissible as proof. The ship, however, in such a case, must be restored, since as a neutral she is under no obligation to refrain from the traffic.

Withdrawal.—A certain time may perhaps be allowed the party to withdraw, without subjecting himself to the penalties of trading with the enemy, or, in the alternative, of acquiring the hostile character.

Thus in *Roberts* v. *Hardy*, (1815) 3 M. & S. 535, Ellenborough held in effect that a British subject living (but not shown to be domiciled or trading) in America was not, pending his return, incapable of suit in England. We need not invoke (with Arnould, *Marine Insurance*, p. 129) the fact that he did not trade in America, to support this leniency. He was not domiciled there. In the *Rapid*,[1] however, the right was denied to the claimant of sending, after the outbreak of war, to the enemy country, to bring away his property. It might have been different, had he or his agent simply withdrawn with it.[2] Considerable division of opinion was manifested on this point in the *Venus*,[3] Marshall, C.J., energetically contending that such liberty ought to be allowed, and Story and Washington, J.J., denying it.

In the *Ocean* and the *Doomhaag*[4] (*Harmsen*) British subjects, removing home from Holland, were allowed to claim their share of goods belonging to their former partnership. But where there was no such personal removal, it was said that a license was the only safe protection for the withdrawal of the goods.[5]

Continuous Voyage.—Of course, English law being alone concerned here, and not the law of nations, the courts are not bound to limit themselves to the rigid presumptions of destination which the law of nations requires. Thus, in the wars against France and Holland, neutral trade with Emden, in Prussia, in whatever goods, was scrupulously respected; but

---

[1] *Supra*, p. 297, (1814) 8 Cranch 155.   [2] P. 163.
[3] 8 Cranch 279.   [4] 5 C.R. 91.
[5] 5 C.R. 140, the *J. Catharina*. *Cf.* the *Dree Gebrocders*, (1802) 4 C.R. 234, and the *S. Lawrence*, (1814) 8 Cranch 434.

British trade with the same place was stopped whenever the goods appeared to be ultimately destined for Holland, a few miles distant.[1] The same principle was followed in America, in the case of *Jecker* v. *Montgomery*,[2] where a U.S. ship was condemned for trading with Mexico, although actually going to Honolulu. (In this case, however, the charter-party was to deliver expressly to a Mexican port.)

Allies.—Allies are equally prohibited from trading with the common enemy. Since the only possible penalty in this case is confiscation as prize, this argues that confiscation is the proper and only normal penalty for the offence in all cases.

"**Enemy**" **Character.**—As to the question of who are enemies and who are subjects for the purposes of this chapter, the reader is referred to the discussion at p. 306 *infra*. It should, however, be noted that the national character of the foreign exporter or importer is here as material as elsewhere. It is not enough if the goods are going to, or coming from hostile territory.[3] We shall see in the next chapter but one that an extremely severe view has been adopted in 1914 of all intercourse of a commercial character with the enemy.

[1] *Cf.* the *Jonge Pieter*, (1801) 4 C.R. 79, and T. Baty, *International Law in S. Africa*, ch. i., p. 25.

[2] (1855) 18 Howard 110.   [3] The *Herman*, (1802) 4 C.R. 228. See the *Juno*, *Times*, 15th Dec. 1914: *Duncan Fox & Co.* v. *Schrempt & Bonke*, ibid. 19th Dec. 1914. In the latter case, honey was ordered by one British merchant of another, to be shipped from Chili to Hamburg. This does not seem to be a trade which the older cases would have touched. Cf. *Bromley* v. *Hesseltine*, (1807) 1 Camp. 75, as to lawful delivery in a neutral port to a domiciled alien enemy; and Campbell's contradiction in a note ("Ellenborough's bad law"?).

CHAPTER IV

PERSON AND PROPERTY OF ENEMIES

I. On Land. Person — Property. II. At Sea. Enemy Character—Tests—Nationality—Domicile and House of Trade—Political Enemy never treated as Neutral or Friend, though Subject sometimes treated as Neutral—Domicile means ordinary Civil Domicile, independent of Trade—Scott and Story quoted against Westlake and Dicey—House of Trade: Its Necessary Elements discussed—Mere Agency not Sufficient—Or Branch—There must be Trade *in* the Territory as well as *to* it—Case of Companies operating Abroad—Contracts and Captures—Confusion between Rules which (*a*) invalidate Contracts—(*b*) confiscate Traffic—Test of Enemy not the same in both—Admittedly, for the test of innocence in the former case is not alleged to be Domicile but mere Tolerated Presence—Technical Rules as to Ownership disregarded — Transfers *in transitu*—Ships—Goods—Declaration of London—Enemy Interests in Neutral Property—Neutral in Enemy Property—Charter-parties—Private Seizure—Conquest changes National Character—"At Sea."

I. ON LAND.

Person.—That an alien enemy who remains in this country without any express (individual or general) promise of protection enjoys protection for his person is apparent from what has been already cited from Foster.[1] It might be supposed that the protection

[1] Pp. 251, 253 *supra*.

of the criminal law is all that such an alien enjoys. But Lord Chief Baron Macdonald's opinion, confirmed by Story,[1] is that he has civil rights of suit: and not only in respect of his person, but of his property. "If the right," he says, "of suing for the injuries which they receive were not allowed them, the protection afforded would be incomplete and merely nominal."[2] It is fairly clear that the Lord Chief Baron here contemplates under the name of "injuries" wrongs independent of contract.

Property on Land.—In *Brown* v. *U.S.*[3] a cargo of timber laden at Savannah on board the *Emulous* was seized by a private person when unloaded at New Bedford, where the vessel had put in for repairs. It was released, the Supreme Court thinking that some express act or declaration of the U.S. government was necessary in order to make it confiscable. Story, J., thought that the executive had sufficiently interposed by ratifying the capture.

"Respecting the power of government," said Marshall, C.J., "no doubt is entertained. That war gives to the sovereign full right to take the persons and confiscate the property of the enemy, wherever found, is conceded." But the practice of treating debts as not confiscated, but suspended, showed that some active interposition on its part was necessary. In the absence of that, private persons had no power to effect seizures.[4] In *Fairfax* v. *Hunter* (7 Cranch

---

[1] *Equity Pleadings*, sec. 52. *Cf.* p. 253 *supra*.
[2] *Daubigny* v. *Davallon*, (1794) 2 Anstruther 467.
[3] (1814) 8 Cranch 110, *supra*, p. 44.
[4] *Cf.* (1865) *U.S.* v. 1756 *Shares*, *G. W. R. of Illinois*, 5 Blatch. 231.

603) Story held that an enemy might take by devise. Brooke (*Abr.*, tit. "Property") quotes a case in 36 Hen. VIII. where it was said that if a Frenchman was living in England, and then war broke out, none might seize his goods. This must mean " no private person," for Lushington (the *Johanna Emilie*, Spinks 14) entertained no doubt that the Crown could do so. An information of *devenerunt* seems the proper step.

II. AT SEA.

Enemy Character.—It is with regard to sea-borne traffic—and we are convinced, with regard to sea-borne traffic alone—that the profound modification of enemy character occurs, to which allusion has been made in Chapter I. It is simply impossible, for historical reasons, that the general capacity and status of alien enemies should have depended on where they lived or carried on their business. From the point of view of all but prize law, the alien enemy is the person who owes political allegiance to the enemy sovereign.

Nationality. — But in prize law there is a modification.

It is sometimes expressed by saying that in prize law the main test of national character is not nationality but domicile. And there are even loose *dicta* to the effect that, "if a man is a merchant of two countries, he must be regarded as a subject of each with respect to transactions respectively originating there." But, when examined, all these *dicta*[1] end in condemnation. They all mean that hostile resid-

[1] Subject to what is said *infra*, p. 308, regarding trade with the enemy.

NATIONALITY

ence, or hostile trade, will outweigh mere neutral nationality: not the converse. They do not, in short, mean that domicile (or trade) is *the* test of national character, but that it is *a* test of enemy character. So Chalmers[1] refers to the law of the civilians' courts —"where they hold that persons take their character from the country where they reside. Such is the rule in prize causes, where . . . an enemy's country makes all persons enemies."

It would be difficult to cite any English case in which an enemy's ship or goods have been released because he had a neutral domicile, or was trading in a neutral country.

The *Postillion*[2] was decided on a very special state of facts. Reprisals had been ordered expressly against the ships and goods of persons inhabiting the territories of the French king. This could naturally not extend to persons inhabiting neutral territory, whatever their nationality. The *Liesbet von der Toll*[3] is a curious case of a fishing-vessel. The owner was originally a Dutchman, but he had for seven years been settled in Prussia, and was apparently "a Prussian subject," though this character was conferred on him by residence. His claim succeeded: it is possible that Holland had resigned his allegiance, just as Germany at the present day disclaims those of her subjects who have resided abroad for seven years without leave. Or the indulgence generally extended to fishermen may have operated in his favour. At any rate, this isolated case can be of little authority in modern times, when an

[1] Forsyth, *Cases and Opinions*, 307.
[2] Hay and Marriott 245. [3] (1804) 5 C.R. 283.

emigrant no longer bids farewell to his country, but keeps in close and constant touch with his compatriots, through the medium of the cheap and easy postal and passenger services which unite the world.

Britons treated as Neutral.—There are indeed cases, of which the *Indian Chief*,[1] the *Emanuel*,[2] the *Danaous*,[3] and the *Ann*[4] may be taken as examples, in which a very different principle was asserted, namely, that a British subject might, exceptionally, be allowed to trade with the enemy's coasts, if he were established and trading in a neutral territory. This was an equitable modification of an otherwise rigid principle which bore hardly upon expatriated Britons in days when they could not divest themselves of their British nationality. Thus, an Englishman in Denmark and a Scotsman in America were permitted to trade with France without objection. But the generality of the language in which Sir W. Scott spoke of a merchant as being identified with the country where he lived and carried on business, misled the American court, in the *S. José Indiano*,[5] into giving the dictum a far wider application than was necessary, and into releasing the goods of a hostile Englishman because he was settled and carrying on business in Spain.[6]

Enemy not treated as Neutral.—This seems never to have been imitated in England, although it is fair

---

[1] 3 C.R. 22. [2] 1 *ibid.* 296. [3] 4 *ibid.* 255*n*.
[4] 1 Dods. 223. [5] (1814) 2 Gallison 268.
[6] In the *Conqueror*, 2 C.R. 307, the domiciled Danish owner had a French-sounding name. But he was evidently a Danish subject (*ibid.*, App. 4), "Peter Peschier of Copenhagen, a subject of H.M. the King of Denmark."

to remark that it seems equally impossible to find a case where such goods have been condemned.

Speaking of an export to England from Holland, Scott says: "A breach of native allegiance it could not be, as Mr Ravie does not appear to be a native subject of this country."[1] This plainly suggests that allegiance is important and domicile not conclusive.

In *Harman* v. *Kingston*,[2] Ellenborough, C.J., observed: "You have given no evidence where these persons were born, nor proved that they were living in a hostile territory at the time of action brought. You have not shown them to be enemies *either by birth* or domicile." Why mention birth, if domicile is the exclusive test?[3] And Lord Davey, in *Janson* v. *Driefontein Consol. Mines*,[4] says plainly that an alien enemy is "a person owing allegiance to a government at war with the king." So, again, in the *Indian Chief,* Sir W. Scott observes: "Mr Johnson is an American gentleman by *birth*, which is the circumstance that first impresses itself on the mind of the Court."

Long ago, in 12 Hen. VI. c. 7, dealing expressly with prize, the distinction is taken between "liege people" and "aliens." Domicile can hardly therefore plead the ancient and inveterate supremacy in Admiralty which Westlake would invest it with.[5]

Bramwell observes, *arguendo*, in *Esposito* v. *Bowden*, that the cargo there in question "might, even after

---

[1] The *Jonge Klassina*, (1809) 5 C.R. 301.   [2] 3 Camp. 152.
[3] This, however, was a case of suit, not of prize.
[4] [1902] A.C. 499.
[5] *Journ. Soc. Comp. Leg.* ix. 265 *sqq*. *Cf.* also 4 Hen. V. c. 7 : 2 Hen. V. c. 6.

the notice of the declaration of war, have been legally purchased from a British subject in Odessa, though not from a neutral." And Campbell, C.J., goes further, and says that, "even after the declaration of war, there was a possibility that the defendant's factors, without any breach of allegiance to the Crown of England, might have furnished the cargo from even the property of [subjects or allies about to leave Russia], which it might have been meritorious to save from the grasp of the enemy."

Phillimore's cautious statement is that "it appears" that the principal tests of enemy character for prize purposes are domicile and traffic. It is therefore perfectly possible to maintain that the statements of text-writers are too sweeping, and that their inferences are too wide, when they infer that an enemy's goods cannot be captured if his establishment is in neutral or British territory. Especially at the present day, when removal from one country to another is so easy, and when the same business may be conducted simultaneously by the same person in several localities, is it easy to see that the political character of the owner of goods cannot be safely ignored. Moreover, this is the test which is universally applied abroad (except in America).

Tests—1. *Nationality.*—We therefore retain nationality as the first test of enemy character for prize purposes—though with some doubt, on account of the inveterate declarations of authors to the contrary,[1] and the fact that it has not been much regarded by the British courts in the past.

[1] Hall thinks that the personal control exercised by a neutral state over persons domiciled in its territory is a fair

2. *House of Trade.*—The second test is the immediate connection of the goods with a house of trade in the enemy's country: with which may be coupled their being the raw produce of the enemy's land. These tests avail to condemn,[1] but not to release. Wheaton explicitly says so.[2] The fact that they are the property of a neutral house of trade will not save the goods if the owners are personally domiciled in an enemy's territory.

3. *Domicile.*—Quite apart from his place of business, a person's ordinary civil domicile may, through being in a hostile country, confer an enemy quality on his goods (though a neutral domicile will not take it off). It may, we think, be safely taken that ordinary civil domicile is meant—the same domicile which is the test of capacity to make a will or to take divorce proceedings. Attempts have been made, by the highest authorities, to prove that domicile has an esoteric meaning in this connection: that it means residence, or trading residence, of a comparatively slight degree of permanence. Since we already have set down the possession (whether resident or not) of a house of trade in the enemy country as a ground of enemy character, it is obvious that the trading element in this asserted special kind of domicile may be neglected. If the individual is indeed trading in

ground for releasing their goods, even if they are of belligerent nationality. But the control exercised by the national state, in these days of conscription and taxation, is not less stringent.

[1] The *Harmony*, (1800) 2 C.R. 322.

[2] *Int. Law*, sec. 335, citing the *Vigilantia*, 1 C.R. 1: the *Susa*, 2 *ibid.* 255: the *Portland*, 3 *ibid.* 41: the *J. Klassina*, 5 *ibid.* 297: the *Venus*, 8 Cranch 253.

the enemy country—(and no hired house[1] of bricks and mortar is necessary for this purpose)—the goods connected with the trade are enemy goods, wherever he resides. If then, we eliminate this element, we get the assertion reduced to a proposition that mere residence of a somewhat settled character in the enemy country will suffice to condemn a man's goods.

That the idea of trade must be eliminated as a necessary ingredient in the conception of domicile as a criterion of national character appears sufficiently clear from what has been said. But we may cite authority.

Domicile is independent of Trade.—Domicile is sharply distinguished from the possession of a house of trade in the *Vigilantia*.[2] "Unless it could be maintained as a rule without any exception whatever, that the domicile of the proprietor constitutes the national character of the vessel, this ship must be condemned:"—the exception, in fact, applied, that it was engaged in a purely Dutch trade. Sir W. Scott speaks of "that character which mere personal residence will give him," as distinct from the character stamped on an individual by the vocation of his trade. (Domicile is often loosely called residence: the *Citto*, infra, p. 325.)

And again, in the *Embden*,[3] Scott considers it possible to become Prussian by domicile, *if a family connection* be established. This is surely remarkable, if domicile means trading residence.

The mere permanent residence of a British subject

---

[1] "How much business is done in coffee-houses!"—per Sir W. Scott in the *Jonge Klassina*, 5 C.R. 297. Thompson (*Laws of War* (1854), p. 27) appears to be the first formally to identify domicile with trade.   [2] (1798) 1 C.R. 1.   [3] (1798) 1 C.R. 16.

in a belligerent country, without trading, was held to fix her with the hostile character in *De Luneville* v. *Phillips*,[1] where a lady, resident in Paris, was refused the right of entering up judgment on a warrant of attorney. A case of prize to the same effect is the *Amado*,[2] where the domicile was in the United States, and the ownership of the goods by an asserted house of trade in neutral South America was insufficient to save traffic with Mexico. *Cf.* Kent, *Comm. Lect.*, 4.

That domicile has nothing to do with trade is further apparent from a judgment of Story's. "It is not," says Story, J., in *The Society for the Propagation of the Gospel* v. *Wheeler*, (1814) 8 Cranch 132, "the private character or conduct of an individual which gives him the hostile or neutral character. . . . He may be *retired from all business*, devoted to mere spiritual affairs, or engaged in works of charity, religion, and humanity, and yet his domicile will prevail over the innocence and purity of his life."

Ordinary Domicile intended.—This can be none other than ordinary civil domicile, and the case of the *Jonge Ruiter*[3] is decisive. The trade had nothing to do with Papenberg. But the owner's wife lived there, and he sometimes spent half the year with her —being at sea the rest of the time. Held, he was domiciled there, and neutral, and not domiciled in the enemy country to which he traded. In fact, the domicile is the place where the individual, being permanently established, contributes permanently to the national resources. This is brought out with

[1] (1806) 2 N.R. 97. [2] (1847) Newberry 400.
[3] (1809) Acton 116.

masterly force by Wheaton.[1] A casual resident is here to-day and gone to-morrow; but a domiciled resident is known, and his resources are known, to the government. Knowledge is a pre-requisite of effective taxation.

In the *Harmony*[2] this was established beyond all doubt. The claimant's house of trade was in America. But he was himself resident in France. And on the ground that he was there domiciled, in the strict sense of civil law, Sir W. Scott condemned his share of the American house's goods.

"Of the few principles that can be laid down generally, I may venture to hold, that time is the grand ingredient in constituting domicile. I think that hardly enough is attributed to its efforts; in most cases it is unavoidably conclusive." He goes on to deal with and repel the contention that to go to a country for a special purpose (*e.g.*, to pursue claims) necessarily prevents the acquisition of a new domicile. The very fact that such a contention could be raised shows that nothing less than ordinary civil domicile was in question. The slender and peculiar "trade domicile in war" which Westlake and others assert to be the "domicile" of prize law, could obviously be readily gained by residence for a limited purpose.

"It cannot but happen," concludes Scott, "but with few exceptions, that mere length of time shall not constitute a domicile."

The contention in the *Harmony* was that the claimant had merely gone to France to settle particular affairs. The Court held that he had gone to

[1] *Captures*, ch. iv., pp. 102-150.   [2] (1800) 2 C.R. 322.

ORDINARY DOMICILE INTENDED

engage in trade, *and therefore* for an indefinite period.

A very similar case to the *Harmony* is *Elbers* v. *Krafts*.[1] The house of trade of A and B was in a Swedish island. B was living in America. He went there for his health ("which, however, he soon recovered"), but he did business there and had agents there on behalf of the partnership. Personally, he had no counting-house. Was a cargo consigned to A and B in the island Swedish or American property? Certainly it was Swedish as to A's moiety: but what as to B's?

"The only question," says Spencer, J., "is, whether Krafts was temporarily here, or whether he was here *animo manendi*. He having remained in the U.S. for such a length of time (two or three years), the presumption of law is that it was his intention to reside there permanently[2]: and he is bound to explain the circumstances of his residence, to repel that presumption. . . . The fact of a person's residing in the country for a considerable period, leads to the conclusion that he has adopted it as *the* place of his residence. . . . It seems to me not to admit of a doubt that by the well-understood law of nations, the absence of all proof that B was here temporarily or that he intended to return at any future time to St Bartholemew's, is decisive that he had an indefinite intention to remain here; and especially as he was actually engaged in superintending the business of his house in their concerns in this country."

Commerce is, therefore, only a subordinate indica-

[1] (1819) 16 Johnson (Amer.) 128.
[2] No doubt, in these days of general travel, the period would be somewhat increased.

tion of the decisive factor—the indefinite intention to remain. And this is simply the criterion of ordinary civil domicile.

"It is an established principle . . . that shipments made by merchants actually *domiciled* in the enemy's country . . . partake of the nature of the enemy's trade, and, as such, are liable to belligerent capture."[1]

So, Washington, J., in the *Venus*, 8 Cranch 279: "On this ground it is, that the courts of England have decided that a person who removes to a foreign country, settles himself there, and engages in the trade of the country, furnishes by these acts, such evidence of an intention permanently to reside there, as to stamp him with the national character of the state where he resides." Evidently, trading is here treated as an element, but not a necessary element, in establishing domicile. Permanence of residence is the sole essential: and that is precisely what it is in ordinary civil domicile. Marshall, C.J., in the same case, understands domicile in precisely the same sense[2]: though he reasonably contends that a domicile acquired for commercial reasons may readily be abandoned on the outbreak of war.[3]

It should be added, however, that in prize cases, there is a presumption that the domicile is where the residence is. The onus lies on the claimant to show that there is no *animus manendi*.[4]

But that *animus* is necessary and sufficient, as is apparent from the position of Mr Whitehill, whose property was confiscated, because he had arrived in

[1] (1819) 16 Johnson (Amer.) 132.　　[2] *ibid.* p. 290.
[3] *Cf.* also the *Diana*, 5 C.R. 60.
[4] The *Bernon*, (1798) 1 C.R. 103.

a Dutch island (S. Eustatius) with the intention of settling and remaining there,[1] only a day or two before the island was captured by the British under Rodney.

It was not until many years subsequently, that the theory was propounded that prize-law domicile was anything other than domicile as commonly understood.[2] For us, it is decisive that cases on the one and the other are quoted by judges and counsel indiscriminately. No higher authority on civil domicile is cited than Scott's judgments in the *Harmony*.[3] No later authority exists of equal importance with *Udny* v. *Udny*,[4] where prize-cases were cited over and over again.

"It has been sometimes said," remarks Twiss,[5] "that there is a peculiarity about domicile in time of war, as distinguished from domicile in time of peace, and that as a person may have establishments in two countries for commercial purposes, he may have in time of war for commercial purposes both a neutral domicile and a belligerent domicile. . . . [But] an individual can only have one domicile for international purposes, in the sense in which domicile is a criterion of a person being a friend or an enemy, for no person can be at the same time both a friend and an enemy under the law of nations." One may have houses of trade in different countries, and if the domicile is neutral, the neutral houses will be safe. But a hostile personal domicile will be fatal to them all.

[1] Cited in the *Diana*, (1803) 5 C.R. 65.
[2] *Cf.* T. Baty, *Trade Domicile in War, Journ. Soc. Comp. Leg.*, ix. 157 ; x. 183. Westlake, *ibid.*, ix. 265. T. Baty, *Juridical Review*, Oct. 1909 (Edin.), p. 209. (Reprinted 1914.)
[3] (1800) 2 C.R. 322.   [4] (1869) 1 S. & D. App. 441.
Law of Nations, ii. 306. *Cf.* also Pitt-Cobbett, *Cases*, i. 209.

House of Trade.[1]—But the main criterion in these cases of sea-borne trade will always be the fact of the goods being the property of a house of trade in the enemy country.[2] Where that can be proved, it will be decisive. Where it cannot be proved, it will only be in a minority of cases that the civil domicile of the owner in the enemy country—(or, if we are right, his enemy allegiance)—will be invoked to condemn.

What, then, is a "House of Trade"? The words do not in any way imply, though they suggest, a partnership. They do imply the carrying on of business in the enemy territory, whether personally or by agents. But they imply more. A merchant in A who sends goods on his own account to be disposed of in B, and who naturally has an agent or partner in B to receive and dispose of them, and maybe to procure cargoes in return, does not thereby possess a "house of trade" in B. It is as a merchant of A that he carries through the transaction. Were it otherwise, every export to the enemy country would be an export of enemy goods. It is difficult to say what would constitute him an importing merchant of B; but the mere finding of a customer for the goods in B cannot possibly do so. The question, however, has not often arisen with regard to the country of import: and with respect to the country of export, it is considerably simplified by the auxiliary rule which treats the raw produce of the enemy's soil as hostile [3] goods, whatever the owner-

---

[1] See particularly Wheaton on *Captures*, chap. iv.: an admirable and unique discussion.

[2] The *Bernon, ut supra*, p. 316.

[3] *Bentzon* v. *Boyle, infra*, p. 330.

ship—(until they have been incorporated into the commerce of a neutral country). Apart from that auxiliary rule, it is to be supposed that a mere purchaser, whose principal establishment is in a neutral country, will not be considered as having a house of trade in the enemy country, because he or his agent makes purchases there and sends them home. But in either case, if the neutral in the enemy country goes beyond the strict limits of an importer-vendor, or a purchaser-exporter—if he is interested in the production, manufacture, or distribution of the goods—his activity will be stamped with an enemy character, and he or his principal will become a belligerent " house of trade."[1]

The same will be true if he habitually imports from other countries than his own, or if he exports to them. And a great adverse factor will be his maintaining no permanent trade establishment in his own country, dealing, instead, with mere correspondents.

The *Vigilantia*[2] was the case of a Prussian ship, with no cargo on board, the asserted property of a neutral Emden merchant. Scott found that she was really the property of the former Dutch owner; but even had it been otherwise, this was a vessel trading regularly from Holland to Greenland, bought in Holland, fitted out from Amsterdam, and having a Dutch captain and crew. " If a vessel purchased in the enemy's country is, by constant and habitual occupation, continually employed in the trade of that country, commencing with the war, continuing during the war, and evidently on account of the war, on

[1] *Cf.* the *Syria, Times*, 19th Jan. 1914 (import).
[2] (1798) 1 C.R. 1.

what ground is it to be asserted that she is not to be considered a ship of that country, just as if she belonged to the inhabitants of it?[1] Suppose the naval arms of France had been triumphant . . . suppose a neutral country should offer her charitable assistance, and her merchants should say 'we will purchase your vessels, but they shall still navigate to Greenland; they shall still continue under your management and be fitted out in your ports; they shall still contribute to the industry of your artificers; they shall be conducted by the skill of your own navigators, by the attention of your merchants, and they shall still supply your manufactures and revenue'—in my apprehension the enemy would be justified in saying—'you, the neutrals, are in this transaction, mere merchants of Great Britain.'"

In two cases,[2] he observes, the shares of partners domiciled in neutral countries had been restored, where the trade was carried on in a hostile one. But in *Coopman*, (1798) these had been authoritatively explained as cases of the mere prompt withdrawal of his property by the neutral at the beginning of a war. Unfortunately, there are no details given of the description of trade carried on in the last case.

In the *Susa*, there was much conflict of fact, and it is difficult to draw any certain conclusions from it. But Scott alludes to a case as having been recently decided, where persons were carrying on the whale fishery of France under the name of an American — "without any footing in America or any visible

[1] It is to be observed that this Dutch-Greenland trade was not, and could not be, a privileged or close trade (*vide* p. 388 *infra*).
[2] The *Jacobus Johannes* (1785): the *Osprey* (1795).

connection with it: but carrying back the produce to France, and supplying the manufacturers and industry of France, without any communication or intercourse with America." Persons employed in such a trade were to be considered as merchants of France, " be their personal residence what it might."[1] The conclusion might be drawn, that a substantial connection with the neutral country would save the traffic. But that is not the case. In the *Portland*,[2] the claimant to cargo, a Mr Ostermeyer, had been a merchant of Ostend, and had removed to Hamburg on the irruption of the French, having his private residence at Blankenese. Sir W. Scott repudiated strongly the idea that, even if the claimant did in fact retain an interest in the Ostend house, this would make him an enemy in respect of all his concerns wherever carried on. He even suggested that the neutral concerns of a domiciled belligerent would be exempt from enemy character (though this suggestion was subsequently abandoned). But Scott distinctly contemplated that if the claimant retained a connection with the house of trade at Ostend, he would be liable *quoad hoc* to be treated as an Ostend merchant.

Agents and Managers.—But to constitute a house of trade, there must be something more than the mere stationing of an agent or manager to conduct seaport trade:[3] (or, presumably, than the mere temporary, undomiciled presence of a partner to do the like). There was in the *Anna Catharina* a resident agent in the hostile country, whose duty was to manage the import and export trade of the claimants: to distribute

[1] 2 C.R. 256.   [2] (1800) 3 *ibid.* 41.
[3] The *Anna Catharina*, (1802) 4 C.R. 119.

their goods, and to collect their return cargoes. If the trade had not been a privileged one, Scott would not have regarded this as constituting an enemy "house of trade" in the hostile territory. It is not a self-subsisting entity: it is a mere channel of the main neutral business. In Wheaton's *Elements* (citing his Reports, ii. App. 27, 28, 29, but inaccurately) several English cases of about 1800 are cited,[1] in which the property of a Mr Dutilth, an American, was condemned or restored, according as he was, or was not, in Holland, at the moment of capture. He had no office in Holland, but merely arranged with Dutch merchants to sell for him on commission. Here, something more was done than the mere import into hostile Holland: the importer retained no establishment in neutral America.

In the *Adriana*,[2] the claimant, Boland, asserting an American character, showed no subsisting connection with America. He was in France, and his shipment was one of wine and brandy from France to Hamburg. Scott was prepared to consider him as a French merchant (apart from any question of domicile) had it not been unnecessary to do so; in fact, his name had merely been used as a blind to protect undoubted French traders. In the *Dree Gebroeders*[3] Mr Grant, being in America to recover debts, took it upon himself to purchase French prizes and to lade them for England. These were restored on being captured, as being property withdrawn by a retiring merchant. But Grant returned to

[1] The *Hannibal* and the *Pomone*, (1800) 3 C.R. 16 (*n*); the *Fair American*, (1796) *ibid*.
[2] (1799) 1 C.R. 313.   [3] (1802) 4 C.R. 232.

France, and began to send French butter to Lisbon. He had ceased to carry on business in America, and he was now held to be trading as a merchant of France, though his family remained in England. It is difficult to distinguish this from the case of the *Herman*,[1] where a Mr Rudolf sent a cargo from Amsterdam to London, and it was seized as on a trading with the Dutch enemy. Dr Laurence, appearing (exceptionally) for the captors, contended that as R. was a partner in the house of trade in London, to which the cargo was consigned, the transit was a trade between Amsterdam and London, and illegal. It was argued *contra* that he was not a merchant of Amsterdam, but of Emden, where he had a domicile, and where his wife resided. He swore that his shipment was solely on account of his Emden business, and that his house in London (consignees) had no interest in it. "That he may carry on trade with the enemy from his house at Emden cannot be denied, provided it does not originate from his house at London, nor vest an interest in that house."[2] Even had he been in London, it would not have mattered. "I cannot think that . . . giving orders during his stay here for a shipment in the enemy's country, on account of his house at Emden, would bring his property into jeopardy."

An instructive case is the *Jonge Klassina*,[3] where the character of a merchant was split up into those of exporter and importer. The claimant, Ravie, had a license to import certain goods from Holland to

---

[1] (1804) 5 C.R. 228. [2] *Per* Sir W. Scott, p. 231.
[3] (1804) 5 C.R. 297.

England, where he carried on business. In his character of a Dutch merchant, he exported them to himself: a transaction which was held not to be permitted by the license. As a Birmingham man, he was "engaged very extensively in the manufactures of this country, in the employment of our artizans, and in the export and import trade." There was nothing to prevent his getting goods from Holland, or going there for them, under the license. But he did more. "The broker on being employed by the master to procure a freight, goes to Mr Ravie, as a man would go to a known merchant of the place. He contracts with the broker under the description of 'Ravie & Co., merchants of Amsterdam.'" That Ravie had no fixed counting-house in the enemy's country was held immaterial. He had agents there, and he went frequently there himself. It cannot be doubted, however, that what fatally told against him was the description in the charter-party as "merchants of Amsterdam."

Much will turn, therefore, on the fact of there being a connection with a subsisting house in the neutral country. If there is none, it is almost impossible to avoid the imputation of the hostile character. But if there is, it would seem that the operations in the belligerent territory must be limited, so as to "stop at the shore," if we may so express it. There is no harm in trying to sell one's own imports from one's own country. And, if the order proceeds from the house in one's own country, there is no harm in receiving and marketing goods from other countries. But the line is crossed when the neutral merchant (or his agent) established in the belligerent country, not only sends for goods from home, but orders them from abroad. By that, he becomes a merchant of the belligerent, and the goods involved in his business are marked with the belligerent character. (*Cf.* the *Citto*, 3 C.R. 38.)

What is commonly called a "branch," "filiale," or "succursale," is only an agency with more or less extended powers. It is subject to precisely the same rules (unless separately incorporated) as the agent-manager of a foreign business.[1]

Companies.—The particular application of this to companies is readily made, and solves the question propounded in *Janson* v. *Driefontein Consolidated Mines*.[2] So far as prize-law and sea-borne goods are concerned, the national character of a corporation does mainly depend—as Lord Lindley infers—on where it carries on its business. But it is further true that if it carries on its business in a neutral country, its goods may still be subject to capture, just as a private person's would be, if the company is substantially identified with the enemy country. As it can have no true nationality or domicile, we suggest that this identification must be inferred, not so much from its mere place or places of incorporation, as from its substantial composition, and the chief seat of its activity.[3]

The principle that the place of business is not decisive was laid down in *Robinson* v. *I. L. A. (London)*. That case shows how misleading it is to talk of the place where a company "carries on business." It may carry it on by an agent in such dependence

---

[1] The *Syria*, supra, p. 319. [2] *Supra*, p. 64, [1902] A.C. 484.
[3] *Supra*, p. 20.

upon the central directorate, or upon a local managing board, that no "house of trade" in the actual place of operations exists.

In *Robinson* v. *Int. Life Assoc. Society (London)*,[1] it was held that the authority of the agent of the neutral corporation in Virginia (a Confederate state), was not revoked or suspended by the civil war, merely because he was in fact instructed by an agency and local board of directors in New York, one of the Federal states. The habit of the agent had been to give receipts signed by the general agents in New York, and to transit moneys to New York by draft. It was argued that the neutral corporation was domiciled in New York, by its officers and board of directors, and could not therefore have intercourse with the enemy. "The principal in this contract was in no sense a resident of the state of New York. The defendant was a British incorporation, organised by virtue of an Act of Parliament, carrying on its business in London as its home office, and doing business also in this state, strictly and professedly as a foreign corporation. Whether its business here is transacted by one agent or many, and whether such agent has extended or restricted authority, can have no effect upon the domicile of the company."[2]

"The argument of the defendant's counsel throughout is based upon the idea that the status of the insured and of the defendants, in a legal and actual sense, was that of enemies. . . . The fact assumed does not exist. The *status* of the defendant

---

[1] (1870) 42 N.Y. 54.
[2] *Ibid*. 62.

was simply that of a neutral, contracting or continuing a contract with a citizen of a belligerent country. . . ."[1]

Contracts and Captures.—The close connection of commerce with contracts is, however, such that it has led authorities of great eminence to confuse the two rules of law which respectively (1) invalidate contracts with an enemy, and (2) subject to confiscation an enemy's goods at sea. It has been assumed that the criterion of enemy character is the same in each case: and it has been laid down broadly that the test of national character, at any rate in commercial matters, is the place where the party carries on business. That is not so, even with regard to prize-captures. The goods of a neutral house may be captured if the partners are personally settled in a hostile country. So that, if the criterion of friendliness is to be the same in both cases, it must not be the place of business alone, but the place of business *plus* the domicile.

But no one suggests that British or neutral domicile (even if we admit the attenuated domicile styled "trade-domicile") is conclusive as to the power of an enemy to enter into contracts. The only possible contention is that mere temporary presence, so long as it can be said to be licensed, in British territory, is enough to clothe the alien enemy with power to contract: and there is certainly no reason why the alien enemy should have any less capacity if he is in a neutral country. Nobody proposes that only the alien enemy who is actually domiciled away from his state shall have power to contract. But

[1] (1870) 42 N.Y. 63.

it certainly is only the alien enemy who is domiciled away from his state (whatever meaning we may attach to "domicile") who can thereby (if at all) save his goods from prize-capture.[1]

Clearly, therefore, the two rules, contract and capture, have quite different tests of what they respectively mean by an enemy. To argue from one to the other would be to commit a gross solecism.

It is easy to slide from the consideration of cargoes to the consideration of the contracts under which those cargoes were produced and shipped. It is tempting to do it without making the necessary adjustments of definition. But to do so introduces an element of error which may lead to disastrous conclusions.[2]

---

[1] If, of course, they are not the produce of a belligerent "house of trade."

[2] The difference between trading with the enemy and contracting with an enemy is thrown into relief in the *Anna Catharina*, (1802) 4 C.R. 107. A contract to ship provisions to Venezuela, made between a Dutchman (Robinson) and the Venezuelan (Spanish) government, was rendered impossible of performance by the British conquest of Curaçoa, whereby Robinson became a British subject. To have sent goods to a Spanish colony, from whatever port, would have been to trade with the enemy. But the benefit of the contract was transferred to a neutral Hamburger, and its fulfilment then became perfectly lawful. "It has been argued that, the contract becoming illegal in the hands of Robinson, the illegality would travel over with it, and attach on those persons carrying it into execution. I am not disposed to hold that it would affect them. . . . The immediate shippers are neutral persons, acting under the contract, as it was devolved upon them to supply the goods and receive the return cargoes, in the same manner that Robinson was to have done. No duties of allegiance bound them to abstain from a direct commerce

Disregard of Technical Ownership.—The legal ownership of goods being *primâ facie* established to be neutral, it is a question whether it will invariably be respected. The usual course of trade is for the property to pass to the purchaser as soon as it is delivered to the carrier. Take the enemy to be the importer. No private arrangement varying the usual rule, even if it makes the risks of sea-transit the vendor's risks, will be recognised by the captor.[1] Hall even thinks it is doubtful whether a pre-war trade usage to the contrary will be recognised. But this view rests on a slavishly literal reading of a phrase of Story's, and ought certainly not to be sustained.[2] If the trade usage can be proved, it should prevail. But whether the goods have or have not been paid for makes no difference to the principle. And it is not necessary that the ignored arrangement should have been made during the war; if it was made in contemplation of it, or the shipment takes place during the war, it is enough.[3] Nor does it matter that a neutral agent is to take charge of the goods on arrival.[4]

with the enemy of this country, and it cannot be inferred that any violation of duties of that species on his part could at all be transferred to others who are neutral merchants standing indifferent to both parties." See also the *V. Anna Catharina*, (1804) 5 C.R. 161.

[1] The *Ann Green*, (1812) 1 Gallison 291; the *Francis, ibid.* 450; the *Anna Catharina*, (1802) 4 C.R. 114 (*a*), citing Sir L. Jenkins, ii. 729, (1666).

[2] The *Packet de Bilboa*, (1799) 2 C.R. 133: here, however, the shipment was prior to the war. The *Miramichi*, 23rd Nov. 1914.

[3] So Halleck, ii. 103. *Cf.* the *Atlas*, (1801) 3 C.R. 299.

[4] The *Anna Catharina*, (1802) 4 C.R. 115.

Take the enemy to be the exporter. Here, the common rule would save the goods in the majority of cases. We therefore get the sub-rule that the native produce of the belligerent can always be captured, at any rate on its first voyage, no matter whose it is[1]—and the further doctrine that the captors are at liberty to make out, if they can, the existence of any arrangement between vendor and purchaser, by which the ordinary rule is varied,[2] and that strict proof of ownership will be required from the neutral in such cases. Any power of the enemy to resume possession of the goods (except the universal one of stoppage *in transitu* in a case of insolvency) will be as a rule fatal.[3]

It is not impossible for the goods, shipped as the enemy's goods, to be accepted *in transitu* by a neutral contemplated at the time of shipment.[4]

Transfers.—Transfers of goods to a neutral *in transitu* are otherwise regarded with suspicion, and will not be recognised if made during or in contemplation of war,[5] whatever the motive of the purchaser.

---

[1] *Bentzon* v. *Boyle*, (1815) 9 Cranch 195; the *Phœnix*, (1803) 5 C.R. 20; the *V. Anna Catharina*, (1804) *ibid.* 167. The rule dates from 1783 (the *Phœnix*, p. 21).

[2] Hall, *Int. Law*, p. 501.

[3] The *Aurora*, (1802) 4 C.R. 219; the *Josephine*, *ibid.* 25; the *Noydt Gedacht*, (1799) 2 *ibid.* 137; the *Carolina*, 1 *ibid.* 304; the *Merrimac*, (1814) 8 Cranch 528; the *Venus*, *ibid.* 253.

[4] *Per* Sir W. Scott, in the *Cousine Marianna*, (1810) 1 Edw. 346.

[5] The *Jan Frederick*, (1804) 5 C.R. 128. (The case was one where the goods were the produce of the hostile colonial soil, and this may have weighed with the Court. Probably, if the transfer had been in the colony, the cargo would still have been confiscable, p. 85 *supra*.)

TRANSFERS

Transfers of ships to a neutral, if made after or in immediate contemplation of the outbreak of hostilities,¹ are also scrutinised with great suspicion. Theoretically competent (unless, perhaps, when the ship is at sea), they are investigated so closely as to be almost impracticable,² if the slightest interest or control remains to the enemy.

French practice is said to be exactly the opposite: refusing to recognise any transfer of a ship, but more lenient as regards goods in transit.³

The principle of continuous voyage applies to sales to a neutral *in transitu*.⁴

The Declaration of London consolidates these presumptions in regard to the transfer of vessels. If unconditional, complete,⁵ and reserving no control

---

¹ The Privy Council, in the *Ariel* (*infra*) (and also Dr Lushington, the *Baltica*, Spinks 269), speak of the cases as to the illegality of the sale of ships *in transitu*. It does not appear that the fact of the ship being at sea makes any difference, and in fact they appear to have been in port; the *Jemmy*, (1801) 4 C.R. 31, "purchased at Dunkirk"; the *Samuel*, (1802) 4 C.R. 284 (*n*). "The locality of the ship will not affect the legality of the sale." The suspicion of fraud may be a little inflamed by the ship being actually at risk.

² *Per* Sir W. Scott, in the *Sechs Geschwistern*, *ubi infra;* the *Welvaart*, (1799) 2 C.R. 122; the *Omnibus*, 6 C.R. 71. "Where a ship, asserted to have been transferred, is continued under the former agency and in the former habits of trade, not all the swearing in the world will convince the Court that it is a genuine transaction."

³ Oppenheim, *Int. Law*, ii. 207. *Cf.* the *Sechs Geschwistern*, (1801) 2 C.R. 100.

⁴ The *Carl Walter*, (1802) 4 C.R. 207.

⁵ Is a transfer "complete" when the purchase-money remains outstanding?

or profits, the transfer cannot be challenged if it took place more than thirty days before war. Under such favourable circumstances it could not, under the received practice, be challenged at all. The fact of the bill of sale not being on board is reduced from a possible ground of condemnation to a ground for further investigation, and then only if the transfer was within sixty days of the outbreak of war.[1] Transfers after the outbreak of hostilities are, contradicting the French rule, permitted; but the Court is left free to regard them as effected in order to avoid the consequences of the ship's belligerent character. And a transfer *in transitu* is to be always fatal. So is a transfer in a blockaded port (why?), and a transfer reserving a right of pre-emption or recovery.[2]

Transfers of goods *in transitu* are absolutely barred[3] (except in case of stoppage in the event of insolvency), and even subsequent transfers may be impeached.

New Orleans residents, when the city was in Federal hands, bought cotton from Confederate parts of Louisiana. This was set aside, as involving trading with the enemy, and the title of neutral *bonâ fide* purchasers for value ignored, the contract being invalid in its inception.[4] This is justifiable when only one nation is concerned in the war. But a transaction in a really independent state could not on principle be so ignored.[5]

Interests.—Interests of third parties (neutrals) in an

---

[1] Art. 55. Art. 56. [3] Art. 60.
[4] The *Ouachita Cotton*, (1867) 6 Wall. 521.
[5] *Castrique* v. *Imrie*, (1870) L.R. 4 E.I.A. 414; *Cammell* v. *Sewell*, (1860) 5 H. & N. 728.

enemy ship will be ignored, *unless they are open and obvious*.[1] The same seems in general to be true of neutral interests in enemy cargo. The captors lay their hands on "the gross, tangible property," in Lord Stowell's phrase.[2] A prize court would do more injustice than justice if it incurred the enormous expense and delay of attempting to decide intricate questions depending on foreign law and foreign witnesses. On the other hand, an enemy's interest in a neutral ship may, if it is sufficiently substantial, condemn the whole. But it has been held that a mere lien for unpaid purchase money will not have this effect. This case (the *Ariel*[3]) was principally restored on an argument of the captors in the *Tobago*:—" Suppose a bond of this nature given upon a neutral ship, and to a person now become an enemy, could a proceeding of prize be instituted against the neutral ship, or any part of it, as the property of the enemy? Certainly not." Drs Laurence and Adams replied that "it would not be reasonable or just to seize the ship itself on account of such an accessorial interest which an enemy might have in it." Both sides may have meant to refer to a possible condemnation of the neutral ship, on account of the enemy's interest in it—and perhaps not to deny that that interest might, by some process, be confiscable. But Sir W. Scott says in judgment, that —"[The captor's] rights of capture act upon the

---

[1] The *Tobago*, (1804) 5 C.R. 218 (bottomree).
[2] The *Marianna*, (1805) 6 C.R. 24 (vendor's lien).
[3] (1857) 11 Moo. P.C. 119 (Leigh, Ryan, Patteson, and Dodson). *Cf.* the *Baltica*, Spinks, 264, 279 (the original case decided by Lushington, whom the P.C. reversed).

property, without regard to secret liens possessed by third parties: In like manner his rights operate on no such liens where the property itself is protected from capture [1] . . . The consequence of allowing generally the privilege here claimed would be that the captor would be subject to the disadvantage of having neutral liens set up to defeat his claims upon hostile property, whilst he himself could [owing to his ignorance of the facts] never entitle himself to any advantage from hostile liens upon neutral property. This Court therefore excludes all consideration of liens or incumbrances of this species."

Scott might have condemned the *Ariel;* but it would apparently have been on the ground of the suspicion that the whole transaction was intended as a protection of the hostile vendor's trade. It would not have been a condemnation of his slender interest still remaining, amounting to a lien for £90 unpaid purchase-money. Had he remained a part owner to the extent of £90, doubtless that share would have been condemned.

The distinction is taken by Halleck [2] to be that between rights *in personam* and rights *in rem*,[2] provided that, if the latter, it is immediate and visible on the ship's papers. If the party, neutral or enemy, has a right *in personam* only (and a bottomree bond is taken to be such; also the maritime liens for collision, salvage, etc.[3]), the

[1] The *Tobago, supra,* p. 223. *Cf.* The *Frances,* 8 Cranch 419.
[2] *Int. Law,* ii. 115.
[3] *Cf.* Takahashi, *Int. Law in the Russian War,* p. 551. Even a formal mortgage was ignored in the *Hampton,* (1866) 5 Wall. 372. Miller, J.'s reasoning is faulty, since he relies on the ease with which an owner, on the approach of war, could protect

interest will be disregarded, and the property restored or condemned. If the interest is *in rem*, it will be restored on the claim of its neutral proprietor, and condemned as the interest of its enemy proprietor, as the case may be. Sometimes, but apparently by indulgence only, British claimants who have advanced money or supplied necessaries to a ship lying in a British port which vessel becomes hostile, have been recouped.[1]

Charters.—Must the Court recognise the interest of a time charterer who has possession? This is an obvious interest, apparent on the ship's papers. Yet the neutral charterer has so closely identified himself with the hostile flag, that we think he cannot claim to save his interest.[2] He not only has an interest in the *res*, but he navigates it, and thereby submits to hostile control. On the other hand, an enemy charterer clearly forfeits his interest, the charterparty is cancelled (if the ship is British or allied), and the ship should be restored to the owners. Sailing under the enemy's flag and pass is always a ground of condemnation. It is difficult to see, indeed, why

his ships by neutral mortgages. But such transactions would never stand. The *Hampton* was followed in the *Marie Glaeser* (*Times*, 17th September 1914). But the true ground on which these cases rest is that the mortgagee identifies himself with the hostile flag. Cf. *per* Evans, P., in the latter case *ad fin.*

[1] The *Belvidere*, (1813) 1 Dods. 351. Lushington's distinction between recouping native claimants and repaying aliens really obscures the true point, which appears to be that the claim is made in the country where the ship is and where the services were rendered. But see the *Nigretia*, Takahashi, *ubi supra*, 552 : the *Russia*, *ibid*. 557.

[2] *Cf.* Latifi, *Effect of War on Property*, p. 80.

the neutral's interest, even *in rem*, in an enemy ship should ever be restored; but possibly a case might arise where the ship was non-fraudulently under neutral colours. In our judgment, however, the formal adoption in profound peace of a foreign-owned vessel into the mercantile fleet and protection of a state which is in the sequel neutral, ought to exempt such a vessel from capture altogether.

Effect of Private Seizure.—Of course, an enemy's goods, so defined as above, must not be seized by an invasion of neutral territory (including a neutral ship): and although we deal with this topic under the general head of "The Subject and the Enemy," it remains to be said that although an enemy's sea-borne commerce lies open to seizure by subjects of the opposing power, so far as International Law is concerned, yet they may commit an offence against their own law in effecting a capture. It does not appear that it is any offence by the law of England—but the result in England is to confer no legal title on the captors. It vests it in the Crown as a *droit* of Admiralty. Kent maintains the right of private ships to make such captures. Oppenheim denies it, and certainly since privateering was abolished, in 1856, it seems at first sight difficult to admit the right. But it is a very different thing to authorise a private ship to cruise for gain (which is what was forbidden), and to admit that a private ship may on her own initiative effect a capture from patriotic motives. Attack may be the best, or the only, defence. And in the particular case of a ship chartered to a British subject, it may be the clear duty of his master and crew to effect a seizure.

In cases such as the above, although no claim for prize can be put in by the private and uncommissioned captors, they may generally be awarded something liberal by way of salvage; and that, although the property has never been in the power of the state before the so-called salvage services were rendered. In an American case, where a private person had fitted out a boat and captured British cargo on board a Spanish schooner, he was allowed one-half its value. As one-third is the usual limit allowed for the most meritorious peace salvage services, this was a recognition of the fact that the capture as well as the subsequent preservation of the vessel is due to the so-called salvors. In the *Haase*, (1799) 1 C.R. 286, they were given the whole.[1]

Conquest.—The fact of cession to, or even military occupation[2] by, the other belligerent or its ally will invest territory of an enemy with a friendly character, and *vice versâ*. So, trade with Hayti became lawful when it revolted from France (*Blackburn v. Thompson*, 3 Camp. 61), and trade with Leghorn unlawful when the French invaded it (*Bromley v. Hesseltine*, 1 *ibid.* 75). But such a change in the status of the land will not work an automatic change in the liability to prize capture of a ship or cargo already at sea.[3] Nor will it necessarily affect the personal

---

[1] *Cf.* the *Amor Parentum*, (1799) 1 C.R. 303; the *Abigail*, (1802) 4 C.R. 72; the *Charlotte*, (1804) 5 C.R. 280; the *Cape of Good Hope Ships*, (1799) 2 C.R. 274; the *Daijin*, Takahashi, *ubi suprä*, 338.

[2] As in Antwerp: cf. *per* Bailhache, J., *Mitsin v. Mumford*, 21st Dec. 1914.

[3] The *Danckebaar Africaan*, (1798) 1 C.R. 107; the *Negotie en Zeevaart*, (1782) *ibid.* 109, 116; the *Herstelder*, (1799)

allegiance of persons connected by birth or residence with the territory. The *Fana* (5 C.R. 113) shows that the cession must not be *in fieri*, but must actually have been carried out.

In case of such a conquest, the original character will remain in those persons who decide within a reasonable or a stipulated time to remove.[1]

"**At Sea or Afloat.**"—Since the mode of dealing in practice with the enemy's property is so different, according as it is found on land or at sea, it becomes important to determine what being "at sea" is.

Wheaton[2] says:—"The private property of the enemy taken at sea, or afloat in port, is indiscriminately liable to capture and confiscation;" and the Admiralty jurisdiction also extends to captures by naval force in foreign territory: *Lindo* v. *Rodney*.[3] In supposed accordance with this principle the *Thalia*[4] was dealt with in the prize courts of Japan, being captured by a naval lieutenant. But it does not follow that other captures on land should be so regarded. The *Canary Merchant* in *Key & Hubbard* v. *Pearse*[5] was held to be at sea; but she was afloat in New York harbour when seized by *H.M.S. Hamburg*.

---

ibid. 113. These cases were decided largely on the authority of Lord Camden, and have been much criticised: even Sir W. Scott, in the first-named, does not seem to have liked the principle. "I am bound down by the decision of the Lords, and I think myself obliged to say . . . that the ship is Dutch property."   [1] The *Diana*, (1803) 5 C.R. 60.
[2] *Elements*, sec. 335.   [3] [1781-2] 2 Dougl. 614.
[4] [1905] Takahashi, *ubi supra*, 605. The actual ground of the decision in the inferior court appears to have been that a dock (and therefore a ship) was a normal position for a ship.
[5] (1742) Dougl. 606.

It was urged that she was "within the body of the City of New York," "and not on the sea." But the Court held that the cause being one of "prize or no prize," the Admiralty could not be prohibited.

"The jurisdiction of a court of admiralty is generally limited to matters arising *super altam mare* . . . yet I do not take it to be so in cases of prize; for the jurisdiction does not depend on locality but on the nature of the question, which is such as not to be tried by any rules of the common law but by a more general law, which is the law of nations"— *per* Lee, C.J.

His view was adopted and extended by Mansfield. "Every reason which created a prize court, as to ships taken upon the high seas, holds equally when they are taken on land."[1] But this broad proposition is not unlimited. He lays stress on two further elements. The capture was made virtually by a force at sea. It was also in *enemy territory* where no court could give satisfaction and apportion the shares of prize. Wheaton[2] sums up the position accurately by saying that prize courts have jurisdiction over goods taken on shore by a naval force.

Long before, in *Brown & Burton* v. *Franklyn, K.P.*,[3] the King's Proctor had libelled in Admiralty concerning a ship called the *Francis* and her furniture, 6000 sequins of foreign money, 200 elephants' teeth, 300 pieces of muslin, 300 pieces of calico, etc. She was a French ship, stranded in the East Indies, and two enterprising H.E.I.C. captains had gone to attack her. Finding her a wreck, they attacked the crew

[1] *Lindo* v. *Rodney*, ubi supra.   [2] *Captures*, 278.
[3] Carthew, 474 (10 Will. III.).

on land, took the sequins from them, and pillaged the ship of the other goods. The King's Proctor obtained a sentence of condemnation of the ship and goods as prize, and proceeded to require an account from the captains. They moved for a prohibition, but it was refused. "Prize or no prize was not triable by the common law, but altogether appropriated to the jurisdiction of the Admiralty." Here, again, the capture was (1) by or from a ship, and (2) effected *dehors* the realm.

If the contention were made that the Admiralty has jurisdiction over all alleged prize seized within the realm, the whole jurisdiction of the common law courts might be ousted. The plaintiff might claim anything as prize: whether it has some connection with shipping or not would be immaterial, for any goods might be libelled as enemy's property.

Fortunately, the *Ooster Ems*[1] is an authority against any such proposition. The ship was stranded on the Goodwins. The cargo was sent on shore, and claimed by the warden of the Cinque Ports as a perquisite. The Admiralty obtained a monition removing the cause into the High Court of Admiralty, which condemned the cargo as prize. On appeal, this judgment was reversed. It was resolved—"that the High Court of Admiralty had not a jurisdiction over the goods seized and proceeded against"—*per* Thurlow and the other Lords Delegate. And in the *Two Friends*[2] Stowell remarks:—

"Another question arises, whether the jurisdiction

[1] (1799) 1 C.R. 284.   [2] (1799) 1 C.R. 281.

is ousted by the landing of the goods? . . . I know of no other definition of prize-goods than that they are goods taken on the high seas, *jure belli*, out of the hands of the enemy. . . . Such goods, when they come on shore, may be followed by the process of the Court." The *Ooster Ems* is distinguished, "because there the goods were landed before seizure." There was no act of capture afloat, and therefore they were not to be considered as prize."[1] Probably as wreck—he was not entitled to prize droits. Prize taken in port or harbour is a "droit of Admiralty," and passes to the Lord High Admiral by special grant: while other prize went to the captors. At present, both go to the Crown, but from separate funds. Such droits are only a particular sort of prize.

Floating Goods.—It is by no means necessary that the "goods" referred to in Stowell's definition should be a ship, or taken in a ship. Floating goods will generally be abandoned goods. But if they are the unabandoned goods of an enemy, there is no need that they should be libelled as part of a ship's cargo.[2]

[1] In the *Roumanian* (7th December 1914) it was held that goods landed within the limits of a port were within the Admiralty jurisdiction. It is true that prize seized on the high seas is prize in the narrower sense, as distinguished from "droits of Admiralty," which include prize seized in port. But it is submitted that the goods must be afloat to be prize (*i.e.*, subject to the Admiralty jurisdiction in prize) at all (subject to *Lindo* v. *Rodney*). Cf. the *Marie Française*, 6 C.R. 282. The MS. cases cited are not conclusive. In one only is it clear that the property was on land, and it was only temporarily so.

[2] *Cf.* (1865) 78 *Bales of Cotton*, 1 Lowell 11.

CHAPTER V

THE PROCLAMATIONS OF AUGUST, SEPTEMBER, AND OCTOBER 1914

Failure to distinguish Contract from Trade—Successive Proclamations of 5th August, 12th August, 9th September—Circular of 21st August, and Statute—Retrospective—Analysis of these—Novel Criterion of Enemy Character for Proclamation Purposes—Branches—Agents.

FROM what has been said it is apparent that trading with the enemy and contracting with an enemy are two entirely different things. The first concerns the "gross, palpable fact" of sea transit. The second turns on a peculiarity of civil status. The one is a matter for a commander and a Court of Prize. The other concerns the utmost delicacies of legal subtlety.

It may be doubted whether this distinction is properly appreciated. The Proclamation against "Trading with the Enemy" of 5th August was drawn in such exceedingly ambiguous terms as to trench on the sphere of contracting with enemy subjects. It occasioned, on the one hand, widespread and wholly unnecessary alarm as to the vague penalties which it mentioned, and which made employers hesitate to pay their German workmen, or to continue to deal

PROCLAMATION AS TO TRADE

with German customers. On the other hand, it was supposed in some quarters to operate as a license to alien enemies elsewhere than in enemy territory to enter into contracts, and to enforce contracts, in the same way as a British subject.

The attempt to mix up two separate things, or rather the failure to distinguish them, led to a veritable chaos. This it was attempted to remedy by the Treasury circular of 20th August, which only made matters worse. Next came the Proclamation of 9th September, which was somewhat more illuminating; and having cleared up the situation to this extent, the Government took its courage in its hands, and passed the Trading with the Enemy Act, which imposed considerable penalties on such trade.

5th August.—The first proclamation affected to apply to "all persons resident, carrying on business, or being, in" the British dominions, and to regulate their intercourse with persons similarly situated with regard to Germany. It did not apply to commercial intercourse carried on solely from a house of trade or a branch established in a neutral country, where the party has also a house of trade in the British dominions or in Germany. But it will be observed that it refrains from excepting from its operation the case in which the party (who may be a German or domiciled in Germany) has his *sole* houses in neutral territory. In the common case of a German trading only in Italy, China, or South America, therefore, the Proclamation does not apply at all.

Where it applies, it warns persons[1] resident,

[1] Including firms and corporations. It is difficult to say what an "unincorporated body" (also included) is.

carrying on business, or being, in the British dominions, from supplying goods to or obtaining goods from, persons in a similar situation in Germany: or to or from German territory (see *Fox* v. *Schrempt*, p. 303). This is certainly too sweeping. A non-trading Spaniard cannot be prevented from getting goods at Barcelona from Germany because he happens to "be," or even to be resident, in Eastbourne. An Englishman cannot be prevented from buying goods from an American in London, merely because the latter is carrying on business in Germany. On the other hand, it is not wide enough. As Dr Schuster has pointed out, it says nothing about the transmission of cash and securities.

But in warning the public against making contracts with or for the benefit of such persons, the Proclamation certainly exceeds its proper scope. Why a contract cannot be made with the agent of a Swiss at Liverpool, because the principal happens to be for the moment in Germany, is incomprehensible. It may be said that the saving clause comes into play. But it does not. It is only directed to the commercial operations of neutral houses. And the contract need *not* be a commercial one, nor will the Swiss necessarily have a neutral house if it is one. To have an agent in a country is not necessarily to have a branch there.

Lastly, the Proclamation permits all that it does not (where it applies) prohibit, in the way of "transactions to, with, or for the benefit of" persons resident, carrying on business, or being, in Germany. What "transactions to" a person are, we cannot state, any more than we can say what a "branch of business" is. The words, however, are far too wide, permitting almost all personal communications actually with Germany except the making of contracts. The performance of all contracts [1] (except by delivery or acceptance of goods), the management of companies, the voting of shareholders, the conduct of partnerships and agencies, the resolution of conditions—these and many other things remained permitted.

But another very important class of persons connected with Germany was altogether outside the Proclamation—German subjects in the British dominions.

In our view it was not "trading with the enemy" to have dealings with them. But in our opinion such persons could not sue: so that it was optional whether to fulfil contracts made with them or not. On the whole, except in small accounts, such as for wages, food, and the like, it was preferable to avoid doing so. The question of payment to the agent of a trader in Germany created further difficulty. Could such payments be supported as against the principal after the conclusion of peace? The very contract of agency had probably been dissolved; and there was no subsisting British partner (as there often was, in the case of a partnership) to wind things up.

21st August.—In these circumstances the Treasury circular of 21st August was issued. It should be remarked that it has no authority to operate as a license. The authority of the Commissioners of Customs was insufficient in the *Hoop*,[2] that of a

---

[1] Except insurance contracts where the loss is due to belligerent action of the Crown and its allies.

[2] (1799) 1 C.R. 196.

minister plenipotentiary, in the *Joseph*,[1] that of the high military authorities in the *Ouachita Cotton*,[2] and that of the consul and the fleet commander in the *Amado*.[3]

It explained, in the case of foreign traders, that the residence *and* place of business (combined) is "the important thing to consider" in deciding on what transactions are permissible.[4] It thus lumps contracts and import together, and adopts a new criterion both to uphold and to condemn, viz.: residence *plus* place of business. It definitely rejects the criterion of nationality, for both purposes, and would apparently admit a German temporarily resident and trading in Rotterdam to sue in our Courts: for in permitting contracts with him it must include permission to sue for them. It is indeed *possible*, that all that these proclamations deal with is the penal aspect of the matter; and, if so, the situation is very much simplified. If they only "permit" certain transactions in so far as to remove penal consequences from them, the point as to their executory validity remains unaffected. And this is a sustainable interpretation. The Proclamation only affects to deal with "trade with the enemy," *i.e.*, with improper communication with the enemy territory. In some cases it removes its penal consequences. But it may not thereby necessarily operate as a license to *both* sides, validating their otherwise

---

[1] (1813) 1 Gallison 546.   [2] (1867) 6 Wall. 521.
[3] (1847) Newberry 400.
[4] In para. 2 of the Statement, the Treasury uses the term "established," apparently as equivalent to the phrase used in their explanation, viz.: "Resident and carrying on business."

invalid transactions, and conferring a power of suit on the alien enemy. The German in Rotterdam is an alien enemy. It may not be penal to contract with him or to send him goods. But it does not follow that he can sue like a Dutchman.

The Treasury proceed to deal with the question of branches. They take the case of a firm (including, we suppose, a person) with headquarters in hostile territory. They assert that trade with a "branch" in neutral or British territory is permissible, so long as no transaction with the head office is involved. This is really extraordinary. A branch is no more than an agent. Its dealings are for the benefit of the principal. The permission is quite contrary to Scott's and Story's doctrine of the impossibility of saving the proceeds of a neutral house when the owner is personally established in a hostile country, as in most cases of this kind he will be. It cannot be supposed that such a casual statement can avail to make transactions with such firms though their neutral branches are valid.

Finally, the Statement observed that there was no objection to the payment of sums due to establishments, even in enemy territory, under contracts already completed. Cf. *Orenstein*, p. 351 *infra*. Altogether, the Statement cannot be taken as a document possessing any legal force.

9th September.—On 12th August 1914 the Proclamation had been declared applicable to Austria-Hungary.

But on 9th September it was revoked and an entirely new one issued.

Branches — whatever they may be — are hurled

from their privileged position (except where existing in British, allied, or extra-European territory).

The definition of "enemy" is restricted to persons resident or carrying on business in enemy territory. Even so, it is too wide. A person may be resident without being domiciled. Why should one not pay a London Bank a Spanish lady's annuity, because she happens to be temporarily resident at Carlsbad? Yet it is a payment "for the benefit of an enemy."

The mysterious "permission" disappears.

Enemy character is attached to those companies only which are incorporated in the enemy country. Alien enemies who neither reside nor carry on business in the enemy country have not that character, although they may be domiciled and keeping up a large establishment there.

The most important new transaction[1] which persons "carrying on business, resident, or being," in the British dominions are warned[2] against carrying out, is the payment of money to or for the benefit of an "enemy." Payment to an enemy's agent is of course payment for the enemy's benefit, if, indeed, it is not "to" the enemy. Exempted "branches" are in a curious position. When does an agent acquire such independence that he can safely be termed a "branch"?[3] It would be safer not to pay, in case of doubt: but does the Proclamation enable the principal, in such a case, to sue? We prefer to read it as relieving subjects against novel penalties, but not as affecting to determine a difficult question of law which is properly for the courts, or as conferring

---

[1] *Vide* Appendix.   [2] *N.B.*, not in terms "prohibited."
[3] *Vide* p. 351 *infra*.

upon Teutonic enemies in Brazil and China the novel power of enforcing payments in England.

It should be added that, apart from the new statute to be mentioned, the mere payment of money for the benefit of a person resident or carrying on business in a hostile country (or even an alien enemy by allegiance) has never in itself been seriously regarded as an offence, apart from treasonable motives. The same remark applies to the "warnings" which follow, against (2) compromising claims; (3, 4) dealing with negotiable instruments; (5) dealing in stocks and shares; (6) insurance, reinsurance; (7) import and export; (8) voyages; and (9) contracts. In the debate of 1747, when treason was a recent memory, it was still gravely doubted whether insurance of enemy ships was even a misdemeanour. And subsequent statutes only made it an offence subject to a six months' penalty. The present legislation giving [1] magistrates power to impose twelve months' imprisonment, and admitting of seven years' penal servitude on indictment for all these commercial transactions, is absurdly vindictive, especially considering that it is extremely doubtful whether such things as the making of contracts with the enemy are, at common law, anything worse than mere nullities. *L'appétit vient en mangeant;* and the section of the Act which makes that penal which was, rightly or wrongly, prohibited by *previous* proclamations, is a departure from constitutional precedent. *Ex post facto* legislation is not our *forte*. Lastly, the Secretary of State, in conjunction with the Privy Council, has power under the Proclamation to bring what trans-

[1] 4 & 5 Geo. V. c. 87 (18th Sept. 1914). *Cf.* Northey, p. 296 *supra*.

action with the "enemy" he chooses under its provisions—which, as we observed, are hortatory only.

It seems strange, but it is apparently true, that payments and other transactions completed between foreigners abroad, one of whom is carrying on trade in a hostile country, are prohibited if the other happens to be for the moment in England, or resident in England, or carrying on a totally different business there.

Payments "by or on account of" [*i.e.*, "for"—not "to"[1]] "enemies" to persons resident, being, or carrying on business in the Empire are expressly saved, if arising out of pre-war transactions "or otherwise permitted." There seems no reason for this express saving, unless payment is made by a dealing with a negotiable instrument, or constitutes the completion of a transaction in stocks or shares.

The amazing permission (para. 6) of transactions[2] of all kinds with a branch of an enemy house "locally situated in British . . . territory," is likely to give rise to very regrettable consequences and to much litigation. If it is meant merely as a relief from penal consequences, it is perfectly right. No one can be penalised for assuming that a customer or merchant is not going to betray the hospitality he is receiving. But, if it means that all transactions with such "branches" are to be valid in law, and British subjects compelled to complete them, it is safe to say that it cannot long remain unaltered. As Dr Coleman Phillipson well comments on an American case, which allows the agent of an enemy to sue during war, such

[1] *Orenstein*, [1914] 2 Sc. L.T. 293.
[2] This term does not include payments, which are separately dealt with: *ibid*.

a principle provides a ready means of "carrying on" for the benefit of the enemy. It may be that it is the agent's duty to transmit nothing to him: but he will not impossibly find a means of doing so. He can even remit direct to an American "branch" of the same business. The innocent assumption that it is the agent's affair if he remits funds to his principals, is almost too childlike to be seriously discussed.

"Branches."—Besides, what is a branch? So important, and indeed crucial a matter, ought not to rest on any vague popular notion. Is every manager a branch? Is every agent?[1] (*Contra*, *Orenstein*, p. 350.) Is a balance-sheet a necessity of a branch? Is the undertaking of business with third countries sufficient or necessary? In some respects a branch is better treated than a resident. For if a thorough American happens to have a share, however slender, in an Austrian house, or happens to be living at Vienna, his transactions are not protected, even if (in the first case) he is carrying on an independent business in England or Philadelphia, or (in the second case) he is permanently settled there.

Yet if a domiciled German subject has one sole business, and runs it in England through a "branch," it can be carried on as before!

Trading in Enemy's Produce.—The most recent pronouncement (9th October 1914) on behalf of the Government goes far beyond the prohibition of trade with the enemy and (if valid) extends to prohibiting

[1] *Cf.* the *Syria*, supra, p. 319. It will be understood, that in speaking of "agents" we do not include commission agents, except when acting within the scope of their commission. As this depends largely on their own mental attitude, it is hard to establish.

a principle provides a ready means of "carrying on" trade in the enemy's products. Certificates of origin are required to be produced by the importer,[1] showing that the goods are not of enemy manufacture or production.[2] What is to happen when the goods are partially the one or the other is not stated. Nor are the consequences plain. Are the goods to be confiscable in transit? or forfeited on arrival? Or are the penal consequences of trading with the enemy alone applicable? The penal statute (4 & 5 Geo. V. c. 87) subjects to its penalties all who infringe (or have infringed) any proclamation "dealing with trading with the enemy." This must certainly mean a proclamation in so far as it deals with the matter in question; and it seems to be going somewhat beyond the subject of trading with the enemy (a perfectly well-understood head of international law) to lay down restrictions on trading in goods which at one time belonged to the enemy. All that the announcement expressly says is that the goods will be "detained."

The same intimation (which is perhaps not a "proclamation" within the meaning of the Act) prohibits exports[3] unaccompanied by a declaration that they are not ultimately to reach the enemy. Whether this can be supported is equally doubtful.

[1] From Europe or the Mediterranean or Black Seas (except British, Allied, or Peninsular ports). Provisionally, certain ports alone are specified, comprising all the Norse, Swedish, Danish, and Dutch ones of any consequence; also Genoa, Spezzia, and Savona in Italy.

[2] "Production" probably applies to the case of raw materials.

[3] To similar localities, without any specification of individual ports.

ENEMY PRODUCTS

Provisionally, foodstuffs and parcels under £100 in value are exempted in the case of imports only. For subsequent variations in the notice, see Appendix. The sanction of the procedure appears to be that no damages can be claimed from the Customs for detention.

Patents, Banking, and Insurance. — But even branches cannot carry on the business of banking[1] or insurance. The question of enemy patents is dealt with by Statutory Rules of 21st August,[2] under which (on application by an intending manufacturer) an enemy's patents may be avoided or suspended, on any terms the Board of Trade may direct. Similar provisions were made in respect of designs and trademarks, by sets of rules issued on 5th September (Designs) and 21st August (T.-M.). In the case of patents and designs, further provision was made on 7th September for the granting of temporary or permanent licenses to use such patents and designs (but not trade-marks). The first Act under which these rules were made (4 & 5 Geo. v. c. 27) contained no reference to designs or grant of license: consequently c. 73 was passed on 28th August. The Act presumes that the license is to be exclusive and the monopoly continued: it speaks of patents "liable to" avoidance. The rules speak of "licenses" to use avoided patents: which is quite absurd, besides being *ultra vires*.

[1] Proc. of 10th Aug.: *vide* Appendix.
[2] *Vide* Appendix.

PART V

THE CROWN AND THE NEUTRAL

CHAPTER I

PRIZE-COURT PROCEDURE

Essentially different from Common-Law Trial—Not a Contest, but a Confession—An International Court, with an International Practice — Whether bound by Local Regulations—Cannot sit in Neutral Territory—Captors' Evidence only admitted if Flaws in Claimant's Evidence —"Further Proof"—Story—Scott—Lushington—Phillimore—Twiss—Claims and Evidence of Enemies.

THE object of a prize court is to give a title to the captured property which will be internationally recognised. The orders "for detention" which have recently been made are otiose. They do not in any way affect the property, and the more regular course would have been for the captors in such cases to have left it for the claimants to move, when the circumstances authorising continued detention would have afforded a valid answer to the claim.

The proceedings are *in rem*, and bind all persons who have any interest in the property or cargo concerned. Consequently, and in order that the decrees of the Court shall secure respect in all countries, the law which the prize court administers, and the procedure which it employs, are of an international character, and are not modelled on the principles of English common law.

International Courts.—The question has been much agitated whether the Court is bound to accept and act upon the proclamations of the British Government as to prize. In the *Maria*[1] Lord Stowell used the often-cited and memorable language which follows :—

"I trust that it has not escaped my anxious attention for one moment, what it is that the duty of my station calls for from me; namely, to consider myself as stationed here, not to deliver occasional and shifting opinions to serve present purposes of particular national interest, but to administer with indifference that justice which the law of nations holds out without distinction to independent states, some happening to be neutral and some to be belligerent. The seat of judicial authority is, indeed, locally here, in the belligerent country, according to the known law and practice of nations; but the law itself has no locality. It is the duty of the person who sits here to determine this question exactly as he would determine the same question if sitting at Stockholm; to assert no pretensions on the part of Great Britain which he would not allow to Sweden in the same circumstances, and to impose no duties on Sweden, as a neutral country, which he would not admit to belong to Great Britain in the same character."

It is true that in the *Fox*[2] the same distinguished authority held that he ought to apply the British

---

[1] (1799) 1 C.R. 349*a*.
[2] (1811) 1 Dods 314. *Cf.* the *Diligentia*, (1814) *ibid.*, 404.

Orders in Council, which were inconsistent with the ordinary rules of International Law. But he did so expressly on the ground of their being justifiable as reprisals.

"A question has been stated, What would be the duty of the Court under Orders in Council that were repugnant to the Law of Nations? It has been contended on one side, that the Court would at all events be bound to enforce the Orders in Council: on the other, that the Court would be bound to apply the rule of the Law of Nations adapted to the particular case, in disregard of the Orders in Council. I have not observed, however, that these Orders in Council, in their retaliatory character, have been described in the argument as at all repugnant to the Law of Nations, however liable to be so described if merely original and abstract. . . .

"These two propositions, that the Court is bound to administer the Law of Nations, and that it is bound to enforce the King's Orders in Council, are not at all inconsistent with each other, because these orders and instructions are presumed to conform themselves, under the given circumstances, to the principles of its unwritten law."

They are, he proceeds to say, either applications of known principles to particular cases, the facts of which could be only imperfectly known to the Court; or else they are reductions to an exact measure of a general principle which in itself, though known, is somewhat vague. He proceeds to invoke the analogy of parliament, which (as was commonly thought at that date) cannot contravene the approved principles of national reason and justice.

In the particular case of the orders and instructions in question, he proceeds:—

"The Court has not heard it at all maintained in argument that as *retaliatory* orders they are not conformable to [principle]—for *retaliatory* orders they are. They are so declared in their own language, and in the uniform language of the government which has established them. I have no hesitation in saying that they cease to be just if they ceased to be retaliatory."

It is difficult to see how a belligerent can "retaliate" on neutrals: and Phillimore[1] holds that the Orders did contravene the law. But that eminent authority is clear from these cases, that "it has never been the doctrine of the British Prize Courts, that because they sit under the authority of the Crown, the Crown has authority to prescribe to them rules which violate International Law. The Orders in Council of 1807 did, in the opinion of the writer, contravene that law; but in the opinion of the Judge of the Prize Court they were, as has been seen, consistent with it; and therefore his decrees carried them into execution."

Much less can a subordinate executive or legislative authority have power to prescribe rules to a prize tribunal. H.M. "Instructions" of 1803 were read by that great jurist, Sir James Mackintosh, as Recorder of Bombay, in a sense which was probably not intended. In order to make them consistent with principle, "colonies" was read "colonies with which neutrals might not trade during peace."[2]

[1] *Int. Law*, iii. sec. 436, p. 655.
[2] The *Minerva: Life of Mackintosh*, i. 317. Wheaton, *Captures*, p. 50 (with whom Story collaborated), entirely agrees with Phillimore and Mackintosh.

"Something," he said, "had been said of the obedience due to the letter of these 'Instructions.' . . . As to the doctrine that courts of prize were bound by illegal instructions, he had already in a former case (the *Erin*) treated it as a groundless charge by an American writer against English courts.[1] In this case (which had hitherto been, and he trusted ever would continue, imaginary) of illegal instructions, he was convinced that English Courts of Admiralty would as much assert their independence of arbitrary mandates as English Courts of Common Law. . . . In such an imaginary case, it would be the duty of the judge to disregard the 'Instructions,' and to consult only that universal law to which all civilised princes and states acknowledge themselves to be subject, and over which none of them can claim any authority." Phillimore adds that Mansfield had, long before, declared from the King's Bench that an Act of Parliament could not alter the Law of Nations.[2] Of course, as the *Walsingham Packet*[3] shows, a

---

[1] See the *Venus*, 8 Cranch 263; "The British Court of Admiralty—a mere political court—a prerogative court regulated by the King's Orders in Council, designed to give Great Britain the sovereignty of the ocean, to subject the whole commerce of the world to her grasp, and to make the law of nations just what her policy would wish it to be." Cf. *De Wolf* v. *N.Y. Fire In. Co.*, (1822) 20 Johnson (Am.) 228: "The doctrines advanced by that eminent judge in the British Admiralty were the result of power forgetting right, and the offspring of state policy created for the occasion."—*Per* Spenser, J.

[2] *Heathfield* v. *Chilton*, (1767) 4 Burr. 2016. Cf. *Bernardi* v. *Motteux*, (1781) 2 Dougl. 581.

[3] (1798) 1 C.R. 84.

British subject may be held, in the Court of Prize as elsewhere, to be bound by a British statute.

The Prize Court, in short, resembles, as Dr T. A. Walker[1] has remarked, a divisional court, sitting in a particular country, of a great International tribunal. It may, and should, accept the instruction and guidance, in doubtful points, of the local sovereign—but it must not enforce his contradictions of established principle.

Protected States.—A Prize Court must not be set up in a neutral (though it may be in an allied) jurisdiction. And a protected state is neutral unless and until the protecting Power, if enabled to do so, puts it in a position of hostility to the enemy.[2] Accordingly, British Prize Courts cannot be set up in Egypt, Malaya, or Zanzibar.[3] Nor can they be set up in countries of capitulations (conceded consular jurisdiction), such as China. For, as Sir F. T. Piggott shows, the consular courts in China or Persia, though administering a peculiar law, are none the less Chinese or Persian courts, exercising their peculiar jurisdiction under the authority of the Chinese or Persian state. The fact that English people are

---

[1] *Science of International Law*, p. 46.

[2] The *Ionian Ships*, Spinks 193.

[3] If these states can really be said to enjoy any independent existence at all. Cf. *Law Magazine*, 1911-12, pp. 334, 470. As to Cyprus and Wei-hai-wei the case is different. There we had definite, though terminable, territorial rights. Power is taken in Stat. 4 & 5 Geo. V. c. 79 to invest the British courts in Egypt, Zanzibar, and Cyprus with prize jurisdiction. But Britain can no more legislate for these territories (which are admittedly foreign) than for France. *Quaere*, therefore, if the decrees of these courts would be respected.

allowed to be tried by English law and judges in Constantinople does not justify England in taking prizes into the Golden Horn and condemning them there. Peculiar privileges do not justify the claim of territorial power. And only territorial power can cover the institution of a prize court.

Captors—no Evidence or Costs.—It should be remarked, in general, that prize-court procedure is wholly different from common-law practice. Costs and damages are seldom allowed to either side, claimants or captors,[1] as the claimant has to establish his interest as a condition of being heard. The case must be decided on the ship's papers, and the answers to the standing interrogatories of her crew. She must be condemned "out of her own mouth." This was definitely laid down by Lord Stowell in the *Haabet* (*Giertsen*[2]), and absolutely confirmed by Dr Lushington in the *Leucade*.[3] It is "the very essence of prize law: and it is a great mistake to admit the common-law notions in respect to evidence, to prevail in proceedings which have no analogy to those at common law." "It is of the last importance to preserve the most rigid exactness as to the admission of evidence."

"The general rule of law is that on all points the evidence of the claimants alone shall be received in the first instance; and if no doubt arises on that view of the case, the Court is bound . . . to take those points as fully demonstrated.

[1] The *Leucade*, (1856) Spinks 217. This international rule cannot be affected by a municipal rule that the Crown *never* pays or gets costs.   [2] (1805) 6 C.R. 54.

[3] Phillimore, *Int. Law*, iii. sec. 473, 474, p. 716. Twiss in 3 *Law Magazine*, 1877-8, p. 1.

"The rule by which this Court has always been guided is, I believe, conformable to the general practice of all the nations of Europe, which directs the evidence to be taken from the persons on board the captured ship. . . .

"If I should accede to this demand [to admit captors' evidence], the consequence would be that I must do it upon a uniform principle of admitting affidavits universally and in all cases, though there should be nothing to excite suspicion in the original evidence, and though the language of all the witnesses is as precise as possible. I can come to no such conclusion. It would, I think, be productive of great mischief on all sides. It might throw into the way of captors a temptation to exceed the line of their duty, and the exact demands of justice and truth; and it could not fail to impose upon the Court a most unpleasant difficulty in the exercise of its judicial functions. For how could the Court decide? Counter-affidavits must be introduced, which would necessarily be contradictory. Which should the Court believe? Can it be maintained that the preference should be given to the captors? and *that*, in opposition to the general rule of law, which gives the preference the other way, and which directs that the property of the neutral claimant shall not be condemned except on evidence coming out of his own mouth, or arising out of the clear circumstances of the transaction.

"If this rule is unsatisfactory to captors, it is nevertheless the rule which the law prescribes. It is my duty to take care that the rules of law are observed, and that the rights of war are not exceeded. And certainly in no cases more than in this particular branch of the

Law of Nations, which must in its nature operate with severe restraint upon neutral commerce. . . .

"If the vessel [really] was within three miles of Dunkirk and within sight of the town, it might have been pointed out in the presence of both crews; it is not to be supposed that out of eight Norwegians, of whom the captain had the right to select the witnesses that should be examined, one might not then have been found honest enough to depose to it."

His Lordship's duty imposed on him the obligation of resisting the captors' attempts to supply the deficiency, and he restored the ship and cargo. (The *Haabet, u.s.*)

In the *Glierktigheit*,[1] Scott repeated (the captor having been allowed to interpose an averment): "If that is positively contradicted, the Court finds itself under a dilemma to which it must always expect to be reduced by admitting such affidavits. When the facts are positively denied, and that denial cannot be invalidated by any adequate means of estimating the credit of the witnesses, there is no other way of proceeding but by laying out of the case all this extraneous matter, and by recurring to the original evidence."

After referring to the conflict of evidence, he proceeds: "This is the state of the dilemma to which the Court is reduced, and it will, I hope, put it upon its guard against the admission of such affidavits in future cases."

Story remarks that "in some few of the district courts it was not unusual, during the late war, to allow the witnesses to be examined *orally*, at the bar

[1] 6 C.R. p. 58, *n.* (1805).

of the Court, long after their preparatory examinations had been taken, and full opportunities had been given to enable the parties to shape any new defence, or explain away any asserted facts. This was unquestionably a great irregularity, and in many instances must have been attended with great public mischief."[1] In the *Dos Hermanos* he remarks: "Witnesses were produced by the libellant and the claimant indiscriminately at the trial, and their testimony was taken in open court upon any and all points to which the parties chose to interrogate them, . . . in fact, there was nothing to distinguish the cause from an ordinary proceeding in a revenue cause *in rem*."[2]

Evidence for the captors was, however, constantly admitted as to facts not connected with the particular individual capture—*e.g.*, the existence of a *de facto* blockade. This is established, if it needed to be formally established, by the recollection of Dr Lushington, as recounted in the *Leucade*.[3] Captors might also lead evidence to escape condemnation in costs; but this was seldom, if ever, necessary, as costs were seldom awarded against them.

Apart from these special exceptions, Lushington says:[3] "The admission would occasion delay, expense, and doubt. There is always difficulty in deciding between conflicting affidavits. How enormously would that difficulty be enhanced when the affidavits came from persons all intermarked in the result; and for the most part, as relates to the

---

[1] Cited, Phillimore, *ubi supra*, iii. sec. 473.
[2] The *Dos Hermanos*, (1817) 2 Wheat. 81.
[3] (1856) Spinks 232.

claimant, prepared abroad, and from translations also."

If the ship's evidence is not satisfactory, it is true that "further proof" may be admitted, either on behalf of claimants or captors. As Dr Lushington observes in the *Aline and Fanny*[1]: " According to my recollection, the practice of the Court has always been to permit both the claimants and the captors to state at the hearing any facts they may deem conducive to their interest, and to pray leave to prove them; and for the Court, after hearing the case on the primary evidence, to deal with such application as it may think fit."[2] And it is on the ground that the original evidence showed discrepancies or deficiencies (such as a blank day in the log) that such cases as the *Charlotte Christine*[3] were decided. So again, in the *Odin*,[4] the witnesses prevaricated. It is fair to observe that Scott's language in the *Romeo*[5] seems to infer that even if the primary evidence is satisfactory, the Court may decline to accept it, owing to "its own private conviction," and order further proof. Such a proposition is strongly combated by Lushington in the *Aline and Fanny*, (1855) Spinks 322, and has no support from Phillimore.

The actual point decided in the *Romeo* was, that papers found on board another captured ship might, in a case where the primary evidence was not satisfactory, be received as "further proof," even though the latter ship was not made the subject of prize

---

[1] (1856) Spinks 322.
[2] *I.e.*, if the primary evidence arouses suspicion, it may order "further proof."
[3] (1805) 6 C.R. 101.
[4] (1799) 1 C.R. 248.
[5] (1806) 6 C.R. 35.

proceedings (at any rate since the paper had been sent in before the capture of the *Romeo*, and was thus subject to no suspicion of fabrication). Had the other ship been libelled as prize, there could have been no question of the admissibility of the paper as invoked primary evidence. Scott's *dictum* in the case must be understood as limited to very extraordinary circumstances indeed. In the *Sarah*,[1] he declined to admit letters (ordering the captured goods) taken in exactly the same way from the ship herself (on the outward voyage). "The practice of the Court would be led away from the simplicity of prize proceedings, and there would be no end to the accumulation of proof that would be introduced in order to support arbitrary suggestions." This was actually a case in which "further proof" had been called for. The *dictum* cannot weigh against a formal decision.

In some cases in the American Civil War, the Court, admitting the claimant's evidence to be true, nevertheless allowed the captors to give evidence, holding the claimant's evidence to be insufficient. Since, for the first time, they were holding as against neutrals that the ultimate destination of the goods to the enemy's use was a crucial factor, it was obvious that the plain and simple answers to the common interrogatories could seldom or never have disproved such an ultimate intention. The true inference should have been, not that further evidence was let in, but that the asserted principle was vicious. The result of admitting the evidence was to assimilate prize proceedings to an ordinary common-law trial,

[1] (1801) 3 C.R. 330.

and to reduce it to a contract of probabilities between the claimant's version and the captor's version. In other words, it amounted to calling on the claimants to prove their innocence. As Twiss shows,[1] this is an entire perversion of prize process. The ship ought to be condemned "out of her own mouth." The grounds of condemnation must be such simple and objective facts as could be put in the standing interrogatories (unfortunately abolished), and answered as matters of fact and not of intention. This is represented as the "immemorial" practice of Europe by the great jurists (Lee, J., Paul, Adv. Gen., Ryder A.-G., and Murray S.-G. (Mansfield)) who drew up the celebrated Report of 1753 (see Wheaton, *Captures*, p. 310.

Enemy Evidence and Claims.—In prize proceedings, the evidence of alien enemies is freely received.[2] Claims by alien enemies may even be made, alleging a license, cartel, or other *commercium belli*. The ordinary objection to suits by enemies does not hold, since *ex hypothesi*, persons fully authorised to deal with the property in all cases of extraordinary accidents and perils are here in the jurisdiction.

Wheaton (*Captures*, p. 39) even states that ships captured illegally from the French before they joined in the war (of the Spanish succession?) were restored to the French by the British Prize Courts *flagrante bello*. It is difficult to extract a clear rule from the *Möwe*.

[1] 3 *Law Magazine* (1877-8), p. 1; Atherley Jones, *Commerce in War*, p. 80; Baty, *Britain and Sea Law*, ch. iv.
[2] The *Fenix*, (1854) Spinks (p. 3). *U.S.* v. 1756 *Shares*, *supra*, p. 289, *per* Nelson, J., citing the authorities.

CHAPTER II

CONTRABAND

Objective Warlike Test—Military Quality—Fluctuations—Test of Port of Destination in Doubtful Cases—"Occasional" Contraband—Pre-emption—Food, Naval Stores—Reversion in Nineteenth Century to Stricter Limit—Nullified by Chase's Doctrine of Intention—The Doctrine examined—Continuous Voyage—Kleen—Declaration of London — Proclamations of 1914 — Declaration of Paris exploded—Penalty of Contraband Carriage.

CONTRABAND is the modern vestige of the bygone assumption to interdict all traffic with the enemy territory.[1]

It denotes certain traffic which a belligerent is still entitled to intercept, and in general to deter by confiscation.

Objective Warlike Test. — It is exceedingly difficult to put the casual reader in a position to appreciate the real nature of contraband. It is true that, on the one hand, it is an elastic conception. It is equally certain, on the other hand, that it is very far from covering (as is sometimes asserted) anything that a belligerent likes to include. What we find is a hard core of articles unmistakably contraband: materials whose sole or characteristic

[1] *Vide* p. 294, *supra*.

use is for war. And if we find a slender penumbra or fringe of other articles thrown in with these, varying from time to time, we shall not therefore conclude that anything whatever may be contraband; but only this, that tentative attempts have from time to time been made to extend the borders of the term in comparatively unimportant directions.

The lists of contraband which various nations published from the seventeenth to the nineteenth centuries,[1] exhibit a striking similarity in their main features. They particularise with great minuteness the various kinds of military equipment, down to trumpets and bridles. This catalogue forms by far the largest part of every one of these lists. In many cases it forms the whole. But in some, it is slightly extended. It was not possible to draw a perfect line of demarcation between what was military and what was not. Many nations included horses. Russia never would. No nation included lead or wagons. At a time when the merchantman of one week was the privateer of the next, ships and their equipment were at least as well within the border line as cavalry. Great Britain began to include naval stores in her idea of contraband. Cordage, sailcloth, and spars were early regarded as such. Tar, pitch, and hemp were also drawn within the ambit of the conception. It is important to remember, moreover, the distinction Sir W. Scott draws[2] between ordinary hemp and best naval hemp, between rough logs and manufactured spars: only the latter is in each case contraband. Still more important was the limitation

[1] *Vide* Atherley Jones, *Commerce in War*, pp. 8-54.
[2] As in *Gute Gesellschaft Michael*, (1801) 4 C.R. 94.

which was put on the seizure of such stores[1] (and which had not been put on the seizure of horses) when they were the raw material and the native produce of the country of the exporting[2] ship. Under the denomination of "occasional" contraband, they were then only subjected to confiscation when the fact of their intended military use was patent: the patent fact being that of avowed and immediate destination to a port of naval equipment.[3] Unless they had that destination they were not confiscated, but might be purchased at a fair rate,[4] with freight to the carrier. When cheeses made to navy pattern, and subsequently other provisions, were included in the category of contraband, it was subject to the same condition that the goods should be avowedly going to a naval or military port: and provisions seem to have been treated somewhat more favourably than home-grown naval stores—*i.e.*, they were not interfered with at all unless going to a naval port.[5]

We do not find that any sweeping captures of provisions were ever made, under these restrictions. Food and clothing destined to ordinary ports were not even as a rule taken up and subjected to pre-

[1] Sometimes (as in the *Apollo* (Bottcher), (1802) 4 C.R. 158) they were simply restored.

[2] *Cf.* the *Jonge Margaretha*, (1799) 1 C.R. 189. It was subsequently recognised as allowable to use the ship of another neutral nation: the *Apollo, ubi supra*.

[3] The *Stadt Embden*, (1798) 1 C.R. 26; the *Neptunus*, (1800) 3 C.R. 108; *N.S. de Begona*, 5 C.R. 97.

[4] The *Sarah and Bernhardus*, (1776) 1 Marriott 96, and many other cases, *ibid.*, pp. 148-287.

[5] The *Haabet*, (1799) 2 C.R. 174 (Cadiz); *Sed. cf.* the *Jonge Margaretha, ubi supra* (Brest); the *Zelden Rust*, (1805) 6 C.R. 93 (Ferrol-Corunna).

emption.[1] But even so, the whole doctrine of interfering with neutral traffic in naval stores and provisions was strongly opposed by every publicist on the Continent during the French wars and until late in the nineteenth century. Their governing principle was to limit the category of contraband strictly to warlike munitions. Hantefeuille and Ortolan's works, published about 1840-50, furnish a good example of the attitude taken up.

"**Intention**" **Doctrine.**—But a case had been decided in America which afforded a foothold for an entirely new conception of contraband. The case itself was not really one of contraband, but one of unneutral service. The vessel (a Swede) was chartered to carry a cargo of grain to a belligerent army, and she was virtually acting as an enemy transport. Spain, where she was destined, might technically be a neutral country to Britain and America; but the hostile British army was there, and Bilbao was its port. The *Commercen* was *avowedly* carrying the supplies direct to the enemy's army, in the territory under its direct control. It was not a matter of inference or conjecture. And it was with reference to these unusual circumstances that Story, J., observed in that case (the *Commercen*, 1 Wheaton 382) that the contraband character of goods depends on the "destination" for which they

---

[1] In one very extraordinary case (1793) this was done, on the express excuse that revolutionary and regicide France was not a state, and could not be dealt with on the ordinary footing of the Law of Nations. For captures of U.S. vessels made on this theory, Britain was obliged to pay damages under Jay's Treaty (Wheaton, sec. 501). And of course the Paper Blockades of 1806-7 were supposed by nobody to be lawful.

are transported. Destination does not here mean "intention"; but "avowed terminus." The intention (that the goods shall assist the enemy's forces) must be established by well-known objective rules, and not by any presumptions based on other indications which commend themselves to the Court. A prize court sits under difficulties, and must not fashion hypotheses.[1]

It will readily be seen how startling and extensive an operation this dictum might have if it was taken out of its context and interpreted to mean that the intention, however manifested, that goods should reach the enemy's forces, was the essential element in contraband. Obviously Story never meant this. By "destination for the use of" the enemy's army, he meant "direct and avowed transmission to" those forces: destination, not a matter of inference but of fact, appearing on the ship's papers.

Continuous Voyage.—The new idea had, in fact, two startling results, which revolutionised the character of contraband, in the ambit of which there had previously been comprised only warlike *matériel*, with naval stores grudgingly annexed, and provisions struggling for a precarious and uncertain inclusion. The way was now open to include everything—and in the American Civil War cases, the courts promptly seized the opportunity. The new Chief Justice (Chase), against the opinion of experienced judges like Nelson, began to treat clothing, boots, medicines, and the like, as contraband,

---

[1] For a fuller discussion, see T. Baty, *Britain and Sea Law*, p. 70. *Cf.* Atherley Jones, *Commerce in War*, p. 80; Twiss in 3 *Law Magazine* (1877-8), 1, and *Ulterior Destination, ibid.*, Sept. 1870, p. 82.

merely on account of their supposed destination for the Confederate forces. Another result was that the courts abandoned the inflexible doctrine of Sir W. Scott, that the ship must be going straight to a hostile port.[1] They held in effect that it was sufficient that the goods appeared to be ultimately destined for the enemy country. This was a travesty of the theory of "continuous colonial voyages" as elaborated by Scott. All that Scott did was to hold a voyage a colonial one, when it was admitted that it had two stages, which together were equivalent to a single voyage from a metropolis to its colony.[2]

Of these novelties, the latter was not unacceptable to later Continental theorists, such as Kleen. So long as the list of contraband was rigidly circumscribed, it could not be a serious interference with neutral trade to capture contraband on its apparent way to a neutral port. All that would happen would be that warlike cargoes would be dangerous, as well as warlike ports of destination. But the dislike of "occasional" contraband persisted. The distaste for allowing prize courts, that is, to interfere, even by pre-emption, with *prima facie* innocent goods was as strong as ever.

Declaration of London.—Yet, when the Declaration of London was framed in 1909, after the abandoned Russian attempt to treat cotton and corn as contraband in the Far East, it was not the theory of

---

[1] The *Imina*, (1800) 3 C.R. 167. See Appendix, *infra*, at end.

[2] Further details will be found in Atherley Jones, *Commerce in War*, p. 253; T. Baty, *International Law in S. Africa*, chap. i. A clear ulterior destination to Ostend was disregarded by Scott in the case of the *Spazemheid*, (1800) 3 C.R. 42, 46.

"continuous voyage," but the doctrine of "occasional" contraband, that was confirmed by the ten Powers that participated in framing it. In exchange for the absolute safety of traffic destined to neutral ports formally established by Art. 35,[1] it was declared by Art. 33 that all commodities going direct to the enemy, except raw materials and fancy articles (the so-called " free list ") should be confiscable as contraband, *and not paid* for, if they could be supposed to be destined for the use of the enemy's armed forces. Two presumptions of that destination were supplied: viz., (1) destination to a "base of supplies"; (2) destination to a government agent or contractor. There could be no others, for the enumeration was exclusive. The serious addition to the troubles of the neutral was made, that carriage of contraband entailed confiscation of the vessel, if it amounted to 50 per cent. of the cargo (Art. 40). This is a serious matter, when the cargo is *primâ facie* innocent, and only held contraband on slender presumptions. Since Britain did not confiscate the vehicle, and the Continent did not recognise "occasional" contraband, it is also an entirely novel infliction for the grain-carrier and other food ships.

The Declaration of London was not ratified by Great Britain. It has been adopted for the purposes of the present war, but with profound modifications.[2] (1) The well-known official Memorandum ("The Renault Memorandum") is to be adopted (though contradicted in the above respects) as a guide to the construction of the Declaration. (2) The rejection of the doctrine of "continuous voyage" is recanted,

[1] For Proclamation, *vide* Appendix, and cf. *Candid Review*, Nov. 1914.

and neutral ports are thereby made unsafe termini. (3) The formal presumption of a warlike destination is extended to all cargoes destined (not only for enemy agents but) to all persons "under the control of" the enemy. Since everyone in his country is under his control, this would seem to amount to a total prohibition to neutrals to deal with the enemy in anything but raw materials and fancy goods ("the free list").

These fundamental modifications of the Declaration [1] do not stand alone.

The next departure from its terms was to impinge on the "free list." By a Proclamation of 22nd September 1914, much crude material is made "occasional" contraband, and therefore confiscable (with the ship) if a court can make out to its own satisfaction that it is ultimately destined for "anyone under the control" of a hostile government. The goods selected are :—Copper (unwrought), lead (pig, sheet, or pipe), glycerine, ferrochrome, hæmatite iron ore, magnetic iron ore, rubber, and hides and skins (raw or rough tanned, but not including dressed leather). The list was enormously extended on 29th Oct. and 28th Dec.—see Appendix. Germany seems to treat timber, cylinder tar, sulphur, and sulphuric acid as conditional contraband (*Times*, 24th Dec. 1914).

None of these things has any special usefulness in war outweighing its peaceful uses. It is understood that Sweden and the United States of America have

---

[1] They were embodied in an Order in Council of 20th Aug. 1914. It also placed aircraft in the category of absolute contraband. Little exception can be taken to this, as by far their most important practical use is military. The addition of their "accessories" is more dubious.

protested against this extension; and it has even been said that the British Ambassador in Washington has offered pre-emption in such cases. In the darkest days of the American Civil War, the President did not venture to declare raw materials contraband; and it is not impossible that some such compromise may have been proposed. Pre-emption was always the line of least resistance in doubtful cases. We do not think, however, that, on any fair interpretation of the analysis of the past, raw material of no particular military significance can be of a doubtful character. Pitch and tar of themselves suggested the sea, and naval conflict. Iron ore, copper ingots, and leather by no means inevitably suggest military apparatus. In point of fact, however, the physical obstacles in the way of trade with German ports make the whole question of contraband insignificant, apart from the doctrine of continuous voyage by overland transit.

Declaration of Paris.—It has been suggested that the real reason of the recent insistence on the element of "intention," instead of the old principle of regarding solely admitted facts, was to evade the Declaration of Paris of 1856, which, in the interest of neutrals, freed from capture the property of enemies found in neutral ships. It can, under our new doctrines, be captured in very many cases; and what is more, very much neutral property, destined for the enemy country, can be captured and annexed without compensation as "contraband of war." It would at once have been much simpler and less harmful to neutrals to have rescinded the Declaration of Paris altogether, as their ships, at any rate, were formerly quite safe (except when transporting dangerous munitions of war).

Take for instance the trade of Holland. So long as a Dutch ship was not freighted with rifles or military equipment, it could trade freely with any mercantile belligerent port, at the risk (at worst) of having its cargo bought. So long as a foreign ship was not trading to a belligerent port, its traffic, even in warlike stores, was safe: consequently, foreign trade with Holland was absolutely uninterrupted. But under the present rules, all trade, no matter in what goods (except raw materials, etc.), is unsafe; trade for Dutch ports can always be subjected to the imputation of enemy destination; and Dutch ships carrying the most innocent of cargoes to their own ports are liable to confiscation if the imputation should be held by an energetic prize judge to be proved. All certainty and security are gone.[1]

This may be beneficial to Great Britain in the immediate present. It is our duty only to point out that it goes far beyond what neutrals have tolerated in the past, and may be calculated to drive them into the arms of a belligerent.[2] Their one consolation is that much of these new contraband cargoes would formerly have equally been seized as enemy goods; but in that case they would have kept their ships and their freight. When once the objective tests were abandoned, real security for the neutral had disappeared.

Penalty.—The ship is free from disturbance on

[1] *Cf.* Twiss, " Continuous Voyage " (*Law Magazine*, 1877-8, p. 1).

[2] T. Baty, *Britain and Sea Law, passim.*

the return voyage. The Declaration of London reversed the curious British rule under which, if the voyage out had been made by the help of false papers, the cargo was held liable to confiscation on the return voyage. It was held to represent the proceeds of the contraband traffic. By the Order in Council of 20th August 1914, this archaic rule is reinstated. The use of false papers also involves the ship in confiscation. But it was not the British practice to confiscate anything but the cargo[1] under ordinary circumstances: and, when it was pre-empted as "occasional" contraband, freight was paid for it as well. This lenity might well be imitated.

If, however, the venture was essentially one—*i.e.*, if ship and contraband belonged to the same owner—the former was involved in the fate of the latter. Any innocent cargo belonging to the owner of the contraband was also condemned.[2]

Bringing In.—The principle of bringing in for examination in port in a case where the papers are not fully descriptive of the cargo was recognised by Sir W. Scott.[3] "Torse is so like hemp, that . . . it is necessary that such cargoes should be brought in for examination." Presumably the description was "hemp,"; and the question would arise whether it was best (naval) hemp or the inferior sort known as torse. So, if the papers named no definite consignor: the *Abo* 24 L.T., O.S. 5; or consignee: the *Jonge Pieter* 4 C.R. 79; or are "to order": the *Atlas*, 3 *ibid.* 299.

---

[1] Ignorance of the nature of the cargo was not requisite. *Cf.* the *Charlotte*, (1804) 5 C.R. 275; the *Sarah Christine*, (1799) 1 C.R. 237.   [2] The *Stadt Embden*, (1798) 1 C.R. 26.
[3] The *Jonge Hermanus*, 4 C.R. 95.

CHAPTER III

BLOCKADE

History — "Paper" Blockades — Modern Uselessness of Blockade—Notification—British and French Variance—Declaration of London—Continuous Voyage—Penalty of Blockade—Maintenance of Blockade—Impartiality—Spurious "Blockades"—(really instances of Contraband, Reprisals, etc.) — Infringement by Entry or Exit—Warships.

BLOCKADE is a survival and extension of siege. It is plainly impossible to allow a neutral to throw provisions or other commodities into a beleaguered place. Doubtless the practice of capturing (and in this case confiscating) vessels and cargoes, which attempt to enter or leave a port of the enemy, was in its origin auxiliary to siege operations. It has, however, been extended so as to prevent intercourse on the part of neutrals with a port against which no immediate naval or military operations are being conducted. Such a "commercial" blockade has been condemned (*e.g.* by Hall) as an abuse; but the practice is too well established to be rejected as contrary to the Law of Nations.

"**Paper**" **Blockades.**—It would be an easy means of interdicting neutral trade with the enemy, if it could be established by mere declaration. But since the stand made by the Armed Neutralities of 1780 and 1800, it has generally been recognised that "paper" blockades bind nobody. And this was embodied formally in the Declaration of Paris (1856), which provided that blockades must be maintained by a force sufficient to make communication with the port in question evidently dangerous. The precise force required in each case must of course depend on circumstances. It need not be very near the port if it can control the traffic, and if its presence is obvious. Great—perhaps undue—lenity has been shown to blockaders since the introduction of steam. A cruiser with a wide radius of action may indeed make access to a port as dangerous as half a dozen old sailing frigates. But she is not so obviously visible.

Notification.—The main use of blockades in future will be to cut off export trade and the import of raw materials. They may be imposed by the government, or by an adequate naval authority on the spot. The Declaration of London provides machinery for their due notification in each case: and it abolishes the rule by which the mere sailing for a blockaded port was held, in principle, sufficient in Great Britain for condemnation. Under the Declaration, it is necessary to approach the blockaded region.[1] A vessel can, of course, be condemned for breach of blockade if she has express notice of it. And French practice required that notice should be express and individual, and intimated by a cruiser on the spot. This rule was negatived by the

[1] Art. 17.

Declaration of London (again in this instance, as in that of contraband, unfavourable to neutrals). It was provided that it should be sufficient that the vessel should have had opportunity of hearing of the blockade. In the case of a blockade by government, it would be sufficient [1] if the ship called at or sailed from a neutral port after notification of the blockade had been made to the neutral government in time for its existence to be notified at that port of exit or call. What remedy there may be for a neutral's laxity in intimation is not apparent. In cases of blockades by naval officers no such presumption was established. The Declaration did not deal with the cases in which the ship had visited an allied or hostile port. The recent Proclamation [2] provides a rule in such cases. (1) If the vessel left a British or allied port, it is presumed to know of all blockades published at the time (where and by whom is not stated—is a declaration in London supposed to be known at the Turks and Keys?). (2) If it left a hostile port, it is presumed to know of all blockades notified to the local authorities [? of the port blockaded] in time to enable the enemy government to make the existence of the blockade known [at the port of call?]. This confused provision appears to refer to the case of blockades established by naval authority, which (Declaration of London, 11) have to be notified to the local authorities of the port blockaded. How they are to communicate with their government is not explained.

But these rules appear to be mere presumptions

[1] Art. 15, Declaration of London.
[2] 20th August 1914.

which can be rebutted, though, it is supposed, only in strong cases, and by clear evidence.

Continuous Voyage.—The doctrine of "continuous voyage" (where the destination of the ship, evidenced by her papers, and not contradicted by the depositions, was for an unblockaded port) was applied in the American Civil War to blockade. But this attempt has been universally reprobated, and finds no sanction in the Declaration of London (Arts. 18, 19).

Penalty.—The usual penalty is confiscation of ship and cargo. But the cargo may sometimes be saved. If the master takes upon himself to run the ship into a blockaded port, this may have been contemplated by nobody at the time of shipment. The shipowners are bound by his act, and therefore cargo belonging to them is confiscable: and after some hesitation Lord Stowell held that cargo of other persons, not appearing to be destined by them for the blockaded port, will also be involved,[1] unless they *could* not have known of the blockade [2] when the vessel sailed.

Maintenance. — A blockade, however formally imposed, if once interrupted becomes non-existent, and must be as formally reconstituted. In the early part of the American Civil War, it is clear that neutrals acquiesced in much disregard of this rule, blockading ships being distant for days from their stations. The justice of it is clear: neutrals are entitled to assume, if the ships are not there, that

---

[1] The *Adonis*, (1804) 5 C.R. 256; the *Alexander*, (1801) 4 C.R. 93. Cf. *Baltazzi* v. *Ryder*, (1858) 12 Moo. P.C. 168.

[2] The *Exchange*, (1808) 1 Edw. 43; the *Mercurius*, (1798) 1 C.R. 84.

entry is free. Short interruptions due to storm or sickness are supposed to leave the blockade subsisting. But if the ships are driven off the station by the enemy, or are withdrawn for service reasons, for however short a time, the blockade is dissolved.[1]

Equality.—Besides being uninterruptedly maintained, the blockade must not be subject to relaxations. This is not to say that an occasional vessel may not be allowed to enter or leave under a safe-conduct.[2] But any general permission to vessels of some particular nation or nations, or carrying some particular kind or kinds of cargo, would invalidate the blockade.[3] Such a measure would be unfair to the traffic debarred from these favours; and, since a blockade must be open and obvious, the undisturbed arrival and departure of vessels would probably lead mariners to infer that the blockade was suspended generally.

Attempts to enforce blockades "against arms," or "against the Greek flag," can only be considered as cases, not of blockade, but of (1) reprisals; (2) contraband; (3) municipal (*i.e.* national) regulations enforced within the limits of national territory; (4) flat illegality or mistake.[4]

Infringement.—Infringement may be by entry or exit. In principle it appears that exit in ballast is not inconsistent with the object of blockade. And

---

[1] The *Juffrow M. Schroeder*, (1800) 3 C.R. 155. Atherley Jones, *Commerce in War*, p. 197.
[2] The *Juffrow M. Schroeder, ubi supra.*
[3] The *Rolla*, (1807) 6 C.R. 364. *Cf.* Declaration of London, Art. 5. The *Franciska*, (1855) 10 Moo. P.C. 37.
[4] Atherley Jones, *Commerce in War*, pp. 172-184.

there is nothing in the Declaration of London to contradict this: indeed, Art. 19 expressly says that "a vessel cannot be captured for breach of blockade if she is on her way to an unblockaded port"! In principle, also, the visit of foreign men-of-war (entry or exit) is equally unobjectionable.[1] And the U.S.A. in the nineteenth century claimed the right of visiting blockaded ports in South America. "Blockades have never been deemed to extend to public ships. Great Britain, almost perpetually at war, and numerically superior at sea to any other nation, never for a moment pretended that neutral ships of war could be affected by blockades. . . . In 1811, in the U.S. ship the *Hornet*, I myself went into Cherbourg, then blockaded by a British squadron." Other cases are cited by the writer (Commodore Elliott). More recent practice has made it obligatory to obtain permission: and it is always more courteous to do so. The Declaration of London, Art. 6, says entry "may" be permitted.

A limited time is generally allowed for exit, and the exigencies of loading a complete cargo are not respected, though communication with a blockaded port is always allowed to a ship in actual distress.

[1] *Cf.* Raguet to Elliott, 18th March 1826, *Brit. State Papers*, xiv., p. 1169: Same to St Amaro, 13th December 1825. Cited, Atherley Jones, *Commerce in War*, p. 134. *State Papers*, xv., 1120, 1123.

CHAPTER IV

UNNEUTRAL SERVICE

Four Cases: (1) Aiding Enemy's Warlike Operations—(2) Participating in Close Trade—(3) Carriage of Troops and High Officials — (4) Carriage of Despatches. Declaration of London: Dangers of its Wide Interpretation—Neutral Flag an Asylum for Isolated Individuals.

UNDER this head are grouped certain cases, where the penalty is that of forfeiture of the ship. Apart from this unusual feature, the cases are not easily distinguished from contraband.

They may all (with one exception) be reduced to the head of taking enemy employment. The contraband trader supplies an enemy person or the enemy sovereign with goods, but he carries them as a trader and not as a transport. In the cases to which we now refer, the vessel is put at the service of the belligerent. The common view, that it is the carriage of a peculiarly objectionable kind of contraband that gives rise to confiscation, is almost certainly wrong.

Four Cases.—Four cases may be distinguished: (1) engaging in the close trade of the enemy; (2) carriage of enemy troops; (3) carriage of enemy despatches; (4) participation in hostilities under belligerent orders.

The last requires no comment, and the first may be dismissed with the explanation that to take up at the invitation of the belligerent government a branch of trade which is preserved in normal times for its own citizens is to identify oneself with that belligerent country. An instance of such condemnations in recent times is the *Montara*.[1]

The acceptance by a neutral of a belligerent license to trade has been held to have the same effect,[2] and so has the freighting of a belligerent armed ship— though in this last point the American courts do not follow the British.[3]

Participation in a privileged trade of the enemy may have the same effect[4] of rendering the vessel liable to confiscation.

Troops and High Officials.—The carriage of enemy troops and despatches require a word or two of more detailed explanation. It is believed that the true explanation of all the cases in which condemnation has proceeded for the carriage of troops or military or government officials is that the ship in each case was hired or taken up for that very purpose, and had therefore virtually become an enemy's transport. It is true that in the *Orozembo*,[5] it was held immaterial

---

[1] Takahashi, *ut supra*, p. 633.

[2] The *Julia*, (1814) 8 Cranch 181.

[3] The *Nereide*, (1815) 9 Cranch 438: the *Fanny*, (1814) 1 Dods. 443.

[4] The *Anna Catharina*, (1802) 4 C.R. 118. (Tobacco monopoly.) *The Spanish Register Ships*, (1744) 5 C.R. 168. (Colonial trade.)

[5] (1807) 6 C.R. 439. So in the *Nigretia*, [1905] Takahashi, *Int. Law in the Russian War*. In the *Carolina*, 4 C.R. 258, the ship had been taken up as an enemy transport.

that the master did not know the dangerous quality of the persons he was carrying. That does not alter the fact that he had been specially engaged to carry them. In our view the mere acceptance of passengers, even with knowledge of their official or military quality, has never of itself been held a cause of condemnation. If, said Sir W. Scott, in the *Rapid*,[1] officers were proceeding as mere passengers at their own expense, " it would be a very different case." It is when the ship is actually employed in the service of the enemy, whether by force (the *Carolina*[2]) or fraud (the *Orozembo*) on the master, that confiscation is possible. It was not attempted in the case of the *Bundesrath*.[3] (*Cf.* the *Henrick and Alida* (1 Hay and M. 139), where a ship carrying five military officers was released.)

The carriage of high civil officials was assimilated to that of troops in the *Orozembo*. (6 C.R. 430.)

Despatches.—The carriage of despatches stands on a different footing. There is no need in this case to prove, even by inference, that the ship was hired or taken for the carriage of the despatches.[4] It is enough that they were carried. The case is therefore little more than one of contraband: and it is said that the penalty of confiscation is attached to it, simply because the contraband ship being, according to British practice, released, there would be nothing of any value left to capture.[5] It is more probable

---

[1] (1810) Edw. 228.   [2] (1802) 4 C.R. 256.
[3] *Cf.* Atherley Jones, *Commerce in War*, p. 309.
[4] Calvo, sec. 2801, thinks that the same rule as to the conveyance of troops, etc., prevails.
[5] *Per* Sir W. Scott in the *Atalanta*, (1808) 6 C.R. 459.

that the ship is regarded as lending herself in a special fashion to the enemy's service. Despatches are so easily put on board and concealed, however, that a plea of ignorance on the part of the master is here admitted as an excuse.[1] In the case of a mass of correspondence, such as a mail-ship carries, the principle of this rule may be extended so as to exempt the ship if the master is ignorant of the quality of the letters, although in a sense he knows they are on board. He cannot be expected to examine the contents of letters. But letters addressed to belligerent officials ought, it may be thought, to be refused, or at least examined.

The Declaration of London does not deal with the question of despatches, except where the voyage was specially undertaken with a view to the transmission of intelligence to the enemy. Such a voyage, and also a voyage with a special view to the carriage of military persons, are assimilated to contraband trading; a contraband carrier being, according to the Declaration's extolled favourable treatment of neutrals, subject to confiscation in every event. The suggested exemption of ships carrying military passengers in the ordinary way of business is negatived. If to the knowledge of owner, charterer, or master, a military "detachment" (it might be two or three persons) is carried, or if anyone is carried who, in the course of the voyage, directly assists the enemy[2] (perhaps by

---

[1] The *Rapid*, (1810) Edw. 228.

[2] This is a most objectionable rule, as it leaves it open to a belligerent to say that acts which a neutral might quite properly do are "assisting" the operations of the enemy. The general transmission of intelligence might thus be entirely impeded.

signalling), she is confiscable.[1] A harsher but a legitimate rule is applied to ships which themselves take part in hostilities, or are under the control of the enemy or its exclusive employment, or exclusively engaged in the transport of troops, or the transmission of intelligence in the interest of the enemy. These are treated as enemy ships, and properly so.[2] The line between ships "exclusively engaged in" such acts, and those which have specially undertaken a voyage with a view to their accomplishment, is rather thin. It makes us suspect that the "special" character of the undertaking will be very easily inferred in practice.

The vessel once concerned in such adventures as we have been discussing, becomes liable to confiscation even after their conclusion.[3]

We should add, with the strongest reprobation, that by Art. 47 of the Declaration of London, a member of the belligerent armed forces may be forcibly taken from on board a neutral merchant ship. Since the foreign captor cannot be contradicted, this opens up the way to the most violent abuses, and is in conflict with all that has been maintained by America and Great Britain in the controversies regarding impressment and the *Trent* respectively. There is little doubt, as Dr T. A. Walker says, that Britain was wrong in 1807 and right in 1862. The inviolability of the neutral flag, except under due sentence of a prize court, cannot be too firmly maintained. It is here set at nought in a quite anachronistic fashion.

[1] Art. 45.   [2] Art. 46. *Cf.* the *Commercen, supra.*
[3] The *Julia*, (1814) 8 Cranch 202.

PART VI
MISCELLANEOUS

CHAPTER I

COMMENCEMENT AND END OF WAR

Commencement — Acts of Hostility — "Conditional War" condemned by Balfour, Scarlett, Metternich—End—Treaty of Peace—Possible Saving for Subsequent Acts of Hostility—Effect of War on Treaties.

Commencement.—At what moments does war begin and end? For many years, no formal declaration has been thought necessary, and although by Art. 1 of the Third Hague Convention, 1907, nations have bound themselves to issue them, there is no doubt that war may exist *de facto* before its formal declaration. "War may exist," said Lord Stowell in the *Eliza Ann*,[1] "without a declaration on either side." Neutrals, however, can hardly be bound by the existence of war, until they have been duly notified in accordance with the Convention. As between the belligerents, acts of force (such as the sinking by the Japanese of the Chinese hired transport *Kowshing*), or the invasion of the Palatinate by Louis XIV., or the bombardment of Venezuelan forts by the allied forces of Britain and Germany, are sufficient to constitute war. And it is obviously not enough to prevent war arising that

[1] Dods. 247.

the party so acting should proclaim (as Louis did) that he does not mean to go to war. His acts outweigh his professions. Any attempt to get his way by force exerted on the territory of a stranger, or on the high seas,[1] amounts to war.[2]

The plain fact that he is interfering with his neighbour's territory, and avowedly prepared to overcome any resistance by force of arms, constitutes the *status per vim certantium*, however little he wishes or supposes that actual physical conflict will be the outcome. The untenable nature of the other theory can be seen at a glance by the citation of a single example. It is puerile that the ships of one nation should be refused asylum in the ports of a neutral because they are engaged in a war (the result of which may be at most the cession of a town), whilst the ships of another are freely admitted on their errand of "pacifically" occupying the littoral of an entire province! We may recall Metternich's caustic criticism passed on Marshal Gérard's declaration (1831) that the Dutch garrison of Antwerp were "prisoners of war," while at the same moment he loudly declared that France was not at war with Holland.[3]

Nor can the submissive attitude of the other party be conclusive against the existence of a state of war.

[1] Apart from the obsolete institution of reprisals.
[2] *Cf.* "Conditional War," 24 *Law Magazine* (Aug. 1899), p. 436; *ibid.*, Febr., p. 227; "Westlake on War," 33 *ibid.* (Aug. 1908), p. 451; "Pacific Blockade," 21 *ibid.* (Nov. 1895), p. 285.
[3] *Mémoires*, v. 305. *Cf.* T. Baty, *Int. Law*, pp. 240, 255, citing Mr Balfour's observation: "Does the hon. and learned gentleman suppose that without a state of war you can take the ships of another power and blockade its ports?"

The party attacked is entitled to assume a passive attitude in the face of aggression, without in any way tying its hands or recognising the continued peacefulness of the armed aggressor. Were it otherwise, a strong nation might commit all kinds of assaults on a weak one, stifling its remonstrances by the threat of war. Armed violence is war, whether it be resisted or not. Consent, even extorted consent, is of course a different matter.

The fact of war, in short, is decisive, internationally. Whether or not the municipal courts of either country may be bound to abide by the declarations of their own executive is a totally different question. In *The Amy Warwick, etc.*,[1] the U.S. Supreme Court had to consider whether a certain blockade was legally established, and, since blockade can only be imposed in war time, this involved the question of whether war existed or not. There had been no declaration of war by Congress, but the Court held that a state of war in fact existed, sufficient to justify the institution of blockade. "War," urged Dana, "is a state of things, and not an act of legislative will." Although Congress alone could declare war, war might arise independently of Congress. Four judges dissented, including Taney, C.J., and Nelson, J.

So the capture of a vessel and the declaration of a blockade, on the W. Atlantic coast, on 22nd April, were held to justify a British subject in treating the capturing and blockading power as at war on the 23rd, although no declaration of neutrality appeared until the 26th.[2]

[1] (1862) 2 Black 635.
[2] *U.S.A.* v. *Pelly*, [1899] W.R. 332.

End.—The end of a war is usually marked by the conclusion of a formal supension of hostilities. One war—that between Sweden and Poland in the eighteenth century—is said to have flickered out. But in general the date is well ascertained. It does not follow, however, that acts of war, occurring subsequently, are invalid. A reservation may be stipulated in favour of acts done in ignorance of peace having supervened. In such a case, prizes may still be made, and kept. Express notice from his own government is requisite in order to debar an officer from hostilities during the agreed period.[1]

In the absence, or the inadequacy, of such a special provision, the officer who, in ignorance, continues to commit acts of war may be liable to civil actions, and must fall back on his government for an indemnity.[2]

In *Philips* v. *Hatch*[3] it was held that the Court would take as conclusive the Government Proclamation of 20th August 1866, declaring the civil war at an end in Texas, and would decline to go into the question of fact. This is in accordance with the tendency of the English courts to accept Foreign Office certificates as conclusive on the foreign character of states (such as Malaya) *de facto* subject to the British Crown;[4] but it may be questioned whether an older generation of judges would have regarded it as completely satisfactory.

---

[1] *La Bellone* v. *Le Porcher*, Pistoye et Duverdy, i. 149. Hall, *Int. Law*, 556 (ed. vi.).
[2] The *Mentor*, (1799) 1 C.R. 183.
[3] (1871) 1 Dillon 571.
[4] Cf. *Law Magazine*, vol. 37, p. 334 (May 1912).

TREATIES

Treaties.—A tendency has been shown of late to argue that war does not put an end to public treaties. This is of course true when such treaties are expressly framed to regulate events transpiring in war. It is equally true when the treaty created a *jus in rem*: a right of national property, corporeal or incorporeal, not depending on the will of the other party for its execution, like a promise, but one which could, during peace, be forcibly maintained against all comers. But it has lately been maintained that in principle all treaties remain unaffected,[1] though it is admitted there may be many exceptions. Commercial treaties, postal conventions, and the like, are however supposed on this theory to remain valid in principle, though possibly suspended in operation. The extreme difficulty of discriminating between different classes of treaties, abolished and suspended respectively, and the fact that modern wars frequently hinge on economic and commercial considerations, induce us to prefer the older view, that all treaties resting on the promise of the party only are entirely abrogated, by war, except such as contemplate their own continuance during its existence. So liberal a writer as Vattel maintained this proposition, and it was not seriously questioned until lately.[2] The practice has generally been to revive treaties expressly, though

[1] *Cf.* Resolution of the Institute of International Law, 1912.

[2] Hall (*Int. Law*, p. 379) criticises Phillimore for not very clearly indicating the boundaries of the two classes of treaties which that author takes to be suspended and abrogated respectively (those recognising principles of permanent policy, and those relating to temporary expediency). But his own 4th and 5th classes (p. 381) are practically identical with these, and no better defined.

Hall points out that this was not done between Austria and France in 1859, nor between Japan and Russia in 1905. We do not know the effect attributed to these omissions.

As to treaties involving another power, entirely different considerations arise. Performance may be affected, but the treaties remain in force.

CHAPTER II

THE MORATORIUM

History—Objects—Method—Proclamations of 2nd August, 6th August, 12th August, 1st September, 3rd September, 30th September — Analysis — Bills — Cheques — Contracts — No Moratorium for Delivery of Goods—Pre-moratorium Debts—Cases—Inclusion in Second Moratorium of Debts then first falling due—Interest—Bank Deposits and Notes—Foreign Debts—Current Accounts—Distraint—Cumulative Accounts—Courts Emergency Powers Act—Rules of 8th September 1914.

A WRITER in the *Law Times* traces the moratorium in its present shape to the French financial dispositions of 1870-1; and refers us to *Rouquette* v. *Overmann*, L.R. 10 Q.B. 525, in which such a provision was applied by an English court, as part of the proper law applicable to a contract (that of France as the place of performance).

The suspension of payments by banks has not infrequently been authorised as an emergency measure. But the general suspension of obligations known as a moratorium is a novelty in Great Britain. It was imposed in August 1914, and continued since, as a measure calculated to steady the financial and commercial situation.

Proclamation of 2nd August.—In the first instance, it was applied to bills of exchange only, these being the principal nerves of communication between the financial and commercial worlds. It will be recalled that war was imminent on the eve of a Bank Holiday (3rd August), and declared on Tuesday, 4th August. The holiday was prolonged for three days, and meanwhile the Moratorium Act was passed, enabling the Crown, in the widest terms, to authorise the postponement of any payment in pursuance of any contract, "to such extent, for such time, and subject to such conditions or other provisions" as might be specified. Although the Act was limited in currency to six months, the validity of the proclamation made in accordance with it was in no way restricted. One proclamation had been issued on the previous day (Sunday, 2nd August) and was confirmed (and by mistake ascribed to the 3rd).

That early proclamation only related to bills of exchange. The reasons for it were well put by the *Solicitors' Journal*. Manufacturers and merchants are paid by foreign bills. British houses discount these bills, and pay cash for them. But if the discounter, who has parted with his money, cannot get it from the foreigner, he is driven to ruin his British client, who has parted with his goods long before. The proclamation gives the necessary time for an accommodation. It excluded bills payable on demand (as to which the merchant ought to be prepared); but with regard to others (provided they had been "accepted" before 4th August), it rendered it possible to have the date of payment postponed for the definite term of a month (on payment of interest at a rate which proved to be 6 per cent.). It was only the acceptor who could do this: not an indorser or a drawer. On presentation to him for payment, he could reaccept, and thereby extend the currency of the bill for one month. But this did not relieve drawers and indorsers, if the acceptor chose to pay.

Proclamation of 6th August.—The next step was a much more serious and important one. Bills payable on demand (including cheques) and all other contracts were now dealt with. Here, there is seldom any fixed time for payment; it depends on the creditor to take action. If the bill was drawn, or the contract[1] made before 4th August, the time for payment under it was automatically postponed (without any necessity for reacceptance) for one month, or until 4th September, "whichever shall be the latest." And if demand for payment was made and refused, interest was to be payable until payment at the special rate. No provision was made for raising the rate in the case where the payment carried interest under the ordinary law.

Is an ordinary payment under an ordinary contract "due and payable" before demand? Certainly: the duty of the debtor is to seek out his creditor and pay him. Consequently, the scope of the proclamation was very little limited. Payments under contracts made on and after 4th August were alone not affected by it. To this wide proclamation various special exceptions were made—in particular, claims of £5 and under, wages and salaries, and maritime freight.

[1] Including "other negotiable instruments" dated before 4th August.

No corresponding delay was granted for the performance of obligations, such as the delivery of goods—and it becomes a question whether the postponement of performance as an obligation imports a postponement of performance as a condition. *I.e.*, if A is exonerated from paying B for goods, is B exonerated from delivering them, when cash payment is a condition of delivery? It may be argued that, the date of payment being postponed, the date of delivery, to which delivery payment is a condition precedent, is necessarily postponed with it. But the contrary view is quite capable of logical support.

The situation was further relieved by a State guarantee for approved bills accepted before 4th August 1914.

On 12th August this proclamation of the 6th was extended, as was only reasonable, to bills of exchange which, though not payable on demand, had not been reaccepted by the acceptor under the first proclamation, unless they had been presented for payment and reacceptance expressly refused. Presumably, therefore, (1) if the acceptor paid, the drawer could derive no benefit from the moratorium: (2) if the acceptor refused to reaccept, neither he, the indorsers, nor the drawer could rely on it: (3) if the acceptor reaccepted, all parties could take advantage of it. Simultaneously, the moratorium was extended to debts from banks throughout the dominions of the Crown (and Protectorates).

Proclamation of 1st September.—The policy of the moratorium was much criticised, especially as unduly favourable to metropolitan banks. Much discussion took place as to the desirability of renewing it. But at the end of August it was extended for a second month. The new Proclamation (1st September) provided substantially as follows:—

1. The Proclamation of 2nd August, dealing with the primary liability on "time" bills of exchange, was to be read as if two months had been inserted in it instead of one. No further reacceptance was needed.

2. The Proclamation of 6th August, dealing with other liabilities, was to be read as though the same alteration was made, and the prolongation of the claim to 4th September in any court was to be read as though it were to 4th October.

With regard to old debts, already due before 6th August (the date of the former proclamation), or falling due (under contracts made) before 4th September, this second provision was intelligible. Already postponed for one month, they were now postponed for two. But what of payments falling due *after* 4th September? It will be observed that the original *contract* (or bill) must still be made or dated before 4th August, and that this date was not advanced a month, so as to postpone debts incurred after the first proclamation. But did it postpone for the full *two* months payments falling due after the expiration of the first moratorium period? Such, for instance, as Michaelmas rent? Such rent was not affected by the first moratorium. Yet it would be a payment falling due before 4th October, and consequently postponed for "two months," viz., until 29th November.

This possibility was precluded—and it seems to be the literal effect of the instrument—by the remodelled proclamation which was issued within three days.

Proclamation of 3rd September.—This (issued 3rd September) substituted new provisions altogether:—

1. As to [time] bills which had fallen due and had been reaccepted prior to 4th September. Here, the time for payment was extended to a definite two months from due date, but no provision for reacceptance between 4th September and 4th October was made. On these bills, therefore, if, say, they originally fell due on 6th August, presentation between 6th August and 4th September would (on reacceptance) extend the date of payment to 6th October.

2. As to bills payable on demand, "other negotiable instruments" and ordinary contracts (which needed no reacceptance). Here, the Proclamation of 6th August was made to apply to payments falling due between 4th September and 4th October, in like manner as it already applied to payments falling due between the date of that proclamation and 4th September. And this was to apply not only to payments so falling due for the first time (such as Michaelmas rent under leases existing on 4th September), but also to payments then falling due under the terms of the moratorium.

Did this apply to debts newly contracted after 4th August? It will be remembered that the original Proclamation (6th August) did not. The present proclamation expressly purports to apply to payments which become due and payable between 4th September and 4th October, "whether they become due and payable by virtue of the [earlier proclamation] *or otherwise.*" It may be that this means to refer solely to pre-moratorium (*ante* 4th August) contracts, payments under which fall due between 4th September and 4th October, (1) because of being postponed by the earlier proclamation, or (2) because of naturally falling due between those dates [*i.e.*, "otherwise"]. But it may be read in a wider sense, and quite literally, to bring in all payments whatever, whenever incurred, so long as they fall due and payable between 4th September and 4th October. This construction has been negatived by *Softlaw* v. *Morgan*, (*Times*, 10th November 1914).

In the next place, a further difficulty is created by the admitted inclusion in this second postponement of payments becoming payable *by postponement* between 4th September and 4th October (*i.e.*, those which originally fell due between 4th August and 4th September, or prior to 6th August, which, it will be remembered, were all given a month, or until 4th September in any event). It might be thought that these would now get another month. But all that the Proclamation (3rd September) says is that the Proclamation of 6th August shall apply to them "in like manner as it applies to payments becoming payable between 6th August (its date) and 4th September." Since it gives these payments a month from their *original* date, does it not give them when renewed, the same month from their *original* date: *i.e.*, no more than they had already? This is hypercriticism;[1] it would stultify the proclamation in an important aspect.

[1] See 58 *S. J.*, p. 848.

3. As to time bills (given before 4th August and maturing before 4th September) which have not been reaccepted. These, it will be remembered, were assimilated on 12th August to ordinary contracts,[1] and they are prolonged with them for another month (unless reacceptance was expressly refused).

4. As to time bills given before 4th August and maturing between 4th September and 4th October, or subsequently no postponement was conceded or necessary, since the Proclamation of 2nd August was already couched in general terms.

Proclamation of 30th September.—A third, and presumably final, extension was effected on 30th September.

1. *As to ordinary contracts*, including bills on demand and cheques, and other negotiable instruments other than time bills. Here the same procedure was adopted as in the Proclamation of 3rd September. Only it was made a condition that interest up to date should be paid: and rent and retail traders' business debts were not to be postponed at all.

2. *As to time bills maturing on and after 4th October.* The Proclamation of 2nd August is declared to "continue" to be applicable to pre-moratorium bills so falling due.

And it is now carefully provided that if such a bill is not reaccepted (or paid), then (unless reacceptance is expressly refused), the bill shall for

---

[1] The Proclamation of 12th August refers to bills which "have" not been reaccepted. It most likely means "which shall not have" been reaccepted *on maturity* (possibly subsequent to 12th August).

all purposes, including the liabilities of drawers and indorsers, be taken to be payable a month later than its original date of maturity.

3. *As to time bills maturing prior to 4th October.* If such a bill has already been postponed, within virtue of the Proclamation of 2nd August or 12th August (whether or not further postponed by that of 3rd September), and the bill is not paid, it is to be postponed for a further fourteen days.

Interest, Deposits, Bank Notes, Foreign Debts, Current Accounts, Distraint.—Interest is of course allowed in all cases of postponement; usually at the current rate on the day when payment last became due.

As the relation of banker and customer is that of debtor and creditor, banks were of course protected against withdrawals of *money* deposited on account current as well as on deposit receipts. But they are expressly excluded from relying on the moratorium in respect of their notes. The moratorium did not, however, apply to debts due by foreign residents, or from firms, companies, "or institutions" whose principal place of business is outside the British Isles (unless incurred by an establishment there).

In *Jupp* v. *Whitaker*, 58 S.J. 819, it was held that a current account with a retail dealer "exceeded £5" and was within the moratorium, although composed of small items. This decision has been criticised, we think, with justice; and, as these pages pass through the press, it has been over-ruled (*Auster* v. *London Motor C. Works, Times*, 21st October 1914). A more tenable decision is to the effect that where payment is postponed, it cannot be enforced by distress any more than by suit. *Qu.*, however, whether a forfeiture, being essentially the operation of a condition, cannot be enforced.

Courts Emergency Powers Act.—Closely connected with the moratorium and its discontinuance is this statute, which was passed 31st August 1914. This practically supersedes the law, and leaves it to the judiciary to decide when it is or is not reasonable "in the circumstances of the present war" to enforce a claim. No process of execution, or even of self-help, such as the taking of possession, can be had without the leave of a court. Rules have been made allowing the application to be dealt with in chambers; but a master (or even a judge) in chambers is not a court, and the rule seems to be *ultra vires*.[1] Power is given to stay bankruptcy proceedings; but the right of pawnbrokers to deal with pledges is expressly preserved, and so is the right of sale of a mortgage in possession. It is hard to see why the mortgagee must be in possession in order to exercise this elementary right; and it is also difficult to see why small rents (at a rate of less than £50 per annum) should be excluded from the general provision, which takes out of the scope of the Act contracts made subsequently to 4th August 1914.

According to the rules of 8th September 1914, the proper court to which to apply (if no court is already

---

[1] *An. Pr.* (1915), 1811, citing *Baker* v. *Oates*, (1877) 2 Q.B.D. 171 : *re Davidson*, [1899] 2 Q.B. 103 : *Clover* v. *Adams*, (1881) 6 Q.B.D. 622. The Judicature Acts expressly enable jurisdiction to be exercised in chambers, but no such provision occurs in the Act under discussion.

seised of the case) is (*a*) the High Court of Justice, (*b*) the County Court, if the claim is of £100 or less, (*c*) a police court, in the case of distress for rent, enforcement of a hire-purchase agreement (by either side), or of lapse of certain policies, if the claim is of £20 or less. The county court selected must be one which would have jurisdiction in the case of an action arising out of the subject-matter. But apparently any police court may be selected: thus the Truro magistrates could not decline jurisdiction over an application by a Londoner to distrain for £20 at Dover. Perhaps it may be limited to cases where the respondent is within the justices' jurisdiction. It is to be made "by summons," and there may be no power to serve this elsewhere. The ordinary practice of the Court is to be followed: but this gives little guidance (para. 14).

Power is given for private hearings, as the respondent's whole financial position may have to be disclosed, and the object of the Act is to save credit.

CHAPTER III

FORCE MAJEURE, ETC.

Not recognised in England — Exceptions — Legal Impossibility, Continued Existence of Specific Things — No Freight when Voyage becomes Illegal — Unless Delivery at Equivalent Port — War Dangers may excuse Deviation or Delay — Effect on Contract of Carriage — War Clauses — Foreign Act of State not an Excuse? — "Restraint of Princes" — Boulay-Paty — "War" — Insurance — may be affected by War Clauses — Neutrals can claim for Damage caused by British Seizure, if Traffic Lawful — And perhaps for Risk of *primâ facie* Innocent Articles being held Contraband — Agreements to carry Goods to the Enemy — to Run Blockades — to Contravene Foreign Enlistment Act — Meaning of "Equip" in Sec. 8.

Force Majeure is not recognised in English law as an "event preventing performance," unless it amounts to an absolute supervening impossibility in law,[1] or is tacitly incorporated in the contract, by the fact of the parties contemplating as a condition of its performance the continued existence of a specific thing, or the continued life and health of a particular

---

[1] This seems to include foreign law. *Ford* v. *Cotesworth*, infra ; *Cunningham* v. *Dunn*, (1878) 3 C.P.D. 443.

person:[1] or unless the contract was on the face of it made with reference to (as distinguished from being made in reliance on) a certain state of affairs.[2]

War, therefore, though it may make supplies impossible to obtain, does not excuse a manufacturer or importer from continuing his supplies, or a shipowner from proceeding on his lawful voyage.

Exceptions.—The completion of a voyage which has become illegal will, however, be excused; and so will the performance of a contract of carriage which is interrupted by the capture of the ship. The neutral owner of goods on board will be exonerated from the payment of freight, for the goods have not been delivered. If, however, they are taken by captors to a port almost as convenient as the port of destination, the captors will be entitled to any freight unpaid. The rule is sometimes expressed in the form that any port "in the same country" will do. But this is clearly wrong; in the cases cited the ports were as near each other as London and Plymouth.[3] *A fortiori*, if the captors take the goods to a port where the owners would have preferred to send them to, had it been possible, freight is due.[4]

The outbreak of war and the presence of hostile cruisers may, again, excuse from exact compliance with the terms of a contract. The short principle is that, while a contract of carriage must be executed strictly according to its terms, a ship cannot be

[1] *Taylor* v. *Caldwell*, (1863) 3 B. & S. 826; *Robinson* v. *Davison*, (1871) L.R. 6 Ex. 269.

[2] *The Coronation Cases*, [1903] 2 K.B. 683, 740, 756, [1904] 1 K.B. 493.

[3] *Cf.* the *Vrouw Henrietta*, (1803) 5 C.R. 75.

[4] The *Diana*, (1803) 5 C.R. 67.

expected to put herself in the way of capture. That would not, for one thing, tend to the performance of her undertaking. Thus, in the Franco-Prussian war, a German barque, the *Teutonia*, was bound from S. America with orders for "one safe port in Great Britain or on the Continent between Havre and Hamburg." Calling at Falmouth to ascertain which port, she was ordered to Dunkirk. Off that harbour, she received news of the imminence of war, and, declining to enter, proceeded to Dover, which, it will be observed, is a Channel port, and might have been a proper termination of the voyage. The owners declined to receive the cargo except at a reduced freight. But they were held not to be entitled to do this. The ship had not broken her contract by declining to go into Dunkirk and be captured. The charterers ought to have indicated another and a safe Channel port, at which the ship would have discharged, earning her full freight.[1] But the Council left the question open of what would have happened had there been no alternative port of discharge. Would any *pro rata* freight at all be payable? Certainly the full freight could not be demanded for delivering in England what you had contracted to deliver in France. Transhipment would immensely increase the cost of transport. And it is a general principle that *pro rata* freight is never payable. That would involve a calculation, as Sir W. Scott said, "attended with great trouble in the inquiry and uncertainty in the result." Yet it would be hard on the shipowner to lose his voyage; and perhaps in this instance some equitable accommoda-

[1] The *Teutonia*, (1872) L.R. 4 P.C. 171.

tion could be found. The Admiralty principle of dividing the loss might be invoked. Scrutton (*Charter-parties*, p. 244) would give the full freight whenever the deviation is reasonable; but the voyage might hardly have been commenced.[1]

Where mere delay is in question, the occurrence of risks, which it would be unreasonable to meet, will operate as a temporary excuse. During the Austro-French war of 1859, an Austrian ship arriving from America was held up at Falmouth, French cruisers being in the offing. Consignees directed her to go to Copenhagen, and on the master's demur, to Plymouth. Even this she declined to do, and it was left for a jury to say whether the refusal was reasonable, as exonerating her owners from a charge of breach of contract. They held that it was. But it does not follow that she would have obtained her freight, or a proportion of it. As a matter of fact, the consignees insured her, and she proceeded safely to the ascertained port of destination, Plymouth, and duly delivered her cargo.[2]

War Clause.—When a contract includes an express exception of restraints of prices, blockades, etc., it seems that it is not cancelled immediately upon the occurrence of such events. After a reasonable delay, during which performance is excused, the contract

---

[1] Cf. the *Juno, sup.* p. 303: a case of capture, where full freight might well have been allowed.

[2] *Pole* v. *Cetcovitch*, (1860) 9 C.B. N.S. 430. *Cf.* the *San Roman*, (1873) L.R. 5 P.C. 301, and the *Heinrich*, (1871) L.R. 3 A. & E. 424. In the *Patria*, ibid. 436, the judge failed to take into account the danger incurred by the ship *apart* from blockade. This, and not the absence of the "restraint of princes" clause (as Scrutton argues), appears to explain the decision.

may be cancelled, but not, it seems, at once, unless time can be shown to be of the essence of the transaction. Probably this rule applies to such a case as the prohibition of export of certain goods, notably food-stuffs, under the British Proclamation of 5th August 1914. But a very short delay would, we think, under modern conditions, enable cancellation. The theory that some delay ought to be interposed rests on an old case,[1] where a ship was held obliged to wait for two years to see whether an embargo would not be removed. An embargo is in its nature temporary. It either leads up to war, or is removed, in the normal course of things. And in *Geipel* v. *Smith*,[2] Cockburn, L.C.J., held that it was a sufficient answer that it was impossible to *expect* that the obstacle to performance (a blockade) would be removed within a reasonable time. "It would be monstrous to say that the parties must wait—for the obligation must be mutual—until the restraint be taken off; the skipper with cargo, which might be perishable, or its market value destroyed; the shipowner with his ship lying idle, possibly rotting, the result of which might be to make the contract ruinous." Even where there is no exception of the restraint of princes, it is even possible that, considering this strong opinion, performance may be abandoned: perhaps not so summarily, but when it is clear that it has become commercially impossible.

Foreign Act of State.—Where there is a time fixed for performance of the contract, it is possible that the intervention of foreign authority preventing

---

[1] *Hadley* v. *Clarke*, (1799) 8 T.R. 259.
[2] (1880) L.R. 7 Q.B.D. 104.

FOREIGN ACT OF STATE

such performance may not afford the excuse that British interference would.

In *Ford* v. *Cotesworth*,[1] the defendant was excused for not discharging a cargo at Callao "in the usual and customary manner," when it was in fact impossible to do so, owing to the fact that Callao was about to be bombarded by the Spanish fleet, and the Chilian custom-house was closed in consequence. But it was said by Martin, B., that a positive contract to discharge in a stipulated number of days would have remained enforceable. The actual contract could be complied with by discharging in a reasonable time in the circumstances.[2] As the circumstances included an imminent bombardment, the delay was justified. There was no need to say that performance had become impossible, because performance was proceeding strictly according to the contract. But where no room is left for such elasticity by the terms of the instrument, it appears to be still the better opinion, in accordance with old cases,[3] that interference by authorities of at any rate foreign countries does not exempt from performance. It may be that such a severity might be resisted. Lord Selborne's *obiter dictum* in *Postlethwaite* v. *Freeland*, (1880)

---

[1] (1870) L.R. 5 Q.B. 544. Cf. *Cunningham* v. *Dunn*, supra.

[2] The view that such a contract ought to be performed in what *would* be a reasonable time under ordinary circumstances seems to be exploded by *Hick* v. *Raymond*, [1892] 7 Aspinall 233.

[3] *Flight* v. *Page*, (1801) 3 B. & P. 295 (*n.*); *Barker* v. *Hodgson*, (1814) 2 M. & S. 271. But in the latter case, the contract *might* have been performed before performance became impossible, while the former one is very imperfectly reported.

5 A.C. 608, needs due limitation, and Lord Blackburn (p. 617) seems to have rested the rule on the consideration that the consignee probably knows the facilities of the port of discharge better than the shipowner, and should be held strictly to the time he has himself estimated. He "takes the risk of ordinary vicissitudes;"[1] but we question whether he takes the risk of an extraordinary interposition of political force.

"**Restraint of Princes.**"—Shipowners and others, as above indicated, are in the habit of relieving themselves by a special war clause. If this is stated to cancel the contract in certain events, it must be remembered that, though it may excuse performance, it does not necessarily confer a right to any part of the payment which depends on performance. The common clause providing for the event of "restraint of princes, rulers, and peoples" does not cover hostile acts, which are properly referred to as "acts of the king's enemies";[2] but it would no doubt cover the acts of allies. It also covers the acts of the British Crown. Byles, J., asserts that "the king's enemies, restraint of princes and perils of the sea [including pirates] seem to include every species of *vis major*."[3] Since the king is neither a pirate nor an enemy, his acts would seem to come under "restraints of princes," if this is correct. And in *Crew & Co.* v. *G.W.R.*[4] Field and Wills, JJ., are understood to have held that the expression means seizure by the government

---

[1] *Thiis* v. *Byers*, (1876) 1 Q.B.D. 344.
[2] *Aliter*, Scrutton, *Charter-parties*, 204.
[3] *Russell* v. *Niemann*, (1864) 34 L.J. C.P. 10, 14.
[4] (1887) W.N. 161.

of this or some friendly power for State purposes. Since their authority is Boulay-Paty, who defines it as "l'acte *d'un prince ami* qui, pour nécessité publique et hors le fait de guerre, arrête un vaisseau dans un port ou rade de ses dominions," the inclusion of "this" power seems gratuitous. The same case is an authority to show that the ordinary process of law is not such a "restraint."[1] Probably the true distinction here is not between an act of legal process and an act of legal or illegal force, but between an act depending on the volition of the government, and an act in which the public force is put in motion by a private party through process of law. Such seizures would be included under "capture and seizure,"[2] which are very wide words, and include such a "restraint of princes" as the requisitioning of gold on the eve of war.[3]

The restraint need not take the form of actual force. The mere imminent risk of capture is sufficient.[4]

War.—Another exception frequently introduced is that of "war," or "war preventing performance." In the latter case, the mere outbreak of war will certainly not relieve the parties: the war must "prevent" performance, and few wars of themselves will do so, except in the case of trade with the enemy, when the clause is almost superfluous. Perhaps the clause

---

[1] See also *Finlay* v. *Liverpool & G. W. Co.*, (1870) 23 L.T. 251. [2] Scrutton, *ubi supra*.

[3] *Robinson, Gold, etc.* v. *Alliance, etc., Insce. Co.*, [1904] A.C. 359.

[4] *Nobel* v. *Jenkins*, [1896] 2 Q.B. 326. *Geipel* v. *Smith*, (1874) L.R. 9 C.P. 518.

will be read so as to mean "war making performance commercially unprofitable," or "preventing performance except at a ruinous sacrifice." Where the word "war" is used alone, there is less difficulty. The contract will, however, remain unaffected by wars breaking out in other parts of the world. What would happen if the country where a cargo was to be loaded went to war with a state to which none of the parties in any way belonged? From *Avory* v. *Bowden* it might be inferred that the clause would not come into play.[1] Words making this point clear might usefully be introduced into war clauses: for the trade of a country may be entirely disorganised by war, so as to make it very desirable that contracts for export to or import from it should be cancelled.

Insurance.—The operation of such clauses may, however, prejudicially affect the insurance of ships or goods. In *Nickels* v. *London & Prov., etc., Co.*,[2] a bill of lading gave power to terminate the voyage and land the goods if it was judged imprudent to proceed "on account of war." A special insurance was effected against risks excluded by the ordinary insurance clauses. One of these risks was "all consequences of . . . hostilities." War broke out, and the goods were landed at Liverpool instead of Havana. The plaintiffs thereby sustained loss, and it was held that it was not a loss "in consequence of hostilities," and consequently that the plaintiffs' claim failed.

[1] 6 E. & B. 975. But in this case the charter-party referred to "the event of war *having commenced*" in showing that a *particular* war was contemplated.

[2] [1901] 70 L.J. K.B. 29.

INSURANCE 421

If the voyage is lawful, neutrals (and presumably subjects) who are inconvenienced by a capture, however proper, can recover the loss from the underwriters,[1] unless warranted free of capture.

In *Lubbock* v. *Potts*[2] it was suggested that insurances "against British capture" must mean "against unlawful British capture," or temporary lawful detention.

So far as insurance is concerned, a *bonâ fide* endeavour to avoid capture will not amount to a deviation discharging the insurer.[3] In fact, it is even held that *force majeure* generally will justify deviation: a striking departure from the usual rule applicable to contracts (including charter-parties). Thus duress put upon the ship by a British cruiser was held to be no deviation.[4]

Rotch v. *Edie*[5] has been cited to show that a neutral settled among the enemy can insure in England his interest in property held jointly with an enemy. But as Campbell points out (1 Camp. 75 (*n.*)) the plaintiff was not settled in France, and the policy was effected before the war.

Arnould (sec. 765) thinks that the insurance in England of articles liable to British seizure as contraband is unlawful. That may be admitted, although no case in point is cited. But insurance against the risk of apparently innocent articles being held to be contraband may not impossibly be upheld. In

[1] *Barker* v. *Blakes*, (1808) 9 East 283.
[2] 7 *ibid.*, (1806) 451.
[3] Arnould, *ubi supra*, 560; *O'Reilly* v. *Gonne*, (1815) 4 Camp. 249. See Arnould's note (p. 564) on *O'Reilly* v. *R. Exchange*, *ibid.* 246.   [4] *Scott* v. *Thompson*, (1805) 1 B. & P. N.R. 181.
[5] (1795) 6 T.R. 413.

Gibson v. *Service*[1] the voyage insured was made in pursuance of an obviously fraudulent scheme; it was not a case of contraband. Now that the definition of contraband is so uncertain, and its qualification is supposed to rest on such delicate presumptions of ultimate destination, there seems little harm in allowing the risk to be covered by insurance. In any event, insurers would probably pay; there would seem to be no illegality in doing so, except in cases of an obvious intention to aid the enemy's forces. American, Scandinavian, or Spanish houses would of course be perfectly free to transact such business, as well as the insurance of contraband admittedly such.

Unlawful Traffic.—The outbreak of war, rendering traffic with the enemy country illegal, is one of the few cases of *force majeure* recognised by English law as excusing performance of a contract.[2]

Agreements to run blockades[3] and to carry contraband[4] are valid if the undertakers know the nature of the risk. But it seems clear that, even if a contract is limited as to time, the imposition even of a foreign blockade must discharge the parties from performance. The ship cannot be bound to load a complete cargo at the risk of exceeding the time allowed for exit. The shipper cannot be bound to furnish cargo to a vessel which cannot stay to load it completely. How far a contract for blockade-running must be performed to the risk of the ship, is of course a question for the jury.

[1] (1814) 5 Taunton 433.
[2] Cf. *Barker* v. *Hodgson*, (1814), 3 M. & S. 267.
[3] *Madeiros* v. *Hill*, (1832) 8 Bi. 231; the *Helen*, (1865) L.R. 1 A. E. 1.   [4] *Ex parte Chavasse*, (1865) 34 L.J. Bk. 17.

Agreements for un-neutral service, being contrary to the Foreign Enlistment Act,[1] doubtless stand in a different position. It will be observed that sec. 10 of that Act would be unnecessary if sec. 8 (3) included every casual act of "equipment," as defined in sec. 30, in its prohibition. The "equipment" intended by sec. 8 must clearly be *ejusdem generis* with the "building," "commissioning," and "despatching" contemplated by the rest of that section—*i.e.*, an original setting forth for war. This is apparent on a comparison with the older Act of 59 Geo. III. c. 69, and the corresponding American statute, which were its models.[2] The *force majeure* of our own law, in such cases, dispenses from performance.

Bills of Exchange.—4 & 5 Geo. V. c. 82 excuses delay in the presentation for payment of bills of exchange outside the British Isles, where the delay is directly or indirectly attributable to the war. And when the loss of a bill so payable is reasonably attributable to the same cause, its production may be dispensed with by "the Court" (*sic.*).

Premiums.—When a contract is discharged by becoming impossible in fact (or law?), payments already exigible (whether or not actually made) under it have been held irrecoverable, as in the nature of premiums payable in any event. (*Chandler* v. *Webster* [1904] 1 K.B. 493). This might not, and on principle should not, apply to any payment made merely for convenience at an early stage.

[1] [1899] 33 & 34 Vict. c. 90. Cf. *U.S.A.* v. *Pelby*, 47 W.R .332.
[2] See "Coal for Russia" (*Murray's Monthly Review*), February 1905, p. 128, for a full discussion of the point.

APPENDIX

CONTENTS

A.—*Illustrating Part I., Chapter II.*

		PAGE
1.	Notification of a State of War (Aug. 4, 1914)	429
2.	Order under Aerial Navigation Act (Aug. 2, 1914)	430
3.	Proclamation authorising Lords of Admiralty to requisition British Ships (Aug. 3, 1914)	430
4.	Order in Council taking over Control of Railroads (Aug. 4, 1914)	431
5.	Proclamation calling out Army Reserve and Territorial Force (Aug. 4, 1914)	432
6.	Proclamation regarding the Defence of the Realm (Aug. 4, 1914)	434
7.	Proclamation extending Bank Holidays (Aug. 3, 1914)	435
8.	Army Order as to Billeting (Aug. 4, 1914)	435
9.	Army Order as to Billeting (Sept. 15, 1914)	437
10.	Proclamation warning British Subjects against contributing to German Loan (Aug. 5, 1914)	437

B.—*Illustrating Part I., Chapter III.*

1.	An Act to consolidate and amend the Defence of the Realm Acts (Nov. 27, 1914)	438
2.	Consolidated Regulations under Defence of the Realm Act (Nov. 28, 1914)	441
3.	Special Constables Act (Aug. 28, 1914)	464
4.	Unreasonable Withholding of Food Supplies Act (Aug. 10, 1914)	466
5.	Articles of Commerce (Returns) Act (Aug. 28, 1914)	467

426   APPENDIX

PAGE
6. Army (Supply of Food, Forage, and Stores) Act (Aug. 7, 1914) 469
7. Aliens Restriction Act (Aug. 5, 1914) 470
8. The Aliens Restriction (Consolidation) Order (Sept. 9, 1914). 473
9. Aliens Restriction (Change of Name) Order (Oct. 8, 1914) . 487

C.—*Illustrating Part III.*

1. Despatch of Sir E. Grey as to proposed violation of Belgian neutrality (Aug. 4, 1914) 488
2. Ultimatum of Sir E. Grey to Germany (Aug. 4, 1914) . . 489
3. Memorandum of Foreign Office (Dec. 7, 1914) . . 490

D.—*Illustrating Part IV., Chapter I.*

1. Extract from Declaration of War by William III. (May 7, 1689) 491
2. Extract from Naturalisation Act, 1870 492

E.—*Illustrating Parts IV., V. and VI.*

1. Trading with the Enemy Act, 1914 (Sept. 18, 1914) . . 492
2. Trading with the Enemy Proclamation, 1914 (Aug. 5, 1914) . 497
3. Proclamation regarding Banking Business (Aug. 10, 1914) . 498
4. Treasury Circular (Aug. 21, 1914) 500
5. Board of Trade Notice (Dividends) 501
6. Trading with the Enemy Proclamation, No. 2, 1914 (Sept. 9, 1914) 501
7. Board of Trade Notices (Freight, Fees) (Sept. 25, 1914) . 505
8. Trading with the Enemy Proclamation (Oct. 8, 1914) . 506
9. Customs Order: Certificates of Origin (Oct. 9, 1914) . . 508
10. Trading with the Enemy Amendment Act (Nov. 27, 1914) . 512
11. Postponement of Payments Act, 1914 (Aug. 3, 1914) . . 523
12. Moratorium of August 2, 1914 524
13. Moratorium of August 6, 1914 525
14. Moratorium of August 12, 1914 527
15. Moratorium of September 1, 1914 528

CONTENTS 427

		PAGE
16.	Moratorium of September 3, 1914	530
17.	Moratorium of September 20, 1914	531
18.	Courts (Emergency Powers) Act, 1914 (Aug. 31, 1914)	533
19.	Proclamation regarding Contraband (Aug. 4, 1914)	535
20.	Proclamation against British Carriage of Contraband (Aug. 5, 1915)	537
21.	Order in Council as to Declaration of London	538
22.	Addition to List of Contraband	540
23.	Revision of List of Contraband	541
24.	Revised treatment of Declaration of London	544
25.	Notice as to Discounting Bills	546
26.	Patents, Designs, and Trade Mark Rules	546
27.	Patents, Designs, and Trade Mark Rules, Additional Rule	550
28.	Prize Courts (Egypt, Zanzibar, and Cyprus) Act, 1914	550
29.	Order in Council under Prize Courts Act, 1914	551

F.—*Authors' Notes.*

1.	Continuous Voyage	553
2.	Public Engagements towards Enemy Persons	554

A.—*Illustrating Part I., Chapter II.*

I

NOTIFICATION OF A STATE OF WAR.

A STATE OF WAR.

His Majesty's Government informed the German Government on 4th August 1914, that, unless a satisfactory reply to the request of His Majesty's Government for an assurance that Germany would respect the neutrality of Belgium was received by midnight of that day, His Majesty's Government would feel bound to take all steps in their power to uphold that neutrality, and the observance of a treaty to which Germany was as much a party as Great Britain.

The result of this communication having been that His Majesty's Ambassador at Berlin had to ask for his passports. His Majesty's Government have accordingly formally notified the German Government that a state of war exists between the two countries as from 11 P.M. to-day.

Foreign Office,
    4th August 1914.

(*Reprinted from the* London Gazette *of 7th August* 1914.)

II

AERIAL NAVIGATION.

In pursuance of the powers conferred on me by the Aerial Navigation Acts, 1911 and 1913, I hereby make, for the purposes of the safety and defence of the realm, the following Order :—

I prohibit the navigation of aircraft of every class and description over the whole area of the United Kingdom, and over the whole of the coast line thereof and territorial waters adjacent thereto.

This Order shall not apply to naval or military aircraft or to aircraft flying under naval or military orders ; nor shall it apply to any aircraft flying within three miles of a recognised aerodrome.

R. McKenna,
One of His Majesty's Principal
Secretaries of State.

Home Office,
Whitehall,
2nd August 1914.

III

TRANSPORTS AND AUXILIARIES.

BY THE KING.

A Proclamation for Authorising the Lords Commissioners of the Admiralty to requisition any British Ship or British Vessel within the British Isles or the Waters adjacent thereto.

George R.I.

WHEREAS a national emergency exists rendering it necessary to take steps for preserving and defending national interests :

And whereas the measures approved to be taken require the immediate employment of a large number of vessels for use as Transports and as Auxiliaries for the convenience of the Fleet and for other similar services, but owing to the urgency of the need it is impossible to delay the employment of such vessels until the terms of engagement have been mutually agreed upon:

Now therefore, We authorise and empower the Lords Commissioners of the Admiralty, by warrant under the hand of their Secretary or under the hand of any Flag Officer of Our Royal Navy holding any appointment under the Admiralty, to requisition and take up for Our service any British ship or British vessel as defined in the Merchant Shipping Act, 1894, within the British Isles or the waters adjacent thereto, for such period of time as may be necessary, on condition that the owners of all ships and vessels so requisitioned shall receive payment for their use and for services rendered during their employment in the Government service and compensation for loss or damage thereby occasioned, according to terms to be arranged as soon as possible after the said ship has been taken up, either by mutual agreement between the Lords Commissioners of the Admiralty and the owners, or failing such agreement by the award of a Board of Arbitration to be constituted and appointed by Us for this purpose.

> Given at Our Court at Buckingham Palace, this Third day of August, in the year of Our Lord One thousand nine hundred and fourteen, and in the Fifth year of Our Reign.
>
> God save the King.

IV

RAILWAY TRAFFIC :—NATIONAL EMERGENCY.

Order in Council under Section 16 of the Regulation of the Forces Act, 1871 (34 & 35 Vict. c. 86).

At the Court at Buckingham Palace, the 4th day of August 1914.

PRESENT,

The King's Most Excellent Majesty in Council.

WHEREAS by virtue of Section 16 of the Regulation of the

Forces Act, 1871, it is lawful for the Secretary of State, when His Majesty by Order in Council declares that an emergency has arisen in which it is expedient for the public service that His Majesty's Government should have control over the railroads in Great Britain, or any of them, by Warrant under his hand to empower persons to take such action in relation to any railroad in Great Britain as is mentioned in that section:

Now, therefore, His Majesty, by and with the advice of His Privy Council, is pleased to declare, and it is hereby declared, for the purposes of the said Section 16, that an emergency has arisen in which it is expedient for the public service that His Majesty's Government should have control over the railroads of Great Britain.

Almeric FitzRoy.

V

Army Reserve and Territorial Force—Mobilisation and Calling Out.

By the King.

A Proclamation for Calling out the Army Reserve, and Embodying the Territorial Force.

George R.I.

WHEREAS by the Reserve Forces Act, 1882, it is amongst other things enacted that in case of imminent national danger or of great emergency it shall be lawful for Us by Proclamation, the occasion having first been communicated to Parliament, to order that the Army Reserve shall be called out on permanent service; and by any such Proclamation to order a Secretary of State from time to time to give, and when given, to revoke or vary such directions as may seem necessary or proper for calling out the forces or force mentioned in the Proclamation, or all or any of the men belonging thereto:

DEFENCE

And whereas the present state of public affairs and the extent of the demands on Our Military Forces for the protection of the interests of the Empire do in Our opinion constitute a case of great emergency within the meaning of the said Act, and We have communicated the same to Parliament:

And whereas by the Territorial and Reserve Forces Act, 1907, it is, amongst other things, enacted that immediately upon and by virtue of the issue of a Proclamation ordering the Army Reserve to be called out on permanent service, it shall be lawful for Us to order Our Army Council from time to time to give and, when given, to revoke or vary such directions as may seem necessary or proper for embodying all or any part of the Territorial Force, and in particular to make such special arrangements as they think proper with regard to units or individuals whose services may be required in other than a Military capacity:

Now, therefore, We do in pursuance of the Reserve Forces Act, 1882, hereby order that Our Army Reserve be called out on permanent service, and We do hereby order the Right Honourable Herbert Henry Asquith, one of Our Principal Secretaries of State, from time to time to give and, when given, to revoke or vary such directions as may seem necessary or proper for calling out Our Army Reserve or all or any of the men belonging thereto:

And We do hereby further order Our Army Council from time to time to give and, when given, to revoke or vary such directions as may seem necessary or proper for embodying all or any part of the Territorial Force, and in particular to make such special arrangements as they think proper with regard to units or individuals whose services may be required in other than a Military capacity.

Given at Our Court at Buckingham Palace, this Fourth day of August, in the year of our Lord one thousand nine hundred and fourteen, and in the Fifth year of Our Reign.

God save the King.

VI

DEFENCE OF THE REALM

Proclamation, dated 4th August 1914, regarding the Defence of the Realm.

BY THE KING.

A Proclamation regarding the Defence of the Realm.

George R.I.

WHEREAS by the law of Our Realm it is Our undoubted prerogative and the duty of all Our loyal subjects acting in Our behalf in times of imminent national danger to take all such measures as may be necessary for securing the public safety and the defence of Our Realm:

And whereas the present state of public affairs in Europe is such as to constitute an imminent national danger:

Now, therefore, We strictly command and enjoin Our subjects to obey and conform to all instructions and regulations which may be issued by Us or Our Admiralty or Army Council, or any officer of Our Navy or Army, or any other person acting in Our behalf for securing the objects aforesaid, and not to hinder or obstruct, but to afford all assistance in their power to, any person acting in accordance with any such instructions or regulations or otherwise in the execution of any measures duly taken for securing those objects.

Given at Our Court at Buckingham Palace, this Fourth day of August, in the year of our Lord one thousand nine hundred and fourteen, and in the Fifth year of Our Reign.

God save the King.

VII

Holidays.

By the King.

A Proclamation for appointing Tuesday, 4th August, Wednesday, 5th August, and Thursday, 6th August, Bank Holidays throughout the United Kingdom.

George R.I.

We, considering that it is desirable in view of the critical situation in Europe and the financial difficulties caused thereby that Tuesday, the 4th instant, Wednesday, the 5th instant, and Thursday, the 6th instant, should be observed as Bank Holidays throughout the United Kingdom, and in pursuance of the provisions of The Bank Holidays Act, 1871, do hereby, by and with the advice of Our Privy Council and in exercise of the powers conferred by the Act aforesaid, appoint Tuesday, the 4th instant, Wednesday, the 5th instant, and Thursday, the 6th instant, as special days to be observed as Bank Holidays throughout the United Kingdom, under and in accordance with the said Act, and We do, by this Our Royal Proclamation, command the said days to be so observed, and all Our loving Subjects to order themselves accordingly.

Given at Our Court at Buckingham Palace this Third day of August, in the year of our Lord one thousand nine hundred and fourteen, and in the Fifth year of Our Reign.

God save the King.

VIII

Army—Billeting in Cases of Emergency.

Army Order 289 of 1914, published 4th August, 1914, promulgating Special Rates to be paid for Billeting in Cases of Emergency.

1. Pursuant to Section 108 A (3) (*c*) of the Army Act, the

prices to be paid to an occupier other than the keeper of a victualling house for billets requisitioned in accordance with the provisions of Section 108 A have been fixed at the rates shown in the subjoined schedule :—

Accommodation to be provided.	Price to be paid to an occupier other than the keeper of a victualling house.
	s. d.
Lodging and attendance for soldier where meals furnished	0 9 per night.
Breakfast as specified in Part I. of the Second Schedule to the Army Act	0 7½ each.
Dinner as so specified	1 7½ each.
Supper as so specified	0 4½ each.
Where no meals furnished, lodging and attendance, and candles, vinegar, salt, and the use of fire, and the necessary utensils for dressing and eating his meat	0 9 per day.
Stable room and ten pounds of oats, twelve pounds of hay, and eight pounds of straw per day for each horse	2 7½ per day.
Stable room without forage	0 9 per day.
Lodging and attendance for officer	3 0 per night.

Note.—An officer must pay for his food.

2. The following special rates have been fixed for troops accommodated in buildings (other than dwelling houses) where bed and attendance are not provided, and for horses where proper stabling is not provided :—

Price to be paid.
For each officer or soldier
For each horse } 3d. per night.

3. A revised form (A.B. 123 M) for payment of billets is now being issued to all units in lieu of A.B. 123.

IX

ARMY—BILLETING IN CASES OF EMERGENCY.

Army Order XXI., *dated* 15*th September* 1914, *as to Special Rates to be paid for Billeting in cases of Emergency.*

With reference to paragraph 2 of Army Order 289 of 1914 the rate payable for troops billeted under Section 108A of the Army Act in empty dwelling houses (unfurnished) is 3d. per head per night; in the case of troops billeted in occupied dwelling houses, but where, in accordance with Appendix H, Mobilisation Regulations, the provision of beds, etc., is not demanded, the full rate of 9d. per head is payable.

Before "dwelling" in line 2 of paragraph 2 of the above Army Order "occupied" should be *inserted.*

X

DEFENCE OF THE REALM—FINANCIAL ASSISTANCE TO ENEMY.

BY THE KING.

A Proclamation notifying that British Subjects contributing to a Loan raised on behalf of the German Emperor or contracting with the German Government, will be guilty of High Treason as adhering to the King's Enemies.

George R.I.

WHEREAS a state of war exists between Us and the German Emperor:

And whereas it constitutes adherence to Our enemies for any of Our subjects or persons resident or being in Our Dominions during the continuance of the state of war to contribute to or participate in or assist in the floating of any loan raised on behalf of the said !Emperor, or to advance money to or enter into any contract or dealings whatsoever with the said Emperor or his Government (save upon Our Command), or otherwise to aid, abet, or assist the said Emperor or Government:

Now, therefore, We do hereby warn all Our subjects and all persons resident or being in Our Dominions who may be found doing or attempting any of such treasonable acts as aforesaid, that they will be liable to be apprehended and dealt with as traitors, and will be proceeded against with the utmost rigour of the law.

Given at Our Court at Buckingham Palace, this Fifth day of August, in the year of our Lord one thousand nine hundred and fourteen, and in the Fifth year of Our Reign.

God save the King.

B.—*Illustrating Part I., Chapter III.*

I

Defence of the Realm Consolidation Act, 1914.

5 Geo. V. c. 8.

[*Royal Assent*, 27*th November* 1914.]

BE it enacted by the King's most excellent Majesty, by and with the advice and consent of the Lords Spiritual and Temporal, and Commons, in this present Parliament assembled, and by the authority of the same, as follows:—

1.—(1) His Majesty in Council has power during the continuance of the present war to issue regulations for securing

DEFENCE

the public safety and the defence of the realm, and as to the powers and duties for that purpose of the Admiralty and Army Council and of the members of His Majesty's forces and other persons acting in his behalf; and may by such regulations authorise the trial by courts-martial, or in the case of minor offences by courts of summary jurisdiction, and punishment of persons committing offences against the regulations, and in particular against any of the provisions of such regulations designed—

- (*a*) to prevent persons communicating with the enemy or obtaining information for that purpose, or any purpose calculated to jeopardise the success of the operations of any of His Majesty's forces or the forces of his allies, or to assist the enemy; or
- (*b*) to secure the safety of His Majesty's forces and ships and the safety of any means of communication and of railways, ports, and harbours; or
- (*c*) to prevent the spread of false reports or reports likely to cause disaffection to His Majesty, or to interfere with the success of His Majesty's forces by land or sea, or to prejudice His Majesty's relations with foreign powers; or
- (*d*) to secure the navigation of vessels in accordance with directions given by or under the authority of the Admiralty; or
- (*e*) otherwise to prevent assistance being given to the enemy, or the successful prosecution of the war being endangered.

(2) Any such regulations may provide for the suspension of any restrictions on the acquisition or user of land, or the exercise of the power of making bye-laws, or any other power under the Defence Acts, 1842 to 1875, or the Military Lands Acts, 1891 to 1903, and any such regulations or any orders made thereunder affecting the pilotage of vessels may supersede any enactment, order, charter, bye-law, regulation, or provision as to pilotage.

(3) It shall be lawful for the Admiralty or Army Council—

- (*a*) to require that there shall be placed at their disposal the whole or any part of the output of any factory or workshop in which arms, ammunition, or warlike stores or equipment, or any articles required for the production thereof, are manufactured;

(*b*) to take possession of and use for the purpose of His Majesty's naval or military service any such factory or workshop or any plant thereof;

and regulations under this Act may be made accordingly.

(4) For the purpose of the trial of a person for an offence under the regulations by court-martial and the punishment thereof, the person may be proceeded against and dealt with as if he were a person subject to military law and had on active service committed an offence under section five of the Army Act:

Provided that where it is proved that the offence is committed with the intention of assisting the enemy, a person convicted of such an offence by a court-martial shall be liable to suffer death.

(5) For the purpose of the trial of a person for an offence under the regulations by a court of summary jurisdiction and the punishment thereof, the offence shall be deemed to have been committed either at the place in which the same actually was committed or in any place in which the offender may be, and the maximum penalty which may be inflicted shall be imprisonment with or without hard labour for a term of six months or a fine of one hundred pounds, or both such imprisonment and fine; section seventeen of the Summary Jurisdiction Act, 1879, shall not apply to charges of offences against the regulations, but any person aggrieved by a conviction of a court of summary jurisdiction may appeal in England to a court of quarter sessions, and in Scotland under and in terms of the Summary Jurisdiction (Scotland) Acts, and in Ireland in manner provided by the Summary Jurisdiction (Ireland) Acts.

(6) The regulations may authorise a court-martial or court of summary jurisdiction, in addition to any other punishment, to order the forfeiture of any goods in respect of which an offence against the regulations has been committed.

DEFENCE 441

2.—(1) This Act may be cited as the Defence of the Realm Consolidation Act, 1914.

(2) The Defence of the Realm Act, 1914, and the Defence of the Realm (No. 2) Act, 1914, are hereby repealed, but nothing in this repeal shall affect any Orders in Council made thereunder, and all such Orders in Council shall, until altered or revoked by an Order in Council under this Act, continue in force and have effect as if made under this Act.

II

DEFENCE OF THE REALM (CONSOLIDATED) REGULATIONS.

At the Court at Buckingham Palace, the 28th day of November 1914.

PRESENT,

The King's Most Excellent Majesty in Council.

WHEREAS by the Defence of the Realm Consolidation Act, 1914, His Majesty has power during the continuance of the present war to issue Regulations for securing the public safety and the defence of the Realm subject to and in accordance with that Act :

And whereas by Orders in Council dated respectively the 12th of August, the 1st and 17th of September, and the 14th of October 1914, His Majesty was pleased to issue various Regulations under the Defence of the Realm Act, 1914, and the Defence of the Realm (No. 2) Act, 1914, and by virtue of the said Defence of the Realm Consolidation Act, 1914, those Orders in Council shall until altered or revoked by an Order in Council under the last-mentioned Act continue in force and have effect as if made under that Act :

And whereas it is expedient to revoke the said Orders in Council and to issue such Regulations as are hereinafter contained :

Now, therefore, His Majesty is pleased by and with the

advice of His Privy Council, to order, and it is hereby ordered, as follows :—

General Regulations.

1. The ordinary avocations of life and the enjoyment of property will be interfered with as little as may be permitted by the exigencies of the measures required to be taken for securing the public safety and the defence of the Realm, and ordinary civil offences will be dealt with by the civil tribunals in the ordinary course of law.

The Admiralty and Army Council, and members of the Naval and Military Forces, and other persons executing the following Regulations shall, in carrying those Regulations into effect, observe these general principles.

Powers of competent naval and military authorities, &c.

2. It shall be lawful for the competent naval or military authority and any person duly authorised by him, where for the purpose of securing the public safety or the defence of the Realm it is necessary so to do—

(*a*) to take possession of any land and to construct military works, including roads, thereon, and to remove any trees, hedges, and fences therefrom ;

(*b*) to take possession of any buildings or other property including works for the supply of gas, electricity, or water, and of any sources of water supply ;

(*c*) to take such steps as may be necessary for placing any buildings or structures in a state of defence ;

(*d*) to cause any buildings or structures to be destroyed, or any property to be moved from one place to another, or to be destroyed ;

(*e*) to take possession of any arms, ammunition, explosive substances, equipment, or warlike stores (including lines, cables, and other apparatus intended to be laid or used for telegraphic or telephonic purposes) ;

(*f*) to do any other act involving interference with private rights of property which is necessary for the purpose aforesaid.

3. The competent naval or military authority and any person

duly authorised by him shall have right of access to any land or buildings or other property whatsoever.

4. The competent naval or military authority may by order authorise the use of land, within such limits as may be specified in the order, for the training of any part of His Majesty's naval or military forces ; and may by such order confer such rights of user of the land, and provide for such temporary suspension of rights of way over roads and footpaths, as are conferred and are exercisable with respect to authorised land roads and footpaths under the Military Manœuvres Acts, 1897 and 1911, and the competent naval or military authority shall have all the powers exercisable by a Military Manœuvres Commission under those Acts.

5. The competent naval or military authority may by order, if he considers it necessary so to do for the purposes of any work of defence or other defended military work, or of any work for which it is deemed necessary in the interests of public safety or the defence of the Realm to afford military protection, stop up or divert any road or pathway over or adjoining the land on which such work is situate for so long as the order remains in force:

Provided that where any such road or pathway is so stopped up or diverted the competent naval or military authority shall publish notice thereof in such manner as he may consider best adapted for informing the public, and where any road or pathway is stopped up by means of any physical obstruction he shall cause lights sufficient for the warning of passengers to be set up every night whilst the road or pathway is so stopped up.

6. The competent naval or military authority may by order require all or any vehicles, boats, vessels, aircraft, transport animals, live stock, foodstuffs, fuel, tools, and implements of whatever description, and all or any forms of equipment and war-like stores, within any area specified in the order, to be removed from that area within such time as may be so specified, or in the case of warlike stores incapable of removal to be destroyed, and if any person being the owner or having control thereof fail to comply with the requisition, he shall be guilty of an offence against these Regulations, and the

competent naval or military authority may himself cause them to be removed, or, in the case of warlike stores, to be destroyed.

7. The Admiralty or Army Council may by order require the occupier of any factory or workshop in which arms, ammunition, or any warlike stores or equipment, or any articles required for the production thereof, are manufactured, to place at their disposal the whole or any part of the output of the factory or workshop as may be specified in the order, and to deliver to them the output or such part thereof as aforesaid in such quantities and at such times as may be specified in the order ; and the occupier of the factory or workshop shall be entitled to receive in respect thereof such price as, in default of agreement, may be decided to be reasonable having regard to the circumstances of the case by the arbitration of a judge of the High Court selected by the Lord Chief Justice of England in England, by a judge of the Court of Session selected by the Lord President of the Court of Session in Scotland, or by a judge of the High Court of Ireland selected by the Lord Chief Justice of Ireland in Ireland.

If the occupier of the factory or workshop fails to comply with the order, or without the leave of the Admiralty or Army Council delivers to any other person any part of the output of the factory or workshop to which the order relates, he shall be guilty of an offence against these Regulations.

8. The Admiralty or Army Council may take possession of any such factory or workshop as aforesaid, or of any plant belonging thereto without taking possession of the factory or workshop itself, and may use the same for His Majesty's naval or military service at such times and in such manner as the Admiralty or Army Council may consider necessary or expedient, and the occupier and every officer and servant of the occupier, and, where the occupier is a company, every director of the Company shall obey the directions of the Admiralty or Army Council as to the user of the factory or workshop or plant, and if he fails to do so he shall be guilty of an offence against these Regulations.

9. The competent naval or military authority may by order require the whole or any part of the inhabitants of any area specified in the order to leave that area if the removal of such

DEFENCE

inhabitants from that area is necessary for naval or military reasons, and if any person to whom the order relates fails to comply with the order he shall be guilty of an offence against these Regulations and the competent naval or military authority may cause such steps to be taken as may be necessary to enforce compliance therewith.

10. The competent naval or military authority may by order require all or any premises licensed for the sale of intoxicating liquor within any area specified in the order to be closed except during such hours and for such purposes as may be specified in the order, either generally or as respects the members of any of His Majesty's forces mentioned in the order, and, if the holder of the licence in respect of any such premises fails to comply with the order, he shall be guilty of an offence under these Regulations, and the competent naval or military authority may cause such steps to be taken as may be necessary to enforce compliance with the order.

11. The Secretary of State or any person authorised by him may by order direct that all or any lights, or lights of any class or description, shall be extinguished or obscured in such manner and between such hours as the order directs, within any area specified in the order and during such period as may be so specified, and if the person having control of the light fails to comply with the order, he shall be guilty of an offence against these Regulations, and the Secretary of State may cause the light to be extinguished or obscured as the case may be, and for that purpose any person authorised by the Secretary of State in that behalf or any police constable may enter the premises in which the light is displayed, and do any other act which may be necessary.

Any such order as aforesaid may provide that vehicles or vehicles of any class or description shall, when travelling within the area specified in the order during the period between one hour after sunset and one hour before sunrise, carry such lamps as may be specified in the order, properly trimmed, lighted, and attached'; and any police officer may stop and seize any vehicle which does not carry lamps in compliance with the order, and the person in charge or having control of the vehicle shall be guilty of a summary offence against these Regulations.

The powers conferred by this Regulation shall be in addition to, and not in derogation of, the powers conferred on the competent naval or military authority by Regulation 12, and the competent naval or military authority may, notwithstanding anything in an order under this Regulation, on any occasion when he may consider lights necessary for any naval or military purpose, require any lights to be lighted or kept lighted.

In the application of this Regulation to Scotland, references to the Secretary for Scotland shall be substituted for references to the Secretary of State.

12. The competent naval or military authority may by order direct that all or any lights, other than lights not visible from the outside of any house, shall be kept extinguished or obscured between such hours and within such area as may be specified in the order; and if any person resident within that area fails to comply with the order he shall be guilty of an offence against these Regulations.

13. The competent naval or military authority may by order require every person within any area specified in the order to remain within doors between such hours as may be specified in the order, and in such case, if any person within that area is or remains out between such hours without a permit in writing from the competent naval or military authority, or some person duly authorised by him, he shall be guilty of an offence against these Regulations.

14. Where a person is suspected of acting, or of having acted, or of being about to act in a manner prejudicial to the public safety or the defence of the Realm, and it appears to the competent naval or military authority that it is desirable that such person should be prohibited from residing in or entering any locality, the competent naval or military authority may by order prohibit him from residing in or entering any area or areas which may be specified in the order, and upon the making of such an order the person to whom the order relates shall, if he resides in any specified area, leave that area within such time as may be specified by the order, and shall not subsequently reside in or enter any area specified in the order, and if he does so, he shall be guilty of an offence against these Regulations.

DEFENCE

Any such order may further require the person to whom the order relates to report for approval his proposed place of residence to the competent naval or military authority, and to proceed thereto and report his arrival to the police, within such time as may be specified in the order, and not subsequently to change his place of residence without leave of the competent naval or military authority, and in such case if he fails to comply with the requirements of the order he shall be guilty of an offence against these Regulations.

15. Where a competent naval or military authority makes an order for the purpose, all persons residing, or owning, or occupying lands, houses, or other premises in such area as may be specified in the order, or such of those persons as may be so specified, shall, within such time as may be so specified, furnish a list of all goods, animals, and other commodities of any nature or description so specified, which may be in their custody or under their control within the specified area on the date on which the order is issued, stating their nature and quantity and the place in which they are severally situate, and giving any other details which may reasonably be required.

If any person fails to comply with any such order, or attempts to evade this Regulation by destroying, removing, or secreting any goods, animals, or commodities to which an order issued under this Regulation relates, he shall be guilty of an offence against these Regulations.

16. The competent naval or military authority may by order require the authority or person controlling any harbour, dock, wharf, waterworks, gasworks, electric light or power station, or other structure, to prepare a scheme for destroying or rendering useless the equipment or facilities of the harbour, dock, wharf, waterworks, gasworks, station, or structure, or such part thereof as may be specified in the order, and if the authority or person fails to prepare such a scheme within such time as may be specified in the order, he shall be guilty of an offence against these Regulations.

17. The restriction on the power to make bye-laws under the Military Lands Acts, 1892 to 1903, imposed by the following provisions of the Military Lands Act, 1892, that is

to say, the proviso to sub-section (1) of section fourteen, section sixteen, and sub-section (1) of section seventeen of that Act, and by the following provisions of the Military Lands Act, 1900, that is to say, the provisos to sub-section (2) of section two and sub-section (3) of section two of that Act, are hereby suspended, and the powers of the Admiralty and the Secretary of State to make bye-laws under the said Acts shall extend to the making of bye-laws with respect to land of which possession has been taken under these Regulations.

Provisions respecting the collection and communication of information, etc.

18. No person shall without lawful authority collect, record, publish, or communicate, or attempt to elicit, any information with respect to the movement, numbers, description, condition, or disposition of any of the forces, ships, or war materials of His Majesty or any of His Majesty's allies, or with respect to the plans or conduct, or supposed plans or conduct, of any naval or military operations by any such forces or ships, or with respect to any works or measures undertaken for or connected with, or intended for the fortification or defence of any place, or any other information intended to be communicated to the enemy, or of such a nature as is calculated to be or might be directly or indirectly useful to the enemy, and if any person contravenes the provisions of this Regulation, or without lawful authority or excuse has in his possession any document containing any such information as aforesaid, he shall be guilty of an offence against these Regulations.

19. No person shall without the permission of the competent naval or military authority make any photograph, sketch, plan, model, or other representation of any naval or military work, or of any dock or harbour work or, with intent to assist the enemy, of any other place or thing, and no person in the vicinity of any such work shall without lawful authority or excuse have in his possession any photographic or other apparatus or other material or thing suitable for use in making any such representation, and if any person contravenes the provisions of this Regulation, or without lawful authority or excuse has in his possession any representation of any such

work of such a nature as is calculated to be or might be directly or indirectly useful to the enemy, he shall be guilty of an offence against these Regulations.

For the purpose of this Regulation the expression "harbour work" includes lights, buoys, beacons, marks, and other things for the purpose of facilitating navigation in or into a harbour.

20. No person without lawful authority shall injure, or tamper, or interfere with, any wire or other apparatus for transmitting telegraphic or telephonic messages, or any apparatus or contrivance intended for or capable of being used for a signalling apparatus, either visual or otherwise, or prevent or obstruct or in any manner whatsoever interfere with the sending, conveyance, or delivery of any communication by means of telegraph, telephone, or otherwise, or be in possession of any apparatus intended for or capable of being used for tapping messages sent by wireless telegraphy or otherwise, and if any person contravenes the provisions of this Regulation he shall be guilty of an offence against these Regulations.

21. No person shall keep or have in his possession or carry or liberate or bring into the United Kingdom any carrier or homing pigeons, unless he has obtained from the chief officer of police of the district a permit for the purpose, and if any person without lawful authority contravenes the provisions of this Regulation he shall be guilty of an offence against these Regulations, and the chief officer of police or any officer of customs and excise may, if he considers it necessary or expedient to do so, cause any pigeons kept or brought into the United Kingdom in contravention of this Regulation to be liberated, detained, or destroyed, or, in the case of pigeons brought into the United Kingdom, to be immediately returned in the ship in which they came.

Any person found in possession of or found carrying or liberating any carrier pigeons shall, if so required by any naval or military officer, or by any sailor or soldier engaged on sentry patrol or other similar duty, or by any officer of police, produce his permit, and if he fails to do so, may be arrested.

22. No person shall, without the written permission of the

Postmaster-General, buy, sell, or have in his possession or under his control any apparatus for the sending or receiving of messages by wireless telegraphy, or any apparatus intended to be used as a component part of such apparatus; and no person shall sell any such apparatus to any person who has not obtained such permission as aforesaid; and if any person contravenes the provisions of this Regulation he shall be guilty of an offence against these Regulations.

If the competent naval or military authority has reason to suspect that any person having in his possession any apparatus for sending or receiving messages by telegraphy, telephony, or other electrical or mechanical means is using or about to use the same for any purpose prejudicial to the public safety or the defence of the realm, he may, by order, prohibit that person from having any such apparatus in his possession, and may take such steps as are necessary for enforcing the order, and if that person subsequently has in his possession any apparatus in contravention of the order he shall be guilty of an offence against these Regulations.

For the purposes of this Regulation any apparatus ordinarily used as a distinctive component part of apparatus for the sending or receiving of messages by wireless telegraphy shall be deemed to be intended to be so used unless the contrary is proved.

23. Where the competent naval or military authority or any person duly authorised by him or an aliens officer has reason to suspect that any person who is about to embark on any ship, vessel, or aircraft is attempting to leave the United Kingdom for the purpose of communicating directly or indirectly with the enemy or with any subject of any sovereign or state at war with His Majesty, he may prevent the embarkation of that person.

Where the embarkation of any person has been so prevented the case shall be reported to a Secretary of State, and the Secretary of State may, if he thinks fit, by order prohibit that person at any time subsequently from leaving the United Kingdom so long as the order is in force, and if any person leaves the United Kingdom in contravention of such an order he shall be guilty of an offence against these Regulations.

24. No person shall without lawful authority transmit, otherwise than through the post, or convey to or from the United Kingdom, or receive or have in his possession for such transmission or conveyance, any letter or written message from or originating with, or to or intended for—

(*a*) any person or body of persons, of whatever nationality, resident or carrying on business in any country for the time being at war with His Majesty, or acting on behalf or in the interests of any person or body of persons so resident or carrying on business ; or

(*b*) any person or body of persons whose sovereign or state is at war with His Majesty, and who resides or carries on business in the United Kingdom ;

and if any person contravenes this provision he shall be guilty of an offence against these Regulations :

Provided that a person shall not be deemed to be guilty of a contravention of this Regulation if he proves that he did not know, and had no reason to suspect, that the letter or message in question was such a letter or message as aforesaid.

This Regulation is in addition to and not in derogation of any provisions contained in the enactments relating to the Post Office, and shall not prejudice any right to take proceedings under those enactments in respect of any transaction which is an offence against those enactments.

25. No person shall without lawful authority be in possession of any searchlight, semaphore, or other apparatus intended for signalling, whether visual or otherwise, or display, erect, or use any signal, and if any person contravenes this provision he shall be guilty of an offence against these Regulations ; and the competent naval or military authority may require any flagstaff or other erection capable of being used as a means of signalling to be removed, and if the owner thereof fails to comply with the requirement, he shall be guilty of an offence against these Regulations and the competent naval or military authority may cause the flagstaff or other erection to be removed.

26. No person shall without the permission of the competent naval or military authority, or some person authorised by him, display any light or ignite or otherwise make use of any fire-

works or other similar device or any fire in such a manner as could serve as a signal, guide, or landmark, and if he does so he shall be guilty of an offence against these Regulations.

27. No person shall by word of mouth or in writing or in any newspaper, periodical, book, circular, or other printed publication, spread false reports or make false statements or reports or statements likely to cause disaffection to His Majesty, or to interfere with the success of His Majesty's forces by land or sea, or to prejudice His Majesty's relations with foreign powers, or spread reports or make statements likely to prejudice the recruiting, training, discipline, or administration of any of His Majesty's forces, and if any person contravenes this provision he shall be guilty of an offence against these Regulations.

Provisions against injury to railways, military works, &c.

28. No person shall trespass on any railway, or loiter on, under, or near any tunnel, bridge, viaduct or culvert, or on or in any road, path or other place, being a road, path or place to which access has been forbidden by order of the competent naval or military authority, and if he does he shall be guilty of an offence against these Regulations.

If any person does any injury to any railway, or is upon any railway, or on, under, or near any tunnel, bridge, viaduct or culvert, or loiters on or in any road or path, or other place near a railway tunnel, bridge, viaduct or culvert, with intent to do injury thereto, he shall be guilty of an offence against these Regulations.

29. The competent naval or military authority may by order prohibit any person from approaching within such distance as may be specified in the order of any camp, work of defence or other defended military work, or any work to which it is deemed necessary in the interest of the public safety or the defence of the Realm, to afford military protection, and if any person contravenes any such order he shall be guilty of an offence against these Regulations.

Provisions as to arms and explosives.

30. The competent naval or military authority may by order

prohibit the manufacture or sale of firearms, ammunition, or explosive substances or any class thereof, within the area specified in the order, either absolutely or except subject to such conditions as may be specified in the order, and if any person without a permit from the competent naval or military authority manufactures, sells, or has in his possession for sale within the area so specified, any arms, ammunition, or explosive substance in contravention of the order, or fails to comply with the conditions imposed by the order, he shall be guilty of an offence.

31. No person shall bring into the United Kingdom any firearms, military arms, or ammunition or any explosive substance, without a permit from the competent naval or military authority, and if he does so shall be guilty of an offence against these Regulations, and any person authorised for the purpose by the component naval or military authority, and any police constable or officer of customs and excise, may examine, search, and investigate any ship or vessel for the purpose of the enforcement of this provision, and may seize any arms or ammunition or any explosive substance which are being or have been brought into the United Kingdom without such permit as aforesaid.

32. If any person by the discharge of firearms or otherwise endangers the safety of any member of any of His Majesty's forces he shall be guilty of an offence against these Regulations.

33. No person, without the written permission of the competent naval or military authority, shall, on or in the vicinity of any railway, or in or in the vicinity of any dock, harbour, or in or in the vicinity of any area which may be specified in an order made by the competent naval or military authority, be in possession of any explosive substance or any highly inflammable liquid, in quantities exceeding the immediate requirements of his business or occupation, or of any firearms or ammunition (except such shotguns, and ammunition therefor, as are ordinarily used for sporting purposes in the United Kingdom), and if any person contravenes this provision he shall be guilty of an offence against these Regulations.

34. Every place used for the storage of petroleum, turpentine,

methylated spirit, wood naphtha, or any other highly inflammable liquid, exceeding in the aggregate one hundred gallons shall be surrounded by a retaining wall or embankment so designed and constructed as to form an enclosure which will prevent in any circumstances the escape of any part of the petroleum or other inflammable liquid.

This requirement shall not apply to any storage place sunk below the level of the ground so as to form a pit, nor to any storage place so situated that the overflow of the petroleum or liquid from the vessel or vessels in which it is contained could not in case of fire seriously endanger life or cause material damage to property.

If any person uses or permits to be used, for the storage of petroleum or other such inflammable liquid, any premises which do not comply with the requirements of this Regulation, he shall be guilty of an offence against these Regulations.

For the purposes of this Regulation "petroleum" means petroleum as defined in section three of the Petroleum Act, 1871, having a flashpoint below 150° F. (Abel).

Nothing in this Regulation shall prejudice the effect of any requirements as to the storage of petroleum or other inflammable liquid lawfully imposed by any local authority, or the taking of any proceedings in respect of the violation of such requirements.

35. No person shall, in any prescribed area, have in his possession or in premises in his occupation or under his control any celluloid or any cinematograph film exceeding the prescribed amount, unless he has obtained the prescribed permit and observes all the prescribed requirements, and if any person contravenes this provision he shall be guilty of a summary offence against these Regulations.

Any police constable or any person authorised in writing by the Chief Officer of Police of the district, may enter, if need be by force, and search any premises in which he has reasonable cause to believe that celluloid or cinematograph film is kept or stored ; and, if the prescribed permit has not been obtained, or if any of the prescribed requirements are not complied with, may remove and destroy any such celluloid or film.

For the purpose of this Regulation "celluloid" includes the

DEFENCE

substances known as celluloid or xylonite and other similar substances containing nitro-cellulose or other nitrated product, but does not include celluloid which has been subjected to any manufacturing process : and "cinematograph film" means any film which is intended for use in cinematograph or similar apparatus and contains nitro-cellulose or other nitrated product : and "prescribed" means prescribed by order made by a Secretary of State, or, in Scotland, by the Secretary for Scotland.

Provision as to navigation.

36. If the master of a ship, or any other person, disobeys or neglects to observe any regulations relating to the navigation or mooring of ships in a harbour or the approaches thereto, or any signals from, or any orders, whether verbal or written, of the competent naval or military authority of the harbour, or any examining or other officer acting under his authority, relating to such navigation or mooring, he shall be guilty of an offence against these Regulations.

37. Every vessel shall comply with such regulations as to the navigation of vessels as may be issued by the Admiralty or Army Council, and shall obey any orders given, whether by way of signal or otherwise, by any officer in command of any of His Majesty's ships, or by any naval or military officer engaged in the defence of the coast.

If any vessel fails to comply with any such regulations or to obey any such orders, the master or other person in command or charge of the vessel shall be guilty of an offence against these Regulations, and if the vessel is at any time subsequently found at a port of, or within the territorial waters adjacent to, the United Kingdom, the competent naval or military authority may cause the vessel to be seized and detained.

This Regulation shall not apply to a vessel not being a British vessel where the non-compliance with the Regulations or disobedience to the orders takes place on the high seas outside the territorial waters adjacent to the United Kingdom.

38. The Admiralty or Army Council may by order prohibit any vessel, or any vessel of any class or description specified in the order, from entering any area which they may consider

it is necessary to keep clear of vessels, or vessels of that class or description, in the interests of the public safety or the defence of the Realm, and if any vessel, or any vessel of that specified class or description, enters any such area, the master or other person in command or charge of the vessel shall be guilty of an offence against these Regulations.

This Regulation shall not apply to a vessel not being a British vessel so far as the area specified in the order extends beyond the territorial waters adjacent to the United Kingdom.

39. The Admiralty or Army Council, or any pilotage authority acting under their instructions, may make orders as to the pilotage of vessels entering, leaving or making use of any port or navigating within any part of the territorial waters adjacent to the United Kingdom, and any such order may provide for pilotage being compulsory for all or any class of such vessels within such limits as may be specified in the order, for the granting of special pilotage licences and the suspension of existing pilotage licences and certificates, and for the supply, employment, and payment of pilots.

Any enactment, order, charter, custom, byelaw, regulation or provision in force for the time being in any area to which any such order relates shall have effect subject to the provisions of the order.

If any person fails to comply with the provisions of any such order he shall be guilty of an offence against these Regulations.

Miscellaneous offences.

40. If any person with the intent of eliciting information for the purpose of communicating it to the enemy, or for any purpose calculated to assist the enemy, gives or sells to a member of any of His Majesty's forces any intoxicant, or gives or sells to a member of any of His Majesty's forces any intoxicant when not on duty, with intent to make him drunk or less capable of the efficient discharge of his duties, or when on sentry or other duty, either with or without any such intent, he shall be guilty of an offence against these Regulations.

For the purposes of this Regulation the expression "intoxicant" includes any intoxicating liquor, and any sedative, narcotic, or stimulant drug or preparation.

41. If any unauthorised person wears any naval, military, police or other official uniform, or any uniform so nearly resembling any such uniform as aforesaid as to be calculated to deceive, or if any person without lawful authority supplies a naval or military uniform to any person not being a member of His Majesty's forces, he shall be guilty of an offence against these Regulations.

42. If any person attempts to cause mutiny, sedition, or disaffection among any of His Majesty's forces, or among the civilian population, he shall be guilty of an offence against these Regulations.

43. No person shall obstruct or otherwise interfere with or impede, or withhold any information in his possession which he may reasonably be required to furnish, from any officer or other person who is carrying out the orders of the competent naval or military authority, or who is otherwise acting in accordance with his duty under these Regulations, and if he does so shall be guilty of an offence against these Regulations.

44. If any person, verbally or in writing, in any report, return, declaration, or application, or in any document signed by him or on his behalf of which it is his duty to ascertain the accuracy, knowingly makes or connives at the making of any false statement or any omission, with intent to mislead any officer, or other person acting under the orders of any officer in the execution of his duties, he shall be guilty of an offence against these Regulations.

45. If any person forges, alters, or tampers with any naval, military, or police pass, permit, or other document, or uses or has in his possession any such forged, altered, or irregular naval, military, or police pass, permit, or documents, or personate any person to whom such a pass, permit, or other document has been duly issued, he shall be guilty of an offence against these Regulations.

46. If any person is found in possession of a false passport, or, being a subject of a Sovereign or State at war with His Majesty, passes under an assumed name, he shall be guilty of an offence against these Regulations.

47. It shall be the duty of every person affected by any order issued by the competent naval or military authority or other

person in pursuance of these Regulations to comply with that order, and if he fails to do so he shall be guilty of an offence against these Regulations.

48. Any person who attempts to commit, or procures, aids, or abets, or does any act preparatory to the commission of, any act prohibited by these Regulations, or harbours any person whom he knows, or has reasonable grounds for supposing, to have acted in contravention of these Regulations, shall be guilty of an offence against these Regulations.

49. It shall be the duty of any person who knows that some other person is acting in contravention of any provisions of these Regulations to inform the competent naval or military authority of the fact, and if he fails to do so he shall be guilty of an offence against these Regulations.

50. If any person does any act of such a nature as to be calculated to be prejudicial to the public safety or the defence of the Realm and not specifically provided for in the foregoing Regulations, with the intention or for the purpose of assisting the enemy, he shall be deemed to be guilty of an offence against these Regulations.

Powers of search, arrest, &c.

51. The competent naval or military authority, or any person duly authorised by him may, if he has reason to suspect that any house, building, land, vehicle, vessel, aircraft, or other premises or any things therein are being or have been constructed, used, or kept for any purpose or in any way prejudicial to the public safety or the defence of the Realm, or that an offence against these Regulations is being or has been committed thereon or therein, enter, if need be by force, the house, building, land, vehicle, vessel, aircraft, or premises at any time of the day or night, and examine, search, and inspect the same or any part thereof, and may seize anything found therein which he has reason to suspect is being used or intended to be used for any such purpose as aforesaid, or is being kept or used in contravention of these Regulations (including, where a report or statement in contravention of Regulation 27 has appeared in any newspaper or other printed publication, any type or other plant used or capable of being used for the printing or produc-

tion of the newspaper or other publication), and the competent naval or military authority may order anything so seized to be destroyed or otherwise disposed of.

52. Any officer, or any soldier or sailor engaged on sentry, patrol, or other similar duty, and any police officer, may stop any vehicle travelling along any public highway, and, if he has reason to suspect that the vehicle is being used for any purpose or in any way prejudicial to the public safety or the defence of the Realm, may search and seize the vehicle, and seize anything found therein which he has reason to suspect is being used or intended to be used for any such purpose as aforesaid.

53. It shall be the duty of any person, if so required by an officer, or by a soldier or sailor engaged on sentry, patrol, or other similar duty, or by a police constable, to stop and answer to the best of his ability and knowledge any questions which may be reasonably addressed to him, and if he refuses or fails to do so he shall be guilty of an offence against these Regulations.

The competent naval or military authority may by order require any person or persons of any class or description to furnish him, either verbally or in writing, with such information as may be specified in the order, and the order may require any person to attend at such time and such place as may be specified in the order for the purpose of furnishing such information, and if any person fails to comply with the order he shall be guilty of an offence against these Regulations.

54. Any person landing or embarking at any place in the United Kingdom shall, on being required to do so by the competent naval or military authority, or any person authorised by him, or by an aliens officer or officer of police, make a declaration as to whether or not he is carrying or conveying any letters or other written messages intended to be transmitted by post or otherwise delivered, and, if so required, shall produce to the person making the requisition any such letters or messages; and the competent naval or military authority, or person authorised by him, or aliens or police officer may search any such person and any baggage with a view to ascertaining whether such person or the person to

whom the baggage belongs is carrying or conveying any such letters or messages.

The competent naval or military authority, or persons authorised by him, or aliens or police officer may examine any letters or other messages so produced to him or found on such search, and unless satisfied that they are of an innocent nature, may transmit them to an officer appointed to censor postal correspondence.

Any person who knowingly makes any false declaration under this Regulation, or on being required to produce any such letters or messages as aforesaid refuses or neglects to do so, shall be guilty of an offence against these Regulations.

55. Any person authorised for the purpose by the competent naval or military authority, or any police constable, or officer of customs and excise or aliens officer, may arrest without warrant any person whose behaviour is of such a nature as to give reasonable grounds for suspecting that he has acted, or is acting, or is about to act in a manner prejudicial to the public safety or the defence of the Realm, or upon whom may be found any article, book, letter, or other document, the possession of which gives grounds for such a suspicion, or who is suspected of having committed an offence against these Regulations.

If any person assists or connives at the escape of any person who may be in custody under this Regulation, or knowingly harbours or assists any person who has so escaped, he shall be guilty of an offence against these Regulations.

Trial and punishment of offences.

56. A person alleged to be guilty of an offence against these Regulations may be tried either by a court-martial or before a court of summary jurisdiction :

Provided that in the case of any offence against these Regulations declared to be a summary offence, the alleged offender shall not be liable to be tried otherwise than before a court of summary jurisdiction.

Where a person is alleged to be guilty of an offence against these Regulations (other than offence declared by these Regulations to be a summary offence), the case shall be referred to the competent naval or military authority, who shall investigate the case and determine whether it shall be tried by court-martial or summarily, or shall not be proceeded with, and if the alleged offender is in custody, he shall if he is to be tried by court-martial be kept in or handed over to military custody, and if he is to be tried summarily, be handed over to or kept in civil custody.

57. A person found guilty of an offence against these Regulations by a court-martial shall be liable to be sentenced to penal servitude for life or any less punishment, or if the court finds that the offence was committed with the intention of assisting the enemy to suffer death or any less punishment, and the court may in addition to any other sentence imposed order that any goods in respect of which the offence has been committed be forfeited:

Provided that a sentence of detention in detention barracks shall not be awarded for an offence under these Regulations, and that no sentence exceeding six months' imprisonment with hard labour shall be imposed in respect of any contravention of Regulations 12, 13, 21, 22, 25, 26, 27, 28 (first paragraph), 35, 53, 60, and 61, if the offender proves that he acted without any intention of assisting the enemy or, in the case of Regulation 27, of causing disaffection or alarm, or prejudicing the recruiting, training, discipline, and administration of any force.

A court-martial having jurisdiction to try offences under these Regulations shall be a general or district court-martial convened by an officer authorised to convene such description of court-martial, within the limits of whose command the offender may for the time being be; but nothing in this Regulation shall be construed as authorising a district court-martial to impose a sentence of penal servitude.

Any person tried by court-martial under these Regulations shall, for the purposes of the provisions of the Army Act relating to offences, be treated as if he belonged to the unit in whose charge he may be; but no such person shall be liable to summary punishment by a commanding officer.

58. A person convicted of an offence against these Regulations by a court of summary jurisdiction shall be liable to be sentenced to imprisonment, with or without hard labour, for

a term not exceeding six months, or to a fine not exceeding one hundred pounds, or to both such imprisonment and fine, and the court may, in addition to any other sentence which may be imposed, order that any goods in respect of which the offence has been committed shall be forfeited.

For the purpose of the trial of a person for such an offence the offence shall be deemed to have been committed either at the place in which the same actually was committed, or at any place in which the offender may be, and the court in Scotland shall be the sheriff court.

Section seventeen of the Summary Jurisdiction Act, 1879, shall not apply to the charge of offences against these Regulations.

Any person aggrieved by a conviction of a court of summary jurisdiction under these Regulations may appeal in England to a court of quarter sessions, and in Scotland under and in terms of the Summary Jurisdiction (Scotland) Acts, and in Ireland in manner provided by the Summary Jurisdiction (Ireland) Acts.

Supplemental.

59. The powers conferred by these Regulations are in addition to and not in derogation of any powers exercisable by members of His Majesty's naval and military forces and other persons to take such steps as may be necessary for securing the public safety and the defence of the Realm, and nothing in these Regulations shall affect the liability of any person to trial and punishment for any offence or war crime otherwise than in accordance with these Regulations.

60. The competent naval or military authority, or any other person by whom an order is made in pursuance of these Regulations, shall publish notice of the order in such manner as he may consider best adapted for informing persons affected by the order, and no person shall without lawful authority deface or otherwise tamper with any notice posted up in pursuance of these Regulations, and if he does so shall be guilty of an offence against these Regulations.

61. Any person claiming to act under any permit or permission granted under or for the purposes of these Regulations shall, if at any time he is required to do so by the competent

naval or military authority or any person authorised by him, or by any naval or military officer, or by any sailor or soldier engaged on sentry, patrol, or other similar duty, or by any officer of customs and excise, officer of police, or aliens officer, produce the permit or permission for inspection, and if he refuses to do so he shall be guilty of an offence against these Regulations.

Any permit or permission granted under or for the purposes of any provision of these Regulations may at any time be revoked.

62. The Admiralty or Army Council may appoint any commissioned officer of His Majesty's Naval or Military Forces, not below the rank of lieutenant commander in the Navy or field officer in the Army, to be a competent naval or military authority, and may authorise any competent naval or military authority thus appointed to delegate, either unconditionally or subject to such conditions as he thinks fit, all or any of his powers under these Regulations to any officer qualified to be appointed a competent naval or military authority, and an officer so appointed, or to whom the powers of the competent naval or military authority are so delegated, is in these Regulations referred to as a competent naval or military authority.

For the purposes of these Regulations the expression "aliens officer" shall have the same meaning as in the Aliens Restriction (Consolidation) Order, 1914.

63. These Regulations may be cited as the Defence of the Realm (Consolidation) Regulations, 1914.

The Interpretation Act, 1889, applies for the purpose of the interpretation of these Regulations in like manner as it applies for the purpose of the interpretation of an Act of Parliament.

The said Orders in Council of the 12th of August, the 1st and 17th of September, and the 14th of October 1914, are hereby revoked:

Provided that the revocation of any such Order shall not—

    (*a*) affect the previous operation of any Order so revoked or anything duly done or suffered under any Order so revoked ; or

    (*b*) affect any right, privilege, obligation, or liability

acquired, accrued, or incurred under any Order so revoked ; or

(*c*) affect any penalty, forfeiture, or punishment incurred in respect of any offence committed against any Order so revoked ; or

(*d*) affect any proceedings or remedy in respect of any such right, privilege, obligation, liability, penalty, forfeiture, or punishment as aforesaid ;

and any permission or direction given, or order, requirement, or appointment made, authority issued, or other action taken under any Order so revoked shall be deemed to have been given, made, issued, or taken under the corresponding provision of this Order. *Almeric Fitzroy.*

III

Special Constables Act, 1914.

4 & 5 Geo. V. c. 61.

[*Royal Assent*, 28*th August* 1914.]

Be it enacted by the King's most Excellent Majesty, by and with the advice and consent of the Lords Spiritual and Temporal, and Commons, in this present Parliament assembled, and by the authority of the same, as follows :—

1.—(1) His Majesty may, by Order in Council, make regulations with respect to the appointment and position of special constables appointed during the present war under the Special Constables Act, 1831, or under section one hundred and ninety-six of the Municipal Corporations Act, 1882, and may, by those regulations, provide—

(*a*) that the power to authorise the nomination and appointment of special constables under the Special Constables

Act, 1831, may be exercised although a tumult, riot, or felony has not taken place, or is not immediately apprehended; and

(b) that any special constables to which the regulations apply shall, in the execution of their duty, act under such direction as may be specified in the regulations; and

(c) for the application to special constables to which the regulations apply of any of the provisions of the Police Acts, 1839 to 1910 (including those relating to the grant of allowances or gratuities to constables injured, and to the dependants of constables killed, in the execution of their duty), subject to such modifications as may be specified in the regulations; and

(d) for giving validity and effect to the appointment of special constables, or any other action taken with respect to special constables, since the commencement of the present war, but before the regulations are made; and

(e) for such supplemental and ancillary matters as may be necessary or expedient for the purpose of giving full effect to the regulations.

(2) His Majesty may, by Order in Council, revoke, alter, or amend any Order in Council made under this section as occasion requires.

(3) In the application of this Act to Scotland the Burgh Police (Scotland) Act, 1892, so far as relating to special constables, the corresponding provisions of any local Act, and the Special Constables (Scotland) Act, 1914, shall be substituted for the Special Constables Act, 1831, and section one hundred and ninety-six of the Municipal Corporations Act, 1882; and the Police (Scotland) Act, 1857, the Police (Scotland) Act, 1890, the Burgh Police (Scotland) Act, 1892, and any Acts amending the same shall be substituted for the Police Acts, 1839 to 1910.

(4) In the application of this Act to Ireland the Special Constables (Ireland) Act, 1832, shall be substituted for the Special Constables Act, 1831; section fourteen of the Dublin Justices Act, 1824, shall be substituted for section one hundred

and ninety-six of the Municipal Corporations Act, 1882 ; and the Acts relating to the Royal Irish Constabulary and Dublin Metropolitan Police, or either of those forces, shall be substituted for the Police Acts, 1839 to 1910.

2. This Act may be cited as the Special Constables Act, 1914.

IV

Unreasonable Withholding of Food Supplies Act, 1914.

4 & 5 Geo. V. c. 51.

[Royal Assent, 10th August 1914.]

Be it enacted by the King's most Excellent Majesty, by and with the advice and consent of the Lords Spiritual and Temporal, and Commons, in this present Parliament assembled, and by the authority of the same, as follows :—

1. If the Board of Trade are of opinion that any foodstuff is being unreasonably withheld from the market, they may, if so authorised by His Majesty's Proclamation (made generally or as respects any particular kind of foodstuff), and in manner provided by the Proclamation, take possession of any supplies of foodstuff to which the Proclamation relates, paying to the owners of the supplies such price as may in default of agreement be decided to be reasonable, having regard to all the circumstances of the case, by the arbitration of a judge of the High Court selected by the Lord Chief Justice of England.

2.—(1) This Act may be cited as the Unreasonable Withholding of Food Supplies Act, 1914.

(2) This Act shall have effect only while a state of war exists between His Majesty and any foreign power.

V

ARTICLES OF COMMERCE (RETURNS, &C.) ACT, 1914.

4 & 5 GEO. V. c. 5.

[*Royal Assent*, 28*th August* 1914.]

BE it enacted by the King's most Excellent Majesty, by and with the advice and consent of the Lords Spiritual and Temporal, and Commons, in this present Parliament assembled, and by the authority of the same, as follows :—

1.—(1) For the purpose of obtaining information as to the quantity in the United Kingdom or in transit to the United Kingdom of any article of commerce, the Board of Trade may, by notice served by registered post or otherwise on any person, require him to make a return to the Board, within such time as may be specified in the notice, giving such particulars of any article of commerce of which he is the owner as may be required by the notice.

(2) For the purpose of testing the accuracy of any return made to the Board under this section, or of obtaining information in case of a failure to make a return, any officer of the Board authorised in that behalf by the Board may enter any premises on which he has reason to believe that there are kept or stored any articles which have been or were required to be included in the return, and of which the person making or required to make the return is or was the owner, and may carry out such inspections of, and examinations on, the premises as the officer may consider necessary for testing the accuracy of the return or for obtaining such information.

(3) If any person—

(*a*) wilfully refuses or without lawful excuse neglects to make a return under this Act to the best of his knowledge and belief; or (*b*) wilfully makes or causes to be made any false return; or

(*c*) obstructs or impedes an officer of the Board in the exercise of any of his powers under this Act; or

(*d*) refuses to answer or wilfully gives a false answer to any question necessary for obtaining the information required to be furnished under this Act ;

he shall be liable on summary conviction to a fine not exceeding one hundred pounds, or, if the court is of opinion that the offence was committed wilfully, to imprisonment with or without hard labour for a period not exceeding three months.

(4) No individual return or part of a return made under this Act, and no information obtained under this Act, shall be published or disclosed except for the purposes of a prosecution under this Act.

2.—(1) If from any such return as aforesaid, or from any other source of information, the Board of Trade are of opinion that any article of commerce is being unreasonably withheld from the market, they may, if so authorised by His Majesty's proclamation (made generally or as respects any particular kind of article of commerce) and in manner provided by the proclamation, take possession of any supplies of the article, paying the owners of the supplies such price as may, in default of agreement, be decided to be reasonable, having regard to all the circumstances of the case, by the arbitration of a judge of the High Court selected by the Lord Chief Justice of England in England ; by a judge of the Court of Session selected by the Lord President of the Court of Session in Scotland ; and by a judge of the High Court of Ireland selected by the Lord Chief Justice of Ireland in Ireland.

(2) Nothing in this Act shall be construed as preventing the Board of Trade exercising their powers under this section without having first obtained, or endeavoured to obtain, returns under this Act.

3. The Board of Trade may make arrangements with any other Government Department for the exercise by that Department on behalf of the Board of Trade of the powers of the Board under this Act with respect to any particular article of commerce, and in such case the Department and the officers thereof shall, as respects such article, have and exercise the same powers as are by this Act conferred on the Board of Trade and the officers of that Board.

4.—(1) This Act may be cited as the Articles of Commerce (Returns, &c.) Act, 1914.

(2) For the purposes of this Act, " owner," in relation to any article of commerce, includes any person who, as factor or otherwise, has power to sell the article.

(3) The Unreasonable Withholding of Foodstuffs Act, 1914, is hereby repealed.

(4) This Act shall have effect only while a state of war exists between His Majesty and any foreign power, and for a period of six months thereafter.

VI

ARMY (SUPPLY OF FOOD, FORAGE, AND STORES) ACT, 1914.

4 & 5 GEO. V. c. 26.

[Royal Assent, 7th August 1914.]

BE it enacted by the King's most Excellent Majesty, by and with the advice and consent of the Lords Spiritual and Temporal, and Commons, in this present Parliament assembled, and by the authority of the same, as follows :—

1. The power of requisitioning carriages, horses, vessels, and aircraft in case of emergency conferred by the Army Act shall extend so as to include a power of requisitioning food, forage, and stores of all descriptions, and, accordingly, at the end of sub-section (2) of section one hundred and fifteen of the Army Act there shall be inserted the words "and also of food, forage, and stores of every description," and all the other provisions of that section and also the provisions of sections thirty-one, one hundred and sixteen, one hundred and seventeen, one hundred and nineteen, and one hundred and twenty-one of the Army Act shall, so far as applicable, apply in relation to food, forage, and stores as they apply in relation to vessels.

2. This Act may be cited as the Army (Supply of Food, Forage, and Stores) Act, 1914.

VII

ALIENS RESTRICTION ACT, 1914.

4 & 5 GEO. V. c. 12.

An Act to enable His Majesty in time of war or imminent national danger or great emergency by Order in Council to impose Restrictions on Aliens and make such provisions as appear necessary or expedient for carrying such restrictions into effect. [*Royal Assent, 5th August* 1914.]

BE it enacted by the King's most. Excellent Majesty, by and with the advice and consent of the Lords Spiritual and Temporal, and Commons, in this present Parliament assembled, and by the authority of the same, as follows :—

1. (1) His Majesty may at any time when a state of war exists between His Majesty and any foreign power, or when it appears that an occasion of imminent national danger or great emergency has arisen, by Order in Council impose restrictions on aliens, and provision may be made by the Order—

(*a*) for prohibiting aliens from landing in the United Kingdom, either generally or at certain places, and for imposing restrictions or conditions on aliens landing or arriving at any port in the United Kingdom ; and (*b*) for prohibiting aliens from embarking in the United Kingdom, either generally or at certain places, and for imposing restrictions and conditions on aliens embarking or about to embark in the United Kingdom ; and

(*c*) For the deportation of aliens from the United Kingdom ; and

(*d*) for requiring aliens to reside and remain within certain places or districts ; and

(*e*) for prohibiting aliens from residing or remaining in any areas specified in the Order ; and

(*f*) for requiring aliens residing in the United Kingdom to comply with such provisions as to registration, change of abode, travelling, or otherwise, as may be made by the Order ; and

(*g*) for the appointment of officers to carry the Order into effect, and for conferring on such officers and on the Secretary of State such powers as may be necessary or expedient for the purposes of the Order ; and

(*h*) for imposing penalties on persons who aid or abet any contravention of the Order, and for imposing such obligations and restrictions on masters of ships or any other persons specified in the Order as appear necessary or expedient for giving full effect to the Order ; and

(*i*) for conferring upon such persons as may be specified in the Order such powers with respect to arrest, detention, search of premises or persons, and otherwise, as may be specified in the Order, and for any other ancillary matters for which it appears expedient to provide with a view to giving full effect to the Order ; and

(*k*) For any other matters which appear necessary or expedient with a view to the safety of the realm.

(2) If any person acts in contravention of, or fails to comply with, any provisions of any such Order, he shall be liable on conviction under the Summary Jurisdiction Acts to a fine not exceeding one hundred pounds or to imprisonment with or

without hard labour for a term not exceeding six months, and the court before which he is convicted may, either in addition to, or in lieu of, any such punishment, require that person to enter into recognisances with or without sureties to comply with the provisions of the Order in Council or such provisions thereof as the court may direct.

If any person fails to comply with an order of the court requiring him to enter into recognisances, the court, or any court of summary jurisdiction sitting for the same place, may order him to be imprisoned with or without hard labour for any term not exceeding six months.

(3) Any provision of any Order in Council made under this section with respect to aliens may relate either to aliens in general or to any class or description of aliens.

(4) If any question arises on any proceedings under any such Order, or with reference to anything done or proposed to be done under any such Order, whether any person is an alien or not, or is an alien of a particular class or not, the onus of proving that that person is not an alien, or, as the case may be, is not an alien of that class, shall lie upon that person.

(5) His Majesty may by Order in Council revoke, alter, or add to any order in Council made under this section as occasion requires.

(6) Any powers given under this section, or under any Order in Council made under this section, shall be in addition to, and not in derogation of, any other powers with respect to the expulsion of aliens, or the prohibition of aliens from entering the United Kingdom, or any other powers of His Majesty.

2.—(1) This Act may be cited as the Aliens Restriction Act, 1914.

(2) In the application of this Act to Scotland the expressions "the court" and "any court of summary jurisdiction" mean the sheriff; and the expressions "enter into recognisances with or without sureties" and "enter into recognisances" mean "find caution."

VIII

ALIENS.

The Aliens Restriction (Consolidation) Order, 1914.

At the Court at Buckingham Palace, the 9th day of September 1914.

PRESENT,

The King's Most Excellent Majesty in Council.

WHEREAS by the Aliens Restriction Act, 1914, power is conferred upon His Majesty in time of war or imminent national danger or great emergency by Order in Council to impose restrictions on aliens, and to make such provisions as may be necessary or expedient for carrying such restrictions into effect;

And whereas a state of war at present exists between Great Britain and Germany and also between Great Britain and Austria-Hungary:

And whereas by Orders in Council dated respectively the fifth, tenth, twelfth, and twentieth of August in the present year, His Majesty was pleased to make various provisions under the said Act, and it is desirable to consolidate the said Orders in Council, with amendments:

Now, therefore, His Majesty is pleased, by and with the advice of His Privy Council, to order, and it is hereby ordered, as follows :—

PART I.

RESTRICTIONS ON ALIENS ENTERING AND LEAVING THE UNITED KINGDOM.

Approved Ports and Prohibited Ports.

1.—(1) For the purposes of this Order, the following ports are approved ports, that is to say :— *Definition of approved ports and prohibited ports.*

Aberdeen,
Dundee,
Newcastle-upon-Tyne,
West Hartlepool,
Hull,
London,
Folkestone,
Falmouth,
Bristol,
Holyhead,
Liverpool,
Glasgow,
Dublin;

and any other port or place in the United Kingdom is, for the purposes of this Order, a prohibited port.

(2) For the purposes of this Order the limits of the approved ports shall be those specified in the First Schedule to this Order, and any part of an approved port outside those limits shall be treated as though it were part of a prohibited port.

(3) A Secretary of State may by order, after consulting the Admiralty and the Army Council, add any port to the list of approved ports, or remove any port from that list, and prescribe or alter the limits of any approved port; and this Order shall thereupon have effect accordingly.

Aliens entering the United Kingdom.

Aliens not to land at prohibited ports.

2.—(1) An alien shall not land in the United Kingdom at a prohibited port:
Provided that—

(a) where a Secretary of State is satisfied that an alien friend has arrived at a prohibited port in ignorance of the provisions of this Order, or in any other circumstances entitling him to special consideration, and may safely be permitted to land, he may grant him permission accordingly; and

(b) subject to the provisions of this Order the foregoing prohibition shall not, unless in any particular case an aliens officer so directs, apply to an alien friend who is the master or a member of the crew of a vessel arriving at a prohibited port, if whilst he is on shore he complies with such requirements (if any) as may be imposed upon him or upon masters and seamen generally by an aliens officer at the port;

and any alien friend who lands in accordance with this proviso, and, if conditionally disembarked, who complies with the conditions, shall not be liable to any penalty for landing at the port in question.

Alien enemies not to land without permits.

3. An alien enemy shall not land in the United Kingdom at an approved port without the permission of a Secretary of State.

4. An alien arriving at an approved port may, if a Secretary of State so directs, or if an aliens officer at the port is satisfied that he cannot safely be permitted to land in the United Kingdom, be treated as though the port were a prohibited port. *Powers with respect to aliens landing at approved port.*

5. An alien landing in contravention of this Order, and an alien arriving at any port in circumstances in which he is prohibited from landing, may, until dealt with under this Order, be detained in such manner as a Secretary of State may direct, and whilst so detained shall be deemed to be in legal custody. *Detention of aliens arriving in United Kingdom.*

6. An alien shall not land at any port in the United Kingdom having in his possession— *Aliens not to enter United Kingdom with firearms, &c.*

(*a*) any firearms or other weapons, ammunition, or explosives;

(*b*) any petroleum spirit, naphtha, benzol, petroleum, or other inflammable liquid in quantities exceeding three gallons;

(*c*) any apparatus or contrivance intended for or capable of being used for signalling apparatus, either visual or otherwise;

(*d*) any carrier or homing pigeons;

(*e*) any motor car, motor cycle, or aircraft; or

(*f*) any cipher code or other means of conducting secret correspondence;

and where an alien lands with any such articles in his possession he shall forfeit the articles and shall be deemed to have imported them in contravention of the provisions of the Customs Consolidation Act, 1876, as though the articles in question were contained in the table of prohibitions and restrictions set out in section forty-two of that Act:

Provided that where an aliens officer considers that an alien friend arriving at any port may safely be permitted to land with any such articles as aforesaid in his possession, he may permit him to land accordingly, and the foregoing provisions of this article shall not apply.

7. An alien conditionally disembarked under the directions of an aliens officer for the purpose of inquiry or examination shall not for the purposes of this Order be deemed to have landed so long as the conditions are complied with. *Conditional landing.*

Aliens leaving the United Kingdom.

Aliens not to embark at prohibited ports.

8. An alien shall not, except in pursuance of an order of deportation under this Order, embark in the United Kingdom at a prohibited port:

Provided that—

(*a*) where a Secretary of State is satisfied that any alien friend who desires to embark at a prohibited port may safely be permitted to do so, he may grant him permission accordingly; and

(*b*) subject to the provisions of this Order the foregoing prohibition shall not, unless in any particular case an aliens officer so directs, apply to an alien friend who is the master or the member of the crew of a vessel leaving a prohibited port;

and any alien friend who embarks in accordance with this proviso shall not be liable to any penalty for embarking in the United Kingdom at the port in question.

Provision as to alien enemies leaving a port without having landed.

9. Where an alien enemy is about to leave any port on board a vessel on which he has arrived at the port, he may for the purposes of this Order, if a Secretary of State so directs, or if it appears necessary to an aliens officer in the interests of public safety, be treated as though he had embarked at that port in contravention of this Order, but shall not be subject to any fine or imprisonment for so embarking.

Alien enemies not to embark without permit.

10. An alien enemy shall not, except in pursuance of an order of deportation under this Order, embark in the United Kingdom at an approved port, unless provided with a permit issued by a Secretary of State:

Provided that an alien enemy about to embark in the United Kingdom at an approved port, even when provided with such permit as aforesaid, may, if a Secretary of State so directs, or if in the opinion of an aliens officer he cannot safely be permitted to embark, be treated as though the port were a prohibited port.

Detention of aliens embarking.

11. An alien embarking or about to embark in the United Kingdom in contravention of this Order may, until dealt with under this Order, be detained in such manner as a Secretary of State may direct, and whilst so detained shall be deemed to be in legal custody.

ALIENS

12.—(1) A Secretary of State may order the deportation of any alien, and any alien with respect to whom such an order is made shall forthwith leave and thereafter remain out of the United Kingdom. *Deportation of aliens.*

(2) Where an alien is ordered to be deported under this Order, he may, until he can, in the opinion of the Secretary of State, be conveniently conveyed to and placed on board a ship about to leave the United Kingdom, and whilst being conveyed to the ship, and whilst on board the ship until the ship finally leaves the United Kingdom, be detained in such manner as the Secretary of State directs, and, whilst so detained, shall be deemed to be in legal custody.

Obligations on Masters of Vessels.

13.—(1) The master of every vessel, whether British or foreign, arriving at or leaving a port in the United Kingdom shall, immediately on the arrival of the vessel at that port, or, as the case may be, not more than twenty-four hours before leaving that port, furnish to an aliens officer at that port, with respect to all persons on board the vessel, or intending to embark on the vessel, such particulars in such manner as the Secretary of State may direct, and shall otherwise take all reasonable steps in his power for securing the enforcement of this Order. *Obligations on masters of vessels.*

(2) The master of a vessel arriving at or leaving any port shall not permit any persons to land or to embark without the sanction of an aliens officer at the port.

(3) Where a person lands or embarks at any port in contravention of this Order, the master of the vessel from which he lands or on which he embarks shall, unless he proves the contrary, be deemed to have aided and abetted the offence.

14. The master of a ship about to call at any port shall, if so required by a Secretary of State or an aliens officer, receive an alien and his dependants, if any, on board his ship and afford him or them a passage to that port, and proper accommodation and maintenance during the passage, and, if the ship is the same or belongs to the same owners as the ship in which the alien arrived in the United Kingdom, shall, if so required as *Obligation to afford passage to aliens.*

aforesaid, afford such passage, accommodation, and maintenance free of charge.

Aliens Officers.

Aliens officers.

15.—(1) The following persons, that is to say—

(*a*) any immigration officers appointed under the Aliens Act, 1905 ; and
(*b*) any persons appointed for the purpose by a Secretary of State ;

shall be aliens officers for the purposes of this Order at the various ports in the United Kingdom, and shall in the exercise of their powers act under general or special instructions from the Secretary of State, and, subject to such instructions, shall have power to enter on board any vessel, and to detain and examine all persons arriving at or leaving any port in the United Kingdom, and to require the production of any documents by such persons, and generally to take such steps as are sanctioned by this Order or as may be necessary for giving effect to this Order.

Exceptions.

Part I. not to apply in certain cases.

16. This Part of the Order shall not apply—

(*a*) to prisoners of war ; or
(*b*) to children appearing to an aliens officer to be under the age of fourteen.

PART II.

RESTRICTIONS ON ALIENS RESIDING IN THE UNITED KINGDOM.

Residence and Registration of Aliens.

Power to order aliens to reside in certain areas.

17. A Secretary of State may by order require any alien enemy to reside or continue to reside in any place or district specified in the order, and the alien shall comply with the order.

Prohibition on alien enemies residing in prohibited areas.

18.—(1) An alien enemy shall not enter, or reside, or continue to reside either temporarily or permanently in any of the areas specified in the Second Schedule to this Order (in this Order referred to as prohibited areas) unless provided with a permit issued by the registration officer of the district, subject to the general or special instructions of a Secretary of State.

(2) A Secretary of State may by order, after consulting the Admiralty and the Army Council, add any area to the list of prohibited areas in the said Schedule, or remove any area or part of an area from that list; and this order shall thereupon have effect accordingly.

19.—(1) An alien residing in a prohibited area, and an alien enemy wherever resident, shall comply with the following requirements as to registration :— *Registration of aliens.*

   (a) he shall as soon as may be furnish to the registration officer of the registration district in which he is resident particulars as to the matters set out in the Third Schedule to this Order :
   (b) he shall, if he is about to change his residence, furnish to the registration officer of the registration district in which he is then resident particulars as to the date on which his residence is to be so changed, and as to his intended place of residence, and on effecting any such change of residence he shall forthwith report himself to the registration officer of the registration district into which he moves :
   (c) he shall furnish to the registration officer of the registration district in which he is resident particulars of any circumstance affecting in any manner the accuracy of the particulars previously furnished by him for the purpose of registration within forty-eight hours after the circumstance has occurred.

(2) Where an alien is lodging with or living as a member of the household of any other person, it shall be the duty of that person either himself to furnish with respect to the alien the particulars aforesaid, or to give notice of the presence of the alien in his household to the registration officer.

(3) Where an alien has a household he shall furnish the particulars as aforesaid, not only as respects himself but as respects every alien who is living as a member of his household.

20.—(1) For the purposes of this Order, the chief officer of police of the police district shall be the registration officer, and the police district shall be the registration district : *Register of aliens.*

Provided that where a prohibited area includes the whole or part of more than one police district, arrangements may be made by a Secretary of State for constituting that prohibited area a single registration district, and for the appointment of a registration officer for that district.

(2) A registration officer shall—
- (*a*) keep for his registration district a register for the purposes of this Act ;
- (*b*) register therein all aliens resident in his district who furnish particulars for the purpose, by entering these particulars on the register ;
- (*c*) enter on the register all other particulars furnished in accordance with this Order with respect to any alien so registered ; and
- (*d*) if a registered alien ceases to be resident in his district, record the fact in the register.

(3) The obligation of a registration officer to enter particulars upon the register shall not be affected by the fact that the particulars may not have been furnished within the time required by this Order, without prejudice, however, to the liability of an alien to a penalty for not furnishing the particulars within the required time.

(4) Every alien shall furnish to the registration officer, in addition to any such particulars as aforesaid, any information which may reasonably be required for the purpose of registering the alien, or maintaining the correctness of the particulars entered on the register.

<small>Prohibition on alien enemies travelling more than five miles from registered address.</small>

21. An alien enemy shall not travel more than five miles from his registered place of residence unless furnished with a permit from the registration officer of the registration district in which that place of residence is situate, which permit shall not cover a period exceeding twenty-four hours from the date of its issue, and shall be returned to the registration officer at the end of the period for which it was issued :

Provided that—
- (*a*) any such permit may, if the registration officer in view of any special circumstances so decides, cover a period exceeding twenty-four hours, but not exceeding four

days, from the date of its issue, subject, however, to the condition that the holder thereof shall on each day during the currency of the permit report himself to the registration officer of the district in which he then is, and subject also to any other conditions which may be prescribed by the registration officer granting the permit; and

(*b*) where any such permit is granted to any person with a view to his leaving one registration district and going to reside in another, the permit may, at the end of the period for which it was issued, be delivered to the registration officer of the new district instead of being returned to the registration officer by whom it was granted; and

(*c*) in the case of an alien enemy having a *bonâ fide* place of business more than five miles from his registered place of residence, the registration officer may, if he thinks fit, grant a permit enabling him to travel to or from his place of business, which shall be renewable from time to time as and when the registration officer so directs.

Possession of Firearms, etc., by Alien Enemies.

22.—(1) An alien enemy shall not, except with the written permission of the registration officer of the district in which he resides, be in possession of— <small>Prohibition on alien enemies having firearms, etc., in their possession.</small>

(*a*) any firearms or other weapons, ammunition or explosives, or material intended to be used for the manufacture of explosives;

(*b*) any petroleum spirit, naphtha, benzol, petroleum, or other inflammable liquid in quantities exceeding three gallons;

(*c*) any apparatus or contrivance intended for, or capable of being used for, a signalling apparatus, either visual or otherwise;

(*d*) any carrier or homing pigeons;

(*e*) any motor car, motor cycle, motor boat, yacht, or aircraft; or

(*f*) any cipher code or other means of conducting secret correspondence ;
(*g*) any telephone installation ;
(*h*) any camera or other photographic apparatus ;
(*i*) any military or naval map, chart, or handbook.

(2) If a justice of the peace is satisfied by information on oath that there is reasonable ground for suspecting any contravention of the foregoing provision, he may grant a search warrant authorising any constable named therein to enter at any time any premises or place named in the warrant, if necessary by force, and to search the premises or place and every person found therein, and to seize any article which is being kept in the premises or place in contravention of this Article.

Where it appears to a superintendent or inspector of police, or any police officer of higher rank, that the case is one of great emergency, and that in the interests of the State immediate action is necessary, he may by a written order under his hand give to any constable the like authority as may be given by the warrant of a justice under this Article.

Restriction on Circulation of Newspapers.

Restriction on circulation of newspapers amongst alien enemies.

23.—(1) The circulation among alien enemies of any newspaper wholly or mainly in the language of a State, or any part of a State, at war with His Majesty, is prohibited, unless the permission in writing of a Secretary of State has been first obtained, and such conditions as may be prescribed by the Secretary of State are complied with.

(2) Any person publishing any newspaper for circulation in contravention of this Order shall be deemed to have acted in contravention of this Order, and where a Secretary of State is satisfied that any newspaper has been, or is about to be, published for circulation in contravention of this Order, he may authorise such persons as he thinks fit to enter, if needs be by force, any premises, and to seize any copies of the newspaper found thereon, and also any type or other plant used or capable of being used for printing or production of the newspaper, and to deal with any articles so seized in such manner as the Secretary of State may direct.

(3) In this article, the expression "newspaper" includes periodical.

Carrying on of Banking Business.

24.—(1) An alien enemy shall not carry on or engage in any banking business except with the permission in writing of the Secretary of State, and to such extent and subject to such conditions and supervision as the Secretary of State may direct, and an alien enemy who is or has been carrying on or engaged in banking business shall not, except with the like permission, part with any money or securities in the bank where he is or has been carrying on or engaged in business, and shall, if so required, deposit any such money or securities in such custody as the Secretary of State may direct. *Restrictions with respect to banking.*

(2) Any constable, if authorised by a superintendent of police, or officer of higher rank, may, for the purpose of enforcing the provisions of this Article, enter, if necessary by force, and search or occupy any premises in which the business of banking is or has been carried on by an alien enemy.

(3) For the purposes of this Article, any person who is a member of a firm or a director of a company carrying on banking business in the United Kingdom shall be deemed to be carrying on banking business.

Provisions as to Clubs frequented by Alien Enemies.

25.—(1) A chief officer of police, if so authorised by general or special order of the Secretary of State, may direct that any premises within his jurisdiction which, in his opinion, are used for the purposes of a club which is habitually frequented by alien enemies, shall be kept closed, either altogether or during such hours as may be required by him; and where any such direction is given in respect of any premises, no alien enemy shall enter or be on the premises at any time when the premises are directed to be closed. *Power to close clubs.*

(2) Any constable, if authorised by the chief officer of police, may, for the purpose of enforcing the provisions of this Article, enter, if necessary by force, and search or occupy any premises to which an order under this Article relates.

PART III.

GENERAL.

Penalty.

26. If any person acts in contravention of or fails to comply with any provisions of this Order, he is liable on summary conviction to a fine not exceeding one hundred pounds or to imprisonment with or without hard labour for a term not exceeding six months, and the court before which he is convicted may, either in addition to or in lieu of any such punishment, require that person to enter into recognisances with or without sureties to comply with the provisions of this Order or such provisions thereof as the court may direct.

If any person fails to comply with an order of the court requiring him to enter into recognisances the court, or any court of summary jurisdiction sitting for the same place may order him to be imprisoned with or without hard labour for any term not exceeding six months.

Disobedience to aliens officers and other offences.

27.—(1) If any alien, master of a ship, or other person arriving at or leaving any port lands or embarks without the permission of an aliens officer, or refuses to answer any question reasonably put to him by an aliens officer, or makes or causes to be made any false return, false statement, or false representation to an aliens officer, or refuses to produce any document in his possession which he is required by an aliens officer to produce, or obstructs or impedes an aliens officer in the exercise of his powers or duties under the Order, he shall be deemed to have acted in contravention of this Order.

(2) If any person furnishes or causes to be furnished to a registration officer any false particulars, or, with a view to obtaining any permit or permission under this Order, makes or causes to be made any false statement or false representation, he shall be deemed to have acted in contravention of this Order.

Persons aiding and abetting.

28. If any person aids or abets any person in any contravention of this Order, or knowingly harbours any person whom he knows or has reasonable ground for supposing to have acted in contravention of this Order, he shall be deemed himself to have acted in contravention of this Order.

ALIENS

29. Any person who acts in contravention of this Order, or is reasonably suspected of having so acted, or being about so to act, may be taken into custody without warrant by an aliens officer or by any constable. Arrest.

30.—(1) A Secretary of State may, if he thinks it necessary in the interests of public safety, direct that any of the provisions of this Order as to alien enemies shall in particular cases be applicable to other aliens, and thereupon such provisions shall apply accordingly. Additional powers of Secretary of State.

(2) A Secretary of State may, if he thinks fit, direct that any powers or duties assigned under this Order to aliens officers or to registration officers shall be discharged by other persons deputed by the Secretary of State for the purpose.

(3) The Secretary of State, with a view to giving full effect to this Order, may direct that passengers on ships entering or leaving any port in the United Kingdom shall be subject to such restrictions, control, and supervision as may appear necessary or expedient, and may impose general conditions as respects ships entering or leaving any such port, and it shall be the duty of all persons to comply with any such direction.

31. For the purposes of this Order— Interpretation.

    The expression "police district" means any district for which there is a separate police force; and the expression "chief officer of police" means the chief constable, or head constable, or other officer, by whatever name called, having the chief command of the police force of the district;

    The expression "alien friend" means an alien whose sovereign or state is at peace with His Majesty, and the expression "alien enemy" means an alien whose sovereign or state is at war with His Majesty; and

    References to landing or embarking shall, unless the context otherwise implies, be deemed to include references to attempting to land or attempting to embark respectively.

32.—(1) In the application of this Order to Scotland— Application to Scotland and Ireland.

    The expressions "the court" and "any court of summary jurisdiction" mean the sheriff;

The expressions "enter into recognisances with or without sureties" and "enter into recognisances" mean "find caution."

(2) In the application of this Order to Ireland—

The expression "police district" means the police district of Dublin metropolis, and any county or other area for which a county inspector of the Royal Irish Constabulary or officer having the rank of such county inspector is appointed; and the expression "chief officer of police" means, as respects the police district of Dublin metropolis, the Chief Commissioner of the Dublin Metropolitan Police; and as respects any other police district, the county inspector of the Royal Irish Constabulary, or officer having the rank of such county inspector as the case may be.

The expression "superintendent of police" includes in the case of the Royal Irish Constabulary a sergeant and any officer of higher rank.

<small>Order not to apply to ambassadors, etc.</small>

33. Nothing in this Order shall be construed as imposing any restriction or disability on any foreign ambassador or other public minister duly authorised, or any servants in actual attendance upon any such ambassador or public minister.

<small>Short title, construction, and revocation.</small>

34.—(1) This Order may be cited as the Aliens Restriction (Consolidation) Order, 1914.

(2) The Interpretation Act, 1889, shall apply for the purpose of the interpretation of this Order in like manner as it applies for the purpose of the interpretation of an Act of Parliament.

(3) The said Orders in Council of the fifth, tenth, twelfth, and twentieth of August, imposing restrictions on aliens, are hereby revoked:

Provided that the revocation of any such Order shall not—

(a) affect the previous operation of any Order so revoked, or anything duly done or suffered under any Order so revoked; or

(b) affect any right, privilege, obligation, or liability acquired, accrued, or incurred under any Order so revoked; or

(c) affect any penalty, forfeiture, or punishment incurred in respect of any offence committed against any Order so revoked ; or

(d) affect any proceedings or remedy in respect of any such right, privilege, obligation, liability, penalty, forfeiture, or punishment as aforesaid,

and any permission or direction given, or order or requirement made, or other action taken under any Order so revoked shall be deemed to have been given, made, or taken under the corresponding provision of this Order.

Almeric FitzRoy.

IX

ALIENS.

The Aliens Restriction (Change of Name) Order, 1914.

At the Court at Buckingham Palace, the 8th day of October 1914.

PRESENT,

The King's Most Excellent Majesty in Council.

WHEREAS by the Aliens Restriction (Consolidation) Order, 1914 (hereinafter referred to as the Principal Order), His Majesty has been pleased to impose restrictions on aliens and to make various provisions for carrying those restrictions into effect:

And whereas it is desirable to extend and amend the said Order in manner hereinafter provided :

Now, therefore, His Majesty is pleased, by and with the advice of His Privy Council, to order, and it is hereby ordered, as follows :—

1. The following Article shall be inserted after Article 25 of the Principal Order :— *Change of name by alien enemies.*

"25A. An alien enemy shall not, after the twelfth day of October nineteen hundred and fourteen, for any purpose assume or use, or purport to assume or use, or continue the assumption or use of any name other than that by which he was ordinarily known at the date of the commencement of the war.

"Where an alien enemy carries on or purports or continues to carry on, or is a member of a partnership or firm which carries on or purports or continues to carry on any trade or business under any name other than that under which the trade or business was carried on at the date of the commencement of the war, he shall, for the purposes of this Order, be deemed to be using or purporting or continuing to use a name other than that by which he was ordinarily known at the date of the commencement of the war.

" Nothing in this Article shall affect the right of a woman who after the commencement of the war marries an alien enemy to use the name which she acquires on her marriage.

"A Secretary of State may, if it appears desirable in any particular case, grant an exemption from the provisions of this Article.

Correction of clerical error in Article 20 of the Principal Order.
2. In Article 20 of the Principal Order, the word "Order" shall be substituted for the word "Act."

Short title.
3. This Order may be cited as the Aliens Restriction (Change of Name) Order, 1914.

Almeric FitzRoy.

C.—*Illustrating Part III.*

I

DESPATCH OF SIR E. GREY AS TO PROPOSED VIOLATION OF BELGIAN NEUTRALITY.

Sir Edward Grey to Sir E. Goschen, British Ambassador at Berlin.

(Telegraphic) *Foreign Office, 4th August* 1914.

THE King of the Belgians has made an appeal to His

BELGIUM

Majesty the King for diplomatic intervention on behalf of Belgium in the following terms :—

"Remembering the numerous proofs of your Majesty's friendship and that of your predecessor, and the friendly attitude of England in 1870 and the proof of friendship you have just given us again, I make a supreme appeal to the diplomatic intervention of your Majesty's Government to safeguard the integrity of Belgium."

His Majesty's Government are also informed that the German Government have delivered to the Belgian Government a note proposing friendly neutrality, entailing free passage through Belgian territory, and promising to maintain the independence and integrity of the kingdom and its possessions at the conclusion of peace, threatening in case of refusal to treat Belgium as an enemy. An answer was requested within twelve hours.

We also understand that Belgium has categorically refused this as a flagrant violation of the law of nations.

His Majesty's Government are bound to protest against this violation of a treaty to which Germany is a party in common with themselves, and must request an assurance that the demand made upon Belgium will not be proceeded with, and that her neutrality will be respected by Germany. You should ask for an immediate reply.

II

Despatch of Sir E. Grey (Ultimatum to Germany).

Sir Edward Grey to Sir E. Goschen, British Ambassador at Berlin.

(Telegraphic) *Foreign Office,* 4*th August* 1914.

We hear that Germany has addressed note to Belgian Minister for Foreign Affairs stating that German Government will be compelled to carry out, if necessary, by force of arms, the measures considered indispensable.

We are also informed that Belgian territory has been violated at Gemmenich.

In these circumstances, and in view of the fact that Germany declined to give the same assurance respecting Belgium as France gave last week in reply to our request made simultaneously at Berlin and Paris, we must repeat that request, and ask that a satisfactory reply to it and to my telegram of this morning be received here by 12 o'clock to-night. If not, you are instructed to ask for your passports, and to say that His Majesty's Government feel bound to take all steps in their power to uphold the neutrality of Belgium, and the observance of a treaty to which Germany is as much a party as ourselves.

III

Belgian Neutrality—Foreign Office Memorandum (7th December 1914).

With reference to statements implying that Great Britain ever contemplated a violation of Belgian neutrality, the Foreign Office issues for publication the following record of a conversation with the Belgian Minister on 7th April 1913. It was sent to the British Minister in Brussels, and a record was communicated by him to the Belgian Minister for Foreign Affairs at the time:—

Sir,

In speaking to the Belgian Minister to-day I said, speaking unofficially, that it had been brought to my knowledge that there was apprehension in Belgium lest we should be the first to violate Belgian neutrality. I did not think that this apprehension could have come from a British source.

The Belgian Minister informed me that there had been talk, in a British source which he could not name, of the landing of troops in Belgium by Great Britain, in order to anticipate a possible despatch of German troops through Belgium to France.

I said that I was sure that this Government would not be the first to violate the neutrality of Belgium, and I did not believe that any British Government would be the first to do so, nor would public opinion here ever approve of it. What we had to consider, and it was a somewhat embarrassing question, was what it would be desirable and necessary for us, as one of the guarantors of Belgian neutrality, to do if Belgian neutrality was violated by any Power. For us to be the first to violate it and to send troops into Belgium would be to give Germany, for instance, justification for sending troops into Belgium also. What we desired in the case of Belgium, as in that of other neutral countries, was that their neutrality should be respected, and as long as it was not violated by any other Power we should certainly not send troops ourselves into their territory.

I am, etc.,

E. GREY.

7th December 1914.

D.—*Illustrating Part IV., Chapter I.*

I

EXTRACT FROM DECLARATION OF WAR (7TH MAY 1689) BY WILLIAM III.[1] AGAINST LEWIS XIV. OF FRANCE.

[2 *Rapin*, 90: *said to be the composition of "the masterly pen of Mr Sommers, afterwards Lord Chancellor."*]

"Being therefore thus necessitated to take up arms, and relying on the help of Almighty God in our just undertaking, we . . . do hereby declare war against the French King . . . hereby willing and requiring all our subjects to take notice of the same; whom we henceforth strictly forbid to hold any

[1] Queen Mary's name is not prefixed to it.

correspondence or communication with the said French King and his subjects. And because there are remaining in our kingdoms many of the subjects of the French King, we do declare and give our royal word, that all such of the French nation as shall demean themselves dutifully towards us, and not correspond with our enemies, shall be safe in their persons and estates, and free from all molestation and trouble of any kind."[1]

"Given at our Court at Hampton Court, the 7th day of May 1869, in the first year of our reign."

II

Extract from The Naturalisation Act (33 Vict. c. 14), 1870, sec. 7, para. 3.

"An alien to whom a certificate of naturalisation is granted . . . shall not, when within the limits of the foreign State of which he was a subject previously to obtaining his certificate of naturalisation, be deemed to be a British subject unless he has ceased to be a subject of that State in pursuance of the laws thereof, or in pursuance of a treaty to that effect. . . ."

E.—*Illustrating Parts IV., V., and VI.*

I

Trading with the Enemy.

4 & 5 Geo. V. c. 87.

[*Royal Assent,* 18*th September* 1914.]

1.—(1) Any person who during the present war trades or

---

[1] Has his present Majesty in any respect so formally "given his royal word"?

has, since the fourth day of August nineteen hundred and fourteen, traded with the enemy within the meaning of this Act shall be guilty of a misdemeanor, and shall—

(*a*) on conviction under the Summary Jurisdiction Acts, be liable to imprisonment with or without hard labour for a term not exceeding twelve months, or to a fine not exceeding five hundred pounds, or to both such imprisonment and fine ; or

(*b*) on conviction on indictment, be liable to penal servitude for a term not exceeding seven or less than three years, or to imprisonment with or without hard labour for a term not exceeding two years, or to a fine, or to both such penal servitude or imprisonment and fine ;

and the court may in any case order that any goods or money, in respect of which the offence has been committed, be forfeited.

(2) For the purposes of this Act a person shall be deemed to have traded with the enemy if he has entered into any transaction or done any act which was, at the time of such transaction or act, prohibited by or under any proclamation issued by His Majesty dealing with trading with the enemy for the time being in force, or which at common law or by statute constitutes an offence of trading with the enemy:

Provided that any transaction or act permitted by or under any such proclamation shall not be deemed to be trading with the enemy.

(3) Where a company has entered into a transaction or has done any act which is an offence under this section, every director, manager, secretary, or other officer of the company who is knowingly a party to the transaction or act shall also be deemed guilty of the offence.

(4) A prosecution for an offence under this section shall not be instituted except by or with the consent of the Attorney-General :

Provided that the person charged with such an offence may be arrested and a warrant for his arrest may be issued and executed, and such person may be remanded in custody or on bail notwithstanding that the consent of the Attorney-General to the institution of the prosecution for the offence has not been obtained, but no further or other proceedings shall be taken until that consent has been obtained.

(5) Where an act constitutes an offence both under this Act and under any other Act, or both under this Act and at common law, the offender shall be liable to be prosecuted and punished under either this Act or such other Act, or under this Act or at common law, but shall not be liable to be punished twice for the same offence.

2.—(1) If a justice of the peace is satisfied, on information on oath laid on behalf of a Secretary of State or the Board of Trade, that there is reasonable ground for suspecting that an offence under this Act has been or is about to be committed by any person, firm, or company, he may issue a warrant authorising any person appointed by a Secretary of State or the Board of Trade and named in the warrant to inspect all books or documents belonging to or under the control of that person, firm, or company, and to require any person able to give any information with respect to the business or trade of that person, firm, or company to give that information, and if accompanied by a constable to enter and search any premises used in connection with the business or trade, and to seize any such books or documents as aforesaid:

Provided that when it appears to a Secretary of State or the Board of Trade that the case is one of great emergency and that in the interests of the State immediate action is necessary, a Secretary of State or the Board of Trade may, by written order, give to a person appointed by him or them the like authority as may be given by a warrant of a justice under this subsection.

(2) Where it appears to the Board of Trade—

(*a*) in the case of a firm, that one of the partners in the firm was immediately before or at any time since the commencement of the present war a subject of, or resident or carrying on business in, a State for the time being at war with His Majesty; or

(*b*) in the case of a company, that one-third or more of the issued share capital or of the directorate of the company immediately before or at any time since the commencement of the present war was held by or on behalf of or consisted of persons who were subjects of or resident or carrying on business in, a State for the time being at war with His Majesty; or

(c) in the case of a person, firm or company, that the person was or is, or the firm or company were or are, acting as agent for any person, firm, or company trading or carrying on business in a State for the time being at war with His Majesty;

the Board of Trade may, if they think it expedient for the purpose of satisfying themselves that the person, firm, or company are not trading with the enemy, by written order, give to a person appointed by them, without any warrant from a justice, authority to inspect all books and documents belonging to or under the control of the person, firm or company, and to require any person able to give information with respect to the business or trade of that person, firm or company, to give that information.

For the purposes of this subsection, any person authorised in that behalf by the Board of Trade may inspect the register of members of a company at any time, and any shares in a company for which share warrants to bearer have been issued shall not be reckoned as part of the issued share capital of the company.

(3) If any person having the custody of any book or document which a person is authorised to inspect under this section refuses or wilfully neglects to produce it for inspection, or if any person who is able to give any information which may be required to be given under this section refuses or wilfully neglects when required to give that information, that person shall on conviction under the Summary Jurisdiction Acts be liable to imprisonment with or without hard labour for a term not exceeding six months, or to a fine not exceeding fifty pounds, or to both such imprisonment and fine.

3. Where it appears to the Board of Trade in reference to any firm or company—

(a) that an offence under this Act has been or is likely to be committed in connexion with the trade or business thereof; or

(b) that the control or management thereof has been or is

likely to be so affected by the state of war as to prejudice the effective continuance of its trade or business, and that it is in the public interest that the trade or business should continue to be carried on ;

the Board of Trade may apply to the High Court for the appointment of a controller of the firm or company, and the High Court shall have power to appoint such a controller, for such time and subject to such conditions and with such powers as the court thinks fit, and the powers so conferred shall be either those of a receiver and manager or those powers subject to such modifications, restrictions or extensions as the court thinks fit (including, if the court considers it necessary or expedient for enabling the controller to borrow money, power, after a special application to the court for that purpose, to create charges on the property of the firm or company in priority to existing charges).

The court shall have power to direct how and by whom the costs of any proceedings under this section, and the remuneration, charges, and expenses of the controller, shall be borne, and shall have power, if it thinks fit, to charge such costs, charges, and expenses on the property of the firm or company in such order of priority, in relation to any existing charges thereon, as it thinks fit.

4.—(1) This Act may be cited as the Trading with the Enemy Act, 1914.

(2) In this Act the expression "Attorney-General" means the Attorney or Solicitor General for England, and as respects Scotland means the Lord Advocate, and as respects Ireland means the Attorney or Solicitor General for Ireland.

(3) In the application of this Act to Scotland the Secretary for Scotland shall be substituted for a Secretary of State, and the Court of Session shall be substituted for the High Court; the court exercising summary jurisdiction shall be the sheriff court; references to a justice of the peace shall include references to the sheriff and to a burgh magistrate; and references to a receiver and manager shall be construed as references to a judicial factor.

(4) In the application of this Act to Ireland, the Lord Lieutenant shall be substituted for a Secretary of State.

(5) Anything authorised under this Act to be done by the Board of Trade may be done by the President or a Secretary or Assistant Secretary of the Board, or any person authorised in that behalf by the President of the Board.

II

Trading with the Enemy.

On this subject the following Proclamation was issued under date of 5th August:—

WHEREAS a state of war exists between Us and the German Emperor:

And whereas it is contrary to law for any person resident, carrying on business, or being in Our Dominions, to trade or have any commercial intercourse with any person resident, carrying on business, or being in the German Empire without Our permission:

And whereas it is therefore expedient and necessary to warn all persons resident, carrying on business, or being in Our Dominions, of their duties and obligations towards Us, Our Crown, and Government:

Now, therefore, We have thought fit, by and with the advice of Our Privy Council, to issue this Our Royal Proclamation, and We do hereby warn all persons resident, carrying on business, or being in Our Dominions:

Not to supply to or obtain from the said Empire any goods, wares, or merchandise, or to supply to or obtain the same from any person resident, carrying on business, or being therein, nor to supply to or obtain from any person any goods, wares, or merchandise for or by way of transmission to or from the said Empire, or to or from any person resident, carrying on business, or being therein, nor to trade in or carry any goods, wares, or merchandise destined for or coming from the said Empire, or for or from any person resident, carrying on business, or being therein:

Not to permit any British ship to leave for, enter, or communicate with any port or place of the said Empire:

Nor to make or enter into any new marine, life, fire, or other policy or contract of insurance with or for the benefit of any person resident, carrying on business, or being in the said Empire, nor under any existing policy or contract of insurance to make any payment to or for the benefit of any such person in respect of any loss due to the belligerent action of His Majesty's forces or of those of any ally of His Majesty:

Nor to enter into any new commercial, financial, or other contract or obligation with or for the benefit of any person resident, carrying on business, or being in the said Empire:

And We do hereby further warn all persons that whoever in contravention of the law shall commit, aid, or abet any of the aforesaid acts will be liable to such penalties as the law provides:

And We hereby declare that any transactions to, with, or for the benefit of any person resident, carrying on business, or being in the said Empire which are not treasonable and are not for the time being expressly prohibited by us either by virtue of this Proclamation or otherwise, and which but for the existence of the state of war aforesaid would be lawful, are hereby permitted.

And We hereby declare that the expression "person" in this Proclamation shall include any body of persons corporate or unincorporate, and that where any person has, or has an interest in, houses or branches of business in some other country as well as in Our Dominions, or in the said Empire (as the case may be), this Proclamation shall not apply to the trading or commercial intercourse carried on by such person solely from or by such houses or branches of business in such other country.

III

Restrictions on Alien Enemies carrying on Banking Business.

Under a Proclamation dated 10th August, it is ordered as follows :—

1. An alien enemy shall not carry on or engage in any

BANKING

banking business except with the permission in writing of the Secretary of State, and to such extent and subject to such conditions and supervision as the Secretary of State may direct, and an alien enemy who is or has been carrying on or engaged in banking business shall not, except with the like permission, part with any money or securities in the bank where he is or has been carrying on or engaged in business, and shall, if so required, deposit any such money or securities in such custody as the Secretary of State may direct.

Any constable, if authorised by a superintendent of police, or officer of higher rank may, for the purpose of enforcing the provisions of this Article, enter, if necessary by force, and search or occupy any premises in which the business of banking is or has been carried on by any alien enemy.

For the purposes of this Article, any person who is a member of a firm or a director of a company carrying on banking business in the United Kingdom shall be deemed to be carrying on banking business.

This Article shall have effect as though it were included and had always been included in the Aliens Restriction Order, 1914.

Note.—A Royal Proclamation of 7th January 1915 provides that—

"transactions entered into by persons, firms, or companies resident, carrying on business, or being in the United Kingdom—

"(*a*) in respect of banking business with a branch situated outside the United Kingdom of an enemy person, firm, or company; or

"(*b*) in respect of any description of business with a branch situated outside the United Kingdom of an enemy bank,

shall be considered as transactions with an enemy.

" Provided that the acceptance, payment, or other dealing with any negotiable instrument which was drawn before the date of this Proclamation shall not, if otherwise lawful, be deemed to be a transaction hereafter entered into within the meaning of this paragraph."

IV

Trading with the Enemy.

The following official announcement was issued by the Treasury on 21st August:—

Some doubts having arisen as to the meaning and application of the Proclamation against trading with the enemy, the Government authorise the following explanation to be published:—

1. For the purpose of deciding what transactions with foreign traders are permitted, the important thing is to consider where the foreign trader resides and carries on business, and not the nationality of the foreign trader.

2. Consequently there is, as a rule, no objection to British firms trading with German or Austrian firms established in neutral or British territory. What is prohibited is trade with any firms established in hostile territory.

3. If a firm with headquarters in hostile territory has a branch in neutral or British territory trade with the branch is (apart from prohibitions in special cases) permissible as long as the trade is *bonâ fide* with the branch and no transaction with the head office is involved.

4. Commercial contracts entered into before war broke out with firms established in hostile territory cannot be performed during the war, and payments under them ought not to be made to such firms during the war. Where, however, nothing remains to be done save to pay for goods already delivered, or for services already rendered, there is no objection to making the payment. Whether contracts entered into before war are suspended or terminated is a question of law which may depend on circumstances, and in cases of doubt British firms must consult their own legal advisers.

This explanation is issued in order to promote confidence and certainty in British commercial transactions, but it must be understood that in case of need the Government will still be free to impose stricter regulations or special prohibitions in the national interest.

V

PAYMENT OF DIVIDENDS TO RESIDENTS IN ENEMY TERRITORY.

The following warning was issued by the Board of Trade on 31st August:—

The Board of Trade warns all joint stock companies and their officers that:

(1) No dividends or interest declared or becoming due after the outbreak of war should be paid during the war to or in accordance with instructions from any person resident in enemy territory.

Such dividends or interest should be paid into a separate account at a Bank to be disposed of after the conclusion of the war.

(2) No transfer of any shares or debentures from any person resident in enemy territory should be registered during the war.

VI

TRADING WITH THE ENEMY.

A Supplement to the *London Gazette*, of 9th September, contains the following Proclamation of that date, relating to trading with the enemy:—

WHEREAS a state of War has existed between Us and the German Empire as from 11 P.M. on 4th August 1914, and a state of War has existed between Us and the Dual Monarchy of Austria-Hungary as from midnight on 12th August 1914:

And whereas it is contrary to law for any person resident, carrying on business, or being in Our Dominions, to trade or have any commercial or financial transactions with any person resident or carrying on business in the German Empire or Austria-Hungary without Our permission:

And whereas by Our Proclamation of the 5th August 1914 relating to trading with the enemy, certain classes of transactions with the German Empire were prohibited:

And whereas by paragraph 2 of Our Proclamation of the 12th August 1914, the said Proclamation of the 5th August 1914 was declared to be applicable to Austria-Hungary:

And whereas it is desirable to re-state and extend the prohibitions contained in the former Proclamations, and for that purpose to revoke the Proclamation of the 5th August 1914, and paragraph 2 of the Proclamation of the 12th August 1914, and to substitute this Proclamation therefor:

And whereas it is expedient and necessary to warn all persons resident, carrying on business, or being in Our Dominions, of their duties and obligations towards Us, Our Crown, and Government:

Now, therefore, We have thought fit, by and with the advice of Our Privy Council, to issue this Our Royal Proclamation declaring, and it is hereby declared as follows:—

1. The aforesaid Proclamation of the 5th August 1914, relating to trading with the enemy, and paragraph 2 of the aforesaid Proclamation of the 12th August 1914, together with any public announcement officially issued in explanation thereof are hereby, as from the date hereof, revoked, and from and after the date hereof this present Proclamation is substituted therefor.

2. The expression "enemy country" in this Proclamation means the territories of the German Empire and of the Dual Monarchy of Austria-Hungary, together with all the colonies and dependencies thereof.

3. The expression "enemy" in this Proclamation means any person or body of persons of whatever nationality resident or carrying on business in the enemy country, but does not

include persons of enemy nationality who are neither resident nor carrying on business in the enemy country. In the case of incorporated bodies, enemy character attaches only to those incorporated in an enemy country.

4. The expression "outbreak of war" in this Proclamation means 11 P.M. on the 4th August 1914, in relation to the German Empire, its colonies and dependencies, and midnight on the 12th August 1914, in relation to Austria-Hungary, its colonies and dependencies.

5. From and after the date of this Proclamation the following prohibitions shall have effect (save so far as licenses may be issued as hereinafter provided), and We do hereby accordingly warn all persons resident, carrying on business, or being in Our Dominions—

(1) Not to pay any sum of money to or for the benefit of an enemy.

(2) Not to compromise or give security for the payment of any debt or other sum of money with or for the benefit of an enemy.

(3) Not to act on behalf of an enemy in drawing, accepting, paying, presenting for acceptance or payment, negotiating, or otherwise dealing with any negotiable instrument.

(4) Not to accept, pay, or otherwise deal with any negotiable instrument which is held by or on behalf of an enemy, provided that this prohibition shall not be deemed to be infringed by any person who has no reasonable ground for believing that the instrument is held by or on behalf of an enemy.

(5) Not to enter into any new transaction, or complete any transaction already entered into with an enemy in any stocks, shares, or other securities.

(6) Not to make or enter into any new marine, life, fire, or other policy or contract of insurance with or for the benefit of an enemy; nor to accept, or give effect to any insurance of, any risk arising under any policy or contract of insurance (including re-insurance) made or entered into with or for the benefit of an enemy before the outbreak of war.

(7) Not directly or indirectly to supply to or for the use or benefit of, or obtain from, an enemy country or an enemy, any goods, wares, or merchandise, nor directly or indirectly to supply to or for the use or benefit of, or obtain from any person any goods, wares, or merchandise, for or by way of transmission to or from an enemy country or an enemy, nor directly or indirectly to trade in or carry any goods, wares, or merchandise destined for or coming from an enemy country or an enemy.

(8) Not to permit any British ship to leave for, enter, or communicate with, any port or place in an enemy country.

(9) Not to enter into any commercial, financial, or other contract or obligation with or for the benefit of an enemy.

(10) Not to enter into any transactions with an enemy if and when they are prohibited by an Order of Council made and published on the recommendation of a Secretary of State, even though they would otherwise be permitted by law or by this or any other Proclamation.

And we do hereby further warn all persons that whoever in contravention of the law shall commit, aid, or abet any of the aforesaid acts, is guilty of a crime, and will be liable to punishment and penalties accordingly.

6. Provided always that where an enemy has a branch locally situated in British, allied, or neutral territory, not being neutral territory in Europe, transactions by or with such branch shall not be treated as transactions by or with an enemy.

7. Nothing in this Proclamation shall be deemed to prohibit payments by or on account of enemies to persons resident, carrying on business, or being in Our Dominions, if such payments arise out of transactions entered into before the outbreak of war or otherwise permitted.

8. Nothing in this Proclamation shall be taken to prohibit anything which shall be expressly permitted by Our license or by the license given on Our behalf by a Secretary of State, or the Board of Trade, whether such licenses be especially granted to individuals or be announced as applying to classes of persons.

9. This Proclamation shall be called the Trading with the Enemy Proclamation, No. 2.

VII

Trading with the Enemy.

The following announcements were made in the *London Gazette* of 25th September :—

1. [Freight.]

WHEREAS by paragraph 5 of the Trading with the Enemy Proclamation, No. 2, dated the 9th day of September, 1914, all persons resident, carrying on business, or being in the King's Dominions were prohibited from doing certain things save so far as licenses might be issued enabling them to do so.

And whereas by paragraph 8 of the aforesaid Proclamation it is provided that nothing in such Proclamation shall be taken to prohibit anything which shall be expressly permitted by the King's license or by the license given on His behalf by a Secretary of State or the Board of Trade, whether such licenses be especially granted to individuals or be announced as applying to classes of persons.

Now, therefore, the Board of Trade hereby announce that British owners of cargo now lying in a neutral port in a ship owned by an enemy may for the purpose of obtaining possession of such cargo pay freight and other necessary charges to the agent of the shipowner at such port.

G. S. BARNES,
A Secretary to the Board of Trade.

2. [Patents, Etc.]

The Board of Trade have given a general license permitting all persons resident, or carrying on business, or being in the British Dominions,

To pay any fees necessary for obtaining the grant, or for obtaining the renewal of patents, or for obtaining the registration of designs or trade marks, or the renewal of such registration in an " enemy country."

506 APPENDIX

And also to pay on behalf of any "enemy" any fees payable on application for or renewal of the grant of a British patent, or on application for the registration of British designs or trade marks or the renewal of such registration.

VIII

Trading with the Enemy.

(Insurance and Colonial Trading.)

A further Proclamation relating to trading with the enemy was issued on 8th October in the following terms :—

WHEREAS it is desirable to amend Our Proclamation of the 9th September 1914, called "The Trading with the Enemy Proclamation, No. 2."

Now, therefore, We have thought fit, by and with the advice of Our Privy Council, to issue this Our Royal Proclamation declaring, and it is hereby declared as follows :—

1. Paragraph 5, heading (6), of the Trading with the Enemy Proclamation, No. 2, is hereby revoked, and in lieu thereof the following heading shall be inserted in the said Paragraph 5 as from the date hereof :—

(6) " Not to make or enter into any new marine, life, fire or other policy or contract of insurance (including re-insurance) with or for the benefit of an enemy ; nor to accept, or give effect to any insurance of, any risk arising under any policy or contract of insurance (including re-insurance) made or entered into with or for the benefit of an enemy before the outbreak of war ; and in particular as regards Treaties or Contracts of re-insurance current at the outbreak of war to which an enemy is a party or in which an enemy is interested, not to cede to the enemy or to accept from the enemy under any such Treaty or Contract any risk arising under any policy or contract of

insurance (including re-insurance) made or entered into after the outbreak of war, or any share in any such risk."

2. (1) The expression "Order of Council made and published on the recommendation of a Secretary of State" in Paragraph 5, heading (10), of the Trading with the Enemy Proclamation, No. 2, shall, as regards persons resident carrying on business, or being in Our Dominions beyond the Seas, be taken to mean an Order of the Governor in Council published in the *Official Gazette*.

(2) The expression "Governor in Council" in this paragraph means as respects Canada the Governor-General of Canada in Council, as respects India the Governor-General of India in Council, as respects Australia the Governor-General of Australia in Council, as respects New Zealand the Governor of New Zealand in Council, as respects the Union of South Africa the Governor-General of the Union of South Africa in Council, as respects Newfoundland the Governor of Newfoundland in Council, and as respects any other British Possession the Governor of that Possession in Council.

3. The power to grant licenses on Our behalf vested by Paragraph 8 of the Trading with the Enemy Proclamation, No. 2, in a Secretary of State may be exercised in Canada, India, Australia, and the Union of South Africa by the Governor-General, and in any British Possession not included within the limits of Canada, India, Australia, or South Africa by the Governor.

4. In this Proclamation the expression "Governor-General" includes any person who for the time being has the powers of the Governor-General, and the expression "Governor" includes the officer for the time being administering the Government.

5. Notwithstanding anything contained in Paragraph 6 of the Trading with the Enemy Proclamation, No. 2, where an enemy has a branch locally situated in British, allied, or neutral territory, which carries on the business of insurance or re-insurance of whatever nature, transactions by or with such branch in respect of the business of insurance or re-insurance shall be considered as transactions by or with an enemy.

6. This Proclamation shall be read as one with the Trading with the Enemy Proclamation, No. 2.

IX

CUSTOMS ORDER: CERTIFICATES OF ORIGIN

On 9th October the following "Notice to Importers and Exporters" was issued by the Board of Trade:—

1. The attention of importers and exporters is directed to the provisions of His Majesty's Proclamation, dated 9th September, relating to trading with the enemy. By paragraph 5 (7) of this Proclamation all persons resident, carrying on business, or being in His Majesty's Dominions are warned "not directly or indirectly to supply to or for the use or benefit of, or obtain from an enemy country or an enemy any goods, wares, or merchandise; nor directly or indirectly to supply to or for the use or benefit of, or obtain from any person any goods, wares, or merchandise, for or by way of transmission to or from an enemy country or an enemy; nor directly or indirectly to trade in or carry any goods, wares, or merchandise destined for or coming from an enemy country or an enemy." It is further provided by paragraph 3 that the expression "enemy" in the Proclamation means "any person or body of persons of whatever nationality resident or carrying on business in the enemy country, but does not include persons of enemy nationality who are neither resident nor carrying on business in the enemy country. In the case of incorporated bodies, enemy character attaches only to those incorporated in an enemy country."

2. With a view to preventing breaches of this Proclamation, it is hereby notified that the Commissioners of His Majesty's Customs and Excise have been authorised by His Majesty's Government to require certificates of origin or declarations of ultimate destination respectively to be presented in respect of all goods, wares, or merchandise imported into or exported from the United Kingdom in trade with any foreign port in Europe or on the Mediterranean or Black Seas, with the

exception of those of Russia, Belgium, France, Spain, and Portugal.

3. Declarations of ultimate destination will consequently be required until further notice in respect of all exports, without regard to value of consignments, to all the foreign ports referred to above.

4. For the present, however (except in regard to sugar), certificates of origin will not be required in respect of imports of foodstuffs, or in respect of any imports from ports other than those specified in Schedule I. below, or in respect of individual consignments not exceeding £100 in value. The certificates and declarations referred to must be in the form prescribed by the Schedules II. and III. hereto.

5. Any goods, wares, or merchandise imported from the above-mentioned foreign ports, except as provided in paragraph 4, unaccompanied by certificate of origin, will be detained by the Commissioners of Customs and Excise until the requisite certificates are produced. The Commissioners are, however, authorised in such cases, and at their discretion, to allow delivery of the goods on the security of a deposit or of a bond to the amount of three times the value of the goods, with a view to the production of the necessary certificates within a prescribed period, provided that they see no reason for suspecting that the goods emanate from any enemy country.

6. Goods, wares, or merchandise sought to be exported to any foreign ports in Europe or on the Mediterranean or Black Seas, with the exception of those of Russia, Belgium, France, Spain, and Portugal, will not be allowed to be shipped until declarations of ultimate destination in the form prescribed have been lodged with the proper Customs authority.

7. The following goods will be exempt from these requirements:—

(*a*) Goods imported or exported under license;
(*b*) Goods shipped for the United Kingdom on or before 19th October;
(*c*) Goods in respect of which Customs export entries have been accepted before the publication of this notice.

Board of Trade, 9th October 1914.

APPENDIX

Schedule I.

List of ports in respect of imports from which certificates of origin will be required (paragraph 4 of Notice).

Norway.—Christiania, Bergen, Arendal, Bodo, Christiansand, Christiansund, Drammen, Flekkefiord, Fredrikshald, Fredrikstad, Hammerfest, Haugesund, Laurvig and Sandefiord, Lofoten Islands, Mandal, Morde, Moss, Namsos, Narvik, Porsgrund, Risor, Skien, Stavanger, Tönsberg, Tromsö, Trondhjem, Vasdö, Vardö, Kragerö.

Sweden.—Stockholm, Borgholm, Gefle, Gotland (Wisbui), Hernösand, Hudiksvall, Kalmar, Lulea, Norroköping, Nyköping, Örnsköldsvik, Oskarshamn, Söderhamn, Sundvall, Umea, Westervik, Skelleftea, Gottenburg, Carlscrona, Halmstad, Helsingborg, Landscroner, Malmö, Strömstad, Uddevalla, Warberg, Ystad and Ahus, Marstrand.

Denmark.—Copenhagen, Nyborg, Aalborg, Aarhus, Bandholm, Elsinore, Esbjerg, Fredericia, Fredrikshavn, Horsens, Castrap, Kolding, Korsör, Lemvig, Odense, Randers, Rönne (Bornholm), Svendborg, Thisted.

Netherlands.—Rotterdam, Amsterdam, Delfzyl, Dordrecht, Flushing, Groningen, The Hague and Scheveningen, Helder, Leeuwarden and Harlingen, Maassluis, Terneuzen, Tiel, Utrecht, Ymuiden.

Italy.—Genoa, Spezia, Savona.

Schedule II.

Form of Certificate of Origin.

I,   , hereby certify that Mr   (Producer, Manufacturer, Merchant, Trader, etc.), residing at   in this town, has declared before me that the merchandise designated below, which is to be shipped from this town to   , consigned to   (Merchant, Manufacturer, etc.), in the United Kingdom, is not of German, Austrian, or Hungarian production or manufacture, and has produced to my satisfaction invoices or other trustworthy documents in proof thereof.

Number and description of cases.	Marks.	Numbers.	Weight or Quantity.	Total Value.	Contents.

This certificate is valid only for a period of not more than   from the date hereof.

(Signature of Consular Authority issuing Certificate and date.)
(Signature of person declaring.)

CUSTOMS ORDER

SCHEDULE III.

Form of Statutory Declaration.

I,   of   do solemnly and sincerely declare as follows:—I have made all necessary inquiries in order to satisfy myself as to the ultimate destination of the goods, particulars of which are set out in the Schedule below, to be exported by me or on my behalf on board   to   , and consigned to   of   , and do hereby declare that to the best of my knowledge and belief none of such goods are intended for consumption in any State at present at war with His Majesty, and I make this declaration conscientiously believing the same to be true and by virtue of the Statutory Declarations Act, 1835.

SCHEDULE.

Number and description of cases.	Marks.	Numbers.	Weight or Quantity.	Total Value.	Contents.

Declaration before me this   day of
(Signature of Commissioner of Oaths or Justice of the Peace.)

(Signature of Declarant.)

[*Note.*—Para. 4 was subsequently modified. Certificates *of origin* were abandoned in the case of (1) food, timber, wood-pulp, iron ore, granite, ice, tar, carbide of calcium, straw-board: (2) goods from places other than Scandinavia, Switzerland, Holland, and Italy: (3) goods under £25 value. Certificates *of destination* were directed to be made by the actual exporter or his representative (not a mere carrier). The exemption in the case of goods exported under license was withdrawn.]

X

TRADING WITH THE ENEMY, 5 GEO. V. C. 12.

[*"Trading with the Enemy Amendment Act,* 1914." *Royal Assent,* 27*th November* 1914.]

1.—(1) The Board of Trade shall appoint a person to act as Custodian of enemy property (hereinafter referred to as "the Custodian") for England and Wales, for Scotland, and for Ireland respectively, for the purpose of receiving, holding, preserving, and dealing with such property as may be paid to or vested in him in pursuance of this Act, and if any question arises as to which Custodian any money is to be paid to under this Act, the question shall be determined by the Board of Trade.

(2) The Public Trustee shall be appointed to be the Custodian for England and Wales, and shall, in relation to all property held by him in his capacity of Custodian, have the like status, and his accounts shall be subject to the like audit, as if the same were held by him in his capacity of Public Trustee, and the Public Trustee Act, 1906, shall apply accordingly.

(3) The Custodian for Scotland and Ireland respectively shall have such powers and duties with respect to the property aforesaid as may be prescribed by regulations made by the Board of Trade with the approval of the Treasury.

(4) The Custodian may place on deposit with any bank, or invest in any securities, approved by the Treasury, any moneys paid to him under this Act, or received by him from property vested in him under this Act, and any interest or dividends received on account of such deposits or investments shall be dealt with in such manner as the Treasury may direct:

Provided that the Custodian for any part of the United Kingdom shall, if so directed by the Treasury, transfer any money held by him under this Act to the Custodian of another part thereof.

ENEMY PROFITS

2.—(1) Any sum which, had a state of war not existed, would have been payable and paid to or for the benefit of an enemy, by way of dividends, interest, or share of profits, shall be paid by the person, firm, or company by whom it would have been payable to the Custodian to hold, subject to the provisions of this Act and any Order in Council made thereunder, and the payment shall be accompanied by such particulars as the Board of Trade may prescribe, or as the Custodian, if so authorised by the Board of Trade, may require.

Any payment required to be made under this subsection to the Custodian shall be made—

(*a*) within fourteen days after the passing of this Act, if the sum, had a state of war not existed, would have been paid before the passing of this Act ; and

(*b*) in any other case within fourteen days after it would have been paid.

(2) Where before the passing of this Act any such sum has been paid into any account with a bank, or has been paid to any other person in trust for an enemy, the person, firm, or company by whom the payment was made shall, within fourteen days after the passing of this Act, by notice in writing, require the bank or person to pay the sum over to the Custodian to hold as aforesaid, and shall furnish the Custodian with such particulars as aforesaid. The bank or other person shall, within one week after the receipt of the notice comply with the requirement, and shall be exempt from all liability for having done so.

(3) If any person fails to make or require the making of any payment, or to furnish the prescribed particulars within the time mentioned in this section, he shall, on conviction under the Summary Jurisdiction Acts, be liable to a fine not exceeding one hundred pounds or to imprisonment, with or without hard labour, for a term not exceeding six months, or to both such fine and imprisonment, and in addition to a further fine not exceeding fifty pounds for every day during which the default continues, and every director, manager, secretary, or officer of a company, or any other person who is knowingly a party to the default shall, on the like conviction, be liable to the like penalty.

(4) If, in the case of any person, firm, or company whose books and documents are liable to inspection under subsection (2) of section two of the Trading with the Enemy Act, 1914 (hereinafter referred to as the principal Act), any question arises as to the amount which would have been so payable and paid as aforesaid, the question shall be determined by the person who may have been or who may be appointed to inspect the books and documents of the person, firm, or company, or, on appeal, by the Board of Trade, and if, in the course of determining the question, it appears to the inspector or the Board of Trade that the person, firm, or company has not distributed as dividends, interest, or profits the whole of the amount properly available for that purpose, the inspector or Board may ascertain what amount was so available and require the whole of such amount to be so distributed, and, in the case of a company, if such dividends have not been declared, the inspector or the Board may himself or themselves declare the appropriate dividends, and every such declaration shall be as effective as a declaration to the like effect duly made in accordance with the constitution of the company:

Provided that where a controller has been appointed under section three of the principal Act this subsection shall apply as if for references to the inspector there were substituted references to the controller.

(5) For the purposes of this Act the expression "dividends, interest, or share of profits" means any dividends, bonus, or interest in respect of any shares, stock, debentures, debenture stock, or other obligations of any company, any interest in respect of any loan to a firm or person carrying on business for the purposes of that business, and any profits or share of profits of such a business, and, where a person is carrying on any business on behalf of an enemy, any sum which, had a state of war not existed, would have been transmissible by a person to the enemy by way of profits from that business shall be deemed to be a sum which would have been payable and paid to that enemy.

3.—(1) Any person who holds or manages for or on behalf of an enemy any property, real or personal (including any rights, whether legal or equitable, in or arising out of property, real or personal), shall, within one month after the passing of this Act, or if the property comes into his possession or under his control after the passing of this Act, then within one month after the time when it comes into his possession or under his control, by notice in writing communicate the fact to the Custodian, and shall furnish the Custodian with such particulars in relation thereto as the Custodian may require, and if any person fails to do so he shall, on conviction under the Summary Jurisdiction Acts, be liable to a fine not exceeding one hundred pounds or to imprisonment, with or without hard labour, for a term not exceeding six months, or to both such a fine and imprisonment, and in addition to a further fine not exceeding fifty pounds for every day during which the default continues.

(2) Every company incorporated in the United Kingdom and every company which, though not incorporated in the United Kingdom, has a share transfer or share registration office in the United Kingdom shall, within one month after the passing of this Act, by notice in writing communicate to the Custodian full particulars of all shares, stock, debentures, and debenture stock and other obligations of the company which are held by or for the benefit of an enemy ; and every partner of every firm, one or more partners of which on the commencement of the war became enemies or to which money had been lent for the purpose of the business of the firm by a person who so became an enemy, shall, within one month after the commencement of this Act, by notice in writing communicate to the Custodian full particulars as to any share of profits and interest due to such enemies or enemy, and, if any company or partner fails to comply with the provisions of this subsection, the company shall, on conviction under the Summary Jurisdiction Acts, be liable to a fine not exceeding one hundred pounds, and in addition to a further fine not exceeding fifty pounds for every day during which the default continues, and the partner and every director, manager, secretary, or officer of the company who is knowingly a party to the default shall on the like conviction be liable to the like fine, or to imprisonment, with or without hard labour, for a term not exceeding six months, or to both such imprisonment and fine.

4.—(1) The High Court or a judge thereof may, on the

application of any person who appears to the court to be a creditor of an enemy or entitled to recover damages against an enemy, or to be interested in any property, real or personal (including any rights, whether legal or equitable, in or arising out of property real or personal), belonging to or held or managed for or on behalf of an enemy, or on the application of the Custodian or any Government Department, by order vest in the Custodian any such real or personal property as aforesaid, if the court or the judge is satisfied that such vesting is expedient for the purposes of this Act, and may by the order confer on the Custodian such powers of selling, managing, and otherwise dealing with the property as to the court or judge may seem proper.

(2) The court or judge before making any order under this section may direct that such notices (if any), whether by way of advertisement or otherwise, shall be given as the court or judge may think fit.

(3) A vesting order under this section as respects property of any description shall be of the like purport and effect as a vesting order as respects property of the same description made under the Trustee Act, 1893.

5.—(1) The Custodian shall, except so far as the Board of Trade or the High Court or a judge thereof may otherwise direct, and subject to the provisions of the next succeeding subsection, hold any money paid to and any property vested in him under this Act until the termination of the present war, and shall thereafter deal with the same in such manner as His Majesty may by Order in Council direct.

(2) The property held by the Custodian under this Act shall not be liable to be attached or otherwise taken in execution, but the Custodian may, if so authorised by an order of the High Court or a judge by whose order any property belonging to an enemy was vested in the Custodian under this Act, or of any court in which judgment has been recovered against an enemy, pay out of the property paid to him in respect of that enemy the whole or any part of any debts due by that enemy and specified in the order:

Provided that before paying any such debt the Custodian shall take into consideration the sufficiency of the property paid to or vested in him in respect of the enemy in question to satisfy that debt and any other claims against that enemy of which notice verified by statutory declaration may have been served upon him.

(3) The receipt of the Custodian or any person duly authorised to sign receipts on his behalf for any sum paid to him under this Act shall be a good discharge to the person paying the same as against the person or body of persons in respect of whom the sum was paid to the Custodian.

(4) The Custodian shall keep a register of all property held by him under this Act, which register shall be open to public inspection at all reasonable times free of charge.

(5) In England and Ireland the Lord Chancellor and the Lord Chancellor for Ireland may by rules, and in Scotland the Court of Session may by act of sederunt, make provision for the practice and procedure to be adopted for the purposes of this and the last preceding section.

6.—(1) No person shall by virtue of any assignment of any debt or other chose in action, or delivery of any coupon or other security transferable by delivery, or transfer of any other obligation, made or to be made in his favour by or on behalf of an enemy, whether for valuable consideration or otherwise, have any rights or remedies against the person liable to pay, discharge, or satisfy the debt, chose in action, security, or obligation, unless he proves that the assignment, delivery, or transfer was made by leave of the Board of Trade or was made before the commencement of the present war, and any person who knowingly pays, discharges, or satisfies any debt, or chose in action, to which this subsection applies, shall be deemed to be guilty of the offence of trading with the enemy within the meaning of the principal Act :

Provided that this subsection shall not apply where the person to whom the assignment, delivery, or transfer was made, or some person deriving title under him, proves that the transfer, delivery, or assignment or some subsequent transfer, delivery, or assignment, was made before the nineteenth day of November, nineteen hundred and fourteen, in good faith and for valuable consideration, nor shall this subsection apply to any bill of exchange or promissory note.

(2) No person shall by virtue of any transfer of a bill of exchange or promissory note made or to be made in his favour by or on behalf of an enemy, whether for valuable consideration or otherwise, have any rights or remedies against any party to the instrument unless he proves that the transfer was made before the commencement of the present war, and any party to the instrument who knowingly discharges the instrument shall be deemed to be guilty of trading with the enemy within the meaning of the principal Act:

Provided that this subsection shall not apply where the transferee, or some subsequent holder of the instrument, proves that the transfer, or some subsequent transfer, of the instrument was made before the nineteenth day of November, nineteen hundred and fourteen, in good faith and for valuable consideration.

(3) Nothing in this section shall be construed as validating any assignment, delivery, or transfer which would be invalid apart from this section or as applying to securities within the meaning of section eight of this Act.

7. Where during the continuance of the present war any coupon or other security transferable by delivery is presented for payment to any company, municipal authority, or other body or person, and the company, body, or person has reason to suspect that it is so presented on behalf or for the benefit of an enemy, or that since the commencement of the present war it has been held by or for the benefit of an enemy, the company, body, or person may pay the sum due in respect thereof into the High Court, and the same shall, subject to rules of court, be dealt with according to the orders of the court, and such a payment shall for all purposes be a good discharge to the company, body, or person.

8.—(1) No transfer made after the passing of this Act by or on behalf of an enemy of any securities shall confer on the transferee any rights or remedies in respect thereof, and no company or municipal authority or other body by whom the securities were issued or are managed shall, except as hereinafter appears, take any cognisance of or otherwise act upon any notice of such a transfer:

INCORPORATION

(2) No entry shall hereafter, during the continuance of the present war, be made in any register or branch register or other book kept in the United Kingdom of any transfer of any securities therein registered, inscribed, or standing in the name of an enemy, except by leave of a court of competent jurisdiction or of the Board of Trade.

(3) No share warrants payable to bearer shall be issued during the continuance of the present war in respect of any shares or stock registered in the name of any enemy.

(4) If any company or any body contravenes the provisions of this section the company or body shall be liable on conviction under the Summary Jurisdiction Acts to a fine not exceeding one hundred pounds, and every director, manager, secretary, or other officer of the company or body who is knowingly a party to the default, shall be liable on the like conviction to a like fine or to imprisonment, with or without hard labour, for a term not exceeding six months.

(5) For the purposes of this section the expression "securities" means any annuities, stock, shares, debentures, or debenture stock issued by or on behalf of the Government, or by any municipal or other authority, or by any company or by any other body which are registered or inscribed in any register, branch register, or other book kept in the United Kingdom.

9.—(1) During the continuance of the present war a certificate of incorporation of a company shall not be given by the Registrar of Joint Stock Companies until there has been filed with him either—

 (a) a statutory declaration by a solicitor of the Supreme Court, or, in Scotland, by an enrolled law agent, engaged in the formation of the company, that the company is not formed for the purpose or with the intention of acquiring the whole or any part of the undertaking of a person, firm, or company the books and documents of which are liable to inspection under subsection (2) of section two of the principal Act; or

 (b) a license from the Board of Trade authorising the acquisition by the company of such an undertaking.

(2) Where such a statutory declaration has been filed it

shall not be lawful for the company, during the continuance of the present war, without the license of the Board of Trade, to acquire the whole or any part of any such undertaking, and if it does so the company shall, without prejudice to any other liability, be liable on conviction under the Summary Jurisdiction Acts to a fine not exceeding one hundred pounds, and every director, manager, secretary, or other officer of the company who is knowingly a party to the default shall on the like conviction be liable to the like fine or to imprisonment, with or without hard labour, for a term not exceeding six months.

10.—(1) Section one of the principal Act shall apply to a person who during the present war attempts, or directly or indirectly offers or proposes or agrees, or has since the fourth day of August nineteen hundred and fourteen attempted or directly or indirectly offered or proposed or agreed, to trade with the enemy within the meaning of that Act, in like manner as it applies to a person who so trades or has so traded.

(2) If any person without lawful authority in anywise aids or abets any other person, whether or not such other person is in the United Kingdom, to enter into, negotiate, or complete any transaction or do any act which, if effected or done in the United Kingdom by such other person, would constitute an offence of trading with the enemy within the meaning of the principal Act, he shall be deemed to be guilty of such an offence.

(3) If any person without lawful authority deals, or attempts or offers, proposes or agrees, whether directly or indirectly, to deal with any money or security for money or other property which is in his hands or over which he has any claim or control, for the purpose of enabling an enemy to obtain money or credit thereon, or thereby, he shall be deemed to be guilty of the offence of trading with the enemy within the meaning of the principal Act.

11.—(1) In addition to the grounds on which an application can be made to the court by the Board of Trade to appoint a controller under section three of the principal Act, such an application may be made in any case in which the Board think it is expedient in the public interest that a controller should be appointed owing to circumstances or considerations arising out of the present war, and that section shall be construed accordingly.

(2) Section three of the principal Act, as amended by this section, shall extend so as to enable a controller to be appointed of a business carried on by a person in like manner as it applies to the appointment of a controller of a business carried on by a firm.

12.—(1) Where, on the report of an inspector appointed to inspect the books and documents of a person, firm, or company under section two of the principal Act, it appears to the Board of Trade that it is expedient that the business should be subject to frequent inspection or constant supervision, the Board of Trade may appoint that inspector or some other person to supervise the business with such powers as the Board of Trade may determine, and any remuneration payable and expenses incurred, whether for the original inspection or the subsequent supervision to such amount as may be fixed by the Board of Trade, shall be paid by the said person, firm, or company.

(2) Paragraph (c) of subsection (2) of section two of the principal Act shall have effect, and shall be deemed always to have had effect as if for the word "trading," there were substituted the word "resident."

13. Where a person has given any information to a person appointed to inspect the books and documents of a person, firm, or company under section two of the principal Act, the information so given may be used in evidence against him in any proceedings relating to offences of trading with the enemy within the meaning of the principal Act, notwithstanding that he only gave the information on being required so to do by the inspector, in pursuance of his powers under the said section.

14.—(1) This Act may be cited as the Trading with the Enemy Amendment Act, 1914, and shall be construed as one with the principal Act.

(2) No person or body of persons shall, for the purposes of this Act, be treated as an enemy who would not be so treated

for the purpose of any proclamation issued by His Majesty dealing with trading with the enemy for the time being in force, and the expression " commencement of the present war" shall mean as respects any enemy the date on which war was declared by His Majesty on the country in which that enemy resides or carries on business.

(3) In the application of this Act to Scotland "real property" shall mean "heritable property"; "personal property" shall mean "moveable property"; "chose in action" shall mean "right of action"; "attached or otherwise taken in execution" shall mean "arrested in execution or in security, or otherwise affected by diligence"; "assignment" shall mean "assignation"; "judgment has been recovered" shall mean "decree has been obtained"; a reference to a vesting order made under the Trustee Act, 1893, shall be construed as a reference to a warrant to complete a title granted under section twelve of the Trusts (Scotland) Act, 1867, and any money paid into the Court of Session in terms of this Act shall be paid in such manner as may be prescribed by Act of sederunt.

(4) Nothing in this Act shall be construed as limiting the power of His Majesty by proclamation to prohibit any transaction which is not prohibited by this Act, or by license to permit any transaction which is so prohibited.

[*Note.*—The following Memorandum is extracted by permission, from the *Journal* of the London Chamber of Commerce.]

THE scheme of the Act is simple. It is to enable an official, called the Custodian, to collect the payments of profits, interest, and dividends due to, and to realise the property belonging to, an enemy. It applies only to the United Kingdom—though this limitation is rather implied than distinctly stated. The property so realised is to be held until the end of the war, and the debts of other enemies than the individuals concerned are not at present to be paid out of it.

Persons who have or control an enemy's property are bound to disclose it to the Custodian, who may sequestrate it, on application to the Court.

Post-bellum transfers by an enemy of securities, debts, and obligations, are deprived of force, unless made *bona fide* and for value before 19th November : or of bills and notes : and it is "trading with the enemy" to pay the friendly transferee. Great difficulty may arise here where the transfer was made (as it could perfectly lawfully be made) in the enemy country, or in a neutral country, to a neutral.

Useful provisions are made regarding the payment of interest, dividends, etc., to enemies, and the transfers of shares to them, also the incorporation of British companies to take over enemies' concerns. It was evident that the power of controlling businesses (now extended to the businesses of individuals) would have to be paid for by someone ; and the objects of the surveillance are now made liable to pay for it.

A useful definition of "securities" is given. The definition of "enemy" contained in the Proclamation, appropriate only to the case of trading with the enemy strictly so styled, *i.e.*, the conveyance of goods to or from the hostile territory, is repeated.

Under Clause 2 (4) it will be noted that the Custodian may require an inspected firm or person to distribute its profits. It will also be observed that partners, as well as companies, must give particulars of their business loans from enemies and of the shares of their enemy partners (Clause 3). It would be straining the Act to apply this to single individuals, all whose former partners were enemies : for they have ceased to be "partners" at all. The war dissolved the firm, and they have no British partners to continue it. Particulars of the interest, as and when payable, will, however, have to be furnished under Clause 2.

Note should be taken of the provision requiring persons to incriminate themselves.

XI

THE POSTPONEMENT OF PAYMENTS ACT, 1914.

4 & 5 Geo. V. c. 11.

[*Royal Assent, 3rd August* 1914.]

1.—(1) His Majesty may by Proclamation authorise the

postponement of the payment of any bill of exchange, or of any negotiable instrument, or any other payment in pursuance of any contract, to such extent, for such time, and subject to such conditions or other provisions as may be specified in the Proclamation.

(2) No additional stamp duty shall be payable in respect of any instrument as a consequence of any postponement of payment in pursuance of a proclamation under this Act unless the proclamation otherwise directs.

(3) Any such proclamation may be varied, extended, or revoked by any subsequent proclamation, and separate proclamations may be made dealing with separate subjects.

(4) The Proclamation, dated the third day of August nineteen hundred and fourteen, relating to the postponement of payment of certain bills of exchange is hereby confirmed, and shall be deemed to have been made under this Act.

2.—(1) This Act may be cited as the Postponement of Payments Act, 1914.

(2) This Act shall remain in force for a period of six months from the date of the passing thereof.

XII

Moratorium of 2nd August 1914.

The Proclamation with regard to bills of exchange (dated 2nd August) was as follows :—

Whereas in view of the critical situation in Europe and the financial difficulties caused thereby, it is expedient that the payment of certain bills of exchange should be postponed as appears in this Proclamation:

Now, therefore, We have thought fit, by and with the advice of Our Privy Council, to issue this Our Royal Proclamation, and We do hereby proclaim, direct, and ordain as follows :—

If on the presentation for payment of a bill of exchange,

other than a cheque or bill on demand, which has been accepted before the beginning of the fourth day of August, nineteen hundred and fourteen, the acceptor re-accepts the bill by a declaration on the face of the bill in the form set out hereunder, that bill shall, for all purposes, including the liability of any drawer or indorser or any other party thereto, be deemed to be due and be payable on a date one calendar month after the date of its original maturity instead of on the date of its original maturity, and to be a bill for the original amount thereof increased by the amount of interest thereon calculated from the date of re-acceptance to the new date of payment at the Bank of England rate current on the date of the re-acceptance of the Bill.

FORM OF RE-ACCEPTANCE.

Re-accepted under Proclamation for £   (insert increased sum).

Signature..

Date...

XIII

MORATORIUM OF 6TH AUGUST 1914.

A further Proclamation *extending* the moratorium was issued on 6th August in the following terms :—

[Reciting the Act and Proclamation.]

NOW, THEREFORE, We have thought fit, by and with the advice of Our Privy Council, to issue this Our Royal Proclamation, and We do hereby proclaim, direct, and ordain as follows :—

Save as hereinafter provided, all payments which have become due and payable before the date of this Proclamation, or which will become due and payable on any day before the beginning of the fourth day of September nineteen hundred and fourteen, in respect of any bill of exchange (being a cheque or bill on demand) which was drawn before the beginning of the fourth day of August nineteen hundred and fourteen, or in respect of any negotiable instrument (not being a bill of exchange) dated before that time, or in respect of any contract made before that time, shall be deemed to be due and payable on a day one calendar month after the day on which the payment originally became due and payable, or on the fourth day of September nineteen hundred and fourteen, whichever is the later date, instead of on the day on which the payment originally became due; but payments so postponed shall, if not otherwise carrying interest, and if specific demand is made for payment and payment is refused, carry interest until payment as from the fourth day of August nineteen hundred and fourteen, if they become due and payable before that day, and as from the date on which they become due and payable if they become due and payable on or after that day, at the Bank of England rate current on the seventh day of August nineteen hundred and fourteen; but nothing in this Proclamation shall prevent payments being made before the expiration of the month for which they are so postponed.

This Proclamation shall not apply to:—

(1) any payment in respect of wages or salary;
(2) any payment in respect of a liability which when incurred did not exceed five pounds in amount;
(3) any payment in respect of rates or taxes;
(4) any payment in respect of maritime freight;
(5) any payment in respect of any debt from any person resident outside the British Islands; or from any firm, company, or institution, whose principal place of business is outside the British Islands, not being a debt incurred in the British Islands by a person, firm, company, or institution having a business establishment or branch business establishment in the British Islands.
(6) any payment in respect of any dividend or interest payable in respect of any stocks, funds, or securities (other than real or heritable securities) in which trustees are, under

MORATORIUM

Section One of the Trustee Act, 1893, or any other Act for the time being in force, authorised to invest;

(7) any liability of a bank of issue in respect of bank notes issued by that bank;

(8) any payment to be made by or on behalf of His Majesty, or any Government Department, including the payment of old age pensions;

(9) any payment to be made by any person or society in pursuance of the National Insurance Act, 1911, or any Act amending that Act (whether in the nature of contributions, benefits, or otherwise);

(10) any payment under the Workmen's Compensation Act, 1906, or any Act amending the same;

(11) any payment in respect of the withdrawal of a deposit by a depositor in a trustee savings bank.

Nothing in this Proclamation shall affect any bills of exchange to which our Proclamation, dated the second day of August nineteen hundred and fourteen, relating to the postponement of payment of certain bills of exchange applies.

XIV

Moratorium of 12th August.

The following Proclamation was issued on 12th August :—

Whereas it is expedient to extend Our Proclamation, dated the sixth day of August nineteen hundred and fourteen (relating to the postponement of payments), so as to cover bills of exchange under certain circumstances, and also payments in respect of any debt from any bank whose principal place of business is in any part of His Majesty's Dominions or any British Protectorate:

Now, therefore, We have thought fit, by and with the advice of Our Privy Council, to issue this Our Royal

Proclamation, and We do hereby proclaim, direct, and ordain as follows :—

Notwithstanding anything contained in the said Proclamation, dated the sixth day of August nineteen hundred and fourteen (relating to the postponement of payments), that Proclamation shall apply, and shall be deemed always to have applied :—

(*a*) to any bill of exchange which has not been re-accepted under Our Proclamation, dated the second day of August nineteen hundred and fourteen, as it applies to a bill of exchange, being a cheque or bill on demand, unless on the presentation of the bill the acceptor has expressly refused re-acceptance thereof, but with the substitution, as respects rate of interest, of the date of presentation of the bill for the seventh day of August nineteen hundred and fourteen ; and

(*b*) also to payments in respect of any debt from any bank whose principal place of business is in any part of His Majesty's Dominions or any British Protectorate, although the debt was not incurred in the British Islands, and the bank had not a business establishment or branch business establishment in the British Islands.

XV

Moratorium of 1st September 1914.

A further Proclamation was issued on 1st September 1914.

Whereas under the Postponement of Payments Act, 1914, We have power, by proclamation, to authorise the postponement of the payment of any bill of exchange, or of any negotiable instrument, or any other payment in pursuance of any contract, to such extent, and for such time, and subject to such conditions or other provisions as may be specified in the Proclamation :

MORATORIUM

AND WHEREAS, in pursuance of that power, We have issued proclamations in relation to the postponement of payments due before We were in a State of war or due in respect of contracts made before that time, dated the sixth day of August and the twelfth day of August nineteen hundred and fourteen; and on the second day of August nineteen hundred and fourteen, We also issued a Proclamation which is confirmed by the said Postponement of Payments Act, 1914, and is deemed to have been issued under that Act:

AND WHEREAS, under the said Act, We have power to vary, extend, or revoke, any Proclamation under that Act by a subsequent Proclamation:

AND WHEREAS it is desirable in the best interests of Our Realm at the present juncture that all persons who can discharge their liabilities should do so without delay, but it is at the same time for certain purposes expedient that Our said proclamations should be varied as hereinafter appears:

NOW, THEREFORE, We have thought fit, by and with the advice of Our Privy Council, to issue this Our Royal Proclamation, and We do hereby proclaim, direct, and ordain as follows :—

1. Our said Proclamation, dated the second day of August nineteen hundred and fourteen, shall have effect as if the period of two calendar months were substituted therein for the period of one calendar month; and the sum mentioned in any form of re-acceptance thereunder shall be deemed to be varied accordingly without the necessity of further re-acceptance.

2. Our said Proclamation, dated the sixth day of August nineteen hundred and fourteen, as extended by Our said Proclamation, dated the twelfth day of August nineteen hundred and fourteen, shall have effect as if the fourth day of October were substituted therein for the fourth day of September therein wherever that date occurs, and as if two calendar months were substituted therein for one calendar month.

3. Nothing in this Proclamation shall affect the payment of interest under the proclamations extended thereby, or prevent payments being made before the expiration of the period for which they are postponed.

XVI

MORATORIUM OF 3RD SEPTEMBER 1914.

[Reciting the above proclamations.]

. . . We have thought fit, by and with the advice of Our Privy Council, to issue this Our Royal Proclamation, and We do hereby proclaim, direct, and ordain as follows :—

1. If on the presentation for payment of a bill of exchange which has before the fourth day of September nineteen hundred and fourteen been re-accepted under the terms of Our said Proclamation, dated the second day of August nineteen hundred and fourteen, the bill is not paid, then, the said Proclamation shall, in its application to that bill, have effect as if the period of two calendar months had been in the Proclamation substituted for the period of one calendar month, and the sum mentioned in the form of re-acceptance under the said Proclamation shall be deemed to be increased by the amount of interest on the original amount of the bill for one calendar month, calculated at the Bank of England rate current on the date when the bill is so presented for payment as aforesaid.

2. Our said Proclamation, dated the sixth day of August nineteen hundred and fourteen, as extended by our said Proclamation, dated the twelfth day of August nineteen hundred and fourteen, shall apply to payments which become due and payable on or after the fourth day of September and before the fourth day of October nineteen hundred and fourteen (whether they become so due and payable by virtue of the said Proclamations or otherwise) in like manner as it applies to payments which become due and payable after the date of the said first-mentioned Proclamation and before the beginning of the fourth day of September nineteen hundred and fourteen.

3. Nothing in this Proclamation shall affect the payment of interest under the proclamations extended thereby, or prevent payments being made before the expiration of the period for which they are postponed.

4. Our said Proclamation, dated the first day of September nineteen hundred and fourteen, is hereby revoked.

XVII

Moratorium of 30th September 1914.

[Reciting the previous proclamations, etc.]

... Now, THEREFORE, We have thought fit, by and with the advice of Our Privy Council, to issue this Our Royal Proclamation, and We do hereby proclaim, direct, and ordain as follows :—

1. The first General Proclamation as extended by paragraph (*b*) of the second General Proclamation shall, subject to the limitations of this Proclamation, apply to payments which become due and payable on or after the fourth day of October and before the fourth day of November nineteen hundred and fourteen (whether they so become due and payable by virtue of the said proclamations or the third General Proclamation or otherwise), in like manner as it applies to payments which became due and payable after the date of the first General Proclamation, and before the beginning of the fourth day of September nineteen hundred and fourteen.

Provided that, if the payment is one the date whereof has been postponed by virtue of any of the said General Proclamations, and is one which carries interest either by virtue of the terms of the contract or instrument under which it is due and payable, or by virtue of the said General Proclamations, then the person from whom the payment is due shall not be entitled to claim the benefit of this Article unless, within three days after the date to which the payment has been postponed by virtue of the said General Proclamations, all interest thereon up to that date is paid.

This Article shall not apply to—

(*a*) Any payment in respect of rent ;

(*b*) Any payment due and payable to or by a retail trader in respect of his business as such trader.

2. The Bills (Re-acceptance) Proclamation shall continue to apply to bills of exchange (other than cheques and bills on demand) accepted before the beginning of the fourth day of August nineteen hundred and fourteen, the date of the original maturity whereof is after the third day of October.

If on the presentation for payment of any such bill the bill is not paid and is not re-accepted under the said Proclamation, then, unless on such presentation the acceptor has expressly refused re-acceptance thereof, the bill shall for all purposes, including the liability of any drawer and indorser or any other party thereto, be deemed to be due and payable on a date one calendar month after the date of its original maturity instead of on the date of its original maturity, and to be a bill for the original amount thereof increased by the amount of interest thereon, calculated from the date of the original maturity to the date of payment at the Bank of England rate current on the date of its original maturity, and paragraph (*a*) of the second General Proclamation shall not apply to any such bill.

If on the presentation for payment of a bill of exchange, the date of maturity of which has before the fourth day of October nineteen hundred and fourteen, become postponed either by virtue of the Bills (Re-acceptance) Proclamation or paragraph (*a*) of the second General Proclamation (whether or not the date of maturity has been further postponed by virtue of the third General Proclamation), the bill is not paid, then the date of maturity shall be deemed to be further postponed for fourteen days from the date of such presentation for payment, and the original amount of the bill shall be deemed to be further increased by the amount of interest on the original amount of the bill for fourteen days, calculated at the Bank of England rate current on the date of such presentation for payment.

4. Save as otherwise expressly provided, nothing in this Proclamation shall affect the application of the General Proclamations to payments to which those proclamations apply, and nothing in this Proclamation shall prevent payments to which this Proclamation applies being made before the expiration of the period for which they are postponed thereunder.

XVIII

COURTS (EMERGENCY POWERS) ACT, 1914.

4 & 5 Geo. V. c. 78.

[Royal Assent, 31st August 1914.]

1.—(1) From and after the passing of this Act no person shall—

(*a*) proceed to execution on, or otherwise to the enforcement of, any judgment or order of any court (whether entered or made before or after the passing of this Act) for the payment or recovery of a sum of money to which this subsection applies, except after such application to such court and such notice as may be provided for by rules or directions under this Act; or

(*b*) levy any distress, take, resume, or enter into possession of any property, exercise any right of re-entry, foreclose, realise any security (except by way of sale by a mortgagee in possession), forfeit any deposit, or enforce the lapse of any policy of insurance to which this subsection applies, for the purpose of enforcing the payment or recovery of any sum of money to which this subsection applies, or, in default of the payment or recovery of any such sums of money, except after such application to such court and such notice as may be provided for by rules or directions under this Act.

This subsection shall not apply to any sum of money (other than rent not being rent at or exceeding fifty pounds per annum) due and payable in pursuance of a contract made after the beginning of the fourth day of August nineteen hundred and fourteen.

This subsection applies to life or endowment policies for an amount not exceeding twenty-five pounds, or payments equivalent thereto, the premiums in respect of which are payable at not longer than monthly intervals, and have been paid for at least the two years preceding the fourth day of August nineteen hundred and fourteen.

(2) If, on any such application, the court to which the application is made is of opinion that time should be given to the person liable to make the payment, on the ground that he is unable immediately to make the payment by reason of circumstances attributable, directly or indirectly, to the present war, the court may, in its absolute discretion, after considering all the circumstances of the case and the position of all the parties, by order, stay execution or defer the operation of any such remedies as aforesaid, for such time and subject to such conditions as the court thinks fit.

(3) Where a bankruptcy petition has been presented against any debtor, and the debtor proves to the satisfaction of the court having jurisdiction in bankruptcy that his inability to pay his debts is due to circumstances attributable, directly or indirectly, to the present war, the court may, in its absolute discretion, after considering all the circumstances of the case and the position of all the parties, at any time stay the proceedings under the petition for such time and subject to such conditions as the court thinks fit.

(4) This Act shall apply to all proceedings for the recovery of possession of tenements under the Small Tenements Recovery Act, 1838, as if they were in all cases proceedings for the payment or recovery of a sum of money due and payable on account of rent.

(5) The Lord Chancellor may make such rules and give such directions as he thinks fit for the purpose of giving full effect to this Act, and may, by those rules or directions, provide for any proceedings for the purposes of this Act being conducted, so far as desirable, in private and for the remission of any fees.

(6) The powers given under this Act shall be in addition to, and not in derogation of, any other powers of any court.

(7) Nothing in this Act shall affect any right or power of pawnbrokers to deal with pledges, or give any power to stay execution or defer the operation of any remedies of a creditor in the case of a sum of money payable by, or recoverable from, the subject of a Sovereign or State at war with His Majesty.

(8) Any stay of execution or of other proceedings, and any postponement of the operation of the remedies of a creditor, which has been granted or ordered by any court since the commencement of the present war and before the passing of this Act shall be as valid as if this Act had been in operation when the stay or postponement was granted or ordered.

2.—(1) This Act may be cited as the Courts (Emergency Powers) Act, 1914.

(2) [Application of the Act to Scotland.]

(3) [Application of the Act to Ireland.]

(4) His Majesty may, by Order in Council, at any time determine the operation of this Act, or provide that this Act shall have effect subject to such limitations as may be contained in the Order; but, subject to the operation of any such Order in Council, this Act shall have effect during the continuance of the present war, and for a period of six months thereafter.

XIX

Contraband of War.

By a Proclamation, dated 4th August, the following articles were to be treated as contraband of war:—

(A) Absolute Contraband.

(1) Arms of all kinds, including arms for sporting purposes, and their distinctive component parts.
(2) Projectiles, charges, and cartridges of all kinds, and their distinctive component parts.
(3) Powder and explosives specially prepared for use in war.
(4) Gun mountings, limber boxes, limbers, military wagons, field forges, and their distinctive component parts.
(5) Clothing and equipment of a distinctively military character.
(6) All kinds of harness of a distinctively military character.
(7) Saddle, draught, and pack animals suitable for use in war.

(8) Articles of camp equipment, and their distinctive component parts.
(9) Armour plates.
(10) Warships, including boats, and their distinctive component parts of such a nature that they can only be used on a vessel of war.
(11) Aeroplanes, airships, balloons, and aircraft of all kinds, and their component parts, together with accessories and articles recognisable as intended for use in connection with balloons and aircraft.
(12) Implements and apparatus designed exclusively for the manufacture of munitions of war, for the manufacture or repair of arms, or war material for use on land and sea.

(B) Conditional Contraband.[1]

(1) Food-stuffs.
(2) Forage and grain, suitable for feeding animals.
(3) Clothing, fabrics for clothing, and boots and shoes suitable for use in war.
(4) Gold and silver in coin or bullion; paper money.
(5) Vehicles of all kinds available for use in war, and their component parts.
(6) Vessels, craft and boats of all kinds: floating docks, parts of docks, and their component parts.
(7) Railway material, both fixed and rolling stock, and materials for telegraphs, wireless telegraphs, and telephones.
(8) Fuel; lubricants.
(9) Powder and explosives not specially prepared for use in war.
(10) Barbed wire, and implements for fixing and cutting the same.
(11) Horse-shoes and shoeing materials.
(12) Harness and saddlery.
(13) Field-glasses, telescopes, chronometers, and all kinds of nautical instruments.

---

[1] The term "conditional contraband" means that the articles referred to are contraband when it is clearly apparent that they are intended to be made use of for military or naval purposes. [*Note in original.*]

XX

British Carriage of Contraband.

By a Proclamation, dated 5th August, British vessels were prohibited from carrying contraband from one foreign port to any other foreign port :[1]—

WHEREAS a state of War exists between Us on the one hand and the German Empire on the other :

AND WHEREAS We have by Proclamation warned all persons resident, carrying on business, or being, in Our Dominions, that it is contrary to law for them to have any commercial intercourse with any person resident, carrying on business, or being in the said Empire, or to trade in or carry any goods, wares, or merchandise destined for or coming from the said Empire, or for or from any person resident, carrying on business, or being therein :

NOW WE do hereby further warn all Our subjects that conformably with that prohibition it is forbidden to carry in British vessels from any Foreign Port to any other Foreign Port any article comprised in the list of contraband of war issued by Us unless the shipowner shall have first satisfied himself that the articles are not intended ultimately for use in the enemy country. Any British vessel acting in contravention of this Proclamation will be liable to capture by Our Naval Forces and to be taken before Our Prize Courts for adjudication, and any of our subjects acting in contravention of this Proclamation will be liable to such penalties as the law prescribes.

---

[1] Query whether this Proclamation applies to articles subsequently included in the list of contraband.

XXI

DECLARATION OF LONDON.

(Partial Adoption.)

Order in Council, dated 20th August 1914 :—

WHEREAS during the present hostilities the Naval Forces of His Majesty will co-operate with the French and Russian Naval Forces, and—

WHEREAS it is desirable that the naval operations of the allied forces, so far as they affect neutral ships and commerce, should be conducted on similar principles, and—

WHEREAS the Governments of France and Russia have informed His Majesty's Government that during the present hostilities it is their intention to act in accordance with the provisions of the Convention known as the Declaration of London, signed on the 26th day of February 1909, so far as may be practicable :

Now, THEREFORE, His Majesty, by and with the advice of His Privy Council, is pleased to order, and it is hereby ordered, that during the present hostilities the Convention known as the Declaration of London shall, subject to the following additions and modifications, be adopted and put in force by His Majesty's Government as if the same had been ratified by His Majesty :—

The additions and modifications are as follows :—

(1) The lists of absolute and conditional contraband contained in the Proclamation, dated 4th August 1914, shall be substituted for the lists contained in Articles 22 and 24 of the said Declaration.

(2) A neutral vessel which succeeded in carrying contraband to the enemy with false papers may be detained for having carried such contraband if she is encountered before she has completed her return voyage.

(3) The destination referred to in Article 33 may be inferred from any sufficient evidence, and (in addition to the presump-

tion laid down in Article 34) shall be presumed to exist if the goods are consigned to or for an agent of the Enemy State, or to or for a merchant or other person under the control of the authorities of the Enemy State.

(4) The existence of a blockade shall be presumed to be known—

(*a*) to all ships which sailed from or touched at an enemy port a sufficient time after the notification of the blockade to the local authorities to have enabled the Enemy Government to make known the existence of the blockade.

(*b*) to all ships which sailed from or touched at a British or allied port after the publication of the declaration of blockade.

(5) Notwithstanding the provisions of Article 35 of the said Declaration, conditional contraband, if shown to have the destination referred to in Article 33, is liable to capture to whatever port the vessel is bound and at whatever port the cargo is to be discharged.

(6) The General Report of the Drafting Committee on the said Declaration presented to the Naval Conference, and adopted by the Conference at the eleventh plenary meeting on 25th February 1909, shall be considered by all Prize Courts as an authoritative statement of the meaning and intention of the said Declaration, and such Courts shall construe and interpret the provisions of the said Declaration by the light of the commentary given therein.[1]

And the Lords Commissioners of His Majesty's Treasury, the Lords Commissioners of the Admiralty, and each of His Majesty's Principal Secretaries of State, the President of the Probate, Divorce, and Admiralty Division of the High Court of Justice, all other Judges of His Majesty's Prize Courts, and all Governors, Officers, and Authorities whom it may concern, are to give the necessary directions herein as to them may respectively appertain.

[1] This paragraph (6) is dropped in No. XXIV. *infra*, which revokes this Order in Council.

XXII

Contraband of War.

Additions to British List of Contraband Articles.

On 21st September, the following Proclamation was issued:—

WHEREAS on the fourth day of August last We did issue Our Royal Proclamation specifying the articles which it was Our intention to treat as Contraband of War during the War between Us and the German Emperor:

AND WHEREAS on the twelfth day of August last We did by Our Royal Proclamation of that date extend our Proclamation aforementioned to the War between Us and the Emperor of Austria, King of Hungary:

AND WHEREAS by an Order in Council of the twentieth day of August 1914, it was ordered that during the present hostilities the Convention known as the Declaration of London should, subject to certain additions and modifications therein specified, be adopted and put in force as if the same had been ratified by Us:

AND WHEREAS it is desirable to add to the list of articles to be treated as Contraband of War during the present War:

AND WHEREAS it is expedient to introduce certain further modifications in the Declaration of London as adopted and put in force:

NOW, THEREFORE, We do hereby declare, by and with the advice of Our Privy Council, that during the continuance of the War, or until We do give further public notice, the articles enumerated in the Schedule hereto will, notwithstanding anything contained in Article 28 of the Declaration of London, be treated as conditional Contraband.

Schedule.

Copper, unwrought.
Lead, pig, sheet, or pipe.
Glycerine.
Ferrochrome.
Hæmatite Iron Ore.
Magnetic Iron Ore.
Rubber.
Hides and Skins, raw or rough tanned (but not including dressed leather).

XXIII

Contraband of War.

Revised List.

The two following Proclamations were issued on 29th October :—

... We do hereby declare, by and with the advice of Our Privy Council, that the list of contraband contained in the schedules to Our Royal Proclamations of the fourth day of August and the twenty-first day of September are hereby withdrawn, and that in lieu thereof during the continuance of the war or until We do give further public notice the articles enumerated in Schedule I. hereto will be treated as absolute contraband, and the articles enumerated in Schedule II. hereto will be treated as conditional contraband.

Schedule I.

1. Arms of all kinds, including arms for sporting purposes, and their distinctive component parts.
2. Projectiles, charges, and cartridges of all kinds, and their distinctive component parts.
3. Powder and explosives specially prepared for use in war.
4. Sulphuric acid.
5. Gun mountings, limber boxes, limbers, military wagons, field forges and their distinctive component parts.
6. Range-finders and their distinctive component parts.
7. Clothing and equipment of a distinctively military character.
8. Saddle, draught, and pack animals suitable for use in war.
9. All kinds of harness of a distinctively military character.
10. Articles of camp equipment and their distinctive component parts.
11. Armour plates.
12. Hæmatite iron ore and hæmatite pig iron.
13. Iron pyrites.
14. Nickel ore and nickel.
15. Ferrochrome and chrome ore.

16. Copper, unwrought.
17. Lead, pig, sheet, or pipe.
18. Aluminium.
19. Ferro-silica.
20. Barbed wire, and implements for fixing and cutting the same.
21. Warships, including boats and their distinctive component parts of such a nature that they can only be used on a vessel of war.
22. Aeroplanes, airships, balloons, and aircraft of all kinds, and their component parts, together with accessories and articles recognisable as intended for use in connection with balloons and aircraft.
23. Motor vehicles of all kinds and their component parts.
24. Motor tyres; rubber.
25. Mineral oils and motor spirit, except lubricating oils.
26. Implements and apparatus designed exclusively for the manufacture of munitions of war, for the manufacture or repair of arms, or war material for use on land and sea.

SCHEDULE II.

1. Foodstuffs.
2. Forage and feeding stuffs for animals.
3. Clothing, fabrics for clothing, and boots and shoes suitable for use in war.
4. Gold and silver in coin or bullion; paper money.
5. Vehicles of all kind other than motor vehicles, available for use in war, and their component parts.
6. Vessels, craft, and boats of all kinds; floating docks, parts of docks, and their component parts.
7. Railway materials, both fixed and rolling stock, and materials for telegraphs, wireless telegraphs, and telephones.
8. Fuel, other than mineral oils. Lubricants.
9. Powder and explosives not specially prepared for use in war.
10. Sulphur.
11. Glycerine.
12. Horseshoes and shoeing materials.
13. Harness and saddlery.
14. Hides of all kinds, dry or wet; pigskins, raw or dressed; leather, undressed or dressed, suitable for saddlery, harness, or military boots.
15. Field glasses, telescopes, chronometers, and all kinds of nautical instruments.

[*Note.*—The following schedule was substituted for Schedule I. on 23rd December 1914. Additions italicised.]

1. Arms of all kinds, including arms for sporting purposes, and their distinctive component parts.

2. Projectiles, charges, and cartridges of all kinds, and their distinctive component parts.

3. Powder and explosives specially prepared for use in war.

4. Ingredients of explosives, viz., *nitric acid,* sulphuric acid, *glycerine, acetone, calcium acetate and all other metallic acetates, sulphur, potassium nitrate, the fractions of the distillation products of coal tar between benzol and cresol inclusive, aniline, methylaniline, dimethylaniline, ammonium perchlorate, sodium perchlorate, sodium chlorate, barium chlorate, ammonium nitrate, cyanamide, potassium chlorate, calcium nitrate, mercury.*

5. *Resinous products, camphor and turpentine (oil and spirit).*

6. Gun mountings, limber boxes, limbers, military wagons, field forges, and their distinctive component parts.

7. Range-finders and their distinctive component parts.

8. Clothing and equipment of a distinctively military character.

9. Saddle, draught, and pack animals suitable for use in war.

10. All kinds of harness of a distinctively military character.

11. Articles of camp equipment and their distinctive component parts.

12. Armour plates.

13. *Ferro alloys, including ferro-tungsten, ferro-molybdenum, ferro-manganese, ferro-vanadium,* ferro-chrome.

14. The following metals: — *Tungsten, molybdenum, vanadium,* nickel, *selenium, cobalt,* hæmatite pig-iron, *manganese.*

15. The following ores:—*Wolframite, scheelite, molybdenite, manganese ore,* nickel ore, chrome ore, hæmatite iron ore, zinc ore, lead ore, *bauxite.*

16. Aluminium, *alumina and salts of aluminium.*

17. *Antimony, together with the sulphides and oxides of antimony.*

18. Copper, unwrought *and part wrought,* and *copper wire.*

19. Lead, pig, sheet, or pipe.

20. Barbed wire, and implements for fixing and cutting the same.

21. Warships, including boats and their distinctive component parts of such a nature that they can only be used on a vessel of war.

22. *Submarine sound signalling apparatus.*

23. Aeroplanes, airships, balloons, and aircraft of all kinds, and their component parts, together with accessories and articles recognisable as intended for use in connection with balloons and aircraft.

24. Motor vehicles of all kinds and their component parts.

25. Tyres for motor vehicles *and for cycles*, together with *articles or materials especially adapted for use in the manufacture or repair of tyres.*

26. Rubber (including raw, waste, and reclaimed rubber) and *goods made wholly of rubber.*

27. Iron pyrites.

28. Mineral oils and motor spirit, except lubricating oils.

29. Implements and apparatus designed exclusively for the manufacture of munitions of war, for the manufacture or repair of arms, or war material for use on land and sea.

Sulphur and glycerine were taken out of Schedule II.

XXIV

Declaration of London.

[*Further modifications*, 29th *October* 1914.]

... His Majesty, by and with the advice of His Privy Council, is pleased to order, and it is hereby ordered, as follows :—

1. During the present hostilities the provisions of the Convention known as the Declaration of London shall, subject to the exclusion of the lists of contraband and non-contraband, and to the modifications hereinafter set out, be adopted and put in force by His Majesty's Government.

The modifications are as follows :—

(i.) A neutral vessel, with papers indicating a neutral destination, which, notwithstanding the destination shown on the papers, proceeds to an enemy port, shall be liable to capture and condemnation if she is encountered before the end of her next voyage.

(ii.) The destination referred to in Article 33 of the said Declaration shall (in addition to the presumptions laid down in Article 34) be presumed to exist if the goods are consigned to or for an agent of the enemy State.

(iii.) Notwithstanding the provisions of Article 35 of the said Declaration, conditional contraband shall be liable to capture on board a vessel bound for a neutral port if the goods are consigned "to order," or if the ship's papers do not show who is the consignee of the goods, or if they show a consignee of the goods in territory belonging to or occupied by the enemy.

(iv.) In the cases covered by the preceding paragraph, (iii.), it shall lie upon the owners of the goods to prove that their destination was innocent.

2. Where it is shown to the satisfaction of one of His Majesty's Principal Secretaries of State that the enemy Government is drawing supplies for its armed forces from or through a neutral country, he may direct that in respect of ships bound for a port in that country, Article 35 of the said Declaration shall not apply. Such direction shall be notified in the *London Gazette*, and shall operate until the same is withdrawn. So long as such direction is in force, a vessel which is carrying conditional contraband to a port in that country shall not be immune from capture.

3. The Order in Council of the 20th August 1914, directing the adoption and enforcement during the present hostilities of the Convention known as the Declaration of London, subject to the additions and modifications therein specified, is hereby repealed.

4. This Order may be cited as "the Declaration of London Order in Council, No. 2, 1914."

XXV

Discounting Bills of Exchange.

On this subject the following official announcement was issued:—

The Bank of England are prepared, on the application of the holder of any approved bill of exchange accepted before the 4th day of August 1914, to discount at any time before its due date, at Bank rate, without recourse to such holder, and upon its maturity the Bank of England will, in order to assist the resumption of normal business operations, give the acceptor the opportunity, until further notice, of postponing payment, interest being payable in the meantime at 2 per cent. over Bank rate varying. Arrangements will be made to carry this scheme into effect so as to preserve all existing obligations.

The Bank of England will be prepared for this purpose to approve such bills of exchange as are customarily discounted by them, and also good trade bills, and the acceptances of such foreign and Colonial firms and bank agencies as are established in Great Britain.

Treasury Chambers, 12th August 1914.[1]

XXVI

Patents, Designs, and Trade Marks.

[Rules, dated 21st August 1914.]

By virtue of the provisions of the Patents, Designs, and Trade Marks (Temporary Rules) Act, 1914,

[1] On 4th September further arrangements were promulgated for securing the success of this attempt to restore normal business relations.

the Board of Trade hereby make the following Rules :—

1. The Board of Trade may, on the application of any person, and subject to such terms and conditions, if any, as they may think fit, order the avoidance or suspension, in whole or in part, of any patent or license granted to a subject of any State at war with His Majesty, and the Board, before granting any such application, may require to be satisfied on the following heads :—

   (a) That the patentee or licensee is the subject of a State at war with His Majesty;
   (b) That the person applying intends to manufacture, or cause to be manufactured, the patented article, or to carry on, or cause to be carried on, the patented process;
   (c) That it is in the general interests of the country or of a section of the community, or of a trade, that such article should be manufactured or such process carried on as aforesaid.

The fee to be paid on any such application shall be that specified in the First Schedule to these Rules and the fee payable on depositing foreign documents or other papers for the purpose of a record not already provided for under the Patents and Designs Act, 1907, and the Trade Marks Act, 1905, shall be that specified in the First Schedule to these Rules.

An application under this section must be made on Patents Form No. 36 contained in the second Schedule to these Rules, and shall be filed at the Patent Office.

The Board of Trade may at any time, in their absolute discretion, revoke any avoidance or suspension of any patent or license ordered by them.

For the purpose of exercising in any case the powers of avoiding or suspending a patent or license, the Board of Trade may appoint such person or persons as they shall think fit to hold an inquiry.

Any application to the Board for the avoidance or suspension of any patent or license may be referred for hearing and inquiry to such person or persons, who shall report thereon to the Board.

Provided always that the Board of Trade may at any time, if in their absolute discretion they deem it expedient in the public interest, order the avoidance or suspension, in whole or in part, of any such patent or license, upon such terms and conditions, if any, as they may think fit.

2. The Comptroller may at any time during the continuance of these Rules avoid or suspend any proceedings on any application made under the Patents and Designs Act, 1907, and the Trade Marks Act, 1905, by a subject of any State at war with His Majesty.

3. The Comptroller may also, at any time during the continuance of these Rules, extend the time prescribed by the Patents and Designs Act, 1907, or the Trade Marks Act, 1905, or any Rules made thereunder, for doing any act or filing any document, upon such terms and subject to such conditions as he may think fit in the following cases, namely :—

(a) Where it is shown to his satisfaction that the applicant, patentee, or proprietor, as the case may be, was prevented from doing the said act, or filing the said document, by reason of active service or enforced absence from this country, or any other circumstances arising from the present state of war, which, in the opinion of the Comptroller, would justify such extension :

(b) Where the doing of any act would, by reason of the circumstances arising from the present state of war, be prejudicial or injurious to the rights or interests of any applicant, patentee, or proprietor as aforesaid.

4. The term "person" used in these Rules shall, in addition to the meaning given thereto by section 19 of the Interpretation Act, 1889, include any Government Department.

5. All things required or authorised to be done by, to, or before the Board of Trade, may be done by, to, or before the President or a Secretary or an Assistant Secretary of the Board, or any person authorised in that behalf by the President of the Board.

All documents purporting to be orders made by the Board of Trade and to be sealed with the seal of the Board, or to be signed by a Secretary or an Assistant Secretary of the Board, or by any person authorised in that behalf by the President of the Board, shall be received in evidence, and shall be deemed to be such orders without further proof, unless the contrary is shown.

A certificate signed by the President of the Board of Trade that any order made or act done is the order or act of the Board shall be conclusive evidence of the fact so certified.

6. These Rules shall come into operation as and from the seventh day of August 1914.

First Schedule.

	£	s.	d.
Fee payable on application under Rule 1 to Board of Trade to avoid or suspend patent rights or license	2	0	0
Fee payable on depositing Foreign Documents or other papers for the purpose of a record not already provided for under the Patents and Designs Act, 1907, and the Trade Marks Act, 1905	0	2	6

Dated the 21st day of August 1914.

Walter Runciman,
President of the Board of Trade.

Approved :—
William Jones,
W. Wedgwood Benn,
Lords Commissioners of His Majesty's Treasury.

Second Schedule.

Patents Form No. 36.

PATENT £2.

PATENTS, DESIGNS AND TRADE MARKS (TEMPORARY RULES) ACT, 1914.

(*a*) I (or We) .... (*a*) Here insert (in full) name, address, and description or calling of person or persons applying.

hereby request the Board of Trade to order the avoidance or suspension of

the Letters Patent No. (*b*)..................of.............................. (*b*) Here insert number and year of Patent, or particulars of License as the case may be.

or the License granted to (*b*).......................under Letters Patent

No. (*b*).......................of..................................

Dated this..................day of...............................

(Signed)................................

XXVII

Patents and Designs.

[*Rule, dated 7th September* 1914.]

In any case in which the Board of Trade make an Order by virtue of the powers vested in them under the provisions of the Patents, Designs and Trade Marks (Temporary) Rules Acts, 1914, and under any Rules made under these Acts or either of them, avoiding or suspending in whole or in part a Patent, or avoiding or suspending the registration and all or any rights conferred by the registration of any Design, the Board may in their discretion grant in favour of persons other than the subject of any State at war with His Majesty, licenses to make, use, exercise, or vend the patented invention or registered design so avoided or suspended, upon such terms and conditions, and either for the whole term of the patent or registration of the design, or for such less period as the Board of Trade may think fit.

[*Note.*—By Orders of the Board of Trade of 23rd September and 4th November 1914, license was given to pay the necessary fees for obtaining the grant or renewal of patents, etc., in an enemy country, and to pay on behalf of an "enemy" fees payable in the United Kingdom on similar applications here.]

XXVIII

Prize Courts in Neutral Countries and Cyprus.

[4 & 5 Geo. V. c. 79.]

[*Royal Assent,* 18*th September* 1914.]

1. If His Majesty is pleased to confer jurisdiction in

matters of prize on any of the following courts, that is to say :—

(a) His Britannic Majesty's Supreme Court for the Dominions of the Sublime Ottoman !Porte in Egypt ;
(b) His Britannic Majesty's Court for Zanzibar in Zanzibar ;
(c) The Supreme Court of Cyprus in Cyprus ;

the Court shall, in respect of the present war, have, under the Naval Prize Courts Acts, 1864 to 1914, the jurisdiction thereby conferred on a Vice-Admiralty Prize Court, and those Acts and any Order in Council made thereunder shall apply accordingly, subject to such modifications (if any) as to His Majesty in Council may appear expedient or necessary.

2. This Act may be cited as the Prize Courts (Egypt, Zanzibar, and Cyprus) Act, 1914.

XXIX

Prize Courts in Neutral Countries.

[Order in Council, dated 30th day of September 1914.]

WHEREAS a state of war now exists between this Country on the one hand, and the German Empire and the Dual Monarchy of Austria-Hungary on the other hand, so that His Majesty's fleets and ships may lawfully seize all ships, vessels and goods belonging to the German Empire or to the Dual Monarchy of Austria-Hungary, or the citizens and subjects of either country or other persons inhabiting within any of the countries, territories, or dominions of the said Empire, or of the said Dual Monarchy, and bring the same to judgment within any such Courts as shall be duly commissionated to take cognizance thereof.

AND WHEREAS by Section 1 of the Prize Courts (Egypt, Zanzibar, and Cyprus) Act, 1914, it is enacted that :—

"If His Majesty is pleased to confer jurisdiction in matters of prize on any of the following courts, that is to say :—

"(*a*) His Britannic Majesty's Supreme Court for the Dominions of the Sublime Ottoman Porte in Egypt ;
"(*b*) His Britannic Majesty's Court for Zanzibar in Zanzibar ;
"(*c*) The Supreme Court of Cyprus in Cyprus ;

"the Court shall, in respect of the present war, have, under the Naval Prize Courts Acts, 1864 to 1914, the jurisdiction thereby conferred on a Vice-Admiralty Prize Court, and those Acts and any Order in Council made thereunder shall apply accordingly, subject to such modifications (if any) as to His Majesty in Council may appear expedient or necessary."

AND WHEREAS His Majesty is of opinion that jurisdiction in matters of prize should be conferred on all of the said courts :

His Majesty is therefore pleased, by and with the advice of His Privy Council, to order, and it is hereby ordered, that a Commission in the form of the draft annexed hereto shall issue under the Great Seal of the United Kingdom authorising the Commissioners for executing the office of Lord High Admiral to will and require His Britannic Majesty's Supreme Court for the Dominions of the Sublime Ottoman Porte in Egypt, His Britannic Majesty's Court for Zanzibar in Zanzibar, and the Supreme Court of Cyprus in Cyprus, and all the Judges of those Courts to take cognizance of and judicially proceed upon all and all manner of captures, seizures, prizes and reprisals of all ships, vessels and goods that are or shall be taken and all other matters of prize falling within the jurisdiction of Prize Courts, and to hear and determine the same and, according to the course of Admiralty and the Law of Nations, and the Statutes, Rules, and Regulations for the time being in force in that behalf, to adjudge and condemn all such ships, vessels and goods as shall belong to the German Empire or to the Dual Monarchy of Austria-Hungary or the citizens or subjects of either country, or to any other persons inhabiting within any of the countries, territories, or dominions of the said Empire of the said Dual Monarchy.

F.—*Authors' Notes.*

I

Continuous Voyage.

Citing *Hobbs* v. *Henning* (17 C.B. (N.S.) 819), a writer in the *Law Magazine* (probably Twiss) infers (p. 374 *supra*) that "if the doctrine of ulterior destination should again come for argument before the courts in England, it would probably be discussed and determined in a spirit less antagonistic to neutral rights than that on which the American judges proceeded, and more in harmony with the decisions of Lord Stowell and Sir W. Grant, which had previously been accepted as the correct exposition of the Law of Nations on this interesting question."

It is true that in *Seymour* v. *London, etc., Insurance Co.*[1] Willes and Keating, JJ., came to a decision entirely contrary to that arrived at by Erle, C.J., Byles and Keating, JJ., in *Hobbs* v. *Henning*[2]—*i.e.*, by the full court. They distinguished that decision with great subtlety on the ground that there was there pleaded no specific intention that the goods should reach any particular belligerent consignee, but merely a general expectation that they would reach the belligerent state. It is clear from the language of Erle, C.J., in *Hobbs* v. *Henning* that he (and probably Byles, J.) entertained no such distinction. They do indeed affirm that a mere vague allegation of an ulterior purpose will not do. But they do not say for a moment that a more precise allegation will. On the contrary, they assert in the plainest terms that "[the defendants] were not liable, unless it distinctly appeared that the voyage was to an enemy's port" (citing the *Imina*, ubi supra).

[1] (1872) L.J. C.P 193.
[2] (1864) 17 C.B. (N.S.) 791.

II

PUBLIC ENGAGEMENTS TOWARDS ENEMY PERSONS.

It is generally accepted that money lent to a government by the subjects of a foreign state will not only be exempt from confiscation if war breaks out between the two Powers, but will even have interest punctually paid upon it—though it may be questioned whether capital would be repaid, according to stipulation, *flagrante bello*. The reason is said to be that loans could never be placed if their interest were liable to be suspended by the outbreak of war (which might indeed be provoked for that very purpose). The classical instance is that of the Russo-Dutch Loan, interest on which was paid throughout the Crimean War.

The principle does not seem to extend to other obligations of the belligerent state. The parliamentary annuity payable to the Grand Duchess of Mecklenburg-Strelitz, aunt of the Queen, has been suspended; though, equally with Consols, reposing on the engagement of the British Crown. The attitude towards Prussia of Her Royal and Grand Ducal Highness is very plain from the letters printed at the end of vol. i. of the life of Princess Mary of Cambridge. The hearts—though not the bayonets—of the Strelitz Court were with the forces of "right and justice" in 1866: and it may confidently be supposed still are so.

It seems, however, that a public treaty may alter the case. H.I. and R.H. the Duchess of Coburg still receives her payments, although the late Duke was a German sovereign. This annuity has been stated by Mr Asquith to be continued because (1) the Duke never ceased to be a British subject (which would be irrelevant, if the Court of Appeal's theory is true, that nationality is immaterial); (2) a public treaty guarantees the payment.

The treaty is printed in 65 State Papers, p. 62. By Art. 12, Great Britain engaged with Russia to pay an annuity to the Duchess when a widow, or to a trustee (*personne en fidéicommis*) for Her Imperial Highness. If, as is probable, the money is paid to trustees, the question of their right to transmit it to the august beneficiary would then arise. Her residence was not stated by Mr Asquith, but her domicile is probably Coburgan.

LIST OF CASES

Abigail, the, (1802) 4 C.R. 72 : 337
Abo, the, (1855) 24 L.T., O.S. 5 : 380
Adam, *in re*, (1837) 1 Moo., P.C., 460, 477 : 55
Adams *v.* Ward (*Times*, 20th Feb. 1914) : 159
Adonis, the, (1804) 5 C.R. 256 : 380
Adriana, the, (1799) 1 C.R. 313 : 322
A. G. *v.* Kissane, 32 Ir. L.R. : 45
A. G. *v.* Tomline, 12 C.D. 214 : 11
A. G. *v.* van Reenen, [1904] A.C. 117 : 21
A. G. *v.* Weedon, Parker 267 : 293
Albrecht *v.* Sussman, (1813) 2 V. & B. 323 : 271, 292
Alciator *v.* Smith, (1812) 3 Camp. 244 : 254, 269, 271
Alexander, the, (1801) 4 C.R. 93 : 384
Alien Enemy Cases, the (*Times*, 20th Jan. 1915) : 254, 266, 293
Aline and Fanny, the, (1856) Spinks 322 : 367
Allen *v.* Russell, 3 Am. Law Register : 276

Alsenius *v.* Nygren, (1854) 4 El. & Bl. 217 ; 1 Jur. (N.S.) 16 ; 24 L.R., Q.B. 19 ; 3 W.R. 25 : 269, 271
Amado, the. (1847) Newberry 400 : 313, 346
Amor Parentum, the, (1799) 1 C.R. 303 : 337
Amy Warwick, etc., the, (1862) 2 Black 635 : 397
Ann, the, 1 Dods. 223 : 308
Ann Green, the, (1812) 1 Gall. 291 : 329
Anna Catharina, the, (1802) 4 C.R. 119 : 321, 328, 329, 388
Antoine *v.* Morshead, 6 Taunt. 237 : 273
Apollo (Bottcher), the, (1802) 4 C.R. 158 : 372
Ariadne, the, 2 Wheat. 143 : 285
Ariel, the, (1857) 11 Moo., P.C., 119 : 331, 333
Atalanta, the, (1808) 6 C.R. 459 : 389
Atlas, the, (1801) 3 C.R. 299 : 329, 380
Aurora, the, (1802) 4 C.R. 219 : 330
Auster *v.* London Motor C. Works (*Times*, 21st Oct. 1914) : 409

558   LIST OF CASES

Avery *v.* Bowden, 6 E. & B. 975 : 420

Baker *v.* Oates, (1877) 2 Q.B.D. 171 : 410
Baltazzi *v.* Ryder, (1858) 12 Moo., P.C., 168 : 384
Baltica, the, (1855) Spink 264 : 292, 331, 333
Barker *v.* Blakes, (1808) 9 East 283 : 421
Barker *v.* Hodgson, (1814) 2 M. & S. 271 : 417, 422
Barrick *v.* Buba, 2 C.B. (N.S.) 563 : 300
Barrow *v.* Arnaud, 8 Q.B. 595 : 13
Bate's Case, 16
Bauvis *v.* Keppel, (1766) 2 Wils. 314 : 18, 157
Belvidere, the, (1813) 1 Dods. 351 : 335
Bentzon *v.* Boyle, (1815) 9 Cranch 195 : 318, 330
Berlin, the (*Times*, 1914) : 222
Bernardi *v.* Motteux, (1781) 2 Douglas 581 : 361
Bernon, the, (1798) 1 C.R. 103 : 316, 318
Blackburn *v.* Thompson, 3 Camp. 61 : 337
Blake's Case, 2 M. & S. 428 : 91
Blundell *v.* Rex, [1905] 1 K.B. 516 : 12
Boussmaker, *in re* : 262
Brandon *v.* Nesbit, (1794) 6 T.R. 23 : 272, 300
Bristowe *v.* Towers, (1794) 6 T.R. 35 : 272, 273
Bromley *v.* Hesseltine, (1807) 1 Camp. 75 : 303, 337

Brown & Burton *v.* Franklyn, K.P. (10 Will. III.), Carthew, 474 : 339
Brown *v.* Hiatt, (1870) 2 Dill. 372 : 293
Brown *v.* U.S., (1814) 8 Cranch 110 : 288, 305
Burdett *v.* Abbott, 4 Taunt. 449 : 30
Buron *v.* Denman, (1842) 2 Ex. 167 : 207

Calvin's Case, 4 Rep. 1 : 250
Cameron *v.* Kyte, (1835) 3 Knapp. 342 : 209
Cammell *v.* Sewell, (1860) 5 H. & N. 728 : 332
Campbell *v.* Hall, (1774) 1 Cowp. 204 : 203, 205, 206, 209
Cape of Good Hope Ships, the, (1799) 2 C.R. 274 : 337
Carl Walter, the, (1802) 4 C.R. 207 : 331
Carolina, the, (1799) 1 C.R. 304 : 330
Carolina, the, (1802) 4 C.R. 258 : 388-89
Carritt *v.* Bradley, [1903] A.C. 233 : 226
Case of Arms, Poph. 121 : 45, 47
Case of Proclamations, 12 Co. 74 : 44
Casseres *v.* Bell, (1799) 8 T.R. 166 : 269
Castrique *v.* Imrie, (1870) L.R. 4 E. I. App. 414 : 332
Charlotte, the, (1804) 5 C.R. 280 : 337, 380
Charlotte Christine, the, (1805) 6 C.R. 101 : 367
Chavasse, *ex parte*, *in re* Grazebrook, 4 De G.J. & S. 662 : 44, 422
Citto, the, 3 C.R. 38 : 325

LIST OF CASES 559

Clarke v. Morey, (1813) 10 Johns. (Amer.) 69 : 270
Clover v. Adams, (1881) 6 Q.B.D. 622 : 410
Commercen, the, (1815) 1 Wheat. 382 : 373, 391
Conn v. Penn, 1 Peter C.C. 496 : 274
Conqueror, the, 2 C.R. 307 : 308
Continental Tyre, etc., Co., Ltd., v. T. Tilling, Ltd. (Times, 24th Nov. 1914, 20th Jan. 1915) : 266
Cook v. Sprigg, [1899] A.C. 572 : 208, 209
Coolidge v. Inglee, (1816) 13 Mass. 26 : 279, 285
Cooper v. Hawkin, [1904] 2 K.B. 164 : 59
Coopman, (1798) : 320
Cope v. Sharpe, [1910] 1 K.B. 496 : 10
Coppell v. Hall, (1868) 7 Wall. 542 : 292
Coronation Cases, the, [1903] 2 K.B. 683, 740, 756 : 413
Cosmopolite, the, 4 C.R. 10 : 298
Cousine Marianna, the, (1810) 1 Edw. 346 : 330
Crew & Co. v. G.W.R., (1887) W.N. 161 : 418
Cunningham v. Dunn, (1878) 3 C.P.D. 443 : 412, 417

Daijin, the, Takahashi, R.-J. 338 : 337
Danaous, the, 4 C.R. 255 n. : 308
Daubigny v. Davallon, (1794) 2 Anstr. 467 : 271, 305
Daubuz v. Morshead, (1815) 6 Taunt. 332 : 273
Dauckebaar Africaan, the, (1798) 1 C.R. 107 : 337

Davidson, re, [1899] 2 Q.B. 103 : 410
Dawkins v. Paulet, 5 Q.B. 108 : 90, 91, 159, 160
Dawkins v. Rokeby, L.R. 8 Q.B. 255 ; 7 H.L. 744 : 90, 159
Dean v. Nelson, (1869) 10 Wall. 158 : 290
De Dohse v. R., (1886) H.L. 66 : 119
De Jager v. A. G. (Natal), [1907] A.C. 326 : 35, 248
De Luneville v. Phillips, (1806) 2 N.R. 97 : 313
Denniston v. Imbrie, (1818) 3 Wash. 396 : 274
Derrier v. Arnaud, (7 Gul. III.) 4 Mod. 405 : 270
De Wahl v. Braune, 25 L.J. (N.S.) Ex. 343 : 277, 292, 293
De Wolf v. N.Y. Fire In. Co., (1822) 20 Johns. (Amer.) 228 : 361
Diana, the, (1803) 5 C.R. 67 : 413
Dickinson v. Lade (Times, 25th April 1914) : 150
Diligentia, the, (1814) 1 Dods. 314 : 358
Don v. Lippmann, (1837) 5 Cl. & F. 6 : 274, 291
Dorsey v. Kyle, (1869) 30 Maryland 512 : 289, 290
Dos Hermanos, the, (1817) 2 Wheat. 81 : 366
Doss v. Sec. for India, (1875) L.R. 19 Eq. 509 : 211
Douglas v. Molford, (20 Edw. IV.) : 268
Dree Gebrocders, the, (1802) 4 C.R. 234 : 302, 322
Duncan Fox & Co. v. Schrempt & Bonke (Times, 19th Dec. 1914) : 303, 344

560 LIST OF CASES

Dunn v. R., [1896] 1 Q.B. 117, 121 : 119, 126

Edwards v. Parcott, Morr. 4535 : 291
Elbers v. Krafts, (1819) 16 Johns. (Amer.), 128, 132 : 315, 316
Eliza Ann, the, Dods. 247 : 395
Elphinstone v. Bedreechund, 2 St. Tr. (N.S.) 379 : 24
Elphinstone v. Bedreechund, St. Tr. (N.S.) 379 : 207
Emanuel, the, (1799) 1 C.R. 296 : 308
Embden, the, (1798) 1 C.R. 16 : 312
English R. C. Colleges in France, 2 Knapp. 23 : 265
Entick v. Carrington, 19 St. Tr. 1030 : 14, 41
Erin, the, Wheat. Capt. 50 : 361
Esposito v. Bowden, (1857) 7 E. & B. 764 : 4, 300
Exchange, the, (1808) 1 Edw. 43 : 384

Fairfax v. Hunter, 7 Cranch 603 : 305
Fanny, the, (1814) 1 Dods. 443 : 388
Fenix, the, (1854) Spinks 3 : 369
Field v. Metrop. Police (Receiver), [1907] 2 K.B. 860 : 25
Filor's Case, (1867) 3 Ct. of Claims 25, 36 : 277, 286
Finlay v. L.G.W. Co., (1870) 23 L.T. 251 : 419
Flight v. Page, (1801) 3 B. & P. 295 n. : 417

Flindt v. Waters, (1812) 15 East 260 : 273
Ford v. Cotesworth, (1870) L.R. 4 Q.B. 127 ; 5 *ibid.* 544 : 412, 417
Fourie, *in re*, 17 Buchanan 173 : 7, 23
Fox, *ex parte*, (1793) 5 T.R. 276 : 127
Fox, the, (1811) 1 Dods. 314 : 358
Frances, the, (1814) 8 Cranch 419 : 334
Francis, the, (1812) 1 Gall. 445, 614, 618 : 329. (Same ship as *Frances*)
Franciska, the, (1855) 10 Moo., P.C., 37 : 385
Franconia, the, (1876) 2 Ex. D. 126 : 203, 206
Freeman v. Fairlie, 1 Moo. Ind. App. : 324
Furtado v. Rogers, (1802) 3 B. & P. 191 : 284

Gamba's Case, (1803) 4 East 409 : 278
Geipel v. Smith, (1880) L.R. 7 Q.B.D. 104 : 416, 419
Gibson v. Service, (1814) 5 Taunt. 433 : 422
Gidley v. Palmerston, (1822) 3 Br. & B. 275 : 126
Glierktigheit, the, (1805) 6 C.R. 58 n. : 365
Goddard v. Swinton, Morr. 4533 : 291
Grant v. Gould, 2 H.Bl. 69 : 20, 88, 89
Griswold v. Waddington, (1818) 15 Johns. (Amer.) 57 ; (1819) 16 *ibid.* 438 : 270, 280
Gute Gesellschaft Michael, the, (1801) 4 C.R. 94 : 371

LIST OF CASES

Haabet, the, (1799) 2 C.R. 174 : 372
Haabet (*Giertsen*), the, (1805) 6 C.R. 54 : 363-65
Haase, the, (1799) 1 C.R. 286 : 337
Hadley *v.* Clarke, (1799) 8 T.R. 259 : 416
Hammersmith Railway Company *v.* Brand, (1868) H.L. 171 : 61
Hampton, the, (1866) 5 Wall. 372 : 334
Handcock *v.* Baker, 2 B. & P. 234 : 26
Hanger *v.* Abbott, 6 Wall. 532 : 277
Hannan *v.* Kingston, 3 Camp. 152 : 273
Harmony, the, (1800) 2 C.R. 322 : 311, 314, 317
Hawley *v.* Steele, (1877) 6 C.D. 526 : 61
Hearson *v.* Churchill, [1892] 2 Q.B. 144 : 92, 125
Heathfield *v.* Chilton, (1767) 4 Burr. 2016 : 361
Heinrich, the, (1871) L.R., 3 A. & E. 424 : 415
Helen, the, (1865) L.R. 1 A. &. E. : 1
Hennen *v.* Gilman, (1868) 20 La. An. 241 : 287
Herman, the, (1802) 4 C.R. 228 : 303, 323
Herstelder, the, (1799) 1 C.R. 113 : 337
Hick *v.* Raymond, [1892] 7 Asp. 233 : 417
Hoop, the, 1 C.R. 165 : 4, 299, 345
Hoppin *v.* Leppett, (1737) Andr. 76 : 270
Hottentot Venus, the, 13 East 195 : 55
Hunter *v.* Coleman, I.R., [1914] 372 : 16, 57

Hutchinson *v.* Brock, 11 Mass. 119 : 284
Hyatt *v.* James, (1867) 2 Bush (Ky.) 463 : 286

Imina, the, (1800) 3 C.R. 167 : 375
Indian Chief, the, 3 C.R. 22 : 308
Inst. of Patent Agents *v.* Lockwood. [1894] A.C. 347 : 74
Ionian Ships, the, (1856) Spinks 193 : 362
Irish R. C. Colleges in France, 2 Knapp. 51 : 265
Isaacson *v.* Durant, L.R. 7 Q.B. 60 : 48, 203

J. M. Schroeder, the, (1800) 3 C.R. 155 : 385
Jacobus Johannes, the, (1785) : 320
Jaffrow Catherine, the, (1804) 5 C.R. 140 : 278, 302
Jan Frederick, the, (1804) 5 C.R. 128 : 330
Janson *v.* Driefontein Cons. Mines, [1902] A.C. 484 : 5, 14, 255, 309
Jecker *v.* Montgomery, (1855) 18 Howard 110 : 303
Jemmy, the, (1801) 4 C.R. 31 : 331
Johanna Emilie, the, (1854) Spinks 14 : 306
Jonge Hermanus, the, (1801) 4 C.R. 95 : 380
Jonge Klassina, the, (1809) 5 C.R. 301 : 309, 311, 312, 323
Jonge Margaretha, the, (1799) 1 C.R. 189 : 372
Jonge Pieter, the, (1801) 4 C.R. 79 : 301, 303, 380
Jonge Ruiter, the, (1809) Acton 116 : 313

LIST OF CASES

Joseph, the, (1813) 1 Gall. 546: 346
Josephine, the, (1802) 4 C.R. 25: 330
Julia, the, 8 Cranch 181: 288, 298, 388, 391
Julius v. Oxford (B.), (1880) 5 A.C. 214: 78
Juno, the (*Times*, 15th Dec. 1914): 303
Jupp v. Whitaker, 58 S.J. 819: 409

Kershaw v. Kelsey, (1868) 100 Mass. 561: 279, 301
Key & Hubbard v. Pearse, (1742) Douglas 606: 338
Kinloch v. Sec. for India, (1886) L.R. 15 C.D.: 137
Kok, *in re*, 9 Buchanan, (S.C.) 62: 7, 15

La Bellone v. Le Porcher, 1 Pistoye et Duverdy 149: 398
Le Bret v. Papillon, (1844) 4 East 503: 284
Leucade, the, (1856) Spinks 217: 363, 366
Levy v. Stewart, (1870) 11 Wall. 244: 293
Liesbet van der Toll, the, (1804) 5 C.R. 283: 387
Lindo v. Rodney, (1781-82) 2 Douglas 614: 338-39
Lubbock v. Potts, (1806) 7 East 451: 421
Ludlow v. Ramsay, (1870) 11 Wall. 581: 290, 293
Luther v. Borden, 7 How. 1: 24, 25
Lyons, Mayor of, 1 Moo. Ind. App. 175: 203

M'Growther's Case, (1746) Fost. Crown Cas. 13: 37, 49
M'Veigh v. U.S., (1870) 11 Wall. 259: 289
Madeiros v. Hill, (1832) 8 Bi. 231: 422
Manilla, the, 1 Edw. 4, and Appx. D: 5
Mansergh's Case, (1861) 1 B. & S. 400: 123
Marais, *ex parte*, [1902] A.C. 109: 6, 7, 23
Maria, the, (1799) 1 C.R. 349*a*: 358
Marianna, the, (1805) 6 C.R. 24: 333
Marie Française, the, 6 C.R. 282: 341
Marie Glaeser, the (*Times*, 17th Sept. 1914): 335
Maxim-Nordenfelt, etc., v. Nordenfelt, [1894] A.C. 534: 99
Maxwell v. Grunhut (*Times*, 25th Nov. 1914): 275
Mentor, the, (1799) 1 C.R. 183: 398
Mercurius, the, (1798) 1 C.R. 84: 384
Merrick v. Van Santrood, (1866) 34 N.Y. 208, 8 Barbour 574: 262
Merrimac, the, (1814) 8 Cranch 528: 330
Metropolitan Asylums Board v. Hill, (1881) A.C. 193: 61
Mighell v. Sultan of Johore, [1894] 1 Q.B. 149: 203
Miller v. Knox, 4 Bi. N.C. 574: 45
Milligan, *ex parte*, 4 Wall. 2: 24
Minerva (*Knuttel*), the, (1807) 6 C.R. 396: 215

LIST OF CASES

Minerva, the, Wheat. Capt. 50 : 360
Miramichi, the (*Times*, 24th Nov. 1914) : 329
Mitchell *v.* Harnony, 13 How. 115 : 24
Mitchell *v.* R., [1896] 1 Q.B. 121 (*n*) : 119, 126
Mitsui *v.* Mumford (*Times*, 2nd Dec. 1914) : 337
Mogul SS. Co. *v.* M'Gregor, Gow & Co., [1891] A.C. : 100
Montara, the, [1902] Takahashi, R.-J. 633 : 388
Moosseaux *v.* Urquhart, (1867) 1 La. An. 482 : 285
Möwe, the (*Times*, 1914) : 369
Munkittrick *v.* Perryman, 74 L.T. 149 : 257
Musgrove *v.* Ah Toy, [1891] A.C. 272 : 54

Nathan, *in re*, (1887) 12 Q.B.D. 461 : 58
Neds Point Battery, *in re*, [1903] 1 R. 2 K.B. 198 : 12
Negotie en Zeevaart, the, (1782) 1 C.R. 109, 116 : 337
Neptunus, the, (1800) 3 C.R. 108 : 372
Nereide, the, (1815) 9 Cranch 438 : 388
N.Y. *v.* Central Ry. of N.J., (1876) 48 Barbour 478 : 262
N.Y. Life Insurance Co. *v.* Clopton, (1870) 7 Bush (Ky.) 185 : 279, 286
N.Y. Life Insurance Co. *v.* Stathem, (1876) 93 U.S. 24 : 261, 279, 286
Nickels *v.* L. & P., etc., Co., [1901] 70 L.J. K.B. 29 : 420

Nigretia, the, Takahashi, R.-J. 255 : 335, 388
Nobel *v.* Jenkins, [1896] 2 Q.B. 326 : 419
Northern Securities Case, 277 U.S.: 99
Noydt Gedacht, the, (1799) 2 C.R. 137 : 330
N.S. de Begona, the, 5 C.R. 97 : 372

O. & M. Ry. Co. *v.* Wheeler, 1 Black 286 : 262
Ocean, the, and *Doomburg*, the, 5 C.R. 91 : 302
Odessa, the (*Times*, 22nd Dec. 1914) : 334
Odin, the, (1799) 1 C.R. 248 : 367
Omnibus, the, 6 C.R. 71 : 331
Ontario (A. G.) *v.* Canada (A. G.), [1896] A.C. 348 : 76
Ooster Ems, the, (1799) 1 C.R. 284 : 340, 341
Oppenheimer *v.* Levy, (2 Geo. II.) 2 Str. 1082 : 269
O'Reilly *v.* Gonne, (1815) 4 Camp. 249 : 421
O'Reilly *v.* R. Exch., (1815) *ibid.* 249 : 421
Orozembo, the, 6 C.R. 436 : 389
Osprey, the, (1795) : 320
Ouachita Cotton, the, (1867) 6 Wall. 521 : 332, 346

Packet de Bilboa, the, (1799) 2 C.R. 133 : 329
Parker *v.* Clive, 4 Burr. 2419 : 125
Parker *v.* Flint, 12 Mod. 255 : 66
Parlement Belge, the, 5 P.D. 197 : 4

LIST OF CASES

Patria, the, (1871) L.R. 3 A. & E. 436 : 415
Patton *v.* Nicholson, (1881) 3 Wheat. 204 : 285
Peacham's Case : 32
Pelican, the, 1 Edw. 4, and Appx. D : 5
Philips *v.* Hatch, (1871) 1 Dill. 571 : 398
Philips *v.* Hatch, (1871) 1 Dill. 574 : 287
Phillips *v.* Eyre, 4 Q.B. 242 : 22
Phœnix, the, (1803) 5 C.R. 20 : 330
Pine, (1628) 3 St. Tr. 363 : 38
Pisani *v.* Lawson, (1839) 6 Bi. N.C. 90 : 268
Poe, *in re*, (1833) 5 B. & A. 688 : 123, 153
Pole *v.* Cetcovitch, (1860) 9 C.B. (N.S.) 430 : 415
Portland, the, (1800) 3 C.R. 41 : 311, 321
Postillion, the, Hay & Marriott, 245 : 307
Postlethwaite *v.* Freeland, (1880) 5 A.C. 608 : 417
Printing Co. *v.* Sampson, (1875) : 99
Prize Cases, the, (1862) 2 Black 635, 687 : 288, 299

R. *v.* Aldred, [1909] 22 Cox 1 : 38
R. *v.* Bowman, [1912] 22 Cox 729 : 38
R. *v.* Brailsford & M'Culloch, 21 Cox 16 : 37
R. *v.* Broadfoot, Fost. *Cr. Cas.* 154 : 47, 127
R. *v.* Charnock, K.S.C. : 32
R. *v.* Crewe, 102 L.T. 760 : 4, 113, 203, 208
R. *v.* Cumming, *ex parte* Hall, L.R. 19 Q.B. 13 : 92, 125
R. *v.* Davitt, (1870) 11 Cox 676 : 33, 37
R. *v.* De Berenger, 3 M. & S. 67 : 4, 81
R. *v.* Geldenhuys, 10 Shiel 369 : 7, 23
R. *v.* Gilliam, Clode, Appx. : 26
R. *v.* Hall, [1891] 1 Q.B. 767 : 78
R. *v.* Harris, (1791) 4 T.R. 202 : 78
R. *v.* Huggins, 2 Raym. 1574 : 109
R. *v.* Hunt, 1 St. Tr. (N.S.) 171 : 47
R. *v.* James, (1837) 8 C. & P. 131 : 150
R. *v.* Lynch, [1903] 1 K.B. 444 : 34
R. *v.* Mulcahy, 7 I.R. I.C.L. 12 : 33
R. *v.* Neale, 9 C.P. 431 : 25
R. *v.* Nelson, Special Rep. : 127
R. *v.* Sec. for War, [1891] 2 Q.B. 326 : 126, 153
R. *v.* Sleep, L. & C. 44 : 109
R. *v.* Smith, 17 C.G.H. Rep. 561 : 150, 155
R. *v.* Suddis, 1 East 306 : 88, 91
R. *v.* Thomas, 3 Russ. Crimes 194 : 150
R. *v.* Tolson, L.R. 23 Q.B.D. 168 : 109, 110, 150
R. *v.* Treasury, (1872) L.R. 7 Q.B. 387 : 126
R. *v.* Treasury, [1909] 2 K.B. 191 : 126
R. *v.* Tubbs, (1776) Cowp. 512 : 127
R. *v.* Waddington, 1 East 143 : 98

LIST OF CASES

R. v. Whitaker (*Times*, 2nd July 1914): 42
R. v. Woodhouse, [1906] 2 K.B. 501 : 97
Raleigh v. Goschen, [1898] 1 Ch. 73 : 11
Rapid, the, (1810) Edw. 228 : 389, 390
Rapid, the, (1814) 8 Cranch 155, 163 : 295, 297, 301, 302
Redford v. Birley, 1 St. Tr. (N.S.) 1071 : 29, 30
Reg. v. Bekker, 17 Juta 348 : 6, 7
Reg. v. Eyre, (Spec. Report) 73 : 18
Reg. v. Grahame, 16 Cox 427 : 25
Reg. v. Nelson & Brand, (Spec. Report) 7 : 18
Roberts' Case (*Times*, 11th June 1879) : 126
Roberts v. Hardy, (1815) 3 M. & S. 535 : 302
Robinson v. C.I.C. of Mannheim (*Times*, 17th Oct. 1914) : 289
Robinson v. Davison, (1871) L.R. 6 Ex. 269 : 413
Robinson, Gold, etc., v. Alliance, etc., Insce. Co., [1904] A.C. 359 : 419
Rolla, the, (1807) 6 C.R. 364 : 385
Romeo, the, (1806) 6 C.R. 35 : 367-68
Rotch v. Edie, (1795) 6 T.R. 413 : 421
Roumanian, the (*Times*, 8th Dec. 1914) : 341
Rouquette v. Overmann, L.R. 10 Q.B. 325 : 401
Russell v. Niemann, (1864) 34 L.J. C.P. 10 : 418
Russia, the, Takahashi, R.-J. 557 : 335

Rutter v. Chapman, 8 M. &. W. 67 : 109
S. José Indiano, the, (1814) 2 Gall. 268 : 308
S. Lawrence, the, (1814) 8 Cranch 434 : 302
Salomon v. S., [1897] A.C. 22 : 257
Saltpetre, 12 Co. 12 : 9
Samuel, the, (1802) 4 C.R. 284 (*n*.) : 331
San Roman, the, (1873) L.R. 5 P.C. 301 : 415
Sandys v. E. I. Co., 10 St. Tr. 520 : 13
Sarah and Bernhardus, etc., the, (1776) 1 Marriott 96, 148-287 : 372
Sarah Christine, the, (1799) 1 C.R. 237 : 380
Scott v. Thompson, (1805) 1 B. & P. N.R. 181 : 421
Sechs Geschwistern, the, (1801) 2 C.R. 100 : 331
Sec. for India v. Kamachee, (1859) 13 Moo., P.C., 75 : 203
78 Bales of Cotton, (1865) 1 Lowell 11 : 341
Shipmoney, 3 St. Tr. 1090 : 16
Sinclair v. Fraser, Morr. 4542 : 291
Softlaw v. Morgan (*Times*, 10th Nov. 1914) : 407
Somersett, 20 St. Tr. 1 : 55
Spanish Register Ships, the, (1744) 5 C.R. 168 : 388
Spazemheid, the, (1800) 3 C.R. 42, 46 : 375
S. P. G. v. Wheeler, (1814) 8 Cranch 133 : 258, 261, 263, 264, 313
Sprigg v. Sigcau, [1897] 4 A.C. 238 : 208
Stadt Embden, the, (1798) 1 C.R. 26 : 372, 380

LIST OF CASES

Stevens *v.* Phœnix Insce. Co., (1869) 41 N.Y. 150 : 263
Susa, the, (1799) 2 C.R. 255 : 311
Sutton *v.* Johnstone, 1 T.R. 509 : 73, 89, 151, 154, 156, 160
Swan, the, 2 C.R. 256 : 320
Syria, the (*Times*, 19th Jan. 1914) : 319, 325, 351

Taylor *v.* Caldwell, (1863) 3 B. & S. 826 : 413
Teutonia, the, (1872) L.R. 4 P.C. 171 : 414
Thalia, the, [1905] Takahashi, R.-J. 605 : 338
Thiis *v.* Byers, (1876) 1 Q.B.D. 344 : 418
Thorington *v.* Smith, 8 Wall. 1 : 268
Thurn & Taxis (P.) *v.* Moffitt (*Times*, 17th Oct. 1914) : 253
Tilonko, *in re*, 27 Natal (N.S.) 570 ; 95 L.T. 853 : 6, 23
Timothy *v.* Simpson, (1835) 1 C.M. & R. 757 : 51
Tobago, the, (1804) 5 C.R. 218 : 333-34
Toronto *v.* Virgo, [1896] A.C. 88 : 76
Tufnell, *re*, L.R. 3 C.D. 164 : 125
Two Friends, the, (1799) 1 C.R. 281 : 341

Udny *v.* Udny, (1869) 1 S. & D. App. 441 : 317
U.S. *v.* Grossmeyer, (1869) 9 Wall. 72 : 274
U.S. *v.* Lane, 8 Wall. 195 : 274
U.S. *v.* Mimmack, 97 U.S. 426 : 124

U.S. *v.* Pelly, [1899] W.R. 332 : 397, 423
U.S. *v.* 1756 Shares, G. W. R. (Ill.), (1865) 5 Blatch. 231 : 289, 305, 369

V. Anna Catharina, the, (1804) 5 C.R. 161 : 329, 330
V. Henrietta, the, (1803) 5 C.R. 75 : 413
Vanbrynen *v.* Wilson, 9 East 321 : 284
Venter *v.* Rex, [1907] T.S. 910 : 54
Venus, the, 8 Cranch 253, 279 : 302, 311, 316, 330, 361
Vertue *v.* Clive, 4 Burr. 2475 : 125
Vigilantia, the, (1798) 1 C.R. 1 : 311, 312, 319

Walker *v.* Baird, [1892] A.C. 492 : 14
Wall *v.* Macnamara, 1 T.R. 509 : 90, 149
Wall's Case, 28 St. Tr. 176 : 160
Walsingham Packet, the, (1798) 1 C.R. 84 : 361
Ward *v.* Smith, (1868) 7 Wall. 447 : 274
Warden *v.* Bailey, (1811) 4 Taunt. 67 : 90, 152
Watford *v.* Masham, (38 Eliz.) Moore 431 : 270
Wells *v.* Williams, (9 Will. III.) 1 L. Raym. 282 : 253, 269, 271
Welvaart, the, (1799) 2 C.R. 122 : 331
West Rand Central Gold Mining Co. *v.* R., [1905] 2 K.B. 391 : 210

LIST OF CASES

Whelan *v.* Cook, (1867) 29 Maryland 1 : 282
Whitbread *v.* Brooksbank, (1774) 1 Cowp. 66, 69 : 58
Williams *v.* Howarth, [1905] A.C. 55 : 115, 153
Willison *v.* Patterson, 7 Taunt. 439 : 282, 283

Woods *v.* Lyttleton, 25 T.L.R. 665 : 124, 153
Wright *v.* Fitzgerald, 27 St. Tr. 765 : 21

Zelden Rust, the, (1805) 6 C.R. 93 : 372

INDEX

A

Act of Indemnity, 21, 22
Act of State, 4, 13, 24, 207-10, 418, 421 ; foreign, 416-18, 422
Actions and suits, 253, 257, 268, 282, 284, 299, 302, 305, 309 *n.*, 346, 410. *See* Pleading and Contract
Admiralty, 75, 132, 139, 225, 309, 336, 339, 340. *See* Navy
Aerial attack, 191
Agent, Government, 376
Agents, 258, 272-75, 276, 285, 291, 318, 321 *seq.*, 325-29, 331, 344, 345, 348, 350
Aircraft, 377
Alabama, the, 214
Alien, 369
Alien, 203-5, 247 *seq.*, 267 *seq.*, 302, 327, 335, 342 *seq. See* Enemy character
Aliens, 203-5
Aliens as defendants, 288 *seq.*
Aliens, protected, 35, 36, 70
Aliens restriction, 93
Aliens Restriction Rules, 252
Allegiance, 33 *sqq.*, 189, 203-8, 247 *seq.*, 262, 268, 289, 306, 309, 310, 318, 338

Allies, 58, 303, 335, 418
Annexation, 24 *n.*, 202 *sqq.*
Appeal, 87, 93, 97, 111, 113, 152
Appendix, 429
Appendix (Contents), 425
Arms, 68, 174, 175, 190
Army. *See* Forces, armed
Army Act, 1881, 65, 83, 117, 129, 130, 131, 143, 146, 152, 157, 160, 161, 177
Army Council, 73, 75, 102, 103, 136 *sqq.*
Arrest, 40, 51, 52, 53, 72, 76, 77, 78, 81, 87, 89, 90, 91, 105, 112, 124, 154
Assistance, 387, 390
Asylum, 391, 396. *See* Sick and wounded
"At sea," 331, 337-38
Attachment. *See* Foreign Attachment
Australia, 129, 131, 132
Austria, 231, 347, 400, 415
Aviation, 63 *sqq.*, 66, 68, 191

B

Bacon's abridgment, 272
Balfour, A. J., 396

INDEX

Ballot, 120-22
Banishment, 54-56, 93
Bankruptcy: insolvency, 260, 332, 410
Banks, 353, 401, 404, 409
Base of operations, 215-16, 232
Base of supplies, 376
Belgium, 230 seq.
Bentwich, Professor N., 276, 289
Berlin and Milan decrees, 221
Bill of sale, 287
Billeting, 62, 64-66, 97
Bills of exchange, 273, 282, 402, 404, 405, 406, 408, 423
Blackstone, 47, 219, 222, 387 seq., 397, 415, 416. See Paper blockade
Blockade, 381 seq., 422. See Paper blockade
Blockade, Pacific, 396
Bombardment, 178, 217, 417
Bottomree, 333
Branches, 325, 342, 344, 347-48, 350, 351
Burke, 243
Bynkershoek, 257, 295

C

Camp-followers, 177
Canada, 129, 131, 132
Canning, 241
Capacity, 306
Capitulations, 362
Capture, illegal, 369
Carriage of troops, 387, 388
Censorship (Press), 83 sqq., 106, 147. See Communications
Certificates of origin, 352
Certiorari, 113
Cession, 337. See Annexation
Chamber jurisdiction, 410

Chaplains, 177
Charter-party, 300, 303, 324, 335, 336, 421
Chili, 417
China, 362
Civil war, 276, 289
Civilians, 18, 20, 21, 26-29, 45, 47, 48, 49, 51, 53, 72, 86 sqq., 89 sqq., 110, 112-13, 149-50, 158, 161, 169, 170, 174, 184, 189, 197, 212 *et passim*. See Non-Combatants
Civilians (lawyers), 307
Clausewitz, 167, 180-81
Close trade, 320 n., 387 seq.
Clothing, 373, 375
Coasters, 222
Coburg. See Appendix (end)
Cockburn, 18, 20, 21, 22, 55, 153, 416
Coke, 5, 9, 10, 250-54, 268
Colonial trade, 388
Colonial trade voyages, 360, 374
Colonies, 115, 127 sqq., 204, 404
Commerce, 252, 269, 270, 284, 285, 287, 294 seq., 306 seq., 342 seq., 399, 401. See Trading with the enemy
Commercial blockade, 381
Commissions, 123-25
Common law, 358, 363, 368
Communications, 73, 74, 81, 85, 106 sqq., 146, 159, 221, 257, 259, 260, 272, 275, 279, 284, 285, 287, 288, 295, 297-300, 346
Companies and corporations, 255 seq., 262 seq., 325 seq., 343 seq.
Compensation, 58, 60, 61, 62, 63, 79, 87
Compromise, 349
Conditions, 404, 410
Conditions, resolution of, 345
Confiscation, 259, 268, 289, 293, 295, 301, 303, 305, 327, 328, 352,

INDEX

372, 376, 380, 384, 387, 389, 390, 391. *See* Capture, Requisition contributions, Purveyance, Defence of the realm
Conquest, 24 *n.*, 337-38. *See* Annexation
Conscription, 311
Consignment in blank, 380
Conspiracy, 31, 37, 42, 81, 83
Constables, 29, 30, 49 *sqq.*, 65, 66, 67, 81, 95, 105. *See* Special constables
Continuous voyage, in trading with the enemy, 302 ; in colonial voyage, 375 ; sales *in transitu*, 331
Continuous voyage, prospective, 368, 376-78, 379, 384. *See* Appendix (end)
Contraband, 370 *seq.*, 385, 387, 389, 390, 421-22
Contract, 210, 401 *seq.*, 412 *seq.*
Contractor. *See* Agent
Contracts, 253 *seq.*, 257, 267 *seq.*, 294, 297, 327, 342 *seq.*, 422
Contracts, pre-war, 277, 350, 412 *seq.*
Contributions, 184, 187
Copper, 377-78
Corporations, non-trading, 258
Correspondence, 41, 146-47, 176, 197, 253, 319, 387-90. *See* Communication
Court-martial, 20, 21, 77, 87, 88, 92, 103, 104, 106, 107, 108, 125, 142 *sqq*. *See* Martial law
Courts Emergency Powers Act, 410
Courts (common law), 73, 74 *sqq.*, 79, 82, 87 *sqq.*, 95, 96, 105, 106, 108, 112, 113, 125, 149, 156-61, 202-4, 348, 358, 361, 397, 410
Criticism, 38, 107, 108, 112, 147
Curaçoa, 328
Current account, 409

Customs. *See* Export, Import
Customs duties, 300, 417
Cyprus, 362

D

Davey, Lord, 309
Debts, public. *See* Appendix (end)
Declaration of London, 215, 331, 375-77, 380, 382-84, 385 *n.*, 386, 390, 391
Declaration of Paris, 378, 382
Declarations of war, 3 *sqq.*, 33, 251-52, 269, 271, 395 *seq.* *See* Appendix D, 1
Deerhound Case, 213
Defence of the realm, 44 *sqq.*, 71 *sqq.*
Defence of the Realm Act, criticism justified, 102
Delay, 415-17, 422-23
Delivery of goods, 404, 413
Denmark, 226, 308, 352
Deposits (bank), 409
Despatches, 387-89
Detention, 357
Devenerunt, information of, 306
Deviation, 421
Devise, 306
Dicey, Professor A. V., 59, 84, 148, 217
Discipline, 142 *sqq.*, 160 *sqq.*, 196
Discovery, bill of, 290
Distraint, 409, 411
Dividends, 260
Domicile, 264, 292, 302, 306, 309, 310, 311 *seq.*, 323, 327, 348, 351
Drilling, 47, 115
Droits of Admiralty, 336, 340-41
Dwelling-house, 61, 65, 76, 79, 180

572 INDEX

E

Egypt, 362
Embargo, 416
"Emergency" doctrine, 8 *sqq.*, 16, 17, 26. *See* Necessity
Emigration, 54, 55
Enemy character, 302, 303, 306 *seq.*, 337, 346, 421. *See* Alien
Enemy claimants, 369
Enlistment, 117 *sqq.*, 127, 173
Enrichment of enemy, 272, 284, 285, 294, 298, 300, 301
Equipment, 423
Evidence, 363 *seq.*, 384. *See* Intention
Evidence, enemy, 369
Evidence of state of war, 5, 6; improperly admitted by court-martial, 87, 158
Execution, etc., 410
Expatriation, 249, 308
Explosive bullets, etc., 190-91
Export, 56, 57, 58, 68, 324, 330, 349, 352, 372, 416, 420. *See* House of trade, etc.
Expropriation of land, 93, 207, 208
Expulsion, 36, 93. *See* Banishment

F

False accusations, 152
False papers, 380
Firm, 343, 347
Fishermen, 222, 307
Flag, 335-36, 391
Flag of truce, 193-94
Flying columns, 183
Food. *See* Provisions
Force. *See* Necessity, Martial law, Riot, Sedition

Force majeure, 412 *sqq.*
Forces, armed, 38, 45, 59, 62, 74, 85, 91, 102, 106, 107, 114 *sqq.*, 127 *sqq.*, 142 *sqq.*, 173, 189, 214, 250, 275, 287, 387-91, 396
Foreclosure, 290
Foreign Attachment, 290, 291
Foreign countries, British Army in, 157
Foreign debts, 409
Foreign Enlistment Act, 5, 423
Forfeiture, 410
Foster, Sir Mich., 5, 32, 34, 35, 46, 49, 251-53 *n.*
France, 238, 239, 253, 265, 308, 314, 320, 321, 322, 331, 337, 373, 400, 401, 415, 421
Fraud, 389
Freight, 372, 388, 403, 413, 414, 415
Further proof, 367

G

Geneva Convention, 42, 177
German theories, 201, 215. *See Kriegsraison*
German War-book, 232-33
Glycerine, 377
Goeben and Breslau Case, 215
Gold, 419
Guarantee, 404
Guarantees of neutrality, 230-31, 236-38
Guides, 170, 184, 189-90

H

Habeas Corpus, 6, 9, 13, 15, 55, 87, 91

INDEX

Hague Conventions, 49, 165 *sqq.*, 213 *sqq.*, 223
Hale, 12, 13, 17, 20, 53
Hanover, 250
Hautefeuille, 373
Hayti, 337
Hemp, 371, 380
Herschell, Lord, 75
Highways. *See* Roads
Hire purchase, 411
Holland, 226, 231, 238, 243, 302, 303, 307, 317, 319, 322, 323, 324, 352, 379
Holland, Dr T. E., 166, 194, 198, 199
Hospital ships, 213-14
Hostages, 185
House. *See* Dwelling-house
House of trade, 311, 312, 314, 317, 318 *seq.*, 343, 347
Hungary, 347

I

Illegal orders, 148 *sqq.* See *Ultra vires*
Illegality of performance, 413, 419, 422
Immigration, 55, 94
Imperial Defence Committee, 133 *sqq.*
Imperial General Staff, 135
Import, 56, 57, 324, 329, 346, 349, 352, 420. *See* House of trade, etc.
Impossibility, 412 *seq.*
Impressment, 47, 66, 67, 126. *See* Guides, Requisitions
Incorporation, 256-59, 260-66, 325-26
India, 129-31, 133, 207
Infringement (blockade), 385

Injunction, 61
Inquisition as to aliens, 95 ; as to commercial stocks, 101 ; as to miscellaneous matters, 105, 113 ; by invaders, 185
Insubordination, 144-46
Insurance, life, 260, 279, 286, 326, 411
Insurance, marine, 273, 278, 283, 345 *n.*, 349, 420
Insurance : reinsurance, 349
Intention, 40, 87, 106, 109, 110, 352, 368, 373 *seq.*, 383, 422
Interest, 409
Interests less than ownership, 332 *seq.*
Internment, 35 ; ships, 214, 215, 216 ; troops and seamen, 216-17
In transitu, 330-32
Invasion, 7, 9, 16, 19, 32, 44 *sqq.*, 175 *sqq.*, 248, 337, 356
Ireland, 15, 30, 47, 57
Iron ore, 377, 378
Irregulars, 173

J

Japan, 338, 395, 400
Japan-Russia War, 221-24
Jurisdiction, 291, 338, 340, 411
Jus in rem, 399

K

Kenny, Mr Justice, 57
Kent, Chancellor, 270-71, 280, 281-82, 285, 288, 296, 336
Kenyon, Lord Chief Justice, 271
Kleen, 375

INDEX

Kriegsrecht, Kriegsraison, 166, 167, 176, 179, 180 *sqq.*, 186, 199, 233 *et passim*

L

Land, expropriation of, 59, 60, 78
Laws of war (land), 165 *sqq.*; (sea), 212 *sqq.*
Lead, 371, 377
Lease, 279
Leather, 377-78
Levée en masse, 173-76
Lex regia, 80, 101
Libel, 253 *n.*, 268
Libel, Press, 84, 108
Liberty and property, 76 *sqq.*, 86, 93 *n.*, 105, 112, 146, 181, 208, 210, 211, 212
License, 252-59, 268-69, 270-71, 281, 285, 324, 333-35, 343, 345-46, 353, 369, 388. *See* Safe-conduct
Licensing (liquor), 96, 109
Lights, 82, 87
Limitations, 277
Littleton, 251, 268
Loans, 37, 69
Luxemburg, 234, 237-39, 240

M

Mackintosh, Sir J., 360
Mails, 222
Maintenance of blockade, 384
Malaya, 362, 398
Management, place of, 259, 264, 326
Managers, 258, 265, 321 *seq.*
Mansfield, Chief Justice, 58-73, 124, 126, 149-50, 209, 283-84, 339, 361, 369
Marshall, Chief Justice, 305
Martial law, 8, 17 *sqq.*, 45, 49, 70, 104, 111-12, 184
Materialmen, 335
Mauritius, 55
Mecklenburg-Strelitz. *See* Appendix (end)
Medical staff, 177, 197, 213
Mens rea, 40, 81, 106, 109, 110 149
Merchant mariners, 222
Merchants, 255, 278, 306 *seq.*, 350
Metals and ores, 377
Metternich, 396
Mexico, 303, 313
Military law, 17, 19, 20, 67, 72-111, 142 *sqq.*, 177
Military offences, 142 *sqq.*
Militia, 46, 50, 62, 119 *sqq.*, 173
Mines, 217-21, 226
Mistake, 67, 272, 388-90
Moratorium, 401 *seq.*
Mortgage, 286, 334 *n.*, 410

N

Napoleon, 225
Nationality, 247 *seq.*, 255, 262-66, 302 *seq.*, 310 *seq. See* Enemy character
Naturalisation, 33, 204, 247-71
Naval stores, 371
Navy, 126, 131, 133, 139 *sqq.*, 160, 215, 217, 338, 383, 386. *See* Admiralty, and Forces, armed
Necessity, 9, 10, 12, 25, 36, 44, 48, 57, 62, 64, 72, 78, 79, 148, 166, 176, 187, 195, 197, 219, 220. *See Kriegsraison*

INDEX 575

Negotiable instruments, 349-50
Nelson, Justice S., 288, 299, 369, 375
Neutrals, 48, 69, 200-1, 213, 214-16, 220, 221, 222, 223-24, 225, 232-35, 236, 262, 276, 295, 301, 303, 308, 310, 313, 317 *seq.*, 343 *seq.*, 360, 365, 370 *seq.*, 381 *seq.*, 387 *seq.*, 395-96, 421-22
Neutralisation, 231, 234, 236, 240
Non-Combatants, 165, 171 *sqq.*, 180, 181, 184, 189. *See* Civilians
"Non-commercial" contracts, 284, 285 *seq.*, 297, 344
Non-commercial traffic, 297 *seq.*
North Sea, 225
Norway, 226, 352
Notification of blockade, 382
Novel usages, 218, 220

O

Obiter dicta, 209-11
Occupation (military), 49, 175, 180 *sqq.*, 203, 337
Officer (military or naval), 28, 64, 65, 80, 89, 91, 103, 105, 113, 123, 124, 174, 208, 388-89, 390, 398
Oppenheim, Prof., 166, 176, 179, 193-94, 238, 336
Orders in Council, 359, 361, 397. *See* Proclamations
Ownership, 329

P

Paper blockades, 373, 381
Parliament, 4, 45, 79, 80, 111, 113, 115-17, 137-39, 140, 208, 359, 361

Partnership, Partner, 259, 262, 273, 281, 315, 318, 321, 327, 345
Passage, 200, 233-34
Passport, 37, 42
Patents, designs, and trade-marks, 353
Pawnbroker, 410
Peace, effort of supervening, 398
Penalties, 346, 348, 350, 352
Penalty, 379, 384
Pensions, 125
Petition of Right, the, 18, 46, 65
Petitions of Right, 58, 125, 211
Phillimore, Judge Sir R., 251, 310, 360, 366-67, 399
Phillipson, Dr C., 350
Piggott, Sir F. T., 247, 362
Pillage, 146, 187-88, 198
Pleading, 269 *seq.*, 272
Police, 49 *sqq.*, 95, 96. *See* Constable
Pollock, Sir F., 268
Port, 413; goods in, 341; naval, 372; seizures in, 340; transfers in, 331, 418
Ports, 12, 15, 68, 214, 215, 217, 221-23, 375-77, 378-79, 382-83
Pre-emption, 372, 378
Preparatory examination, 363, 366
Press. *See* Censorship
Presumptions, 215, 316. *See* Intention and Evidence
Prevention, 81-82, 84
Prisoners, 283
Private captors, 305, 336
Privateering, 336
Privilege, 159
Prize-court procedure, 357 *et passim*
Prize judges, 358 *seq.*, 379, 397
Proclamations, 358, 397-98; defence of the realm, 44 *sqq.*, 67; railways, 67; food export, 67; arms export, 67; enemy loans,

69; trading with the enemy, 342 seq.; Declaration of London, 376-77, 383; Moratorium, 401 seq.; prohibition of export, 416. Texts in Appendix

Produce of enemy soil, 330
Produce of neutral soil, 372
Produce of soil, 318, 330, 351
Produce, trade in enemy's, 351
Prohibition, 88, 92
Promissory note, 287
Property and liberty, 252-53, 260, 304
Property at sea, enemy's, 306 seq., 338, 379; enemy's floating, 341; entry on, 78; landed, enemy's sea-borne, 341; on land, enemies', 305, 341
Protected states, 362
Provisions, 58, 68, 97, 100, 187, 372, 376
Prussia, 230, 231, 239, 301, 303, 307, 319
Public policy, 278
Purveyance, 65, 97. *See* Requisitions, Impressment
Public engagements. *See* Appendix (end)

Q

Quarter, 172, 193, 196

R

Railways, 40, 62, 68, 74, 82
Ransom, 188
"Regulate," 75, 76
Relaxation of blockade, 385
Rent, 405, 410
Reports, alarmist, 74, 81, 83, 85, 107, 146

Reprisals, 167, 198 *sqq.*, 359, 385, 396
Requisitions, 49, 62, 97, 181, 186, 187
Rescue, 213-16
Reserve forces, 119, 127, 173
Residence, 201
Restraint of trade, 97-99; of princes, 415-16, 418
Retail debts, 408
Rights of action, 184; *in rem* and *in personam* (*ad rem*), 334, 336
Riot, 25-31, 50, 54
Roads, 59, 61, 63, 72, 113
Rubber, 377
Rule of law, 59, 84
Russell, Earl, 213
Russia, 231, 266, 300, 310, 376, 400

S

Safe-conduct, 251 *seq.*, 268, 270, 271, 385
Sale, 286, 318, 324, 329, 332, 344
Salvage (prize), 337
Scotland, 291, 308
Scott, Sir John, 32
Scott, Sir William (Lord Stowell), 309, 312, 314, 317, 319, 321, 331, 333, 334, 341, 347, 358, 363, 368, 375, 380, 384, 389, 395
Search in port, 380
Secrets, official, 39, 56, 77, 82, 185
Securities, 344, 349
Sedition, 38, 77, 81, 84, 85
Sequestration, 257, 260-61, 293
Ships, 47, 125, 212 *sqq.*, 306 *sqq.*
Ship's papers, 363, 374, 380
Sick. *See* Wounded
Signalling, 221

INDEX 577

"Sniping," 174
Sovereign, 203, 209, 215, 249, 250, 252, 253, 295, 305, 362
Spain, 253, 308, 328, 373, 417, 422
Special constables, 50, 51, 52, 95-96
Spies, 39 *sqq.*, 56, 94, 161, 189, 195 *sqq.*
Standing interrogatories. *See* Preparatory examination
Stanley, Lord, 237
State of siege, 15 *n.*, 82, 94, 156
Stocks and shares, 349, 350
Stocks, commercial, 100
Story, 258, 261, 263, 264, 265, 280, 288, 290, 305, 306, 313, 347, 360, 365, 373
Stratagems, 193-95
Sulphur, 377
Suspects, 72, 76
Sweden, 226, 315, 352, 358, 373, 377, 398

T

Taxes, 184
Territorial Force, 4, 46, 65, 66, 122, 173
Terrorism. *See* *Kriegsraison*, Necessity
Torpedoes, 218-19
Tort, 253 *n.*, 305
Trade, place of, 250, 255, 262, 264, 325-27. *See* House of trade, Domicile
Trading with the enemy, 37, 255, 266, 277, 280, 284, 294 *seq.*, 306, 342 *seq.*, 415. *See* Produce, trade in enemy's
Transfers, 330-31
Transport, 373, 388, 391

Treachery, 193
Treason, 31 *sqq.*, 48, 70, 77, 81, 84, 85, 106, 110, 189, 252-53, 284, 294, 349
Treaty, 207, 209, 230 *seq.*, 311, 314, 399
Trespass, 10, 11, 13, 41, 80
Trust, 265, 272-73
"Twenty-four hours' rule," 215-16
Twiss, Rt. Hon. Sir Travers, 317, 363, 369, 379

U

Ultra vires, 77, 82, 101, 102, 104, 105, 152 *sqq.*
United States, 24, 124, 191, 274, 284 *seq.*, 288, 313, 320, 322, 326, 332, 361, 368, 373-74, 377, 384, 386, 391, 397
Un-neutral service, 387, 423
Usage, 329

V

Vattel, 399
Vendor's lien, 333
Venezuela, 328, 395
Vicarious penalties, 186
Villenage, 268
Volunteers, 121, 123, 127, 173, 178
Voyage, 349, 388, 390, 413, 421-22

W

Wages and salaries, 403
War clause, 415, 418-20

War, commencement and end, 395 *seq.*
War, conditional, 396
War, prisoners of, 172, 177, 193, 196, 213, 217
Warbeck, 250
Warlike *matériel*, 39, 58, 179, 187, 217, 233 *n.*, 371 *seq.*, 374 *seq.*
Warrant, 66, 67, 76, 77, 78, 105, 112
Westlake, 247, 289, 309, 314

Wheaton, 338, 339, 360, 369
White flag. *See* Flag of truce
Winding-up, 259
Wireless telegraphy, 222, 224
Withdrawal, from enemy country, 302, 310, 320, 322, 338
Wounded, 197-98, 213, 214, 216, 240

Z

Zanzibar, 362

www.ingramcontent.com/pod-product-compliance
Lightning Source LLC
Chambersburg PA
CBHW021846230426
43671CB00006B/286